VILLAGE AMONG NATIONS

"Canadian" Mennonites in a Transnational World, 1916–2006

Between the 1920s and the 1940s, the descendants of 10,000 traditionalist Mennonites emigrated from western Canada to isolated rural sections of northern Mexico and the Paraguayan Chaco; over the course of the twentieth century, they became increasingly scattered through secondary migrations to East Paraguay, British Honduras, Bolivia, and elsewhere in Latin America. Despite this dispersion, these Canadian-descendant Mennonites, who now number around 250,000, developed a rich transnational culture over the years, resisting allegiance to any one nation and cultivating a strong sense of common peoplehood based on a history of migration, non-violence, and distinct language and dress.

Village among Nations recuperates a missing chapter of Canadian history: the story of these Mennonites who emigrated from Canada for cultural reasons, but then in later generations "returned" in large numbers for economic and social security. Royden Loewen analyses a wide variety of texts, by men and women – letters, memoirs, reflections on family debates on land settlement, exchanges with curious outsiders, and deliberations on issues of citizenship. They relate the untold experience of this uniquely transnational, ethno-religious community.

ROYDEN LOEWEN is the Chair in Mennonite Studies and a professor in the Department of History at the University of Winnipeg. He is an award-winning author of a number of books on Mennonites and immigrants in North America.

ROYDEN LOEWEN

Village among Nations

"Canadian" Mennonites in a Transnational World, 1916–2006

UNIVERSITY OF TORONTO PRESS
Toronto Buffalo London

© University of Toronto Press 2013
Toronto   Buffalo   London
www.utppublishing.com
Printed in Canada

ISBN 978-1-4426-4685-8 (cloth)
ISBN 978-1-4426-1467-3 (paper)

Printed on acid-free, 100% post-consumer recycled paper with vegetable-based inks

---

Library and Archives Canada Cataloguing in Publication

Loewen, Royden, 1954–, author
Village among nations : "Canadian" Mennonites in a transnational world, 1916–2006 / Royden Loewen.

Includes bibliographical references and index.
ISBN 978-1-4426-4685-8 (bound). – ISBN 978-1-4426-1467-3 (pbk.)

1. Mennonites – Historiography. 2. Mennonites – Canada – History – 20th century. 3. Canada – Emigration and immigration – History – 20th century. 4. Transnationalism. I. Title.

BX8118.5.L65 2013   289.7'710904   C2013-903571-0

University of Toronto Press acknowledges the financial assistance to its publishing program of the Canada Council for the Arts and the Ontario Arts Council.
University of Toronto Press acknowledges the financial support of the Government of Canada through the Canada Book Fund for its publishing activities.

This book has been published with the help of a grant from the Canadian Federation for the Humanities and Social Sciences, through the Awards to Scholarly Publications Program, using funds provided by the Social Sciences and Research Council of Canada.

Contents

Acknowledgments vii

Maps xi

Introduction 3

1 Leaving the "British Empire" in Canada: Promises in the South, 1916–1921 14

2 Drawing Lines on God's Earth: Settlers in Mexico and Paraguay, 1922–1929 40

3 Dreaming of "Old" Canada: Nostalgia in the Diaspora, 1930–1945 66

4 Rethinking Time and Space: East Paraguay and Beyond, 1945–1954 96

5 Meeting the Outside Gaze: New Life in British Honduras and Bolivia, 1954–1972 119

6 Crystallizing Memory: The "Return" of the Kanadier, 1951–1979 151

7 Imagining a Pan-American Village: Reading *Die Mennonitische Post*, 1977–1996 175

8 Homing in on the Transnational World: Women Migrants in Ontario, 1985–2006 205

Conclusion 227

Notes 235

Glossary 271

Bibliography 273

Index 291

Illustrations follow page 144

Acknowledgments

Many people and numerous encounters within a broadly distended community have made this book possible. I am profoundly grateful for their generosity and support.

A Social Sciences and Humanities Research Council grant allowed me to seek the highly valued assistance of committed student and professional researchers. Andrea Dyck spent many months reading and making notes on the entire run of the *Steinbach Post*, from 1916 to 1967. Kerry Fast offered her expertise in oral history, as well as her research in the *Mennonitische Post* and insightful textual criticism. Robyn Sneath unearthed every relevant personal writing at the Mennonite Heritage Centre, translated documents, and wrote a number of thoughtful interpretative pieces. Jason Yaremko and Gustavo Velasco translated valuable materials from the Spanish. Jonathan Klassen, Jonathan Hildebrand, Susie Fisher Stoesz, Doreen Klassen, Luis Enrique Rivero Coimbra, and Lukas Thiessen researched a variety of newspapers across the Americas. Kathryn Boschman indexed the book.

I am deeply grateful to colleagues and friends – Kerry Fast, Susie Fisher Stoesz, Gerald Friesen, John J. Friesen, Doreen Klassen, and Hans Werner – who read the entire manuscript with utmost care and offered invaluable critical comment. I extend this gratitude to anonymous University of Toronto Press readers. I benefited from very helpful conversations with: Alexander Freund, Jake E. Peters, Mary Friesen, Titus Guenther, Karen Warkentin, and John Janzen of Winnipeg; Abe Rempel and Tina Fehr Kehler of Winkler, Manitoba; Abe Warkentin and Otto Loeppky of Steinbach, Manitoba; and William Janzen of Ottawa.

Special thanks to managers of archives: Kennert Giesbrecht of the *Mennonitische Post*; Conrad Stoesz and Alf Redekopp of the Mennonite

Heritage Centre; Sam Steiner and Laureen Harder of the Mennonite Archives of Ontario; Henry Ratzlaff of the Mennonite Archives in Loma Plata, Paraguay; and the staffs of Centro de Estudios Migratorios Latinoamericanos in Buenos Aires and Archivo de La Paz, and Maria Bjerg for enabling access to both.

Too many people to mention in various parts of the Americas opened their homes to my visits and curiosities. In Canada they include: Klaas and Maria Penner and Levi Dueck of Northfield, Nova Scotia; Abe Harms of Aylmer and Marvin Dueck of Leamington, Ontario; Helen Braun of La Crete and George Epp of Taber, Alberta; and Leonard Doell of Saskatoon. In Mexico they include: Peter Enns, Jacob Fehr, Johann Teichrob, Johann Krahn, Jacob Friesen, Franz Rempel, Jorge Reimer, Bram Siemens, Gerhard Unger, and Jacob Dyck and their families of Cuauhtémoc; Arden Dueck, Menno Dueck, Mary Plett, Eddie Plett, and Richard Reimer of Los Jagueyes; Jakob Wall of Nuevo Ideal; and Isaac and Lydia Froese and Bernard and Julia Penner of La Honda. In Bolivia they include: Abram Thiessen, Peter and Sara Wiebe, Anna and Johann Neufeld, and Siegfried Schartner of Santa Cruz. In Paraguay they include: Johan Schmidt of Rio Verde; Peter Klassen and Gundolf Niebuhr of Filadelfia; Alfred Neufeld and Gerhard Ratzlaff of Asunción; and Jacob Heinrichs of Sommerfeld. To name all those who were welcoming and accommodating would fill multiple pages.

I am grateful to colleagues who responded to papers arising from this project at various history conferences of the Canadian Historical Association, Social Science History Association, University of Winnipeg Mennonite Studies, Royal Society of Canada, and Western Canadian History Association, as well as the 2007 Amish studies conference at the Young Center in Elizabethtown, Pennsylvania. These events led to the publication of two pieces that duplicate some materials in this book: "To the Ends of the Earth: An Introduction to the Conservative Low German Mennonites of the Americas," *Mennonite Quarterly Review* 82 (2008); and "Text, Trains and Time: The Emigration of Canadian Mennonites to Latin America, 1922–1948," in *Place and Replace: Essays in Western Canadian History*, edited by Adele Perry, Essylt Jones, and Leah Morton (Winnipeg: University of Manitoba Press, 2013).

I have benefited greatly from engaging conversations with, and generous assistance from, the following professors in Latin America: Maria Bjerg, Universidad Nacional de Quilmes, Bernal, Argentina; Pedro Castro, Universidad Autónoma Metropolitana-Iztapalapa, Mexico City; Paula Peña Hasbún, Museo de Historia y Archivo Histórico de

Santa Cruz, Bolivia; Raul Calderon Jemio of Universidad Mayo de San Andres, La Paz; and Don Arturo, Olga Cabrera, and Ricardo Romo of Campus León de la Universidad de Guanajuato.

A number of people generously offered overnight accommodation and valued assistance: Henry and Susie Bergen of Aylmer, Ontario (Canada); Peter and Margaretha Rempel of Cuauhtémoc, Hein and Mary Heide of Los Jagueyes, Ann and Jake Enns of Nuevo Casas Grandes, Anna and Johann Klassen of Sabinal, and Ben and Margie Giesbrecht of Nuevo Ideal (Mexico); Levi and Rosalie Hiebert of Loma Plata, and Jakob and Sina Warkentin of Neuland (Paraguay); and Dick and Kathy Braun of Santa Cruz, and Jacob and Maria Neudorf and Benjamin and Anna Guenther of Yacuiba (Bolivia).

Mary Ann has been an unfailing companion and helpful critic throughout this project.

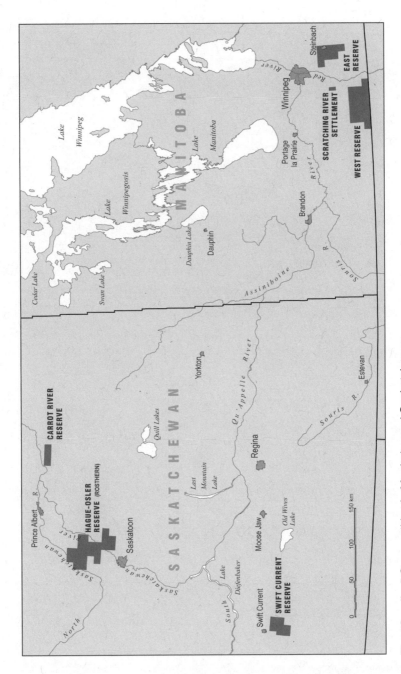

The "Sending" Communities in Manitoba and Saskatchewan

Selected "Canadian" Mennonite Settlements in the Americas

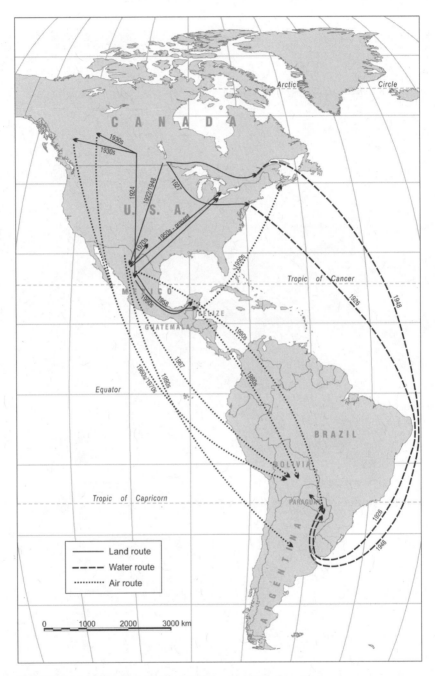

The "Canadian" Mennonite Migrations across the Americas

Mexico Mennonite Communities, 1922 to Present

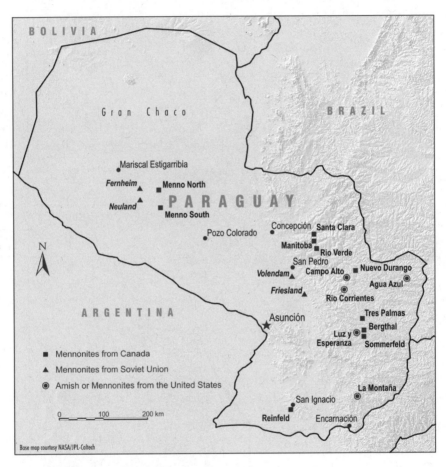

Paraguay Mennonite Communities, 1927 to Present

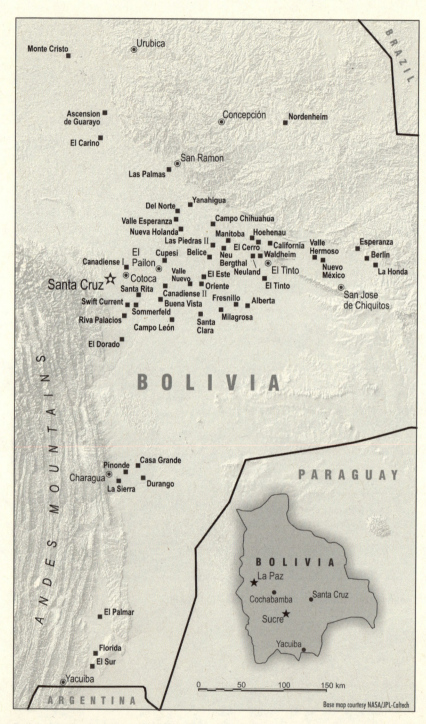

Bolivia Mennonite Communities, 1954 to Present

VILLAGE AMONG NATIONS

"Canadian" Mennonites in a Transnational World, 1916–2006

Introduction

Jakob Wall is an energetic, middle-aged, ex-newspaper man who has returned temporarily to the old red-brick family house in his beloved Mennonite colony in a mountain valley in Durango, Mexico. His wife Neta and seven children are maintaining their other house in Leamington, Ontario, where the oldest of them work at various jobs. In January 2007, I visit Jakob in Durango as he writes a history book on his colony, founded in 1924 by Mennonite settlers from Saskatchewan. Having just left the Old Colony Mennonite church for the more progressive, Canadian-spawned, Evangelical Mennonite Mission Church, he is in a cultural transition. He has exchanged the traditionalist black overalls and long-sleeved shirt of the Old Colony Mennonites for modest, but modern, men's garb. Coincidentally, many of the more traditionalist Old Colony members have themselves just left the church at Durango in a searing schism and migrated southward to even more isolated communities in East Paraguay, Argentina, and Campeche (Mexico), where they hope to maintain an anti-modern "horse and buggy" culture. Durango moderates like Jakob may have established homes in Canada, but many other Durango residents have headed in the very opposite direction.[1]

Maria Penner is a talkative, Low German-speaking grandmother from the parkland of Northfield, Nova Scotia. With her husband and extended family, she lives here in a settlement of Kleine Gemeinde Mennonites who have moved north from Belize, Central America. The move has occurred in part because of violence in Belize; Maria's cousin, for example, has fled to Texas with his family after being kidnapped and held for ransom by drug lords in the 1990s. In July 2005, as her large family sits at Sunday lunch, Maria, dressed in the long, print dress and black head scarf worn by conservative Mennonites, speaks of her scattered family. Four of her brothers and their families farm at Spanish Lookout Colony in Belize. One brother has returned to Belize *after a disappointing sojourn in Nova Scotia; another, after multiple stints in Manitoba. Two other siblings have become urban folk, residents of Winnipeg. Many cousins still live in Los Jagueyes Colony in Chihuahua, Mexico. Maria recalls her own many moves – from Manitoba to Chihuahua in 1948, to British Honduras (Belize) in 1958, and now, recently, back to Canada. She finds the departure of her son and his young family for Ontario, where they hope to establish a chapter of the Kleine Gemeinde, especially difficult.*²

Isaak Goertzen is a friendly, elderly Old Colony Mennonite minister living at the Mennonite senior citizens' home in La Crete, Alberta's most northerly farming community, surrounded by pristine boreal forest. Isaak seems wary at my unannounced visit in August 2004, but after a conversation in Low German, he responds warmly to my questions about the "Kjampf fe dee Jemeend" (the struggle for the true congregation) and the encroachment of the modern world. He tells me about the migration he led from northern Alberta to the Bolivian lowlands in 1972 to join tens of thousands of Mennonite co-religionists, and then his sad return to Alberta in the 1980s. His stories describe exhilarating air travel, land purchases, pioneer pitfalls, and the eventual abandonment of Bolivia. He keeps to himself the more intricate stories of intra-community conflict during these trying years. But he offers a blessing, as he and his son, an Old Colony church song leader, sing from the Oole Gesangbuak (the note-less, German-language Old Song Book *of the Old Colony Church), in lengthy cadences, chant-like sonnets of suffering and faithfulness. Isaak and his son have managed to keep an old tradition alive in modern Canada.*³

This book relates a distinctive transnational experience linked to the history of Canada, but also to half a dozen other countries across the Americas. It focuses on specific aspects in the making of an imagined village, a loosely linked pan-American community of some 250,000 Low German-speaking Mennonites. Its inhabitants, many still possessing Canadian citizenship, are the descendants mostly of traditionalist Old Colony Mennonites (but also of four other smaller groups) who emigrated from western Canada in the 1920s and settled in isolated, rural places in Latin America: 6000 chose mountainous northern Mexico; 1700, the Paraguayan Chaco. There they struggled to reconstruct close-knit farm village life as they had known it in Manitoba and Saskatchewan.

Over the course of three generations, this migrant community became increasingly scattered; in general terms, undergoing a three-part dispersion. Today, about a third of these Mennonites still live in or near the original settlements founded in Mexico and Paraguay in the 1920s.

Another third have travelled even farther south, some from Canada to East Paraguay in the 1940s, but mostly those from northern Mexico, first to Belize in the 1950s, then, beginning in the 1960s to Bolivia, to Argentina in the 1980s, and to southern Mexico's Campeche state in the 1990s. A final third have "returned" north, mostly to Canada, the land of the grandparents, but also to the south-central United States. This scattering, however, is not this simple, and continues to and from each of these places today.

The ninety-year period examined in this book describes these Mennonites as honing a world "among the nations." Socially, they migrated across borders, sometimes with remarkable frequency; they reached back to places from which they came; they pursued "sustained social ties" across borders; oftentimes, they maintained homes in more than one country.[4] Their culture contained elements of what scholars variously dub the "transoceanic," "transborder," "trans-local," "transstatal," "supranational," and or even "nationally indifferent,"[5] but, to my mind, most effectively designated as the "transnational." As such, their lives were shaped by sojourns that dealt directly with various governments along the way, by ongoing struggles with issues of citizenship, and by an ever-present consciousness of life in more than a single nation-state. It is true, they infrequently held dual citizenship, a common strategy of many transnational migrants,[6] but frequently they held citizenship in one country and resided in another. Most often, they retained a singular Canadian citizenship for multiple generations, moving between North and South America, usually without pursuing either social or cultural citizenship in them. In fact, like some ethnoreligious people elsewhere described by Dhiru Patel, Jeremy Stolow, and others, they usually resisted allegiance and emotional attachment to any one country.[7] They were thus not Mexican Mennonites or Paraguayan Mennonites as much as Mexico Mennonites and Paraguay Mennonites, a subtle, but significant, difference.

This particular approach to the nation-state was expressed in specific ways. Their leaders negotiated directly with national governments to secure guarantees that the Mennonites could live outside or beyond the nation, in village communities shaped by their religious faith and non-violent agrarian ideals. Many experienced Canada not as a benevolent place of refuge, but as a way-station country that seemingly had betrayed them in 1916 with laws forcing them to send their children to English-language public schools even though it once had promised them their own private education system. Most resisted any national identity whatsoever, cultivating instead a commonality based on their sectarian faith and a history of migration. Their pacifist ways reflected sixteenth- and seventeenth-century Dutch Anabaptist teachings found in old books they carried with them from one continent to another. Their everyday language was a Low German (*Plautdietsch*) dialect acquired in eighteenth-century West Prussia (Poland), but infused with native Dutch and more recently acquired Russian words.[8] Their evolving ethnic boundaries stemmed from those that defined Mennonite farm communities in nineteenth-century New Russia (Ukraine) and western Canada.[9] Many wore distinctive clothes adapted over the centuries: the women in lengthy, dark floral-patterned dresses and black kerchiefs; the men, mostly clean-shaven, often in black overalls, almost always in long-sleeved shirts, and never with ties. Most were rural householders who cared deeply about fertile land, considering it as a means to sustain traditional village life rather than as a physical asset belonging to one nation. Over the course of the twentieth century, these Mennonites migrated time and again, when economic need dictated or religious teaching called. With the aid of widely circulated texts – published memoirs, local histories, oral recollections, and especially letters in newspapers – they also developed an especially pronounced, however unusual, identity that linked them to an imagined village superimposed on half a dozen nations of the western hemisphere.

A crucial feature in the making of this particular identity was Mennonite religious teaching on non-violence and nonconformity. In fact, their very migrations sent a religious message: the true Christian must not become too settled in one place, linked to one nation-state, or too comfortable in "this world." The New Testament message of Romans 12 – "do not conform any longer to the pattern of this world" – was taken to heart, while the counsel of I Peter 2 – "as foreigners and exiles ... abstain from sinful desires" – was interpreted as a call to contest consumer culture and patriotism.[10] They also invoked a common Old Testament motif of living in exile; that is, "scattered among the nations."[11] Although exile of this kind is most often used in Hebrew scripture to denote God's displeasure and even punishment, these traditionalist Mennonites most often saw it as a virtue, their signal that true citizenship lay beyond the mainstream of this world. They identified first with the close-knit, pacifist Christian community here on earth, and ultimate citizenship lay in a glorious afterworld, in heaven.

If elements of this story are distinctive, others are universal, shared by many millions of twentieth-century migrants, many hundreds of thousands in Canada. It is an account shaped by economic necessity, ideals of better beginnings in yet other lands, and a willingness to undertake not only one but many moves, often with continuing links in more than one country. Employing the ideas of Ann Curthoys and Marilyn Lake, this story considers how "lives and events have been shaped by processes and relationships that have transcended the borders of nation states." As such, this account also inherently critiques nation-centric histories, described by these scholars as "rigid and confining," and rather invokes "metaphors of fluidity, as in talk of circulation and flows ... alongside metaphors of connection and relationship."[12] These flows constitute endless exchanges of information, evolving memories spoken in ethnic media, and counsel on life in new places. In the end, it is a story of a life referenced to multiple locations and affected by varied geographies. In his recent book titled *Transnationalism*, Steven Vertovec focuses on "ways in which conditions in more than one location impact upon such forms of social organization and the values, practices and structures that sustain them."[13] The very act of being on the move and living among nations became a primary defining feature of both these Mennonites and other migrant groups in Canada and, indeed, around the world.

But transnationalism is not only a subject, it is also a methodology or a lens of enquiry, and in this respect, too, this study connects to a wider field of historical enquiry. Isabel Hofmeyr writes that "the key claim of any transnational approach" is not only that it serves "as a theme or motif," but also includes "an analytic set of methods which defines the endeavor itself" that "direct one's attention to the 'space of the flows.'"[14] As a method of historical enquiry, this approach may identify particular, hitherto uninvestigated, events as worthy of study. As Ewa Morawska, Dirk Hoerder, and others have argued, this approach ironically illuminates the local and the seemingly banal in new ways; indeed, these scholars argue that any migration story gains credence when the global and the local are linked,[15] when broader forces are studied for their impact on the local community. The distinctive Low German Mennonite migrant community was, in some respects, merely a variation of what happened elsewhere; in fact, a premise of this book is that its very subject can add insight to the global story of migration.

The general themes outlined in each of the eight chapters identify specific aspects of this broader transborder story. In no respect do they tell a complete story, only a number of crucial aspects of it. Chapter 1 tells of a particular cosmology, as male leaders of emigration expressed a supra-national outlook, shaping a debate on the relative merits of living in one of numerous countries, and offered to exchange proven economic security in one country for religious well-being in another. Chapter 2 outlines how ordinary migrants expressed a worldview that bypassed the nation in favour of the village, street, and field; they were "trans-local" spaces, reincarnated ethnic enclaves on soil that was seen to belong to no one nation, but to a wider and expansive earth. Chapter 3 relates how, in the context of unexpected troubles, an unmitigated nostalgia for the old homeland developed, leading to second guessing, rigorous debate, and even sharp social rift. Chapter 4 considers how time and space were reshaped – both contracting and expanding – as migrants moved out of the local into the chaos of the wider world, and then became entrenched again in the local, albeit in new lands. Chapter 5 describes ways in which the immigrants presented themselves to outsiders – the national media and international experts – who visited to gaze upon, evaluate, illuminate, and interpret the newcomers' success in integrating into national economies and global markets. The sixth chapter shows how the immigrants, seeking order within uncertainty, remember their migrations and thus stake their ground as distinctive people in new societies. Chapter 7 outlines a geographic reimagining as migrants tell their stories, mentally turning a constellation of diasporic villages into a single, imagined, intercontinental village ordered by their particular sense of citizenship. The eighth chapter presents the story in the most localized of spaces – the migrant household – and traces the gendered ways in which women link their domestic space to a wider, transcultural world. These eight themes represent significant aspects of all transnational migrant experiences, and of Canadian-descendant Mennonite migrants in particular.

This lens also illuminates the very existence of a subject, perhaps even giving birth to it. A strictly nation-centred perspective, for example, easily excludes or misrepresents entire groups of people when they do not fit a national teleology. Over time, most histories of ethnoreligious groups such as the Mennonites have anchored their stories to specific nations.[16] A three-volume *Mennonites in Canada* series and a four-volume *Mennonite Experience in America*, for example, present a history of Mennonites in one country only, even though specific denominations in those countries spilled over the Canada–United States border.[17] Even the most noted anti-modern Anabaptist groups – the Amish and the Old Order Mennonites – are typically discussed within a single nation, whether the United States or Canada.[18] Ironically, the valuable secondary studies that provide a base for this book are also often nation-centred: they include histories of these traditionalist groups in Canada and Mexico, sociological works on them in Mexico and Paraguay, and anthropological studies based in Belize, Bolivia, and Argentina.[19]

This book seeks to illuminate a three-generation-long story of a specific group of Mennonites that does not nicely fit a national story. These migrants were Low German-speaking traditionalists, conservative, conserving or old order in nature, sectarian in their identity, and antipatriotic, unwilling to become tied to a specific country.[20] Historically, they experienced relatively short sojourns in a variety of countries, lived in peripheral regions in those countries, and charted pathways outside even the main Mennonite centres. In the 1870s, when 17,000 Mennonites in Russia contested new military conscription laws, the ancestors of the subjects of this book were among the 7000 more conservative Mennonites who chose to settle in newly created Manitoba rather than farther south in the more economically developed and climatically temperate states of the Great Plains. The simple reason for their choice for Canada was Ottawa's promise of military exemption and block settlement, as well as freedom of private education. That it had made these commitments official in an 1873 Order-in-Council, which the Mennonites referred to as their "Privilegium," a special charter of privileges, was especially important; they firmly believed that the Canadian option would enable them to contest any form of national integration.

This resistance shaped the history of the various subgroups of Mennonites making Manitoba their home in the 1870s.[21] The largest and most traditionalist of these various groups, the so-called Old Colony Mennonite Church (officially, the Reinländer Mennonite Church), was organized upon the arrival of Mennonites in Manitoba in 1875 by settlers stemming from the Old Colony (that is, from the Khortitsa Mennonite Colony, the first Mennonite community founded in New Russia in 1789). This church was founded on a vision of Christ-like simplicity and separation from the wider society, including its public schools and municipal governments. At first, the members of the Old Colony Church settled in the Mennonite West Reserve, one of two major Mennonite block settlements, but in the 1890s they also spread westward, to Swift Current and Hague in that section of western Canada later reorganized as the province of Saskatchewan. Four other smaller, somewhat more progressive, groups also became known for their opposition to any form of nation-centric public education. Three of these groups – the Sommerfelder from Manitoba's West Reserve, the Chortitzer from Manitoba's East Reserve, and the Saskatchewan Bergthaler from central Saskatchewan – were cut from the larger so-called Bergthaler Church after a painful schism over public education in Manitoba during the 1890s. The smallest group, the Mennonite Kleine Gemeinde, had been founded in 1812 in the Molochna (or Molotschna) Colony in Russia over questions of simplicity and absolute pacifism. These five subdenominations stand on the periphery of the Russian Mennonite story, dominated by the much larger and more accommodating progressive General Conference and Mennonite Brethren groups whose histories include immigrant settlements in the United States in the 1870s and Canada in the 1920s. They stand in contrast to the more marginal and traditionalist subjects of this book.

Ironically, the transnational lens of this story also sharpens the very outline of the story of Canada. Historians who have placed Canada's social evolution within a wider global and imperial environment have, in the process, also illuminated how borderland cultures were formed, how migrants became racialized citizens, and how the dominant and the dominated were imagined and structured.[22] As C.A. Bayly has argued, nations have always been made in relation to other nations: "The 'nations' embedded in the term 'transnational,'" he writes, "were not originary elements to be 'transcended' by the forces we are discussing," but rather "the products ... of those very processes."[23] The Mennonite diaspora described in this book illustrates Canada's interconnectedness with other parts of the world. In the 1910s and 1920s especially, the young dominion's ambitions of becoming a proud, integrated, and independent power, and not merely a vestige of British imperialism, set it on an ambitious course of assimilating its newcomers to an English-language, nation-centric culture.[24] In the 1940s, Canada demonstrated its maturing international membership by a remarkable war effort, underpinned by unprecedented urbanization, industrialization, cultural engineering, and militarization.[25] Then, during the second half of the twentieth century, Canada's highly developed economy, relatively open citizenship laws, multicultural policies, and social safety net made it a magnet for newcomers, including workers ordered by an international labour market.[26]

This broader focus, however, does critique the nation-centred history that celebrates the coming of beleaguered people to chosen shores of hope. The established migration history of Canada may tell of newcomers leaving places of hardship for a democratic, multicultural, prosperous country,[27] but Canada was also a land of emigrants, not only a receiving nation but also a sending one. Over the course of its history, its difficult winters and limited economy sent farmers, labourers, tourists, professionals, and other social groups southward, especially to the United States. A growing literature on twentieth-century emigrants describes especially the thousands of farmers who headed from Ontario to Michigan, from Quebec to New England, from Manitoba to Kansas, from Saskatchewan to Oregon.[28] Thousands of other migrants left Canada to return home, especially sojourning, single men from disparate places including Italy, India, Chile, Vietnam, and Kenya.[29] Hundreds of thousands of emigrants were passport-carrying Canadians who returned to old homelands with the "golden fleece," while tens of thousands so-called snowbirds found seasonal refuge in the southern United States, Mexico, and other places in the sun. Within this story, the Low German Mennonite group exodus in the 1920s and subsequent diaspora is a noteworthy subject, as much a part of Canada's migration history as the myriad accounts of arrivals in Canada. That the Low German Mennonite story includes a "return" to Canada after a two- and three-generation sojourn away makes it all the more Canadian and simultaneously transnational.

Employing this perspective better illuminates the changing nature of migrant cultures over time. Indeed, scholars have suggested that transnationalism is a dynamic and evolving phenomenon. Vertovec, noting that many theorists exclude "old" migrations of the late nineteenth or early twentieth centuries from the transnational category, argues that one must differentiate "old" and "new" transnationalisms.[30] The former registers early twentieth-century realities – return migration, letter writing, split families, chain migration, remittance payments, compelling homeland politics, and diasporic community life. In contrast, the new transnationalism is associated with changes in communication linked to new media connections, inexpensive air travel, multicultural policies, and an increasingly globalized economy. One could add to this list the increasing trend of dual citizenship, multinational family business links, elastic labour markets, economic border zones, and rapid highway-based transportation.

A three-generational history of the "Canadian" Mennonite diaspora in the Americas exemplifies this increasingly complex world, not only as a juxtaposition of the old and the new, but as an evolving social space over time. A globalizing economy and ever-speedier travel technologies simultaneously sent communities to the far corners of the

Americas and created closer bonds among the dispersed. In the same way that this book's eight chapters illustrate specific building blocks of the transnational experience, they also demonstrate how it gained traction over time, evolving from an old to a new version of international linkage. The first two chapters mark unilinear movement, the story first of Mennonite leaders charting a path from Canada to Latin America, then of the emigration of the people themselves. The next two chapters continue this theme, commitment to life in Mexico and Paraguay despite a sharp exchange of ideas on the benefits and pitfalls of a return to Canada, and then a smaller echo migration from Canada to East Paraguay and northern Mexico during the late 1940s. The last five chapters, though, outline more intense international linkage and multivariate identities, a new transnationalism affected by improved technology, global commodity and labour markets, and repeat migrations. The post-war migration to British Honduras and Bolivia illustrates the ironic symbiotic relationship of a Mennonite search for isolation and globalizing economies. The sustained return to Canada during the second half of the century underscores the importance of a global labour market, while the outlines of pan-American diaspora link it to new technologies of inexpensive air travel and more elastic citizenship laws. The final chapter on the translocal worlds of Mexico Mennonite women in southern Ontario identifies the importance of American interstate highways, a Canadian social safety net, and provincial immigrant services in creating even closer links between Canada and Latin America.

Finally, the transnational turn clarifies the importance of specific texts and the flow of their circulation in the making of an identity. In this regard, Isabel Hofmyer highlights "the movement of objects, people, ideas, and texts," especially "popular media and its global distribution and circulation."[31] Such texts may include media of great circulation, but also localized texts created by the migrants themselves or non-migrant observers. The interrogation of these specific documents illuminates the migrant imagination, the groups' lines of power, their sense of order, and the impact of government policies and global economies in their lives.

This book is based on a specific set of publicly accessible texts, each created by the migrants or direct observers. It begins by considering the memoirs and diaries of Mennonite leaders who sought to shape the religious thinking of a diasporic group. It then analyses hundreds of letters written by settlers in Mexico and Paraguay and published in a Canadian-based, German-language, immigrant newspaper, *Die*

Steinbach Post, and, to a lesser degree, in English-language rural weeklies located in sending communities. It also queries national newspapers in Belize and Bolivia, as well as contemporary fieldwork by visiting American and Canadian graduate students in the disciplines of geography, economics, and anthropology. Two of the final chapters consider narratives produced by oral history, projects that, in 1979 and 2006, respectively, asked Ontario residents about the experience of international migration, about diasporic mindsets, and about adaptations to new lands. Another chapter is based on letters to a recently established immigrant newspaper, *Die Mennonitische Post*, begun by a Canadian Mennonite service agency that inadvertently facilitated the creation of a particular public, that of a transborder Low German peoplehood. While these disparate texts cast light on specific moments in the story, they also give voice to a people who transcended national boundaries.

The story that unfolds in these pages, then, is both unique and universal. It is unique in that any early twentieth-century emigration from prosperous Canada to the underdeveloped countries of Mexico and Paraguay is unusual. The idea that an immigrant would make an economic sacrifice for a specific cultural goal seems strange in a world where middle-class values seem to dictate most social action. Even within the Mennonite world, where non-violence, simplicity, and community cohesiveness tend to shape an ethno-religious self-awareness, the old Anabaptist idea of being "pilgrims and strangers," contesting nationalist lures, has largely disappeared. This story, it would seem, has few counterparts in the modern world.

Yet, in other ways, this story is universal. It can clarify the qualities of any modern nation-state, Canada in particular, by asking how the imperative of national unity and national integration into a globalized economy affect localized cultures. In more general terms, it can illustrate how such modernization affects vulnerable people who do not possess sophisticated cultural or economic defenses. It also sheds light on how these identities are created, how they change over time, and how the very manner of telling their stories affords some measure of agency to peripheral people. Finally, it reveals that collective identities are never exclusive. Local communities, regions, or nations may seem like distinct categories of study, but in fact they are intertwined – with each other and with wider worlds – in more ways than one can imagine. To trace these various currents, these dynamic connections across the Americas, is to describe each society to the other.

1 Leaving the "British Empire" in Canada: Promises in the South, 1916–1921

In his memoir recounting the emigration of Old Colony Mennonites from Canada to Mexico in the 1920s, Isaak M. Dyck emphasized the effect of the 1916 school legislation in Manitoba and Saskatchewan.¹ These laws, a product of the heady and patriotic days of the First World War, gave the government the power to determine what Mennonite children would learn in school. The Canadian federal government had exempted the pacifist Low German Mennonites from military service, but the two provincial governments pressured them in new, systemic ways.² The school legislation, wrote Dyck, entailed more than a simple curriculum change: it grew from "an inextinguishable enthusiasm for the art of war" and planned that "militarism be instilled in every child." Mennonite children were to learn the rallying cry of "one king, one country, one fleet, one flag, one all-British empire: love and sacrifice for the Fatherland," and soon, "even the Mennonites were going to be made into '100 percent Canadians.'" According to Dyck, the Mennonites' only option was to leave the Dominion of Canada, rooted as it was in the hegemonic, imperial culture of the "all-British Empire." Religious rebirth and commitment could occur only in exile, well removed from a land most Canadian Mennonites had come to call home.³

As Dyck saw it, the Mennonites needed to search for a particular kind of land, because a further problem with Canada was that its wealth and middle-class culture were beginning to transform their simple agrarian ways.⁴ Dyck related the mystical experience of another Mennonite minister, Jacob Wiens of Saskatchewan, in 1913, significantly just a year before the outbreak of the First World War. Outside the village of Reinland, "while looking out over a field ... of swaying wheat with its beautiful ears," Wiens had heard "a voice come from above, saying ... 'You will not be able to stay here [in Canada] forever; the [Mennonite] church will once again have to take up the walking staff.'" When Wiens asked, "but where to?," "in his spirit he received the following answer: 'if the church wishes to maintain itself in the pure gospel, it will once again need to settle among a heathen people.'"

Perhaps in 1874, when the first Mennonites migrated from Imperial Russia to western Canada, they had found in its frontier lands a chance to rebuild their farm villages in "simplicity and humility." But the wealth of Canada intervened: houses grew larger and buggies more elaborate, commerce took off, the learning of English followed and then, too, the temptation to accept the nation's schools, resounding with patriotic language of empire and war. A "heathen" land denoted a primitive and strange place, one far removed from the comforts of Protestant, white, Anglo Canada. Only in such a land could the Mennonites secure their cultural independence and eternal salvation.

Dyck's memoir was written in Mexico in the 1960s when he was an elderly *Ältester* (bishop or lead minister) of the large Old Colony Mennonite Church. It was an evocative retrospective, a history lesson recounting the difficult exodus from Canada and pilgrimage to Mexico in the 1920s.

Four other texts by leaders, all extensive daily diaries, offer a somewhat less emotional and more quotidian perspective. The first is a "church diary" by Peter R. Dueck of Steinbach, Manitoba. As the Ältester of the small Kleine Gemeinde Mennonite group, Dueck kept a record of the regular meetings of the church's Ministerial Council (the *Lehrdienst*, consisting of the Ältester and the ministers), and of the church's Brotherhood assembly (the *Bruderschaft*, a voting body consisting of all baptized males), from 1901 to 1919, the year Dueck died during the Spanish Flu. A second diary is a personal writing of farmer David Rempel of Swift Current, Saskatchewan, who was chosen by the Old Colony Mennonites to join a land-scouting delegation to Brazil and Argentina in 1920. A third diary is a more reflective account by Johan M. Loeppky, an Old Colony Mennonite minister from Hague, Saskatchewan; he recalled the final scouting trip to Mexico in 1921 and the historic negotiation for a charter of privileges (or, as Mennonites called it, their *Privilegium*) with Mexican president Álvaro Obregón. A fourth diary, by farmer Bernard Toews of Altona, Manitoba, and a member of yet another church group, the Sommerfelder Mennonite

Church, records in remarkable detail the final scouting trip to South America, an exhausting five-month foray into Paraguay in 1921, with a side trip to Mexico.

The five texts – one memoir and four diaries – reveal a religious understanding that emphasized the biblical idea of being "foreigners and exiles" or "pilgrims and strangers." They convey their authors' intricate knowledge of government and agriculture, and, in several cases, an intense curiosity about the cultures of new lands. Each, however, is undergirded with the biblical premise that the true Christian must not "be conformed to this world" and must chart a life beyond the mainstream culture of the nation-state.

Most of these writings, implicitly or explicitly, created a dichotomy between danger in Canada and redemption in Latin America. Each offered to interpret the historical moment when Canada imposed its "imperialistic" culture on the anti-modern, conservative Mennonites. No doubt, the writings reinforced the male authors' positions as leaders within an overtly patriarchal church, but, as the authors were members of a minority group within nationalistic Canada, their writings also reflected the aims of the dispossessed, or at least those of members of a group on the periphery of mainstream, middle-class society. Ironically, Sidonie Smith's feminist vocabulary describing autobiographies that "resist memory," "talk back," and critique "certain teleological itineraries" may also describe the writings of these patriarchal leaders of an ethno-religious minority out of step with modernity.[5] Perhaps the Mennonite leaders shored up official, church-based memory, but they rejected an official, sanctioned, national memory that heralded imperial culture, a militaristic masculinity, and middle-class ideals. To employ Julie Rak's description of radical pacifist, even anarchist, Doukhobor writers, these Mennonite writers can be said to have "'trouble[d]' the idea of Canada as a nation with an unproblematic history ... foreground[ing] nationhood itself as a problem that preserves some form of injustice."[6] And they brought their texts into conversation with historic writings, not in dissimilar fashion to practitioners of *Agudat Israel*, an anti-Zionist orthodox Jewishness, described by Jeremy Stolow as conceiving "of collective Jewish existence based on cosmological explanations of the state of Jewish exile in the world, as had been elaborated in centuries of canonical writings."[7]

Perhaps a narrative of Canada's growing "sense of power" within the British Empire and steady evolution to full nationhood was celebrated by British-Canadian writers, but, to members of minority religious groups such as the Mennonites, nationalism was problematic.[8] Mennonite leaders in 1916 and its aftermath wrote to explain how they resisted assimilative legislation and how they took up the "walking staff" to resist a powerful cultural incursion into their close-knit worlds. The idea of migration to foreign countries as "strangers in this world" infused these writings. A transnationalism in this instance arose not as an economic consequence of a global economy or rising technologies,[9] but as a religiously informed, financially unfavourable resistance to an incipient nationalism and rapidly encroaching modernity.

Isaak Dyck: A Sermon against Canadian Patriotism

Dyck's memoir was written in German and published in two volumes in 1965 while he resided in Manitoba Colony in Chihuahua, Mexico. Distributed among fellow Old Colony Mennonites throughout the Americas, Dyck's narrative offered an Old Colony Mennonite interpretation of historic events, but one penned with the specific aim of reviving a simple, separate world just as forces of modernity were undermining his church. He was not only the historian, but also the preacher whose memory of the 1920s-era emigration was linked to a plea for a return to old values in the tumultuous 1960s. And, as with any sermon, it was anchored in myriad biblical references.

Dyck's first and foremost point was that the true Mennonite was an "alien in this world," and that, collectively, the Mennonites resembled a modern children of Israel. As such, they chose a difficult pathway. Dyck called his readers to immerse themselves in the *Martyr's Mirror*, the classic 1660 history of persecution endured by the sixteenth-century Anabaptist ancestors of the Mennonites. The book taught the life-altering lesson that the "followers of Jesus were ... born into sorrow, suffering and persecution" and that their calling was to "walk in all humility and lowliness."[10]

This imperative described the migration of the 1920s to Mexico. The emigrants ultimately had been strengthened by the troubling events of the First World War in Canada, a time when "God ... wanted to test his church ... like gold in a fire." Indeed, the threatening school legislation engendered in the Mennonites a new, refined loyalty to the old idea of a visible, separate, steadfast community of non-violent believers.[11] The emigrants, Dyck implied, had exerted their "freedom of conscience" and expressed an authentic faith; of them it could not be said, "as the Lord spoke through the prophet Isaiah: 'these people come near to me with their mouth ... but their hearts are far from me.'"[12] Their action had been informed by true religion. Indeed, propelling them to take this costly step was their sacred baptismal vow, when, as young adults, each one had "promised God obedience to the faith with their hearts and mouths."[13] God's truth, declared Dyck, did not require an elaborate, culturally sophisticated worship, but simple obedience. Elaborate theologies were useless, for "truth is never more beautiful than when it appears totally naked and simply free of human understanding or worldly teaching."[14] Such devotion was the very foundation of the community.

Dyck's retrospective sermon placed the 1920s migration in a wider historical context. He linked it first to the ancient exodus of the children of Israel from Egypt; like the Israelites, the Mennonites had been divinely guided to begin wandering, leaving Canada for a promised land, and their inherited faith had served as their own "clear pillar of smoke by day and a pillar of fire by night," leading them "through the cruel desert of life." Dyck also related the migration to sixteenth-century Mennonite suffering: the faith of "Menno Simons ... [and] our ancestors ... was so firmly based on the path of the cross that they had no doubt that a pilgrim who had followed the path until the end would finally arrive happily at upper Zion."[15] Like the "thousands of martyrs" of the sixteenth century, the emigrants of the 1920s were following Christ in "footsteps of grief," a pathway that took the Mennonites from one country to another, and ultimately to eternal life in heaven, the figurative "upper Zion."[16] Indeed, the migrants of the 1920s were part of a grand narrative of Mennonite diaspora: true religion, wrote Dyck, "has only been spread through the walking staff, namely from Holland to [northern] Germany ... [to] Russia ... to America and Canada, and from Canada to here, our present home in Mexico."[17] The message was clear: the Old Colony Mennonite migration was encased in profound meaning.

Dyck saw a particular parallel between the 1920s emigration from Canada and the 1870s exodus from Russia. "Faith, love and hope in God," insisted Dyck, had enabled "our fathers, elders and teachers ... to leave their dearly beloved home and fatherland, Russia" in 1875 even as compromising, short-sighted Mennonites who stayed behind scoffed at the pilgrims leaving for the Canadian wilderness. Most importantly, as Dyck saw it, both migrations had been divinely ordered and protected.

His own mother's stories of the 1875 migration to Canada, given credence with reference to the veneration of mothers in Jeremiah 15, illustrated divine guidance. The stories "my dear mother would tell me," wrote Dyck, described "the voyage across the big ocean ... on the water for twelve whole days." It was a troubling time, but Mother was comforted by the presence on the ship "of dear Ältester Johan Wiebe," and, "without worry or care," fervently believed that if he "was on her ship, then it could not sink."[18] During a massive storm one night, Mother had "noticed that the loving Ältester went to every room on the ship where our people were and reminded them all of how [in biblical times] the disciples were with the Saviour on the boat" and how the stormy Sea of Galilee had been miraculously calmed. Ältester Wiebe's faith had had its effect: "The next morning as they awoke, the storm had subsided and the ship sailed on the smooth sea. ... They saw the works of the Lord, his wonderful deeds in the deep. ..."[19] The 1875 immigration to Canada had been divinely ordered and so, too, the 1922 emigration from it.

The main focus of Dyck's historical interpretation was the very era that had produced the offending 1916 school legislation. It had been a time of a slow but certain encroachment of modernity, including wealth, greed, and pride. Dyck was unrelenting: "Wealth breeds boldness, boldness breeds high spirits," and high spirits, the haughtiness of "Sodom ... and her daughters," who, before their destruction in the Bible, had been "arrogant, overfed and unconcerned," unwilling to "help the poor and needy." Then the treachery of wealth evolved into the lure of war. True, the Mennonites had been exempted from military service, but the announcement from "the most revered Prime Minister Robert L. Borden ... that the [1873 military exemption] promise to the Mennonites would be honoured" merely served to "pacify the people and lull them to sleep." The unsuspecting Mennonites failed to realize militarism's pervasiveness, and soon they were cajoled in other ways. At first, the government merely coaxed the Mennonites into paying "large sums of money to the Red Cross," but then it tried to force them to participate in the "general [manpower] registry throughout all of Canada." Ältester Johan Friesen at the time had warned his people against registering, declaring that if the Old Colonists offered "but a finger [the government] would take the whole hand." Unfortunately, the Mennonites fell for the scheme, duped by a clever government official who recited for the Mennonite leaders the biblical story of Mary and Joseph obeying Caeser's order to be registered in Bethlehem. As a result, the Brotherhood, which had supported Ältester Friesen at first, "changed their decision" and soon began registering. It was a turning point, wrote Dyck, "peace and fleshly security reigned,"[20] and many Mennonites now moved incontrovertibly towards assimilation.

For the observant Mennonites, said Dyck, the two years after 1916 introduced other matters that signalled the end to the Old Colonists' time in Canada. First, "things continued to decline morally in the congregation; sin was heaped upon sin and the great assimilation to this world seemed to gain the upper hand." Especially worrisome was the raucous behaviour of many young Mennonite men, who carried "in one pocket ... the [military exemption] cards signed by the Ältester verifying that they were [pacifist] Mennonites ... and in the other ... their bottle of Schnapps." To make matters worse, they frequented "pubs and theatres," all the while "dressing and wearing their hair the same way as the 'English.'"[21] The English boys' "hatred and envy" of the Mennonites was a natural response, as the parents of "the English" wondered why their "sons must offer up their blood, body and lives" while worldly Mennonite boys won military exemptions.

The enforcement of the new education laws in 1919 brought "more concern, anxiety and sorrow."[22] The government's increasing harshness, culminating in prison terms for some recalcitrant parents, was especially worrisome. Dyck highlighted Rev. Peter Friesen's two-week prison term in Winnipeg and noted other similar sentences in the nearby British-Canadian town of Morden. Making matters even worse, many moderate Mennonites actually seemed to welcome the new school laws, blindly helping to construct a "Canadian tower of Babel." They might claim that public education would not interfere with their pacifist principles, but their own subsequent embrace of the "automobile and ostentatious clothing," "English" spouses, and military service showed otherwise.[23]

Ominous warnings followed this acquiescence. The Spanish Flu epidemic of 1918 and 1919 devastated Mennonite families: "Homes were turned into houses of mourning [as] ... fathers and mothers were torn from their children and parents were forced to give their children up," wrote Dyck, and even Ältester Friesen became grievously ill.[24] The flu was not just an epidemic, but also a divine message of biblical proportion, "a just judgement of God ... because of our sins," the fall to middle-class lure and nationalistic impulse. Human threats followed this warning as Mennonites faced disdain from mainstream Canada: "The people of Canada began to mock us," for the Old Colonists could not endorse their ambition "to make for themselves a great name among the nations."

Emigration was the only way out: "The only thing that could preserve our simplicity in Christ was our willingness to pick up the walking staff." Thus, when "the dear Ältester Johan Friesen finally asked at a meeting of the Brotherhood how many were in favour of moving, the answer was unanimous – everyone wanted out!"[25] A culmination of events had left the "true" Mennonites with no other choice. Perhaps the Old Colony Mennonites had almost succumbed to the lure of nationalism, but, as Dyck argued in his autobiographical sermon, emigration from Canada ensured a people's quest for religious purity.

Peter R. Dueck: The Concerns of 1916

The details of concern in Isaak Dyck's memoir are substantiated by at least one diary from the tumultuous days of the First World War. Ältester Peter R. Dueck's record of 1916, for example, reveals the perspective of a leader within a close-knit Mennonite community – Steinbach, Manitoba, in the heart of the so-called East Reserve – and recounts a litany of social dangers in Canada.[26] It also reflects the leadership of one of the smaller Mennonite denominations, the Kleine Gemeinde, their thinking and worldview, and their collaboration with leaders from the wider Mennonite community. In the end, perhaps in part because of Dueck's untimely death in 1919, the Kleine Gemeinde wavered and did not leave Canada, although its more conservative wing did leave for Mexico after the Second World War. Nevertheless, the Kleine Gemeinde Mennonites were deeply troubled by the events linked to the First World War, and Dueck's diary suggests why.

His very first entry for 1916 depicted a placid, rural Mennonite settlement, reaching beyond its immediate borders only to embrace a similarly close-knit Mennonite community elsewhere. Dueck announced that the year's first Sunday worship service was held "in Steinbach where Peter Loewen preached" and where Dueck read a letter from Rev. Gerhard Klassen of the Kleine Gemeinde counterpart at Meade, Kansas. On a later Sunday that January, the Brotherhood met to agree on the process of an upcoming minister's election, and then reassembled on yet another Sunday for that election, one in which two farmers – Henry R. Dueck and Peter B. Kroeker – were chosen for the lifetime office of preacher. Immediately after the election, the church leaders from *Jantsied*, the "other side" – literally, the Kleine Gemeinde community of Rosenort located on the other side of the mighty Red River – left for home after having provided oversight on the election.[27]

In February, Dueck's diary took an ominous turn from this communal harmony. His entry for 10 February was curt: "The Kleine Gemeinde Ministerial invited to [the village of] Chortitz for an inter-Mennonite meeting concerning the school legislation of the [provincial] Liberal government which wishes to legislate 'English only' schools; the Mennonites want to resolve this issue with the government." Just four days later, Dueck, accompanied by a lay Kleine Gemeinde member, Jacob Reimer, travelled to "Winnipeg concerning the school business," apparently joining an inter-Mennonite delegation to appeal directly to government officials. Dueck noted that their "presentation to the government" seemed successful, as they received a "promise that the private schools would not be disturbed and that the government would seek the best for the Mennonites."[28]

But peace with the province would be elusive. Indeed, soon after the Winnipeg visit, Dueck recorded a series of events suggesting a highly intrusive state. On 20 February, Dueck returned to Winnipeg for yet another inter-Mennonite gathering, this time to address the government's troubling request for the Mennonites to provide "financial aid for wounded soldiers and widows." Mennonites had their military exemption, but now they faced a war tax disguised as a pitch to assist in humanitarian aid. Then came the national plebiscite on the issue of temperance and again a lure to engage the nation; Dueck put the viewpoint of the Mennonite ministers bluntly: "Christians should not work with the world nor help to rule it." In March, the Kleine Gemeinde ministers assembled again to discuss "private schools" and, in April, to again consider "a request for aid," presumably war-related aid from the government. Although the rest of the year was peaceful enough, on 26 December, the Kleine Gemeinde ministers met to discuss yet another government demand, the national "service cards which all 18–65 year olds must fill out." Any plan to simply ignore the regulation was squelched by "fear of what could happen to those not complying." Again, the Kleine Gemeinde ministers sought help from other Mennonite leaders, and so Ältester Dueck and Minister Heinrich R. Reimer travelled to the West Reserve in south-central Manitoba to attend an inter-Mennonite meeting in Altona. The following day, Dueck recorded the joint decision "not to fill out the cards until it can be determined whether by so doing we will jeopardize our faith stance," and, towards that end, the selection of "three delegates to go to Ottawa to make enquiry with the government." Pressure from government seemed to increase with every turn.[29]

Peter Dueck voiced other concerns in 1916, similar again to those Isaak Dyck remembered years later. In fact, Dueck's references to wealth and "worldly" lifestyles outnumbered the allusions to schools and war. In March, the Kleine Gemeinde ministers met to discuss the social implications of the arrival of "a new fashioned machine," that is, the new, small, gasoline-driven tractors that were replacing the large steam engines. Motorized technology was about to become the mainstay on every farm, a worrisome development for a people committed to humility and plain living. The same meeting also raised a "concern about A. W. Reimer's store" newly opened in Winnipeg, a member's open embrace of urban-based commerce deemed "damaging for salvation." In April, at a Sunday afternoon Brotherhood meeting in Steinbach, Dueck again warned members against "conformity to the world," and, in July, he led the Brotherhood in pondering "the extent to which one can be involved in business with those who are under the ban," and heard them agree "to abide by the rules and not to interact" with a particular excommunicated entrepreneur. In this entry, Dueck recommitted himself, "with the aid of Menno Simons' writings, to discern and compassionately admonish" those who had erred and been banned from membership.[30]

In September 1916, at yet another Brotherhood meeting, Dueck raised the most vexing question of the year: car ownership. The church had disallowed the car because it symbolized pride and vanity, and yet it had seduced several members. In fact, to escape censure, some disingenuous members had sold their cars "quickly before the [last] communion service" and then, in frightful callousness, partaken of the holy sacraments without having confessed their sin. When Dueck and the ministers met that October, they outlined the problem more clearly: "Because the car is pressing itself into our midst we resolve to oppose it even more diligently." After a Brotherhood meeting just a week later in Steinbach, Dueck seemed distraught: "Concerning the car, the resolve among the brethren was very weak and yet we hope for the best." But it must have been only a faint hope, for he expressed "a further concern about pride" seen in worldly dress, specifically some members wearing fashionable "women's hats." The concerns climaxed at a 3 December meeting where Dueck lamented the "wild goings on by the youth" and called on his fellow preachers to "awaken in the parents a resolve to teach their children the Christian way." The world was moving against the Mennonites from the outside, but it was also springing up from within.[31]

Over the next two years, Dueck's small Kleine Gemeinde, like the much larger Old Colony, saw the problems of 1916 increase rather than abate. The temptations of car ownership became intense, the wild youth remained uncontrolled, and the government's early promise to consider the Mennonite concerns on the school question proved false. In 1919, the courts ruled that the provincial governments of Manitoba and Saskatchewan were within their constitutional right to enforce an English-language and publicly inspected curriculum, and to decide unilaterally whether Mennonite schools met the test. Dueck's 1919 death may have undermined the Kleine Gemeinde's resolve to emigrate, but it was a resolve to which the large Old Colony group, and three other small denominations, the Chortitzer, Saskatchewan Bergthaler, and Sommerfelder groups, recommitted themselves.

David Rempel: Diary on the Way to South America

If it was clear to these four groups that they must leave western Canada, it was less clear just where they should go. Scouting trips to a number of locations occurred in 1919 and 1920: they included multiple visits to places in North America (specifically to Mississippi and Quebec) and to various places in Latin America.[32] Each visit was preceded by a Brotherhood meeting, pondering first whether emigration was necessary, then determining a possible location, and finally choosing the scouting delegates. The first of the trips to Latin America was a joint foray by representatives of the smaller denominations to Brazil and Argentina in February 1919. Led by Ältester Aron Zacharias of the Saskatchewan Bergthaler Church, its charge was simple: "Look for suitable land for a closed Mennonite group and ... make contact with governments regarding the conditions of settlement."[33]

Relatively little is known about this trip, but a second journey taken in the late summer of 1919 by delegates of the large Old Colony Church to Argentina, Brazil, and Uruguay was recorded in greater detail. David Rempel, a farmer from Swift Current, Saskatchewan, kept a personal diary and also penned numerous letters to his wife describing the trip. Like that of Peter Dueck, Rempel's diary was never published, but over time it was translated into English, and both the handwritten translation and the original documents in Gothic handwriting were placed in a Mennonite archives in Canada.[34] Unlike some of the other delegates, Rempel was not a religious leader, and much of his diary is remarkably materialist in nature. Indeed, it reveals the habits of a relatively well-to-do traveller, one insisting on at least second- and, sometimes, first-class accommodation on good decks and in fine hotels, and visits to numerous museums and other tourist attractions along the way. But it also reveals a delegate with singular purpose: find good farmland able to sustain a community of committed Mennonites and a willing nation to take them in, and there exchange a stellar reputation as good farmers for religious concessions, especially military exemption and private schools.

Rempel's diary indicates the broad interest in full religious freedom, a curiosity of foreign cultures, and an eye for physical landscape. Indeed, one of Rempel's first notes after pulling out of the train station in Winnipeg and heading east on 6 August was that "soon ... the landscape changed to stony hills and mountains covered with pine trees." And the delegates' first destination was Ottawa, where they planned a last effort to secure Mennonite "freedoms." On 8 August, the delegation checked into Ottawa's "Windsor Hotel" and at once looked up (presumably to seek legal counsel) a trusted British-Canadian lawyer from Manitoba who happened to be in Ottawa. Rempel noted, "McLeod from Morden [Manitoba] was very friendly and very helpful," and gratefully prayed that "the dear Lord repay him." Rempel and his party could not quite ignore picturesque Ottawa itself, and thus they strolled the Rideau Canal, visited an expansive flower garden, and toured the famed Eddy Match factory in nearby Hull. The delegates, in fact, seemed to enjoy the capital: one "evening we walked in a [new] direction ... [and] from there we returned on a street car [on which] a friendly Irish stranger paid for our ticket."[35] But, mindful of their ultimate purpose, on Sunday, 10 August, Rempel noted that after yet another day of sightseeing, "we returned to the hotel where we then meditated on God's word."

A similar set of interests infuses Rempel's description of the next stop along the way, New York City. Not only was this the point of departure for the voyage to South America, it was home to Samuel McRoberts, a well-to-do and well-connected financier with strong South American ties, of whom they had heard after South Dakota Hutterites moved en masse to Manitoba during the First World War. The Mennonite delegates now were interested in McRoberts's business and government ties and sought his services to locate their place in South America. Again, Rempel and his party found time to partake in the marvels of the city; they were impressed with New York's "electric" subway trains, they visited the fifty-seven-storey Woolworth Building, they walked the Brooklyn Bridge – 80 feet above the water, 550 feet long, he reported – and they visited the zoo and several museums. In a letter to his wife, Rempel noted that in New York, they saw "so much that one could not even have imagined."[36]

Still, Rempel soon had his fill of urban North America. He began his entry for 18 August with the curt statement: "The rushing begins early." On another day, he described seeing a brutal attack on a sailor who lost an eye in the process; a shaken Rempel declared: "We cannot be thankful enough that dear God has so graciously protected us till now."[37] New York had its wonders, but, as he wrote to his wife, the departure date for South America, 31 July, arrived none too soon: in "this Babylon," he exclaimed, "there is no peace. ... I would love to take my farewell from ... all American places."[38]

This mindset, at once temporal and sacred, continued en route to South America. In Rio de Janeiro, Rempel described a beautiful city located among "high hills with some forest cover," and one that at night was "an artist's delight with its millions of lights" outlining the hills.[39] In Sao Paulo, after a day of business, Rempel described "a nearby park; where we saw many different types of trees and flowers, a splendour that cannot be described,"[40] and mentioned seeing a deer, several apes, and a peacock with a wingspan of eight feet. Because of their mandate to secure good farmland, Rempel and the delegates then visited several potential settlement sites. In the Curitiba region in southern Brazil, Rempel saw quality German farms, and, in Uruguay, he noted a highly developed economy, apparently well suited to sustaining modern agriculture.

But overall, South America proved to be a place of deep disappointment. First, the tragic death in Curitiba of one of the delegates, Rev. Johan Wall, on 28 September, rattled the delegates. Rempel described the heart-wrenching sadness with which the delegates hovered over Wall as he "said goodbye to us ... and wished us a blessed passing into eternity." Then, in a makeshift funeral, "according to our custom ... we buried him in the Protestant cemetery, there ... to rest until ... awakened by the archangel."[41] Rempel continued with a disheartening portrait of all of South America. In Argentina, he raised significant doubts about the whole idea of emigration after speaking to German immigrants:

> It is very sad in the old country, where many old people and children are dying from hunger. In comparison we are protected under a cover [of wealth] in Canada. Now they [the German immigrants] are in Argentina

and are met with disappointment as things down here are not as had been expected. That would also be the case for many of our people if we should emigrate. It would probably be like the children of Israel experiencing [great fear] when their spies came back from [scouting] the Promised Land [with stories of formidable giants].[42]

Even greater uncertainty followed the long-awaited 15 October meeting with an Argentine government official, who bluntly informed the delegates that a private school system was "against the constitution." Instead of a welcoming hand, they received a lecture that, in Argentina, "everyone has the same privilege and no one has more rights than anyone else," and that the national "constitution stipulates mandatory military service for all men."[43] On 26 October, the delegates began their journey back to Canada, stopping in Rio de Janeiro on the 28th. Here, they received a similar answer from Brazil's immigration officials: "They could not agree to the Mennonites' immigration requests saying that it was 'impossible to make any exceptions.'"[44]

Ironically, on 9 November, one of their last days on South American soil, the Mennonite delegates who had left the ease of Canada and travelled south in a struggle to secure German-language education attended "an English church service" in Sao Paulo and heard a sermon of how "it is easy to stay in Christ." On 24 November, the Old Colony Mennonite delegates arrived home, empty-handed, to "our beloved Canada under snow and ice." Two days later, Rempel made his final, heartfelt summation: "With God's help we arrived home safely from this long trip. Oh, if the trip to eternity could also end so fortunately and a happy reunion with God and Jesus Christ and the angels. We travelled approximately 8955 [miles] according to the railroad and ship lines, from here to Buenos Aires, South America."[45] Finding a new home in the South would be fraught with difficulty, anything but "easy," but the promise of finding a particular citizenship "among the nations" seemed worth the cost.

Johan M. Loeppky: Tears of Affection for Mexico

The various 1919 and 1920 trips to Mississippi, Quebec, Brazil, and Argentina proved unsuccessful, but two visits to Mexico by Old Colony Mennonite delegates seemed promising. Thus, in 1921, the Old Colony Mennonites turned their primary attention to Mexico. Here, at the conclusion of their third visit to Mexico in February 1921, they met success, and a six-man delegation entered into an historic agreement with the Mexican authorities.

Johan M. Loeppky of Saskatchewan was one of the six delegates – two from each of three communities of Swift Current and Hague-Osler in Saskatchewan, and the Altona–Winkler area in south-central Manitoba.[46] His account of the trip parallels Rempel's descriptions of strange new lands, but it shares the overtly religious and biblical vocabulary of Isaak Dyck's memoir. Loeppky opens with a poem, firmly establishing the sacredness of the Mennonite migration: "He who travels only with His God / He finds a way is always made / A direction always pointed out to him."[47]

But Loeppky moved quickly to spell out the specific reason for the emigration. First, it had become evident that the Canadian government had granted only a conditional religious freedom with its Order-in-Council of 1873; evidently, its guarantee of freedom of religion pertained only to freedom of worship, not, as the Mennonites had thought until 1916, to the education of their children. The consequent fact was that "the time here [in Canada] has expired in which we enjoyed freedom with regard to education." Second, the community had been strained by its own quickly assimilating youth, especially in the prosperous days of the First World War; "already very wild and unruly, often unrestrained ... living freely and happily in the world," wrote Loeppky, they would surely not improve under the new English-language school system. Finally, the "Word of God" had spoken: Loeppky quoted Matthew 10:23 – "when you are persecuted in one place, flee for another" – and he recalled the biblical promise that if one does "flee [and] ... touch no unclean thing ... I will take you in and be your Father."[48] Any emigration from Canada would be divinely blessed.

For Loeppky, the trip to Mexico was nothing short of a search for freedom and eternal salvation. As he noted, the six delegates were not merely land scouts "travelling in the world ... to survey one region and [moving] from one place to the next. No, we went to seek freedom for our faith."[49] The trip to a strange land seemed to overwhelm Loeppky; he requested prayer "from my dear wife on the morning we left; I encouraged my daughters to pray for me too," that "I might return [safely] to my dear loved ones and to the whole congregation."[50] But he was less concerned with safety than with success, and he inserted his own prayer: "Do not let our tears, which we shed before you, fall unproductively to the ground." For Loeppky, the migration's ultimate purpose was to procure a heavenly "homeland": his starkly expressed religious hope was that they "might one day arrive [in heaven] because of grace, where all of your people are, who made it through great affliction ... [with] clothes bright in the blood of the lamb."[51] He felt deeply humbled at the thought that he had been chosen for such a weighty mission, "an important trip, but I am only dust and ashes, yes, a sinful person ... [with] a mind bursting with fear."[52]

The trip itself was a mixture of misadventure, worry, and unexpected sources of comfort. In Winnipeg, the delegates faced a tough United States consular office where "we had a lot of work trying to get our travel documents" and where we "were thoroughly interrogated."[53] Then, after departing Winnipeg, Manitoba representative Klaas Heide discovered he had forgotten his passport in the city and had to return to fetch it. Soon, Loeppky's co-representative from Hague-Osler, colony mayor Benjamin Goertzen, experienced such pain in his leg that he worried he might have to turn back. Renewed resolve came from various quarters. In Manitoba, Loeppky met his siblings, a brother and a sister and their families, "with tears in their eyes," and felt renewed after "a lot of singing." On the day of departure, Manitoba's Ältester, Johan Friesen, came to the railroad station "and gave us many beautiful words of encouragement for the journey."[54]

But Loeppky especially appreciated the words of a young widow, a Mrs. Knelsen, whom the delegates met on the train. Knelsen was en route to Rochester Clinic in Minnesota to seek medical treatment, and she tearfully told Loeppky and his companions her story of intense physical suffering and her ceaseless faith. Loeppky wrote of gratitude that this woman, with a "repentant and contrite heart ... gave us many weighty things [to think about] on this trip; it helped me – a weak person – a lot whenever I thought about this widow."[55]

In the succeeding days, Loeppky gladly viewed the scenery, but he never lost sight of the deeper meaning of the journey. At El Paso, he compared the "difference between the beautiful south and the cold north," but he was also concerned that "the children were scrawny and thin."[56] On Mexico's western coastal plain, at a place he identified as "Razolus," he wrote that "we encountered modern irrigation and big fields of rubber," and he again took note of people, "terribly thin," loudly trying to sell food.[57] At Guaymas, he saw a beautiful bay, "a wonderful place for a city," but he reminded himself that "in the world many things are incredible." Outside the city, he "beheld Mexico's fields with wonderment," noting a plantation of "several thousand acres of sugarcane," but again he found another meaning and quoted Isaiah 45: "He who fashioned ... the earth ... did not create it to be empty, but formed it to be inhabited."[58]

He had quite a different impression of Culiacán City, especially the nightlife, "a wild striving among the world's children," corrupt enough to qualify for God's warning of Genesis 6: "I am surely going to destroy them and the earth."[59] In Mazatlán, he walked the beach and "observed the ways of the great ocean," a sight that reminded him of the "miracles of God."[60] At Tepeyac, where the delegation stopped to see its dormant volcano, "walking to the top, near the precipice" and glancing down to the "dark at the bottom," Loeppky recalled Psalm 104: "[God] looks at the earth and it trembles, he touches the mountains and they smoke."[61] At every turn along the way, the delegation considered agricultural potential, but Loeppky never wavered from the ultimate objective, telling one land agent that "everything depended upon the freedoms – the land was not the most important."[62]

The culmination of the trip was Mexico City and a scheduled meeting with President Álvaro Obregón in the evening of 17 February 1921. Loeppky was in awe when the delegates arrived at the presidential palace – the row of guards, the "shiny laces" on the uniform of the president's attaché, and the "Mexican seal ... an eagle with a snake in its mouth." But these features paled in comparison to the importance of the meeting with the president. In the moments before the historical encounter, the delegates were all "quiet in contemplation about how it would be and what we would say in front of men of such high position." The delegates agreed that Ältester Julius Loewen should "lead the talk and present our wishes" to the president.[63]

Upon meeting President Obregón, the delegates began actual negotiations. They outlined ten requests, and the president and his officials responded. The Mennonite requests were all intended to ensure their right to a self-sufficient agrarian settlement, free from any form of military service or government intrusion. First, the delegates requested exemption from the Mexican law requiring civil marriages in addition to church marriages, a request the president initially balked at, but then accepted. Second, the Mennonites wanted their own egalitarian inheritance practices following their centuries-old, partible, bilateral system, a matter on which the president readily agreed, declaring that Mexico itself disparaged a patrilineal system. Third, the Mennonites requested their own church-run, German-language schools. When the president suggested how "advantageous [it would be] to learn the national language at a later date," the delegation re-explained the Mennonites' commitment to full separation from the wider world, and, as Loeppky recalled it, the president "praised our steadfast reasoning." Fourth, the Mennonites asked for military exemption, and the president agreed, even in the event that the Mennonites became naturalized citizens. Fifth, the Mennonites requested "the admittance of the elderly, the weak and the crippled"; again the president agreed, noting that, as a military commander, "he himself had lost an arm and yet he served as president." Items six to ten were economic in nature: exemption from import duties, assistance in obtaining final land titles, permission for future land acquisitions, support for travel inland, and legal provisions enabling the nine preceding items. Each was easily agreed to.[64]

The negotiations that night ended on an emotional note. Loeppky himself addressed the president, thanking him for his "very merciful government" and assuring him that his kindness "would find reward ... in eternity." The president in turn welcomed the Mennonites to Mexico and, according to Loeppky, insisted "this should be our promised land." As they left the palace, Loeppky and his party became reflective: they quietly "praised and thanked the one who can steer and govern the hearts of those who are high in the world." Loeppky had seen that even the president was "visibly moved." That night, Loeppky could not contain himself; he had observed in Obregón what the Queen of Arabia had seen in King Solomon in the Bible: "It is true what I have heard in my land, about your nature and your wisdom. ... Blessed be your people and ... praise be to the Lord."

Loeppky was certain that Mexico's president had been divinely placed to help the Mennonites; he was impressed by Obregón's actions, not his trappings of power. The next day, when the delegates accepted an invitation to complete their tour of the presidential palace, Loeppky acknowledged "all of the splendour a president possessed in his life," but he declared, "I am not interested in the splendour of this house, only in the freedoms." His wish for Obregón was that when this earthly "splendour would some day decay," he would experience the transformation of "that life into eternal splendour according to Revelation 21:24."[65]

The final task of the delegates was to examine the north-central state of Durango, where farmland was less expensive than the productive soils of the western coastal plain. A day's travel north of the city of Durango, they visited a region that impressed Loeppky: "There were stream beds, some of them with some water ... and the land was light. ... There was grass everywhere and also large gardens of fruit, trees, and many horses, mules, donkeys, sheep and goats." Again, Loeppky reminded himself of the delegation's priorities: "We thought this was the land for us," but first they "wanted to hear what the congregation at home would say regarding the [promised] freedoms."[66] Before they left Durango, they met the state governor, who assured them the Obregón accord would be respected in his state. They also received official copies of the document, one each for the three Old Colony Mennonite communities, the one in Manitoba and the two in Saskatchewan.

The final hurdle was crossing into the United States, where border officials "did not want to let any Mennonites in." The barrier was lifted only after the delegates insisted that they "only wanted to travel through" and once their luggage had been thoroughly searched. Heading north, Loeppky felt relieved to be on the way home but Mexico had left its mark: "Now we sat on a different train than we had in Mexico," he observed. And, even though it was superior to Mexican technology, the train felt strange, for "we had grown accustomed to the Mexican manner among the people." A day into their travels north, Loeppky and his party received a pleasant surprise, a modicum of familiarity in the heart of America. On the day they travelled through southwestern Kansas, "quite suddenly a [conservative Kleine Gemeinde Mennonite] father and his daughter [boarded the train] and entered into our car, a Mr. Heinrich Reimer [of Meade, Kansas]," returning from a trip to see a local doctor. Reimer and Loeppky had never met but evidently immediately recognized one another as Mennonite. Speaking in Low German, Reimer seemed overcome with curiosity "about the successes we had had in Mexico." After the father and daughter disembarked at Meade, Loeppky pondered how "the dear God knows how to sustain his own everywhere, even in the United States."[67]

Loeppky arrived home on 13 March, two and a half months after leaving Canada. He was relieved to find his family healthy, but thoughts of the momentous trip – a "time among a totally foreign people" – preoccupied him. He even recalled the enticement of the Mexican people: true, the Mexicans had "often stared at us," the strange visitors from the North, but the glances had never been cast "with malice." In his conclusion, as in his introduction, Loeppky returned to overtly pietistic language: "How good it is to walk with Jesus; he has led me from place to place. ... My Jesus for the travel mercies ... I give thee thanks ... I am a pilgrim here on earth. ... Lead me safely ... through the world, to you, my Saviour, into heaven's firmament."⁶⁸ The emigration from Canada was no mere relocation; for Loeppky, it was a broader travel to eternity.

Bernard Toews: The Promise of Paraguay

In February 1921, just as the Old Colonists were concluding an agreement with Obregón in Mexico, another Mennonite delegation left for Paraguay and an eventual meeting with its president, Manuel Gondra Pereira. This delegation consisted of representatives from the three smaller traditionalist Mennonite groups – the Chortitzer and Sommerfelder from Manitoba, and the Saskatchewan Bergthaler. The 1920 Old Colony delegation visit with financier Samuel McRoberts in New York (reported on by David Rempel) had born some unexpected fruit. Some time after meeting those delegates, McRoberts, by chance, met Paraguay's president-elect Manuel Gondra on a ship en route to South America and raised the idea of locating the Mennonites in the vast, semi-tropical Paraguayan Chaco. As Gondra expressed interest, McRoberts sent his emissary, the experienced land scout, Norwegian-American Fred Engen, who was familiar with the Mennonites, to explore the Chaco. By August 1920, McRoberts had visited Paraguay himself, receiving a promise from Gondra that the Chaco awaited the Mennonite settlers. Engen's report, rejected by the Old Colonists, who had sent one of their various delegations to Paraguay, nevertheless became the impetus for the Chortitzer, Sommerfelder, and Bergthaler groups to visit Paraguay in 1921.⁶⁹

One of the delegates, farmer Bernard Toews of the village of Weidenfeld, near Altona, Manitoba, kept a detailed travelogue that later served as a basis for his report to his Sommerfelder congregation.⁷⁰ Like delegate David Rempel, farmer Toews was on a mission in South America that combined a search for the physical requirements of a farm settlement with a search for a charter of privileges, their *Privilegium*, that recognized the Mennonite teachings on pacifism, educational autonomy, and other practices. Toews's description of the point of departure put the trip into perspective: "On Friday, the 11th of February 1921, at 10:30, I, Bernard Toews ... left my beloved family for an approximately four month long trip to South America and Mexico, regarding religious concerns; our wish and prayer is that the beloved God will bless our pioneering work, and will return us safely to our families."[71] This religious sentiment infused his writing, although by far the greatest portion of the text of his diary is given to recording the marvels of the wider world.

New York especially was impressive, with its buildings towering to fifty-four storeys, its elaborate streetcar system, and especially its "museum," most likely the American Museum of Natural History, featuring artefacts from as early as 3000 BC. On the voyage to South America, Toews was enthralled by both the endless sea and the mechanics of the massive ship – 498 feet long, 60 feet wide, propelled by a 7000-horsepower steam engine. True, he complained, "As I have never liked city life, I did feel that we lived here [on the ship] in a locked down city."[72] But, in Rio de Janeiro, he was impressed by city life, in this case by one "lying beautifully within steep mountains"; he was especially impressed by Corcovado Mountain, the Mimosa Pudica plant, and women carrying large baskets of fruit on their heads. In Buenos Aires, the delegates rested on Good Friday, but visited the zoo on Saturday and marvelled at the size of this bustling city of 1,800,000 inhabitants and 6000 automobiles. Although Toews concluded that ultimately the Argentines were no different from the Mennonites, "the people, large or small, are more or less like us, one is fat, the other thin."[73] In Asunción, he noted lively bands of brass music, a German-language evangelical Lutheran service, rich floral life, primitive traffic of two-wheeled carts, and a vibrant open market that reminded him of life in Russia when he was a boy.

For Toews, as it was for Rempel and Loeppky, the route into the strange lands of the South followed a network of meetings with those who could facilitate an ultimate migration. In New York, the delegates met with McRoberts to discuss the Paraguayan land deal and even partook in a gala evening at his house: "We sang a German song for him, and then Jakob Neufeld and I also sang a Russian song."[74] Upon arriving in Buenos Aires, they were met by McRoberts's land agent, Engen, with whom they spoke "earnestly." Then, on 22 March, the delegation finally met with German-speaking plantation magnate José Casado, whose family had acquired much of the Paraguayan Chaco, the largest tract of privately owned land in the world, from a cash-hungry Paraguayan government following the War of the Triple Alliance.[75] The delegates presented Casado with their wish list, most specifically "what kinds of freedoms we wanted from the Paraguayan government, before we proceeded with the inspection of the land." The moment reminded Toews of the delegation's ultimate purpose and, at the end of the day, he penned that "our wish and prayer is, that the beloved God would direct us so that this will serve to the salvation of us and our descendants, and we are in the firm belief, that at home many prayers join ours and will reach the throne of God."[76]

Casado gave the delegates the assurance they were seeking. He had no doubt that in Paraguay, "we would be able to obtain our freedoms and hoped that we would appreciate the region." But he also had a warning and a challenge: while the Chaco "was a wild region, where no white person resides," he "had no doubt that good wheat could be grown out there." He also spoke of the "absence of any winter," of the plentiful and nutritious manioca plant, of a climate of "25 degrees in summer, in winter 12 degrees, and 79 days ... of rain, totalling 60 inches."[77] The Chaco, as presented, was a veritable utopia.

On Easter Sunday, the party, accompanied by Casado and Engen, boarded a riverboat for the 1000-kilometre trip up the Paraná River to Asunción. Again, Toews turned reflective, writing, "My thoughts are at home with the Easter celebration." He pondered fellow traveller Jakob Neufeld's sermon based on the biblical story of the disciples on the "road to Emmaus," a trip on which the disciples encountered Christ after the resurrection.[78] The sermon seemed especially relevant to Toews, the delegate on his own journey. In travelling up the Paraná, however, Toews's primary attention turned to the physical environs: he noticed the "peaceable ... black haired" fellow travellers and especially their exceptionally good teeth, the supposed result of the "water and climate"; he observed "good, high land, also corn and gardens, also a railroad."[79] Toews even seemed to connect the richness of the Paraguayan environment to the historical tenaciousness of its people; with a hint of admiration, he recounted the story of Francisco Solano López, the country's dictator during the War of the Triple Alliance in the 1860s, the five-year-long war against three of Paraguay's mightier neighbours, Brazil, Uruguay, and Argentina.[80]

The climax of the Asunción visit was the 4 April meeting with English-speaking Dr. Eusebio Ayala, Minister of Agriculture (and later the president), and then with President Gondra. Toews's notes on the two fifty-minute-long meetings are cursory: the president "greeted us in friendly fashion," and then, during the meeting, "we presented him with our written requests, following a discussion of our 'privileges', immigration requirements, etc."[81] The specific list, as noted by other sources, included five basic requests: military exemption; the right to affirm rather than swear an oath; church-run schools; freedom to replicate the Mennonites' egalitarian inheritance practice and their own fire insurance agency; and, given their disappointment with school laws in Canada, a specific Paraguayan law guaranteeing the Mennonites their own schools.[82] Later, the delegates added several more requests: a ban on the sale of alcohol in and near the Mennonite colony; exemption from import duties; a tax break for ten years; and permission to bring in their handicapped members, for "such people cannot be left behind for they are part of the population and belong to it."[83]

On 29 March, the delegates, along with Casado and Engen, boarded a riverboat for the next leg of the trip into the heart of Paraguay, 500 kilometres north along the Paraguay River to Puerto Casado, the Casado family outpost and factory town. Again, Toews took note of agricultural potential, the "citrus trees, banana plants and the ever present manioca plants," and the practicality of "carts with 8 foot high wheels." He seemed impressed by the marks of commerce in this wilderness: a modern American-owned meat-packing plant "with cement walls, washed clean, beautifully in order" and the "Calk and Portland Cement Factory."[84] In Puerto Casado, the party settled into the Casado villa and then visited the family's massive wood-products factory and their 22,500-head cattle ranch. Again, Toews was especially interested in how a settlement might survive: he observed the "wild potatoes," the broad "Ukalipse" trees, and "large cotton plants."[85] He recorded the cost of white flour ($9 per 198 pounds) and of beans. He reiterated his admiration for the virulent Paraguayan, exemplified in this instance by a seventy-six-year-old man who had lived there for fifty years, and sired twenty-nine children, the youngest of whom was only seven months of age.[86] As a champion of church-run education, he was especially interested in Casado's private school for his employees' children: "the tables just as we have them in Schoenau [Manitoba]," the "wall illustrations, just as we have them for the beginners, and the various curriculum materials, what bad things alcohol can do for people, how to calculate percentages, etc."[87] Paraguay, as he had seen it to this point, was promising indeed.

Puerto Casado, however, was but a way station to the heart of the Chaco, another 320 kilometres west into the "wilderness." On 2 May, the delegates, accompanied by an entourage of Casado's men, left for a month-long trip into the interior. The first part of this journey, sixty kilometres in distance, was on the company's slow, narrow-gauge railroad. Then, the delegates transferred to a large caravan of oxen and horses and made their way westward, travelling for days through bush and savannah, sometimes in torrential rain, along treacherous stretches of mud. Occasionally, they encountered the indigenous Lengua or Enhlet people, with whom they traded for peanuts and who showed the Mennonites the bounty of local commodities and the potential of the Chaco's rich soils.[88] Toews was the ever-curious scout: on 11 May, he was fascinated to see a four-year-old indigenous boy catch salamanders and roast them in a fire; on the 12th, they met "ten Indians" and "also saw their gardens," and then, an hour later, another "seventeen Indians" with "sheep, goats and dogs"; on the 13th, he discovered "'Palosanto' wood which burns intensely [from] the oil which oozes out"; on the 14th, he was impressed by an "Indian grave" and the elaborate funeral rituals that "to their beliefs" assured that "the dead can go to the other world";[89] on 17 May, the party hit good soil: "high land, the soil is red, sandy, grass two to three feet high";[90] on the 18th, Toews observed how the "hard working," muscular, and well-proportioned "Lengua Indians" thrive on "sweet potatoes, beans and manioca."[91] The understanding was clear; Mennonites might well thrive here, too.

Finally, on 20 May, they reached their destination, a place where a settlement could take root: "open land, large fields and ... wells, or springs ... fresh water ... one foot from the surface." They had reached the future site of what would become Menno Colony. Here, Engen, their guide, declared that they had seen enough and that it was time to return home. On a particular tree, they affixed an historic sign that Casado himself had sent along, an abbreviation of the words "McRoberts, Engen, Mennonite Expedition, May 1921";[92] they had made their mark and claimed this land as their future home. On 30 May, the scouting party arrived back at Puerto Casado and, in Toews's words, got to work at once "to arrange everything with José Casado, as much as we could."[93] Three days later, they reached Asunción and telegraphed Canada that they had just found a promising settlement site.[94] In Asunción, the delegates met with Gondra a final time, receiving a promise that a railway would be constructed into the Chaco and, most importantly, an official welcome from him to Paraguay.[95]

On 24 July, Toews and his fellow delegates docked in New York. To ensure that they covered all their bases, they took a lengthy rail trip southwest across the United States and through Mexico, obtaining their own fifteen-minute audience with President Obregón in Mexico City. They also inspected potential settlement sites in Durango and Chihuahua. If the Old Colonists had rejected Paraguay for Mexico, the Chortitzer-Sommerfelder-Bergthaler party concluded that Mexico seemed more dangerous and its promises of school freedoms more tenuous than Paraguay's.

38 Village among Nations

Therefore, they headed north back to Canada, planning to recommend Paraguay to their congregants. On 2 September, the party crossed into Manitoba at Emerson and made their way at once to report to "our beloved Ältester Abram Doerksen" in the village of Sommerfeld. After the session with the Sommerfelder Mennonite leader, "it was on home" to Weidenfeld. As always, Toews mixed the poetic with the scientific: at precisely "8:10 ... I had the joy of greeting my dear family after a separation of 6 months and 22 days" and a trip of "27,000 miles."[96] He then recorded a final personal prayer: "Gracious God and heavenly father, I thank you from the bottom of my heart, that you have allowed my trip to have come to an end, and through the protection of your beloved angels, joyfully brought me back to my people."[97]

On 7 September, Toews and fellow Sommerfelder delegate Isaak Funk reported to their own Brotherhood "on both lands, what we had seen and heard."[98] Later that fall, Fred Engen arrived in Manitoba to help boost Paraguay. In September, the West Reserve-based Sommerfelder and the East Reserve-based Chortitzer Mennonites in Manitoba voted on the settlement location: the Sommerfelder voted 125 to 123 for Mexico; the Chortitzer, 277 to 3 for Paraguay.[99] The migration to Paraguay would be dominated by Chortitzer Mennonites. In the end, Toews himself did not migrate, and most of the congregants of his denomination, the Sommerfelder Church, chose Mexico over Paraguay.

Conclusion

The migration mentality that Mennonite leaders attempted to re-instill in their people after 1916 was rooted in a particular reading of Dutch-North German Mennonite history. The ancestors of these Mennonites had migrated before, most recently from Russia to Canada in the 1870s. It never mattered to them that the reason the Mennonites had been welcomed in Canada at that time was to advance a national agenda. Ironically, while the Mennonites had emigrated from a modernizing Russia in the 1870s because it was considering the introduction of universal military service, integrated local government, and the partial Russification of schools, Canada had been open to the immigration of the very same Mennonites in order to modernize the prairie West, placing commodity-producing farmers on government-surveyed lands within striking distance of eventual railroads and burgeoning farm-service centres.

It was no different in the 1920s: the Mennonites – isolationist, Low German-speaking, pacifist agriculturalists – were fleeing Canada because its prairie provinces were advancing the cause of a modern nation-state (public education in the language of the nation), but were being welcomed to settle in Mexico and Paraguay by their respective governments for national reasons of their own.

Historian Martina Will has argued that President Obregón, despite his socialist roots, had long advocated for foreign farmer immigrants and, with the arrival of the Mennonites, hoped to signal to a wider world that Mexico possessed a modern and peaceful frontier, settled with successful, industrious farmers of northern European descent, employing the most recent technology.[100] Significantly, Obregón's was a highly racialized policy, one that was as demonstrably hostile to Chinese Mexican merchants as it was welcoming to European-descendant farmers.[101] Mennonites might have come to Mexico to escape modernity, but, ironically, Obregón embraced them because they had the expertise and technology he believed Mexico required to gain full entry into a Western-oriented modernity.

This irony was also evident in Paraguay. Even local Mennonite historians in Paraguay acknowledge that President Gondra's "government passed the law," the historic Law 514, exempting Mennonites from national schools and military service, "for purely pragmatic reasons," especially for the ability and willingness of the Mennonites to settle the intemperate Chaco and develop a modern, rural economy.[102] Other Mennonite scholars have argued that Gondra's national agenda was even more aggressive, nothing less than using the Mennonites to lay claim to the central Gran Chaco, a territory also claimed by Bolivia.[103] Certainly, the Mennonite presence in this part of the Chaco was one of the main factors that ignited the conflict between the two countries in 1932.

Ironically, the Mennonites, presumably unaware of these national agendas, were seeking to escape involvement in state institutions and national sentiments in any country. Their singular idea was that the true Mennonite must always be prepared to leave countries that required assimilation to national cultures of the type now being promoted in Canada. For the Mennonites, it was a religious duty that called for a life in a "village" that existed beyond any one national society. This outlook infused the narratives – autobiographies and diaries – produced by the emigrant leaders. They had troubled the history of Canada, challenged the way Canadians viewed themselves within their history of Canada, and done so with their own religiously informed, transnational mindset. They had rejected a nation-centric culture and were determined to secure their groups' futures in an act of emigration.

2 Drawing Lines on God's Earth: Settlers in Mexico and Paraguay, 1922–1929

Having chosen their land, two streams of Mennonite emigrants began making their way southward. In March 1922, the first of several chartered trains of migrants from Manitoba and Saskatchewan left for Mexico. On board, about 6000 Old Colony and Sommerfelder Mennonites travelled across the American Midwest to El Paso and then into "old" Mexico, entering the broad mountain valleys of the eastern Sierra Madre, specifically Bustillos Valley in Chihuahua state and Guatimapé Valley in Durango state. At railroad sidings beyond the capital cities bearing the names of their respective states, they transferred their supplies onto horse-drawn wagons they had brought from Canada and headed out to their newly acquired lands on the open, semi-arid grassland of the broad mountain valleys. Beginning in 1926, a second stream of migrants – almost 1800 Chortitzer, Sommerfelder, and Saskatchewan Bergthaler Mennonites – followed suit, although they travelled from western Canada by rail via Minneapolis and Chicago to New York, then south by ship on a two-week voyage to Buenos Aires. Their arrival in Argentina was immediately followed by an almost 2000-kilometre voyage into Paraguay, north up the Paraná and Paraguay rivers, past Asunción to the outpost of Puerto Casado, and then west by primitive train and ox cart, into the hot and lush "green hell" of the Paraguayan Chaco.

In both Mexico and Paraguay, the Mennonite settlers built their exclusive ethno-religious colonies, divided into farm villages, the mediaeval-based *Strassendorf*, according to practices well established on the Canadian prairies and in New Russia before. Ironically, these close-knit agrarian places, linked by a commitment to insularity and parochialism, were established within a particular "old transnational" mindset, to employ Steven Vertovec's term, one that placed the migrant within a refashioned social network and one that honed a specific view of the natural environment.

Certainly, the migration introduced a moment of social networking across nations, a time of stretched kinship ties, expanded diaspora, and flows of information between two countries. Reflecting the experience of immigrants elsewhere, a central medium expressing this new social web was the homeland newspaper, a local paper rapidly turned into a novel site of diasporic exchange. But, as importantly, the newspaper allowed migrants to reinforce an old spatial and environmental idea, one that imagined the replicated farm community as a separate ethno-religious space rooted in soil beyond any one nation-state. The Mennonites seemed to view agricultural land as an asset of the ethno-religious community, a parcel on God's earth, not as the possession of any one nation. Land, for these Mennonites, was both a material site and, as Mennonite theologian Waldemar Janzen has argued, "a sacred plot by virtue ... of God's choice of it as an instrument toward his purposes."[1] The very founding of agrarian communities on land soon to be turned to agricultural use held "divine purpose" seemingly coupled indelibly to their traditional values of simplicity and self-sufficiency, a modicum of the "kingdom of God" on earth.

Perhaps this sense of space reflected a pre-industrial, even antimodern, idea, but, in one respect, this view of land was indistinguishable from ideas undergirding "the great land rush" described by John Weaver, and affecting Canadian ethnic settler groups as outlined by Gerald Friesen, Frances Swyripa, Lyle Dick, John Lehr, and others in complex ways.[2] In this "land rush," European-based people claimed the right to settle on land – mostly mid-latitude regions such as the Argentina pampas, the Siberian steppe, and the North American plain – convinced that this acquisition advanced civilization. For many white settlers, civilization spelled democracy and capitalism, nuanced perhaps by ethnic identities; but for traditionalist Mennonites, civilization constituted the close-knit, pacifist, ethno-religious community. In both instances, agricultural land was "made," a process in which land deemed wilderness was acquired by some means, oftentimes unjustly from native dwellers, always surveyed and mapped, turned into a legal commodity, and "improved" – that is, cleared and ploughed – and all in language that made this process seem natural and inevitable.[3] In a complex cultural process, the very acts of building farm villages and ploughing soil legitimized the process for the farm settler. The final result for the Mennonites, though, was not the integration of an agricultural settlement into a nation-state as much as it was the advancement of a Mennonite village envisaged to transcend the very boundary of the nation-state.

The Transnational Subject in Diary and History Book

Both the expanded social network and the specific view of the earth were expressed in an immigrant newspaper, the *Steinbach Post*, a local Manitoba newspaper turned into a transnational medium during the 1920s. Not able to shape a broad reimagining of community, two other texts, the diary and the contemporary observer's history book, nevertheless clarify the evolution of the culture described within the newspaper letters. Unlike the newspaper letters, the daily diaries examined below gave only cursory expression to a migrant mindset; the history book highlighted it, but only as a fleeting aspect of the migration.

Two personal diaries, both by Manitoba farmers who migrated to Mexico, focused on the quotidian even in a context of uprooting and transplanting. The diary of farmer Johan A. Thiessen, who left for Mexico from the village of Neuhorst sometime after October 1923, features a three-line entry for every day of the year. His extant diary, running seamlessly from 1902 to 1923 and then again from 1931 to 1951, is similar to most other Mennonite diaries of the time, offering but a rudimentary factual account of daily life.[4] It reveals a person close to nature, recounting daily weather patterns and farm work, a six-day workweek broken only by the weekly note that "today is Sunday." Thiessen's diary for 1921 and 1922, however, also records events leading up to the emigration, albeit in cursory form. On 12 March 1921, when the six-man delegation, including Johan M. Loeppky, returned from Mexico with the Obregón agreement, Thiessen notes simply: "Today the men are back from Mexico," followed by a similarly short note five days later: "Today we drove to Reinland for a Brotherhood meeting," presumably to hear the travel report. Two months later, on 19 May, Thiessen was only slightly more precise: "This afternoon we were in Reinland for a worship service [and] today the Brotherhood met regarding emigration." His reflective year-end poem in 1921 hints at times of uncertainty: "The old year has passed by; we thank you Lord Jesus Christ that you have kept us from great danger, protecting us this entire year."

Thiessen's next entry relating to emigration appears on 11 February 1922, but now with a hint of friction within the community: "Those who presently wish to respect the emigration assembled in Reinland." Just two weeks later, Thiessen notes the departure of the first train from the town of Gretna, Manitoba, for Mexico, and, a day later, the second train. For an unknown reason, Thiessen lingered in Manitoba, slowly preparing his family's own departure. On 13 May, he attended a meeting regarding the youth who were bound for Mexico; on 29 May, another meeting at the village mayor's office regarding the "Mexico delegates"; and on 7 July, he and neighbour Abram Wiebe drove to Reinland to attend to details regarding the sale of their land. Thiessen notes the departure of more trains from Gretna in 1922: on 17 and 23 October, and 23 November. But on 4 October 1923, his diary ends abruptly without a word about his specific plans. When the diary resumes in October 1931, the Thiessen family has settled in Mexico.[5]

Another personal diary, kept by Jacob J. Peters, one of the delegates on the 1921 scouting trip to Brazil and Argentina, resides amidst a 300-page compendium of statistics and scattered notes that covers a period of twenty years. Like the diary of Thiessen, Peters's contains mostly references to daily events. Even as a delegate to South America, he recorded only a basic outline of the trip, noting places along the way and offering fewer anecdotes and less analysis than did fellow delegate David Rempel. After his scouting trip, Peters's diary moves rather seamlessly back to life in Canada, with regular entries, each in the typical fashion of an agrarian diary, noting the weather, social encounters, work routines, and church services. Peters, too, makes only passing reference to preparations for the move to Mexico, the auction sales and train departures. The references seem almost clinical: "11 July [1922] today, another train of emigrants on twelve cars left for Mexico. ... At 9:30 a.m. the train departed and by 12 noon we [having gone to bid our farewells] were back [at home]. It was cloudy the entire day."

His own move to Mexico, however, receives full shrift. Indeed, the moment of emigration propels a sudden change in the nature of the diary, with more emotion and greater detail. On 22 September, Peters notes, "What can I write? ... It has come to the point that we will leave this land for Mexico; may the Loving God guide us to our land according to his will." Then, perhaps because he had time on the train, he writes of the day of departure in the same vein: "12 October 1922 was a clear and beautiful morning. At 5 o'clock in the morning we rose, the last morning in Canada. What a lovely meal time and then we hoped [that] we were ready for departure. ... The siblings, the parents, the nephews, friends came to bid farewell. ... As everything was ready, at

9 o'clock we began to move, slowly," from Gretna, on the Canadian side, "to Neche, USA ... for a mile and a half, and then all the people on the entire train began to call out."

At this point, Peters's writing turns intentionally into a travelogue, in fact, under the title "On the Trip to Mexico, October 1922." He notes the sequence of towns passed through – Grafton, St. Cloud, St. Paul, Kansas City, and El Paso. At the Mexican border, he records an unusually long stop, but then, as the trip continues into Mexico, he resumes listing the names of place names – Warries [Juárez], Chihuahua, where they purchase supplies; San Antonio, which awaits them on the other side of the mountain range. Then, quite suddenly, after they disembarked and unloaded supplies, Peters's farm diary, with its agrarian pattern, resumes. For the next year, Peters dutifully records the daily routine of life in the Bustillos Valley – the weather, the local market, the work, church services – at least until 1 January 1924, when, for an unknown reason, his daily diary ends abruptly.[6]

A much more analytical reference to the wandering nature of the Mennonites who headed south is found in a specific section of a history written by a contemporary observer of the migration. The history of the Mennonite migration by Walter Schmiedehaus, the German consul then resident in Chihuahua, reflects his close friendship with Mennonite leaders and his enthusiastic support for German-speaking immigrants in northern Mexico. But it also reflects his position of authority as a social commentator, at once offering details on the migration and valorizing the newcomers. These immigrants who "embarked on a journey ... not over the ocean but across half a continent," writes Schmiedehaus, were a people of means, "not poor, afflicted or persecuted who were at the mercy of others ... rather they are affluent, self-sufficient farmers who with written 'Privilegium' in hand embarked on an eight day journey as a closed community, in order to take up ownership of the estates purchased in a foreign country with precious money." They did not travel with government assistance, nor did they travel "with the single bundles of humble possession." Rather, "they rented for themselves entire trains ... brought into service in order to resettle an entire people, on extra long trains to cross the stretch between Canada and Mexico." They purchased their land, for "unlike Canada and Russia before it," Mexico did "not make the land available for free. That is not what they ask for. They have the money and they are proud to be able to pay it, to stand and walk on their own feet and even to take their own poor with them."[7] The Mennonite settlers were accorded particular agency in Schmiedehaus's rendition, masters of their relocation, financing and directing it. They had "discovered" Mexico at a time when few North Americans were casting about in Central America. The significance of their migration was made with reference to the culture of migration among Mennonites, including sojourns in Canada and Russia.

While both the diary and the history book illuminate aspects of a migrant mentality, letters in the *Steinbach Post* best capture the outlook of the ordinary Mennonite migrant. As a local, privately owned, Canadian Mennonite newspaper, the *Post* described the migration to, and settlement in, Mexico and Paraguay first for a Canadian audience. It evolved rapidly to become the central repository of reports back to Canada, including numerous accounts from observers in Canada as the migrants left. Most significantly, it consisted of a corpus of over 500 letters sent home from Mexico and Paraguay in the 1920s. Writers to the *Post* outlined the qualities of their emerging international social network and they offered a view of land as a supranational physical feature, no matter that the nation itself might have viewed the newcomer farmers as fulfilling a national agenda.

"We are all very curious about Mexico"

Lengthy reports on the migration to Mexico, complete with references to emotion-laden separations, appeared in the *Steinbach Post* at the first sign of emigration. Some writers reported on the departure of the very first train in 1922 in terms of broken social ties: "On the 1st of March the first train with Old Colony Mennonite emigrants left for Mexico. Such [a move] cannot occur without a great deal of pain, especially when one thinks of leaving all that one loves and taking leave from so many loving friends."[8] Other writers spoke of the migration in more hopeful terms: "Concerning the migration to Mexico," noted one correspondent in October 1922, "one can report that between eighteen and twenty families have ordered cars for themselves so that they can leave on November 8 and by winter time will be happily living there."[9] Precise details about the migration were important for many other correspondents. In January 1923, a writer from Gouldtown, Saskatchewan, set out to "provide the names of the emigrants, as perhaps it might interest some folks." He then listed twenty-eight families and explained that "together these have loaded a total of seventeen cars with three cars reserved for the colonists themselves."[10] No doubt, it was an impressive scene. Different writers stationed in Canada emphasized different aspects of the migration, but all spoke to its importance and wide-ranging social effect.

Soon, too, reports were posted from Mexico itself. A few were by members of a small Soviet Mennonite community that had settled in northern Mexico just before the arrival of the Old Colony Mennonites. One such report by an Abram Rempel described the arrival of Canadians at the border town of Juárez on a train that included five passenger cars:

> Mennonites, large and small, old and young, ... all showing happy faces ... have finally arrived in Mexico. ... Their five passenger cars were attached to an endless row of freight cars ... over thirty, with horses, cows, dogs, cats, geese and chickens. All were loaded with all possible types of cultivation equipment and household goods; at one platform I noticed a massive tractor with a plough and fine threshing machine. The whole train offered up quite a treasure and was no small matter for Mexico. After completing their official formalities they will continue their trip, leaving at 10 p.m. for San Antonio [Cuauhtémoc].[11]

Most other *Post* letters relating to Mexico came from Mennonite settlers from within the newly founded agrarian colonies: the largest in Chihuahua state were Manitoba Colony and Swift Current Colony, named after Canadian locations; the smaller ones, Santa Clara and Santa Rita colonies, bore Mexican place names; the colony in Durango state, founded in 1924, was usually referenced by its Saskatchewan antecedent, Hague Colony, but also by its location near the Mexican village of Patos.

Often, the letters from Mexico provided specific information on the process of settlement. In one, Rev. Abram Goertzen, originally of Morse, Saskatchewan, emphasized the day of arrival: "We left for Mexico on 16 December 1922 from Herbert and Morse, Saskatchewan; twenty-seven families" on several passenger cars, and "an additional seventeen freight cars." After an eleven-day trip, they arrived at their destination on the morning of 28 December, a "trip that seemed slow," wrote Goertzen, "but God be thanked, everything went well." He expressed gratitude that at San Antonio, "the railroad company was very accommodating and allowed us three freight cars in which we could live as long as we wished." Then began the settlement process: "At first, we moved into the large [ranch] house, which stood on the land, of course built in Mexican style, of red clay bricks; but we did have our shelter ...

[Then] we began the scouting and surveying the village sites, and then the construction of the houses." He added that "the construction wood here is only half as expensive as in Canada, but neither is it as good," and concluded that "once ... most people live on their own place, some land will be broken."[12] It was an account of pioneering on a frontier, transplanting the old Mennonite custom of living in villages, including the initial consideration of wooden houses according to Canadian custom. Canadian readers could now imagine the worlds of their kin in Mexico.

These initial reports in the *Steinbach Post* initiated a rapid transformation of the local newspaper into a lively medium of transborder exchange. Settlers in Mexico wrote to subscribe to the *Post*; a typical early letter from Chihuahua linked the old and new homelands with a request "whether our *Steinbach Post* which was always sent to Box 161, Morse, Saskatchewan, could also be read here in Mexico, if it isn't too expensive." The writer explained that "from time to time" he wished to "send in a short report as we still have many relatives out there in the old homeland, as well as a beloved elderly mother, Widow Abram Hamm of Grunthal, Manitoba, [and] three married children in Saskatchewan ... from whom we would very much like to hear."[13] Mexico Mennonites, oftentimes self-reflexive and certainly self-conscious, undertook the new task of newspaper writing, all the while being encouraged by those in Canada. In August 1923, immigrant Peter Schulz thanked the editor for the *Post* and promised to "send something to the *Post* even though I will have to write only in pencil as [in semi-arid Chihuahua] my ink has dried up"; the editor retorted, "With a pencil it works too. ... So please continue to write in that manner, for we are all very curious about Mexico and want to share in your experiences."[14] In July 1924, the *Post* editor articulated the obvious: the *Post* had clearly outgrown its original mould. "Even though our paper is named *Steinbach Post*," wrote the editor, "it does not mean that it is of only local interest in [Manitoba's] East Reserve"; indeed, the paper had found "its way across the border of Manitoba, following the emigrants from [Manitoba] ... to Saskatchewan, Alberta, BC and to the United States and Mexico." Anticipating further expansion, the editor invited "correspondence from every corner of the Americas," and explained that the *Post* did "not require professional reports, no, every farmer, every representative, any vocation is fine" for the task of writing in the *Post*.[15]

Indeed, letters began pouring in. Writers from Mexico especially enquired about family members back in Canada and sent cross-border greetings. Peter Schulz's July 1923 letter was typical for its outreach to kin in the old northern homeland: "Hearty greetings to my beloved father, Aron Schulz, who is in care at David Friesens'. ... Also I herewith greet Peter Banmans, Dietrich Harders and the sister, Widow Jacob Kehler of Steinbach [Manitoba]. And many other friends and acquaintances are herewith greeted, including brother Aron Schulz of Niverville [Manitoba]." Schulz also hailed his old neighbours, especially "those at Main Centre, Saskatchewan, where my old residence stands and where just eight months ago I still lived."[16] The tone of the letters could be very personal. In his December 1923 letter, Johan A. Friesen of Gouldtown, Saskatchewan, addressed his brother Jacob directly, having heard that "you out there in Sommerfeld have been ordained as a minister; we wish you good success."[17] Letters also served as newscasts, reporting joyous and tragic events, often intended for relatives back in Canada: a typical letter from August 1923 announced "a death, namely that of Cornelius G. Wiebe from here who died on May 13. His sickness was dropsy and he suffered from it for three months and five days. ... He leaves behind his deeply grieving wife of 27 years; he was father to fifteen children."[18]

Dozens of such letters helped settlers imagine a new translocal geography that spanned specific sites in Canada and the new colonies in Mexico. They cultivated an ethno-religious space spread across two international borders. Their conversations – of birth and death, illness and well-being, loss and gain – within a single newspaper hearkened back to a time when the Mennonites who remained in Canada and those in Mexico shared life in a single physical location. Infused in the details of these reports was a consciousness of distance, of diaspora, of life in a transnational world.

"The Mexicans leave us entirely alone, only the ploughing is hard"

The early letters from Mexico published in the *Steinbach Post* not only described a broadening Mennonite social network; they positioned the new settlements in Mexico itself, its people and its geography. But the newcomers also drew strict social boundaries between themselves and the host society, as well as between themselves and the new physical environment – the strange land, the red soil, the dry climate, and the temperate weather. They described not so much a transplantation of settlers in a new land as a sojourn in it by pilgrims. Mexican soil and culture needed to be discovered and understood, but they did not constitute a new homeland.

Indeed, letters describing the relationships between Mennonite settlers and their Mexican neighbours often were presented in racialized language that reasserted an ethno-religious social boundary.[19] The letters described distant neighbours and even "primitive" strangers. In an early letter, P.K. Doerksen, a young, single visitor from Manitoba, wrote with astonishment: "I had never thought that Mexico was so backwards, some of the people say that it is a hundred years behind, and I believe it. It has all the appearance of Bible times. ... Here one rides on donkeys, walks bare foot, eats ... and sleeps on the ground. In the middle of the room one has a small fire." Imagining the naysayers, Doerksen declared, "Please, go ... and see for yourself."[20] In the next issue, Doerksen reported again, this time on a car trip through the Old Colony villages and on the settlers' sense of well-being. Again he mentioned social distance: "The Mennonites in Mexico seem to be very happy, and when I asked what should I relay to the people in Manitoba their answer was, 'we are doing well and we are all happy; the Mexicans leave us entirely alone, only the ploughing is hard.'" Doerksen added his own commentary: "I told them that a remarkable difference separated the Mennonites and the Mexicans, in two months to have such [nice] houses, while [the Mexicans] are still sleeping outdoors. Here one can see that it makes a big difference who has learned something in school and who has not."[21] Having rejected assimilation in Canada, the Mennonite migrants would not now assimilate in Mexico.

This same cultural difference marked references to Mexico's social elite, usually government officials, despite a long-standing Mennonite tradition of deference to those in authority. But it was a loyalty they honed as "subjects" rather than as "citizens," for subjugation to governing officials did not entail identification with the nation-state.[22] This sentiment revealed itself in other ways, including Mennonite pride when lauded by authorities. In a May 1924 issue of the *Post*, for example, a writer submitted an article earlier published in a German-language paper, *Die Herald*, a report itself translated from the Spanish press. The missive described a two-day fact-finding mission by Mexican authorities among the Mennonite colonies and praised Mennonite industrial and agricultural ingenuity. It lauded the neat houses and barns in orderly villages, and it noted specifically how one Mennonite had built a threshing machine and another harnessed the wind to run a sawmill. The report asserted that these "are certainly the very kind of people suited to the settlement of a new land. They are not afraid of any difficult problem. Their ... way of life shows that they are practiced in the hard school of life. They have taken vast stretches of land which were said to be useless for anything more than meadow and have organized themselves in twenty-five or thirty well organized villages." The writer continued by comparing the Mennonites to no less a person than the "father of Mexico," Hernando Cortez, who, before his legendary 1517 "march inland" from Vera Cruz, "destroyed his ships as a sign of his determination to neither hesitate nor die." In similar fashion, claimed the writer, "these Mennonites have given up everything" to become successful settlers; "they are a frugal people and their needs are few; they are capable of withstanding much."[23] Perhaps the allusion by this Mexican writer was to a national hero, but his message corresponded to the Mennonites' own self-perception that Mennonites were remarkable for being Mennonites, not for becoming Mexican.

Most of the letter writers from Mexico reported not on the new social milieu, but on the new physical context. In particular, they compared the weather and climate of Mexico to that in Canada: how it was better or worse; how it hampered or advanced the farm culture. Abram Goertzen's June 1923 letter heralded Mexico's mild winters and temperate summers; upon arriving in Mexico in December 1922, Goertzen wrote that "the winter seemed very nice," and this spring "we've had very nice weather, and no great heat." Peter Schulz was similarly positive in his July 1922 letter, noting, "Since July 7 we have had rain everyday and the soil now is all wet and the breaking of land goes well, everyone is working mightily hard. The cattle now have green pasture, and the corn by the Mexicans is three to four feet high." But the immigrants also spoke of weather aberrations. Dozens of letters described the terror of high-altitude lightning: a July 1923 letter spoke of "the lovely July rain" that turned tragic when an "ox was killed by a bolt at Johann Schulzes' and a horse at Franz Zachariases'";[24] one letter from August 1924 reported on successive thunderstorms, including one with "a lightning bolt [that] killed two cows at neighbour Heinrich Bergen's place." Other letters reached back to Canada with happy reports of snowfall in the high-altitude mountain valley: on "the 10th of this month as we rose in the morning," wrote Peter Schulz in December 1924, "the earth had a white snow covering and it snowed till noon, so that we had a snow covering of eight inches,"[25] although he added that the snow disappeared in rainfall just a few days later.

Most often, the allusions to climate pointed not to idle conversation but to a central challenge Mennonites faced as farmers in a new land. Their main concern was the successful adaptation to a new geography. In December 1924, P.B. Zacharias took an atypical turn at weather reporting by offering an overview of an entire year. He recalled that when his group arrived in Mexico on 9 November 1922, they lived in tents for a short time, but soon lumber from the numerous sawmills in the region allowed for the rapid construction of wooden shelters. Equally important was the breaking of new land. Zacharias noted that his quality horses from Canada had enabled him to break "twenty acres of land before the winter." Learning the rhythm of Mexico's climate was also important, for, although Zacharias broke some land in November, it could not be planted until 27 March, when rain dampened "the top five inches of soil." Still, by the middle of April, when he "planted four acres of corn, germination was poor as it was too dry." On 19 June, it rained again and he now "seeded six acres of the best broken land into wheat, but it too stagnated for lack of rain." Not until 8 July, however, did the community receive "a thorough rain so that everything could grow." Zacharias's report then focused on the state of the crops: "Now it rains often and very hard. Everything grew very well. Too bad that in the garden, hail damaged some wheat. From October 15 to 16 during the night we had frost, ruining the flax and corn, although the oats and barley still produced a little; the wheat had too much rust."

Zacharias had gained valuable knowledge by observing annual weather patterns, but he also learned from his neighbours and reported that the "Mexicans who had 'old' land under cultivation, planted their wheat in the middle of April really deep and it has moisture to grow."[26] Other Mennonites wrote about learning from the Mexicans, especially not to count on freshly ploughed land to yield good crops. Rev. Abram Goertzen wrote of the disappointment in April 1923 when "we planted a few potatoes and some corn" on land broken in December and discovered that while "the freshly broken soil did not have moisture, [and the plants] did not progress ... what the Mexicans ... planted in the old soil grew very well." Clearly, a little patience would bring success. The Mennonites also learned just when to plant: "According to the Mexicans, the rainy period is yet to begin (after June 14), and it is then that we really want to plant and seed."[27] Counter-intuitively, they changed a fifty-year practice perfected in western Canada of rushing to plant just before, and not after, it rained. References to failure highlighted the few unable to learn. An August 1923 letter, for example, announced that despite fine rainfall and the author's belief that "everything is happy and hopeful. ... Brothers Johann and Abram Thiessen ... find pioneering too hard and they are selling their goods for cash and wish to return to Canada."[28]

Certainly, some complained that northern Mexico's semi-arid climate made agriculture unsustainable. Most of these reports, however, came from migrants returning to Canada, reports disseminated paternalistically by Mennonites who had never left Canada. A February 1923 letter from Bernard Friesen of Renata, BC, sounded a dire warning: "News from Mexico ... does not sound very pleasant; it seems many would come back if only they had the means to do so. In many families one has a very 'small table,' indeed only corn and water. It is at least as bad as [the present famine] in Russia ... [especially] the elderly are dying in large numbers."[29] But other letters, including several from 1924, were only slightly more upbeat. In August, David Redekopp of Aberdeen, Saskatchewan, reported that some fifty families were planning to return to Canada, all because wheat in Mexico had grown only six inches high and few vegetables survived in the garden; his adult children had told him "that it is impossible to live out there ... and that the land they have [in Mexico] will be lost."[30] Other Canadian letters carried similar reports: two from Gouldtown, Saskatchewan, for example, pondered the news of return migration, having heard that "the food there is in short supply" and that "not much of a crop will be harvested out there."[31]

Still, as the fifth anniversary of the settlement approached, a sense of cautious optimism prevailed and most letter writers spoke of Mexico as a place of promise. A June 1926 writer even seemed buoyant: "It appears that this year could produce a good harvest. The saying is, 'all good things three times,' and it is the third year in which we are seeding. We hope we will prosper. ... Still one cannot praise the day before the evening arrives. It has rained here several times. ... The people are working ... diligently ... Uncle Klaas Heide of Blumenort has already cut his winter wheat."[32] Another writer, in comparing life in Mexico in August 1926 to the apparent ease of Manitoba, mitigated any seeming difficulty with humour and a bit of irony: "It is not all gold, oh no here there is enough work for both hands, and the weeds are no less here than in Manitoba. ... No one here can sit down and simply have the 'cooked goose fly into one's mouth'. ... However in the hope that one can live here, most are embracing the future."³³ Mexico would be no utopia, but its soil would certainly reward Mennonite efforts.

By the end of the 1920s, most letter writers described their community as a place of normalcy. In spring 1927, a Santa Clara colonist wrote as if the cycle of farming had become routine: "Overall little news can be reported from our small settlement, presently the people are very busy planting corn, potatoes, and peanuts. Oats, barley and flax are mostly planted in the beginning of June."³⁴ Other letter writers had grown accustomed to periodic droughts; a letter from San Antonio in the summer of 1927 noted that although the month of July was turning out to be especially dry, "there isn't much of importance to report from here. At places marriage fever is raging ... and the stork also often stops by here for visits."³⁵ Adaptation to Chihuahua's semi-aridity was well underway.

After five years, Mennonites had also seemingly decoded the local and regional Mexican economy. Writers increasingly spoke of the marketing of commodities. A typical letter from 1927 reported on "daily work now of hauling grain to market" and described how "last week Julius and Daniel Harder, each took two loads to Chihuahua, and this week we ... want to ... haul a rail car load's worth of oats to San Antonio and next week others [will haul grain] to Chihuahua."³⁶ Certainly, marketing grain in northern Mexico was challenging. As P.A. Unrau noted in a September 1927 letter, "Last week again several drove to Chihuahua with corn, receiving seven centavos per kilo; it is a long journey, about ninety-five miles, taking from seven to eight days."³⁷

Most farmers were not only learning to negotiate the Mexican marketplace, they were becoming active contributors to it. The Mennonite presence around San Antonio had propelled this once-lowly railway siding into a commercial centre. One writer described the town in September 1926 as possessing "three oil and gasoline outlets, three lumberyards, twelve stores and two banks."³⁸ Other letter writers explicitly credited the town's growth to the Mennonites. In December 1927, one farmer wrote that "if one sees the people in town on their festival days, one can quite clearly see how they have improved themselves with money from the Mennonites. ... Townsfolk make most of their money from the farmers."³⁹ In a few cases, Mennonites even joined the merchant class in town. In December 1927, a *Post* writer announced that "John F. Wiebe of Herbert [Saskatchewan] is establishing himself here ... [and] will have an elevator built in San Antonio to purchase the wheat from the farmers, as the price is good enough for him to sell it."[40] Mennonites had come to claim the town as their market centre. A February 1928 *Post* story that brought more news on Wiebe's elevator also noted how humble San Antonio, named for a Franciscan monk, had been renamed Cuauhtémoc, with reference to an Aztec warrior.[41]

Adaptation to Mexico, however, did not spell integration into it. During the very first years, Mennonites wrote of learning about soil preparation from their Mexican neighbours; now, in the late 1920s, letters described a wider range of lessons learned from them. In a December 1927 issue, for example, several letter writers voiced appreciation for Mexican ways. In one, the writer commented on having learned to smoke tobacco that came rolled up in a sack.[42] Two other writers explained how Mennonites had replaced their first wooden houses with ones built of homemade, red clay bricks; one contributor explained that the brick house was not only "cheaper to construct," it was of better quality, "warmer in winter and cooler in summer" than houses of wood.[43] These adaptations, however, marked but small steps towards assimilation to Mexican society. The Mennonites had survived the first five years in part because they willingly learned from their neighbours and negotiated the local economy. Still, their very presence in Mexico was based on an identity beyond the nation. The vocabulary used in an April 1924 letter from "I. and H. Hiebert" described an ironic affection for Mexico. The writer complained of depressed egg prices in San Antonio, but insisted that we "still love Mexico ... [for] we have the freedom here with our schools, we are still happy that we are here."[44] Their love for Mexico depended on being left alone.

Paraguay, "on the other side of the equator yet"

By 1927, letters to the *Steinbach Post* began to tell an additional story.[45] The Mennonites in Mexico were no longer the only ones who had moved south. A correspondent in a June 1927 issue declared that "from almost every region one reads about migration as the Mennonites in particular spread themselves through the whole world," most specifically to northern Alberta and into the heart of Paraguay.[46] During the same month, another Mexico writer noted, in passing, the joyful reception of the first "letter from Paraguay,"[47] and, soon, Mexico writers reached not only northward to Canada, but southward to kin in Paraguay. In November 1927, for example, Heinrich A. Friesen of Santa Clara, Mexico, announced midway through a letter, "Yet to Paraguay, to sister [Mrs.] P. F. Krahn; how are you doing out there? Let us hear something from you! Each time, I search through the *Post* wondering if I might find something about you. ... That your daughter Maria died out there, we did learn through the *Post*."[48] Friesen even expressed good-natured competition between his Latin American site and that of his sister's: "I read that Mexico is taking a backseat to Paraguay," wrote Friesen, "but one must remember that all beginnings are difficult; without [money] progress can't be made, neither in Mexico nor in Paraguay."[49]

The Mennonite diaspora had expanded and now truly reached across the Americas. Just as the 1922 move to Mexico became a central concern in the *Steinbach Post*, so, too, did the late 1926 move to Paraguay. Again, the initial exodus was detailed by the *Post* editor: "On Wednesday, the 24th of November, in the early morning hour, the first train set out from Niverville [Manitoba] where the Paraguay emigrants from our East Reserve had gathered to travel to a new homeland." But it was immediately clear that the move to Paraguay differed substantively from the move to Mexico; as the writer noted, "the project was even more controversial."[50] He pondered the meaning of the epic move by a group of "humble farmers," and considered the immense energies required and the pain of separation the mothers must have felt. How strange for Mennonites to entrust themselves to the good graces of non-Mennonites who "lead them into the wilderness of Paraguay."[51] Those who remained behind, he wrote, "wondered who their new neighbours would be," and felt sadness that the "Steinbach area ... had to lose many of its own kind," so many that "a sort of depression hung over the entire reserve." Especially worrisome was how "widely, very widely indeed, the Mennonites have spread," and particularly the fact of "settlement on the other side of the equator, that is something new in our history." He warned that "as a German people the Mennonites are a northern people, and their ability to adapt to subtropical lands such as Paraguay, to Spanish culture and to other classes of Paraguayans, has yet to be determined." Certainly, he argued, the traditional ways transplanted from Russia, still remembered by the elderly, would need to be discarded. The writer's parting hope was that "the Mennonite communities on the other side of the equator will make for themselves at least as good a name, as in all the other lands to which their world migrations have taken them."[52] It was one thing that their parents had migrated from Europe to North America; quite another matter to migrate from North to South America.

By April 1927, the Paraguay settlers' voices in the *Post* attested to a rapidly expanding diaspora, a social network now reaching across the continents. The very time span between letters written and letters published spoke of immense geographic distance traversed. Correspondents who, in December 1926, wrote about arriving at Puerto Casado, the tannin factory outpost on the Paraguay River, saw their reports published three months after being mailed north. Their relocation in July and August of 1927, 200 kilometres inland to nascent Menno Colony, lengthened the time to publication even more. The first Paraguay letters also emphasized the distance by dwelling on the difficulty of the epic journey south. Some writers were fatalistic, others expressed trust in God, and yet others used biting humour and irony to mitigate the hardships. The sheer distance travelled had been breathtaking, according to A.A. Bergen's April 1927 letter; it had been a "very long" trip resulting in "much illness, of which I too was not spared." Perhaps the "wonders on the trip were remarkable, but none of it interested me, and I gave no room for such thoughts," wrote Bergen. In fact, he was certain that "the next trip I want to take in a hot air balloon, as more misfortune I cannot endure."[53] In a letter published in the same month, Johan G. Klippenstein wrote that the "journey was fine, except the riverboat [on the Paraná and Paraguay rivers] was too small. Many became ill as not all could sleep in it, forty persons had to sleep on the deck, although it was better there than below, where it was very stuffy. We did make very good progress though, as we had a good crew."[54]

Both Bergen and Klippenstein also emphasized the early difficulty in the strange environs of Paraguay, especially of the first months sequestered at primitive Puerto Casado. However indirectly, they were the first to criticize their hosts, including Samuel McRoberts's Corporación Paraguaya formed in 1926 to oversee the land purchases but also to facilitate all aspects of the settlement process in the Chaco.[55] In his April 1927 letter, Bergen noted curtly that "we have been here for three weeks and the work is proceeding slowly. ... We are living in tents next to the Casado factory, and live from 'pocket to mouth', without being able to earn anything." And yet, the letter writers seemed as worried about the new physical realities of life in Paraguay. In his letter from the same month, Klippenstein also mentioned the lack of income, but highlighted other concerns of climate, cost, and health. His note, written "16 days after having arrived on the morning of 31 December 1926 in Puerto Casado," began with a description of the task of disembarking, but moved quickly to the weather. In fact, the newcomers could not finish "getting our belongings in good order [on that last day] in the old year ... as it was simply too hot," as much as "37 above," according to the Réaumur gauge used by the Mennonites.[56] The suffocating heat required immediate adaptation, and the Mennonites learned that "at night it cools off somewhat" and that "over noon no one works."

Other problems ensued. Klippenstein, for one, was painfully aware of the cost of food and supplies: "Potatoes are five dollars a pound and butter too is very expensive, as are plums, raisins and coffee. To date we have not yet had flour milled for ourselves and it costs eleven dollars for a 150-pound bag. ... Carpentry tools and similar items are very expensive here. If we had known this, we would have brought more materials with us."[57] But the illnesses and deaths were most difficult: "To date twelve children have died, all from diarrhoea, and we others have acquired many boils, perhaps from mosquitoes, more likely related to malaria." The search for "school freedoms" in Paraguay was coming at an unanticipated cost.

The long, albeit temporary, halt at Puerto Casado proved especially frustrating. The settlers were impatient to get on with the settlement in the Chaco and yet it seemed that their hosts were simply unprepared for them. Klippenstein explained that wagons required for the inland journey had not arrived, "making for much trouble, for we can hardly start anything without them." He was concerned that no one had even "established a site for the settlement or determined the availability of water." His impatience grew "as always more [settlers] come and yet our wagons have not arrived." And he repeated the overarching concern: "We cannot plant. ... many have so little and sustenance is expensive." On a more hopeful note, Klippenstein reported that experimentation was possible, and that "several here have small gardens of beans" and that the "buckwheat already has flowers and the flax grows as well." By the time he completed his lengthy letter, written over several days, he had received word that "tomorrow, if it is God's will, we leave early for the land [in the Chaco], six families and several men, in order to make wells and also to plant gardens on 168 NW, according to the measurements of the land surveyors." He was confident that the Chaco's wildlife would provide a good food source on the trip inland, given that "Mr. Engen has lent me his small rifle."[58] At long last, the Mennonites would see their new land.

"The line cutters are supposed to be from our people"

Spirits lifted when survey lines began outlining the sites of villages in the Chaco. On 10 May 1927, Johan Wiebe wrote to the *Steinbach Post* with guarded optimism: "We are still in Puerto Casado as the land has not yet been surveyed, but it is to begin now; yesterday the land surveyor arrived and a caravan is to leave shortly for the Chaco. The line cutters are supposed to be from our people."[59]

Significantly, the story of settling the Chaco as told in the *Steinbach Post* highlighted the role of the Mennonite settlers themselves rather than other parties, like the agents of the Corporación Paraguaya, who ultimately would have been in charge of the land surveys.[60] Significantly, the first marks of "civilization" were to be made by the Mennonites. As Wiebe drew the narrative, Mennonite men were now poised to take control of the settlement project. Stories of progress followed: "In the Chaco several have dug for water, and even if the water at first was a little salty, now it is good, and usable for anything." Other letter writers that May echoed Wiebe's stories of a difficult but manageable foray inland: an advance caravan took twelve days to travel the long kilometres to Loma Plata – ninety by company train and seventy by oxen pulling *carettes*, the high, two-wheeled wagon.[61] By the early South American winter, Puerto Casado was almost empty of Mennonites: one writer, referring to the narrow-gauge company train that took the families on the first leg inland, noted that the "little train has it very busy; oftentimes it takes three groups a week out" into the Chaco.[62]

The first correspondents from the Chaco itself seemed filled with new energy as they settled the unbroken land, even though pioneering difficulties and tragedies abounded. One farmer, writing in September 1927, noted, "There is so much to report I hardly know where to begin." He described the gardens, the beans that bloomed brilliantly and the peanuts that withstood the dry conditions. But he also noted problems. A "night time frost" of −5 degrees on 15 August had frozen the garden vegetables. The building of the access road to the end of the rail line was very slow, reflecting the Paraguayan adage that "everything has time." Only a caterpillar tractor capable of towing twenty tonnes of material through the low-lying bush could be relied on to bring in supplies. Then, too, the land surveying took so long that some families moved onto their properties before it was finished, settling as agreed in specific areas – one each for settlers from the East Reserve in Manitoba, from the West Reserve in Manitoba, and from the Mennonite reserve north of Saskatoon, Saskatchewan – but doing so without full knowledge of just where the internal boundaries would be. The writer also noted the tragic death of a little girl who drowned while her mother was chopping wood for the morning fire and her father was away hauling products. In the end, the writer returned to self-effacing humour: "I will describe how we are building our 'palace', 15 x 22 with seven foot high walls," built with "nine foot long timbers placed vertically in the ground" and home-kilned bricks stacked up between the timbers. He also returned to the promise of Paraguayan soil: "red, and the redder the better."[63]

Other correspondents writing in the Paraguayan spring of 1927 were almost boastful in their exuberance. In October, one writer noted that "I had never realized that so much unbroken land lay here in the south; thousands ... or in fact millions of acres of land can be found [in a region] where it is summer twelve months of the year. ... The [only] difference between summer and winter here is that the latter is not so unrelentingly hot."[64] Two things missing in Canada offset the heat of Paraguay's summer: a mild winter and plenty of land. In another letter published in November, the writer spoke in almost idyllic terms of the large, open areas of luscious meadow, the many springs and pools of water, the small trees. He recognized that "overall we will have to learn a great deal before we will know just when the best time for seeding and planting is." But the area was promising in every way: west from Puerto Casado, the "land became completely different than what we had seen before; the scrub bush became less and less. ... And even though the whole region looked like a wilderness ... where no plough had ever made a furrow, it seemed to be a region very suitable for a Mennonite settlement."[65] Then, in a December letter, a writer reported on a thriving early agriculture:

> [We are] progressing quickly to the end of the year and the anniversary of the arrival of the first group at Puerto Casado. As it appears now, we are all anticipating the future. ... The water problem has been solved as in all of the so-called villages wells have been dug and almost all have ... good water. Also the fruitfulness, with few exceptions, leaves little to want ... . In the gardens, which were successfully planted, one can find onions, corn, melons and watermelons, cabbages, carrots, ruben and a variety of other plants; ... wheat, flax and especially peanuts do well.[66]

The Chaco seemed charged with possibility: familiar crops could be expected to flourish, but the newcomers were also adopting new crops.

The letters did acknowledge that some settlers were unhappy in Paraguay and felt stymied by the high cost of a return trip to Canada. Most letter writers, however, seemed to dismiss any returnees as malcontents who had not given Paraguay the chance it deserved. In April 1927, one writer, still stationed in Puerto Casado, recounted that "a particular Peter Peters, formerly of Saskatchewan, Canada, last week turned his back on Paraguay"; the writer quipped that "such a move is expensive 'fun'" and that "of Peters it can truly be said, 'I've been to Rome but not seen the Pope,' I've been to Puerto Casado but not to the Chaco. ... From our future home, he has stayed away by 200 kilometres."[67] Other letter writers describing return migrants were less derisive: a September missive simply announced that "again this week several families have moved from Puerto Casado to the Chaco and some have gone back to Canada."[68] But most writers saw the returnees as turncoats. A September letter was slightly dismissive: "There are those who are thinking of yielding, of leaving it, and so seven families have again left for their old home, Canada. Oh well, things out here are not for everyone."[69] An October writer used positive language to report on a "higher" and "cooler" Chaco region, words of grief for the "many [children who] have died," but less than flattering language in relating that "another seven families returned" to Canada, as "evidently they had not thought through the implications of pioneering."[70] Clearly, many Mennonites were affirming the Chaco bush as their new home.

Still, as most of the newcomers settled down to hard work, they did not forget the old homeland. The *Steinbach Post* remained a central medium of news for both the Mexico and Paraguay settlers. In May 1927, Johan Wiebe argued that "as the *Post* goes so far and wide, it should include something for readers from far and near, as we know that the people in the old homeland very much would like to learn something from here."[71] Letters from Canada confirmed his curiosity; in a typical letter that June, Katherina Friesen went on an imagined visit "to my sister in Paraguay," pleading, "So beloved siblings, how are you doing?; do write me a really nice long letter, about how everything out there is." She followed empathetically: "Actually one can imagine that in the beginning not everything will go all that well. But you will have to comfort yourself that dear God is with you and will not forsake you." She concluded her letter by affirming the *Post*'s important role in keeping her family connected: "I don't know how to write you except through the *Steinbach Post*; that you yourself are reading it, I have learned from reading in the *Post*. ... Do write a really nice long letter ... even if only in the *Post*. ... Letters must be!"[72]

Over time, the letters in the *Post* continued to express the ever-widening Mennonite diaspora in the Americas. In August 1929, a Chaco writer responded to a query from "someone from Peace River [Alberta], noting ... that he was almost the most northerly *Post* reader ... and wondered who might be the most southerly *Post* reader." The Paraguay writer had the answer: "Well, if the *Post* does not go farther south than here in Paraguay, it means that I will presumably have the honour ... as no *Post* reader in our colony lives farther south than me." The writer closed by wondering "and just how long might the distance then be between us?"[73] The answer was about 12,000 kilometres, but behind the question was a statement that, no matter the actual distance, here were two Low German-speaking Mennonite men within a single cultural sphere.

Most letter writers seemed to imagine this cultural space, but many drew specific attention to it. Often, the correspondents tried to relate the stranger features of Paraguay to common knowledge about Canada. In a May 1927 letter, for example, Johan Wiebe appealed to Canadian readers with both the familiar and the unusual. He reported on good rain amidst cool weather, so much so that "we have to cover ourselves quite a lot at night," reminding him of Manitoba, where he imagined farmers seeding, leading to the empathetic quip, "So also seed something for me." But Wiebe also reminded his readers just how different Paraguay was from western Canada: at Paso Azul, where "some of our people live ... a tiger has killed a foal and a calf. The Indians took up the hunt and have pursued the tiger. Eventually we will cage 'Mr. Tiger.'"[74] In June 1927, another writer reached out to Manitobans, defending the Paraguayan climate, but then making Manitoba seem the more strange and difficult land: "The weather changes here as in Manitoba," he wrote, "one day clear with sunshine, the other day rainy, the third ... so cold and windy." But then he turned acerbic: "It sounded in number 18 of the *Post* as if no one can still live here" in Paraguay, but readers should note, he continued, that "on account of the animals and insects, which are in abundance, no one will lose his life." True, unlike in Manitoba, "occasionally we see crocodiles or foxes," but at least "we don't have twelve feet of water here as they do in Manitoba [in the springtime], even in the river it isn't twelve feet deep!"[75]

Mostly, the letters served to inform readers that the Mennonite settlement was taking root in the Chaco. As the decade drew to a close, the letters increasingly expressed successful adaptation. Old ideas of growing wheat, flax, and barley fell by the wayside as farmers successfully experimented with new crops. In a June 1929 letter, signed "Abr. und Katherina Doerksen," the writer outlined the range of new farm commodities:

> Corn we harvested five bags, peanuts four bags, white beans we have enough for ourselves, cucumbers, melons and watermelons we received in good supply. With the cotton harvest we are not yet finished, need to pluck for some time yet. We planted it on October 1 and already sold 1000 pesos worth and wish to sell another 500 pesos. ... For next spring we have more acres prepared for corn, sweet potatoes, manioca and will also try some sugar cane. We have also ordered mulberry bushes that we want to plant in spring.[76]

Mennonites had also learned the cycle of two harvests per year. A June 1929 writer related that "the cotton which had promised such a good yield last time, will be completely lost as the young knobs have suffered much under the frost. ... But we shouldn't be completely dismayed, thinking that we have only one crop as in Canada ... [We] are awaiting a good harvest of beans and maize. ..."[77]

Certainly, in 1929, a sense of pioneering still pervaded the community. In a letter published in August of that year, one writer described how "several horses have died on account of the cold weather, due in part to the absence of barns."[78] Lack of proper fencing was also an issue as cattle strayed. In June 1929, a correspondent reported that "Johan F. Wiebe, whose ox wandered off some time ago, has searched almost the entire colony, but cannot find him," and that "Peter Kauenhoven of Weidenfeld recently was fortunate to have recovered his ox, which had wandered off about a year and a half ago; Mr. Casado noticed it in his herd and at once shipped it back to the Chaco by rail."[79] Arduous trips were still required to the "end of the rail line," 145 kilometres distant, to pick up "flour, lard and sugar and such items."[80] And some concern regarding malaria lingered: "As far as I know [malaria] is abating," wrote one colonist in a September letter, "although here and there sick ones can be found."[81]

Despite these difficulties, Mennonites had made an indelible mark on the Chaco landscape by 1929. They had also established a dominant, racialized position vis-à-vis the approximately 200 indigenous, semi-nomadic Enlhet neighbours. The Enlhet, whom the Mennonites referred to simply as *Indianer*, had once offered their knowledge of the Chaco environment to uninformed Mennonites, but quickly they became a subordinate people, seemingly compelled to offer the newcomers only their wage labour.[82]

The few accounts in the *Post* of indigenous–Mennonite relations tended to reflect this employee–employer relationship. The need for labour on any farm frontier is legendary, and, arguably, the Mennonites quickly became dependent on the Enlhet. In a May 1929 letter, Franz Froese reported that "from Hoffnungsfeld a road directly to the east is being built" with "the work, as always, done by the Indians. ... Later a [mechanized] grader will do the rest."[83] A single August 1929 letter from Philip U. Kehler noted three different encounters with the indigenous people: one that "[Samuel] McRoberts is using the labour of the Indians, is building roads and opening more land [owned by the Corporación Paraguaya] for new settlers behind our land"; another that "last week I received a visit from six Indians, looking for work, willing to work for one shirt per week";[84] and a third that the Paraguayan military had come to ask if "the Indians ... or any Bolivians were hurting us," an allusion suggesting an abiding distrust of the indigenous people.[85] Other notes referred to the indigenous as a people of the bush. It seemed natural that when Johan Neufeld's and Cornelius Wiebe's oxen disappeared one day in mid-1929 during a visit to the village of Hoffnungsfeld, they "sent the Indians to find their oxen."[86] That closer relationships did exist between some of the Chaco settlers and the indigenous people is evident from an August 1929 note announcing that Fred Engen, the Canadian-Norwegian explorer whom Mennonites dubbed "the founder of our colony," had died of cancer in Puerto Casado, leaving many friends at Menno Colony as well as "many friends here among the native born Indians, who ... had stories to tell about him." Similar notes on any close Mennonite–Enhlet friendships eluded the *Post*.

By 1929, the *Post* writers were describing a Low German Mennonite settlement in the Chaco wilderness as if it had existed for decades. Writers identified the new villages in the colony with familiar-sounding place names, mostly German, but also Russian and English, all referring to Mennonite villages or districts in Canada, all anchoring familiar work and social activity. Three typical letters from August and September 1929 reflected the cultural landscape that carried in its place names the story of Mennonite migration over the previous century and a half. One related that "Jacob and Franz Thiessens and Johan Kehlers and Widow Katherina Sawatsky, earlier this week, went to visit the sick at Chortitz," a Ukrainian place name designating the first

Mennonite colony in the Russian empire. Another reported that "Klass Wienses and Heinrich Wiebes and others from Strassbach last Saturday night travelled to visit their siblings in Bergthal," two German names, the latter denoting the third colony founded in Russia. And a third announced that "early on Thursday the young widow, Mrs. Heinrich Harder of Schoenthal arrived here unannounced via Halbstadt from Lowe Farm," a village named after a British-Canadian railroad siding in Manitoba.[87]

Other writers portrayed an almost idyllic Low German-speaking community. In August 1929, Franz Froese reported that "as one drives through Weidenfeld and Gnadenfeld, one sees the people occupied with a variety of tasks; the one builds, the other ploughs, a few others are cutting boards, although [the elderly] Uncle Peter Krahn, one sees ... doing nothing other than engage in the art of furniture making under the shade of his veranda; mostly they are chairs which he constructs for sale."[88] The scene could have portrayed any other Mennonite village, in Manitoba or Saskatchewan back in Canada, or in one of the newly established main colonies in Mexico. In a sense, Froese's report sounded the theme of transplantation, but it also sounded the theme of an expanding diasporic village, one stretched across the nations, from Canada to Mexico and Paraguay.

Conclusion

The Mennonites who migrated to Mexico and Paraguay not only crossed international borders as immigrants, they did so as transnational subjects. Certainly, the very process of migration created a social network that extended back to Canada and was supported by letters published in the Canadian newspaper, the *Steinbach Post*. Writers to the *Post* struggled to maintain ties to the old homeland, despite the distances between the sending and receiving societies. They shared notes on well-being, they reported on family milestones, they sent greetings, and described to loved ones back in Canada the unusual elements in the new land in Mexico and Paraguay. Those letters gave expression to an imaginary "village" that lay superimposed over an entire hemisphere, linking specific points in an international social network.

But the letters to the *Post* marked this mindset in an even more farreaching way. By reporting on the strange new features of Mexico and Paraguay, they revealed a particular view of the environment, geographic features in general and the soil in particular, that seemed to ignore the nation. When the Mennonites drew survey lines across the mountain valleys of northern Mexico or through the savannah and parkland of the Paraguayan Chaco, they took possession of the land for their communitarian purposes. Their letters testify to a perspective in which land and soil that comprised a village territory were seen to belong to no one nation, but rather to a wider cosmos. Ironically, it was a viewpoint commensurate with the parochial act of turning mountain valleys and savannah bushland into farm fields. The Mennonites' choice of settlement site certainly was influenced by national government policies, but that choice did not reflect a new-found loyalty to a particular nation. The soil the settlers found in one country was an asset that could well be found in another.

In some respects, Mennonite migrants of the 1920s were not unique among the migrant farmers of the world. They participated in the "great land rush" of modern times, assuming an implicit right to the land, so long as they improved it and used it for the purpose of advancing a European-based civilization. This civilization was defined by many international migrants as a racialized democracy, a capitalist economy, and a place of law and order. For Mennonites, the cultural project was more specifically the grounding of a separate ethno-religious community somewhere on earth, in the wider world. The very values of this religiously informed community dictated against a close identification with any one nation-state. The settlers seemed ever ready to cross national boundaries in the search for good land and suitable settlement sites.

3 Dreaming of "Old" Canada: Nostalgia in the Diaspora, 1930–1945

By 1930, the majority of the almost 8000 western Canadian Mennonite emigrants had stayed true to their original decision and re-established themselves in the South.[1] The Mennonite communities of Manitoba, Swift Current, Santa Rita, and Santa Clara Colony in the Bustillos Valley in Chihuahua state, and of Hague Colony, near Patos, in Guatimapé Valley in Durango state, were clearly etched in northern Mexico's cultural landscape.[2] And, in Paraguay, Menno Colony had made its mark in the central Gran Chaco savannah. Over time, scholars have focused on the remarkable ability of these settlers to replicate old ways in new lands. H. Leonard Sawatzky's thorough historical geography, *They Sought a Homeland*, is the classic study of the Mennonite transplantation in northern Mexico's semi-arid climate, an outline of the ways in which farm colonies were first established in 1922, complete with orderly villages, familiar house-barn architecture, local governance, and a household economy. Martin W. Friesen's remarkably comprehensive history of the first decade in Paraguay, *New Homeland in the Chaco Wilderness*, recounts turbulent times between 1927 and 1936, but especially the process by which farm villages were established in the challenging Chaco wilderness and the way in which old forms of democratically elected self-government were eventually re-established at Menno Colony.[3]

Perhaps it seemed that the Mennonite settlers were focused singularly on their new ventures in the South. But, just as their migration and pioneering efforts during the 1920s revealed a transnational mindset, so, too, did their lives within established colonies in Latin America during the 1930s and early 1940s. The migrants continued to live outside national cultures and within self-governing communities. They thought of themselves as a people belonging not to any one nation, and their leaders continued to negotiate directly with national governments to secure that separation from national life. Moreover, a steady stream of Mennonites, defeated or distraught, returned north to Canada, more so from Mexico than Paraguay. Then, too, the settlers in the South continued to cultivate close ties to the old homeland of Canada, especially by maintaining the flow of letters to the *Steinbach Post*.[4] Evidently, the settlers could not forget the old homeland of Canada; indeed, it comprised a central feature of their imagined worlds. Their letters reported on visits to and from Canada; they expressed yearnings for the old homeland; they voiced antipathies to it. Whether they saw Canada as friend – home to close kin and spelling safety – or as foe – the country that had betrayed them – it remained an integral part of their worlds; it could not be left behind.

A specific range of events has always shaped such imaginations. Ewa Morawska argues that, depending on their specific circumstances, immigrants have variously seen their homelands with reference to either the idyllic, local village, the *Heimat*, or, in sweeping nationalistic terms, to the more hostile *Vaterland*, relatively, as places "either beautifying / idealizing or unequivocally inimical." And, in most cases, regardless of how one viewed it, the "imaginations of the homeland were complex, often contradictory, dynamic, and 'untidy.'"[5] Mennonite imaginations were no less untidy.

Certainly, insofar as their experiences differed in Mexico and Paraguay, so, too, the specific Mennonite attitude towards, and memory of, Canada varied. The Paraguay Mennonites' encounter with Canada became relatively less intense as insurmountable distance made visits from the homeland and return migration rare. Their focus now included other countries, including Paraguay itself, as increasingly close relations with national leaders evolved during a tumultuous time in the nation's history. Menno Colony's new neighbours, the Mennonite refugees of nearby Fernheim Colony, also brought into focus the Soviet Union, with its stories of suffering, as well as Germany, their temporary abode as refugees in the late 1920s and their cultural suitor during the Nazi regime in the 1930s.[6] In addition, the Paraguay Mennonites were courted by progressive co-religionists from the United States seeking to aid their "brethren of the south."[7] By the early 1940s, Canada was still the old homeland, but now increasingly a place of nostalgic memory.

The Mennonites in Mexico experienced Canada in somewhat different terms, for relative proximity to it encouraged visits back to northern birthplaces. This proximity also allowed for festering doubt regarding the exodus from Canada in the first instance, especially after a wave of theft and violence in the early 1930s, and after the government reneged on granting Mennonites their treasured school autonomy. In the mid-1930s, the Mexico Mennonites considered the merits of migrating a second time and establishing themselves in any one of a number of countries, including Paraguay, the United States, Bolivia, South Africa, and Australia. The nostalgia many Mexico Mennonites felt for "old" Canada included much more than kinship networks, but also the country's reputation for "peace, order and good government." A profound ambivalence about Canada became a feature of Mexico Mennonite culture.

Despite these differences in how Mexico and Paraguay Mennonites related to Canada, they shared a common imagination of the old homeland. Certainly, it differed from the way many other migrants viewed their old homelands. Robin Cohen's *Global Diasporas*, for example, describes the Jewish concern to "return to Jerusalem to rebuild the Temple" and the Sikh or Armenian desire to re-establish the ethno-religious community in old homelands and thus coalesce a fragile diaspora.[8] The Mennonite story is reflected more fully in Takeyuki Tsuda's work, *Diasporic Homecomings*, which argues that both first-generation "return migrants" and "later generation ... ethnic return migrants" have not so much been "driven by the search for ethnic roots and ancestral heritage [as] by global economic disparities."[9] When Mennonites were tempted to return to Canada, it was not for the patria but for profit; they moved because of local circumstances and were affected by an ancestral impulse that disparaged any kind of return to sending societies. In her work on return migration, Morawska explains, "It is at the level of local surroundings" that return migrants "define their purposes ... and undertake actions," albeit conditioned by "original goals in migrating."[10] For the Mennonites, local surroundings – kinship ties, environmental conditions, colony politics, health issues – as well as the staying power of their original idealism mattered.

The economic equation in the story of the Mennonites' return to Canada is clear. For most Mennonites in Mexico and Paraguay, economic difficulty was far greater than they could have anticipated: Chihuahua and Durango were too arid, the Chaco too intemperate, the land deals in both places too unfavourable, and the markets too uncertain or difficult to access. But the nostalgia for Canada, especially during the 1930s, also related to the failure to meet "original goals" of religious faithfulness in the new homeland and the "failure in the host society" to guarantee safety and security. Because these factors were highly subjective, the nostalgia for Canada in the 1930s and 1940s was encased in ambivalence. Intense debates on matters of goals and failures at the local level shaped the volume and nature of the migration back to Canada – indeed, the untidy way Canada was imagined.

The Canadian homeland during the 1930s was, thus, never only a magnetic attraction, the lovely Heimat, but also a place of antipathy, the betraying Vaterland. Perhaps most typologies of diasporic nostalgia do not allow for antipathy towards the homeland as a force for cultural solidarity. Certainly, for the Mennonite migrants, the very subject of Canada revolved around both nostalgia and antipathy. As Charles Tilly has argued, insofar as such conflict and debate rage, they also encourage a common vocabulary, itself a central and coalescing feature of migrant cultures.[11] Even for a people whose religious values discouraged expressions of patriotism and nationalism, and whose ultimate homeland was a heavenly kingdom in the hereafter, images of old Canada retained cultural importance.

Commitment to Paraguay

By the early 1930s, those Mennonite settlers who had survived the intense heat and privation of the Paraguayan Chaco seemed to relegate Canada to the back of their minds. Canada was the place to which the malcontents and failed settlers, sometimes negatively dubbed "bondbreakers," had returned. It was the place from which the returnees could offer their own refutation, lambasting those who remained in Paraguay as "hypocritical." In one report published in the 5 March 1930 edition of the *Steinbach Post*, a writer from Canada ridiculed those still in Paraguay who "self righteously" called themselves "The Quiet in the Land," who claimed that "the Creator created them as a model," and who declared that the move southward had staved off linguistic assimilation. The letter writer was unrelenting: "Do not send such unnecessary babble to Canada," and "Be careful that the Spanish language does not take over, for the devil will plant his seed over there [in Paraguay] as well as here [in Canada]."[12] This letter was a last salvo from the 335 persons (or sixty families, about 20 percent of the migrant group) who returned to Canada from Paraguay in the late 1920s, bitterly complaining that Samuel McRoberts's Corporación Paraguaya had failed to provide the means to settle the Chaco and that the Chaco was uninhabitable in any case.

The very next issue of the *Post*, however, cast the great return northward as a fading phenomenon. A writer in the 12 March issue noted the return in past tense: "Yesterday it was three years since the first immigrant group landed in Puerto Casado. How quickly this time has passed by. Much has happened. ... as many have taken the wanderer's staff to 'return' and abandoned us. In recent times many again have ... left us to return to Canada. Thus, as we have been told, Peter Krahns of Gnadenfeld and Franz Giesbrechts of Blumengard wish to be gone from here."[13] Even as the letter highlighted the return migration of two families, it placed them into the context of "time passed." Another letter from October that year even had the tide turning: it announced that "Jakob Wiebes ... who moved to Asunción in order to seek an opportunity to return to Canada, have, so to speak, changed their minds about the Chaco, and are presently living in [the Mennonite village of] Bergthal."[14] The busy return path to Canada was, it seemed, subsiding, and even reversing itself.

The early difficulties at Puerto Casado and the sizable return northward had dominated the Paraguayan story during the late 1920s. The preoccupation of the 1930s and 1940s was the building of the economic base of the colony, creating an efficient administrative system, welcoming new neighbours from the Soviet Union at nearby Fernheim Colony, and adjusting to Paraguay's national politics and military ventures. Most letters to the *Steinbach Post* from the 1930s had a singular intent, that of reporting on the conditions at Menno Colony. Stark details reminded readers of just how difficult matters were in Paraguay – its climate, its primitive economy, its marauding soldiers – but these problems all seemed surmountable. The basic conditions – the fertility of the land and the support of the government – were never in doubt.

The most regular of the contributors to the *Post*, farmers Franz Funk and Philip Kehler, usually depicted Menno Colony in overtly positive terms, even while acknowledging the 1930s years as difficult ones. In his 1929 Christmas letter, Funk wrote whimsically that "the Christmas man [Santa Claus] is naturally not especially rich at most places and has mostly presented gifts of personal story telling," except for "several places where he has presented beautiful dolls," in the form of newborn babies.[15] Then, too, these were times of continued physical challenge, of drought, dust storms from the north, and continued reliance on imported flour. In a typical letter, Funk reported in April 1931 of "another shipment of [500 sacks of] flour from Buenos Aires" that had "arrived at Kilometer 145," still the nearest rail terminal some sixty-five kilometres east of Menno Colony.[16] Poverty would not disappear easily. Correspondent Johann Harder reported in January 1936, "This year more flour is being borrowed, and [although], as in all years, flour debt is being paid."[17]

The 1930s also marked intense inner political turmoil at Menno Colony, although this problem was not readily acknowledged in the *Post*. Other sources suggest that the colony's *Fuersorgekomitte* (the "Welfare Committee" in English, later redubbed the *Chortitzer-Komitee*), which Paraguay's Law 514 designated as the colony's central administrative unit, faltered due to a stalemate within the governing group's undemocratic base.[18] Its ill-thought-through structure, which granted equal representation to the Chortitzer (of Manitoba's East Reserve), the Sommerfelder (of Manitoba's West Reserve), and the Saskatchewan Bergthaler groups, despite the Chortitzer's 80 percent majority, was rewritten only after an appeal to Paraguay's president, Eusebio Ayala, in September 1934 and April 1935.[19] Then, too, this was a time of testing and eventual dissolution for the Corporación Paraguaya, which had overseen both the sale of the Mennonites' land in Canada and land purchases in Paraguay, and, by contract, had worked to provide an economic lifeline to the new colony. The Corporación was accused of profiteering in the land deals, failing to survey Menno Colony in timely fashion, never completing the railroad it had promised, and cutting off credit prematurely. Only its 1936 sale to the Mennonite Central Committee based in the United States and the establishment of the Menno Colony Co-operative ended long-standing bitterness.[20]

The news in the *Post* on these institutions seemed all rather more positive. In a February 1930 letter, Franz Funk described the corporation's power to tax as a matter of fact, describing how "Ed Fehr is again traveling through the colony in the interest of the Corporation, which he does monthly, to tax, or to remove from the tax roll, the gardens or fields, together with the cattle and buildings."[21] In his May 1931 letter, Funk again reported on the corporation without complaint: he began by announcing that each cotton-producing family had now received sixteen centavos per kilo from the corporation, and noted that even if the "sum is small, it brought happy faces, as until recently we had not been able to sell our cotton." In the same report, he heralded the decision of the "Corporation Committee" to build a massive cotton-storage shed in Hoffnungsfeld, the colony's eastern entrepôt.[22]

Other letters reported on a seemingly well-functioning set of colony institutions. In September 1930, Funk commented briefly on the colony's church-directed educational system, announcing that "a meeting of teachers and preachers was held in Osterwick last Friday," and noted the near completion of the new schoolhouse at Silberfeld.[23] Other reports highlighted village government: in a typical letter, Philip Kehler reported on a 30 December 1931 *"Schulzenbott* [village council] meeting here in Schoenthal where a *Waisenvorsteher* [estates administrator], *Komiteeman* [colony committee representative] and *Dorfsschulze* [village mayor] were elected," the latter office being filled by Abraham Doerksen.[24] Similarly benign reports regarded church life: sometimes individual ministers were highlighted, as in 1931, when Funk announced that the young minister "Abram B. Toews of Weidenfeld will preach his first sermon on Easter ... God willing."[25] Sometimes it was another significant event, as the action at Osterwick in 1932, where the colony's first "church building is to be constructed; just how large I cannot report, but evidently not too small."[26] Rarely was there a hint of church friction or the malcontented settler.

Even the extraordinary insularity of Menno Colony and its immense distance from any market centre garnered few complaints in the *Post*, although all links to the outside world were along the wilderness route to Asunción, some 400 kilometres to the southeast. Indeed, the only route to the city was along a rough road sixty-five kilometres east from Hoffnungsfeld, typically five to seven hours by truck in dry conditions,[27] to the rail terminus at Kilometer 145 (also known as the Fred Engen station); then, after a wait of some time, a five- to seven-hour train ride took the traveller to the outside world even farther eastward to Puerto Casado, followed by a thirty-six-hour riverboat trip south on the Paraguay River to the national capital.[28] Notwithstanding these difficulties, *Post* writers made frequent references to individuals making this journey for business purposes. They also highlighted visits from the outside world. In February 1929, two American Mennonite missionaries stationed in Argentina visited the colony at the behest of their American leaders, including Orie O. Miller, head of the US-based Mennonite Central Committee (MCC), who wrote to enquire about the colonists' difficulties.[29] On the occasion of a second such visit in late 1929, Franz Funk noted the visit of "two distinguished gentlemen from Argentina. ... to inspect our agriculture as well as our colony operation. ... And they spoke in laudatory terms of our endeavours and apparently were completely surprised about our progress to date."[30] Few reassurances were as convincing as the praise from well-connected and sympathetic outside observers.

Another such reassurance, though, was the news of coming neighbours. Especially reaffirming for Menno Colony was word that some

500 Russländer Mennonites, refugees from the Soviet Union, were en route to the Chaco with support from US Mennonites. In his April 1930 letter, Philip Kehler described the "Corporation's preoccupation with surveying land for the Russländer who departed from Hamburg, Germany on 15 March," and he wrote with anticipation of the imminent arrival of "200 families, traveling in three groups."[31] The very coming of the Soviet refugees introduced further links to the outside world. In his April 1930 letter, Franz Funk announced that MCC's G.G. Hiebert from California had arrived in Paraguay to "receive the Mennonites from Russia, who we have learned, arrived in Buenos Aires on Wednesday." Funk also described Menno Colony's close connection to the coming Europeans, including "much work being done at the new colony site by our people [from Menno Colony] and the Indians; houses are being built, roads constructed and roots removed for ploughing," in addition to which, "on April 20, some forty wagons are supposed to arrive at Kilometer 145 to pick up the newcomers."[32] New ties to Germany and the United States had, for the moment, eclipsed Canadian connections.

While Menno Colony was refocusing on Mennonites from these countries, it was also establishing closer relations with its neighbours within Paraguay. Both Funk and Kehler reported regularly on encounters with non-Mennonites and most often in rather positive, albeit racialized, terms. The approximately 300 indigenous Enlhet in the vicinity of Menno Colony drew most comment. Despite some accusations of thievery, the *Post* writers seemed to defend their indigenous neighbours. Funk, for one, recounted in February 1930 that local Mennonites had assembled a "40 person work force of Indians found at Stassbourg," and editorialized that "overall the Indians are good workers, unlike the Indians of Canada, who to my knowledge, did not want to work."[33] Philip Kehler noted in June 1931 that the local natives seemed restive; some had stolen potatoes, with Mennonites giving chase, and then, on the 20th, "some 30 souls, Indians, passed through here" quietly, without any social exchange, but he was quick to add that the Mennonites had no fear of them as they "did not have hostile appearances in their faces, as [did the natives] in Canada."[34] Despite racialized language used to describe indigenous people in both countries, Kehler's implicit argument seemed to be that Canada and not Paraguay was now the exotic "other."

Agents of the Paraguay government were among the other non-Mennonite visitors who received positive references. Government medical workers were especially welcomed at Menno Colony. In a

1933 report, Funk explained, "Two men are traveling" the colony "by order of the government, to compel the people to be vaccinated, thus stemming illnesses."[35] In a 1935 missive, farmer Johan Harder was almost laudatory when he noted that "a government doctor is traveling through Menno Colony to inspect eyes," and explained that about one half of all colonists "suffer from eye sickness, mostly Trachoma," concluding that "this is a significant overture from the government."[36]

Even bitter experiences with the Paraguayan army during the bloody Paraguay War or War of Thirst, which raged between Paraguay and Bolivia from 1932 to 1935, seemed to leave the Paraguayan government's reputation unblemished in the eyes of the pacifist Mennonites. Perhaps it was because Mennonites were said to have profited from the war; indeed, their provision of water and foodstuffs supposedly aided the Paraguayan defeat of Bolivia, a military force the Mennonites seemed to have considered foreign interlopers despite its being led by German-speaking Bolivian generals.[37] In fact, the first of thousands of Paraguayan soldiers to set foot on Menno Colony, most en route to battle stations at the northern war front, were described positively, sometimes even as symbols of order. When Philip Kehler reported in February 1930 that "here in Blumgard sixteen soldiers armed with machineguns have set up in the bush," he explained that they were on the lookout for "several Bolivians who were in the neighbourhood to recruit Indians for reconnaissance."[38] At a later date, when the army created encampments and began training at Hoffnungsfeld and other nearby places, Kehler again extolled the soldiers, highlighting their orderly marches to "music that sounds very pleasing."[39]

These laudatory images, of course, were challenged as reports surfaced of the military's requisitioning colony buildings, soldiers stealing from the colonists, and occasional renegades even raping and murdering. In January 1933, Funk wrote bluntly, "We have a plague in our community, which one must openly oppose, namely the plague of soldiers. They have given us a lot of trouble. At night they go around and rob and steal, especially in the gardens, where they take melons and watermelons." Funk added, "Here in Halbstadt an officer has taken over the schoolhouse with a dozen soldiers. ... In Blumengard and other villages the soldiers have shot cattle, cut off some meat and left the rest."[40] Over the next two years, such reports became common. In April 1934, Funk described an incident on the main road to the northern front, one traversing the heart of the colony: "On Sunday some 125 trucks loaded with soldiers drove through Halbstadt heading to the front; as a 'farewell' they left indelible tracks ... in that they broke into several granaries" and entered "our garden where they helped themselves to many mandioca and sweet potatoes."[41]

But marauding soldiers were overtly lambasted when they engaged in sexual assault. Funk, for one, described as "ferment" those soldiers stationed at the Halbstadt School who sometimes "break into houses at night and molest women and girls."[42] The problem escalated with a "horrible murder" on 1 February 1934; Funk described the event:

> In [the village of] Chortitz, between 10 and 11 at night, three soldiers took hold of Abram Giesbrecht's daughter, with whom they undertook their disgraceful mischief. At the sound of her screams several neighbours hurried over to help the girl. After the neighbours had freed the girl, the soldiers began firing at the Mennonites ... whereby a bullet hit Abram F. Giesbrecht [the recently widowed father of small children], killing him right at the spot.[43]

And this report matched another in which young Fernheim Mennonite women were molested en route to Kilometer 145. As correspondent J.A. Esau put it in a letter published in March 1934, the soldiers stationed at Hoffnungsfeld are "always becoming more wicked ... including the hijacking of a wagon en route to Kilometer 145" and, in one case, kidnapping a girl on her way home from being a domestic and "for several hours took her as their prize."[44]

Despite the terrible shock of these events, neither Funk nor Kehler seemed to blame the Paraguayan government. Funk found it significant that, at the time of his writing, the soldiers who killed Giesbrecht had "already been found and received their just reward," presumably imprisonment or even summary execution. Even in January 1933, when he declared soldiers to be a "plague," Funk appended a note that "the government is still very favourably disposed towards us [Mennonites] and we have no complaints against it."[45]

In the years after the war and once the colony had become established, an even stronger loyalty to the new homeland ensued, and Canada passed gracefully from a compelling physical reality, one to which malcontents had returned in the late 1920s, to one that was merely celebrated as an old homeland, a Heimat. In his September

1938 letter, Johann P. Ginter begged for some news from old friends in Canada:

> [In my mind] I travel to Ebenfeld to Uncle Abram Ginter's [and wonder] if the Uncle is still living? If not, can his children write us? If neither the Uncle nor the children read the *Post* can a neighbour pass this message onto him? Is Aunt Johan Ginter still alive? ... Of Uncle Peter Falk, Morse [Saskatchewan], we hear nothing. ... Someplace out there, sister-in-law Jakob Ginter must also be alive. ... Who can report on these? ... Johann, write us a long letter, even if it is in English; there are still those here who can read it.[46]

Other writers pined for a visit to their birthplace, knowing full well that such a visit could never occur. In his July 1944 report, correspondent Jakob D. Harder began with a declaration that "I still remember much about Canada, even where I left my cradle standing, and especially of Manitoba and the Rural Municipality of Tache where I was born and later farmed. Even the very last events [the farewell gatherings] are very clear in my mind."[47] For Paraguay Mennonites, Canada had evolved into just that, a place of continued kinship ties and a site of one's mythological cradle, a Heimat rather than Vaterland.

Ambivalence in Mexico

It was a different matter for the much larger Mennonite community in Mexico, where, letters in the *Steinbach Post* suggest, debate continued about the merits of actually returning to Canada. The 1930s especially marked a time of incessant debate. While many Mennonites defended life in the new homeland of Mexico, others castigated it. This intense divide was apparent at several levels of discourse.

Neighbourly letters of the everyday, for one, were infused with a current of uncertainty. Many letter writers seemed slightly defensive in describing Mexico, oftentimes implicitly addressing those Canadians who were skeptical of the settlement in the South. One writer may have begun his 1934 letter with a humorous salutation in a German-English hybrid, but his message was curt and brusque: "'Viel-beloved Big Bill,' it has been ten years since we came to this land, and you could not believe how good we have it here!"[48] Similarly positive, but hinting at malcontent, was a 1933 correspondent: "Things are very good in Mexico; there is much building this year, as it now seems, quite a few will settle down here; we think this is a very good land."

Other writers seemed to acknowledge the problematic semi-arid climate of Mexico, all the while countering Canadian skeptics. If Canadians thought Mexico a dry place, joked one householder in December 1931, they should take stock of two remarkably successful pig slaughterings, one at the J. Wiebe household where "two pigs produced 20 gallons of lard and one at J. Friesens' where three pigs gave 30 gallons." Perhaps, punned the writer, "the Canadians can see that in Mexico it is not all that 'dry', at least not at these people's places, for they will certainly be able to spread their lard thickly [on their morning bread]."[49] Other writers offered a reverse analysis, boasting of Mexico's temperate climate but hinting of economic difficulty. In his November 1934 report, regular correspondent Abram Wolf chirped that "the weather here is still 'Mexican,'" characterized by "warm sunshine," and added a personal note to an acquaintance, "Well Justina … if in winter you want to have sunshine, then … come to Mexico." But Wolf joked that when Justina did visit, she should "come with chickens, turkeys and pork and serve us dinner, for we still know how to eat in 'German.'"[50] Canada perhaps had the inhospitable climate, but it was still a land of bounty.

Mexico Mennonites also were of two minds regarding Mexican culture and society. Some letters suggested a tentative acceptance of Mexico as an adopted land. In a 1933 report in the *Post*, correspondent Wolf wrote a full exposé of Mexican farming methods, declaring that in "many ways the Mexican is ahead of us." Wolf recalled a recent intense rainstorm that had destroyed earthen brick walls of many Mennonite buildings, and confessed that "at first we wondered why the Mexicans built their houses of such thick walls, but one always learns more. … We Mennonites know how to save money, but not at the right places; in house construction we … constructed the walls only 12 inches thick, when it would have been better at 18–24 inches." Wolf even suggested that Mennonite farmers could learn from Mexican peasants: "In the first years we found their farming methods comical, but today we see that they get along with little expense. In some years the modern machines are far too costly for this region." While Mennonites suffered financially, wrote Wolf, the Mexicans, with their primitive farm equipment consisting of "a plow made of wood, a piece of steel as the share, a harrow made of shrubs," seem "satisfied."[51] Mennonites might well be ahead by abandoning Canadian capitalist attitudes.

Other writers commented on the deep cultural divide between the Mennonites and Mexico. In May 1932, one writer began his report by highlighting this social boundary: "Today all of Mexico is celebrating National Day, but we celebrated this day as *Himmelfart* [Ascension

Day]."⁵² As Mexicans embraced their nation, Mennonites looked heavenward. They could also look askance at their Mexican neighbours, employing such words such as "primitive" and "disorderly" to describe Mexicans. In a lengthy April 1933 report, a writer signing "H. P." described Mexico as inhabited by an indigenous people who "are overall uncivilized and may well be a hundred years behind people of other lands." He described the meagre diet and crude cooking methods on neighbouring ranches:

> Corn marks a national standard. ... Small cakes are baked from it and laid on fires till they are done. ... Nearby is a pot of coffee and a box of peppers. The women in preparing food don't fuss a lot; the men eat once things are hot, sitting on a crate ... they feast. Pigs are not slaughtered according to our customs ... the beef is hung on trees till dry.

He described the Mexicans' houses in a similar tone: "Very few rooms are graced with windows ... the house is of bricks, 14 x 16 feet for one family. The roof is covered by dirt and in few houses does one see furniture." He concluded by highlighting Mexico's class divide: while one person "transports everything by donkey – corn, firewood, fruit cases," another drives "the nicest car ... manufactured in the United States"; here, "one person might own a thousand acres, the other nothing."⁵³ Mexican society was strange in every way.

Racialized divides often accompanied class division. Descriptions of Mennonite relations with Mexicans, for example, suggested brisk economic exchange, but rarely on equal social footing.⁵⁴ Mennonites deferred to merchants and professionals in the cities, but held a significant economic advantage over their immediate neighbours. Mexican natives or indigenous people, the *Einheimische*, as Mennonites called them, were described in racialized terms as "coming around wanting to work, and if there is no work they beg for bread."⁵⁵ But Mexicans of Spanish descent more often fit a class-based employer–employee relationship. A 1932 letter from Hague Colony in Durango state reported that "Uncle Peter Redekopp has again traveled to the city of Durango for medical help," indicating the Mennonites' respect for the modern Mexican medical profession in the distant city. But the reporter also noted that in Redekopp's absence, he "has hired" fellow Mennonite "Aron Buekert to supervise his ... ten Mexican workers,"⁵⁶ suggesting a position of Mennonite power. A similar order was apparent even in the symbolic heart of the Mennonite community: a 1933 letter reported "a real building boom" at the village of Gnadenthal, including news of "a large new church ... being built of bricks" made on-site, providing "the Mexicans with work and the chance to earn a little money."[57] Clearly, the Mennonite trustees felt charitable, but the fact was that Mexican workers came cheaply. Then, too, they were more easily steered to difficult tasks: at places where "corn is being husked," noted a 1936 correspondent, the work is provided "by Mennonites during the day and by Mexicans at night."[58]

This kind of social divide was also evident in descriptions of commercial exchange. As a 1933 reference to "Mennonites ... trading young cows [heifers] for Mexican wild horses" signalled, two peoples existed in the Bustillos Valley: Mennonite farmers and Mexican ranchers.[59] Other reports reflected a divide between the mechanized Mennonites and their non-mechanized Mexican neighbours. The *Post* carried frequent references to a variety of technical services provided by the Mennonites to Mexican customers: in 1935, it was that "Bernard Schmidt of Campo 113 is at this time in the mountains with his well driller and is drilling a well for a Mexican";[60] in 1936, that "for some time Johann Ginter has been in [name illegible] and there threshes wheat for the Mexicans."[61] Rather atypical was an October 1933 letter describing one Mennonite's business trip "with a Mexican friend who ... wanted me as a travel companion" to Santiago, west of Cuauhtémoc, a place the Mennonite had long wished to visit.[62] Even though oral history suggests occasional primary relationships in which young Mennonite women or men eloped with Mexican counterparts, such reports did not appear in the *Post*.[63] For the most part, the social boundary between the Canadian newcomers and Mexican host society was impermeable.

Of Two Minds on Canada

If Mexico Mennonites expressed ambivalent feelings towards their adopted country, they also did so towards Canada. On the one hand, Canada was seen as the old homeland, the Heimat full of familiar sites and kin; on the other, it was the Vaterland of repressive, nationalist school legislation. The Great Depression intensified the production of repelling images of troubled times in Canada.

Letters in the *Steinbach Post* from the early 1930s, for example, were replete with descriptions of Canada's depression. Mexico writers seemed to indulge in *schadenfreude* as they repeated stories of Canadian Mennonites complaining about poor commodity prices.

Mexico Mennonites could respond tauntingly: "Uncle A. A. Hiebert of Hochfeld," joked one Mexico Mennonite in May 1932, "if the pigs [in Canada] are so cheap, then why not come out here with a truck load."[64] More often, the Mexico Mennonites decried the Canadian Mennonites' response to that country's economic crisis, especially farmers' reliance on government "relief," an English word the southern writers used pejoratively in untranslated form within their German letters. A May 1934 letter announced that life in Mexico was good; not only had President Abelardo L. Rodriguez "visited [the Mennonite colonies] and reaffirmed Mennonite [religious] privileges," but, in Mexico, "the kind of 'relief' we hear Canada has to pay out is not needed";[65] the Mexico Mennonites would gladly take their President Rodriguez over Canadian Prime Minister Bennett. Another writer in May 1933 chided the Canadians for self-righteous talk. In response to a Canadian letter writer's criticism that Mexico Mennonite men had adopted a new custom of wearing workaday overalls to church, the Mexico writer reminded readers that "in Canada 125,000 persons live on 'relief' and another much larger group lives enclosed in hobo camps." In such a context, the writer argued, Canadian writers "should not be too concerned about clothing" in Mexico.[66]

A much sharper criticism of Canada appeared in a lengthy letter in May 1935 by regular correspondent Bernhard Penner. He noted that if Canadians were alarmed to read about banditry in Mexico, they should realize that "our danger here has been much exaggerated ... and is not greater than that in Canada, indeed there it is worse." Penner declared that he was "grateful to be in Mexico, away from the Bolsheviks, Communists and other demonstrators in Regina." In fact, as Penner saw it, "It is my responsibility to alert you [Canadians] to your danger ... of Communist assemblies, demonstrations in the streets of the big cities, so large that the police ... have to move aside." Penner had read that "at places, such as in Saskatoon, mounted police officers have had to be called in" and had even heard that "in Ottawa, at the Parliament buildings, machine gun fire has broken all the windows." He listed other dangers: "The dependence on 'relief' ... seems dangerous to us as it is completely ... misused," leading to corruption and laziness. "Moreover," charged Penner, "those who take 'relief' give their trust to the government ... [a reliance] forbidden by Mennonite faith confessions." Immorality was also rampant in Canada, where the "Bolsheviks ... seek to bury all order, morals, and beliefs in order to incite revolution." In a veiled reference to the Winnipeg General Strike of 1919, Penner said that he had seen such leftist tendencies "even while we were still in Canada." He concluded unequivocally: "I see danger here, I see danger in Canada, and ... within the whole world. So, further responses to these charges [against life in Mexico] I intend to ignore completely."[67]

Writers came to Mexico's defence on other controversial issues. In 1931, Mennonites began reporting that Mexico had closed its border to immigrants, seriously inconveniencing certain Mexico-bound families from Canada.[68] The letter writers were highly critical: "The immigrants from Canada ... have not yet arrived" because they "are having difficulty coming across the border," stated one *Post* writer in November 1931.[69] Mennonite leaders responded quickly to this infringement of Mennonite rights. A December writer noted that "the Canadians who are stranded on the Mexican border" are "to be helped across, if at all possible" by "our *Vorsteher* and by *Ältester* Julius Wiebe, who have gone out there."[70] Numerous other reports of the border closing and new obstacles followed.[71] After weeks of such reports, a contributor in February announced that "the poor people at the border in El Paso, five families who are land owners, have after seven months returned to Canada; what they have all experienced during the last year one can only imagine, but it was impossible for them to enter Mexico."[72]

But even in this charged context, Mexico writers reserved their sharpest rebukes for their Canadian counterparts, and offered charitable thoughts on the Mexico border authority. One writer in early 1932 explained that the border closure did not reflect Mexico's view of the Mennonites but was simply a directive involving all foreigners, and that Canadian Mennonites had no right to an exemption from the law.[73] Another writer added that Canadians who complain about Mexico's border "should note that Canada's border is also closed" to immigrants, and they should recognize that "Mexico's border was [only meant to be] open [to Mennonites] for a ten year period."[74] Another writer blamed the border closure not on Mexican policy but on two disreputable Canadian Mennonites, P.P. Klassen and Gerhard H. Hiebert, who had shamefully competed for the business of transporting Mennonites to Mexico; Mennonite reputation had suffered from Klassen's charge that Hiebert had "smuggled" Mennonites, bringing "many people from Canada without passes," and it had been further damaged by Hiebert's accusation that Klassen was an "obsessive drunk."[75] Mexico in this equation was friend; Canada remained foe.

If Canada was a country of cold climate and social unrest to the Mennonites in Mexico in the early 1930s, it nevertheless remained a country of kith and kin. Canada, with its progressive, rapidly anglicizing Mennonite churches, could be rejected, but blood relations in the old homeland, the Heimat, could not. Indeed, most issues of the *Steinbach Post* carried references to visits by Mexico Mennonites to their relatives in Canada, or by Canadian visitors to kin in Mexico. Many issues included lengthy travelogues or references to the brisk business of ferrying Mennonite "tourists" on the 3000-kilometre road trip. A July 1935 issue, for example, carried the notice that "Hildebrandt thinks of going again to Canada," that is, "as soon as he has a truck full of passengers."[76] A June 1938 issue similarly informed readers that "Johann Wiebe of Halbstadt returned recently from a trip to Canada, having taken guests there and back." It went on to explain that "he is planning another trip out there on the 31st with five passengers."[77] Many other travellers crammed into cars, sat in the back of large trucks, or boarded transcontinental buses. Active links with Canada continued.

The itinerary in Canada, as described by the visitors in the *Post*, followed a common template, an agenda full of visits with as many relatives as possible, with short side trips to birthplaces, to the homes of old classmates, or to regional cities to obtain necessary travel documents, and, occasionally, even a bit of amusement.[78] A typical report in December 1937 by Gerhard D. Neufeld and his wife illustrates a whirlwind nine-day, two-province tour, visiting old friends and tracing their kinship network. The tour began with friend Daniel Teichrob of Rosenort taking the Neufelds to the "Old West" (Hague, Saskatchewan), where they visited one set of in-laws, plus an elderly aunt, "as well as many nephews and nieces, and acquaintances." They then travelled south to Swift Current, where "Friend D. D. served us very well with his old Ford" by taking the couple around to visit friends and relatives. Next, the couple headed east to Winnipeg, spending an entire Sunday in a "city, still as we knew it thirteen years ago, with much running, driving and bustle." On Monday, they "took the train to Winkler" in southern Manitoba, visiting more relatives, including the "Peter E. Neufelds, where ... we gave them a joy filled and startling surprise visit." Then, it was on to Gerhard's "birth village" and to Hochfeld to see the families of other siblings, including adult siblings "Heinrich and Susanna. ... still unmarried, living in the parental home." At each place, wrote Neufeld, "we refreshed many old memories and met many acquaintance, friend and relative."[79]

The visits invariably revived old memories. Many travel accounts contained images of emotional remembering and recognition. A 4000-word travelogue by Helena Thiessen in July 1945 recounted a visit to Manitoba after a fourteen-year absence. She, too, noted the visits with dozens of relatives, including her "old schoolteacher." But the report highlighted the first of many stops she and her husband made. At the home of Heinrich Klassen and his wife, the two couples were so excited about meeting each other, they "forgot all about eating 'Faspa,'" the cold, late-afternoon meal, and "spoke till late into the night." The most poignant moment at the Klassens', however, occurred when Helena's niece, a young married woman, dropped by and, although not recognizing or expecting the Thiessens, intuitively knew them and uttered, "Uncle David and Aunt Helena!" The specific moment of meeting any relative inevitably brought overwhelming emotion. On the way to visit the Buhlers, whom "we had not seen in fourteen years," Klassen could not contain her feelings: "When one comes closer and closer" to the house of any loved one, "the heart beats hard, as if it does not have nearly enough room." And it intensified as she approached "the parental home" where she met her elderly mother: there in the doorway of the "old house on the hill was the actual mother. ... Only the person who has experienced it can know what kinds of feelings this produces!"[80]

Lending a sense of occasion to these visits, the travelogues often highlighted the road trips through the American Midwest. Although most travellers followed a standard route from El Paso north to central Kansas on Highway 54 and then along Highway 81 to the Canadian border, some trips varied. After a ninety-nine-day stay in Canada, A.W. Peters returned to Mexico by car in December 1938. The importance of the US section of the trip for Peters was illustrated by the descriptors he used. For one, he knew precisely that the trip south covered 2172 miles, that each day he began driving at 6 a.m. and travelled until 10 p.m., that on the days within the US he covered distances of 484, 342, 458, and 430 miles, respectively, and that he stopped for the night at Moorhead (Minnesota), Northfolk (Nebraska), Newton (Kansas), Amarillo (Texas), and El Paso (Texas). Travel by truck was slower than by car. In their return to Mexico in January 1942, Jakob T. Klassen and his wife spent fourteen days on the road. Klassen's interest was also in the time it took to cross the American Midwest, and he recorded in detail every delay – the times a battery died, a tire became flat, a radiator overheated. Travelling by a combination of overnight bus and train, and using a taxi to cross the border, could cut the trip down to five days, and travelogues describing these traverses were similarly detailed.[81]

Significantly, these accounts spoke of the distance "in between" two "transcultural" nodes, to quote Dirk Hoerder's terminology. They recounted the crossing of a hostile outside world linking two parts of a transnational village. They focused in particular on the two national borders that separated the relatives in Canada and those in Mexico. Not surprisingly, their crossings invariably received special mention, even when they occurred without trouble. When Jakob Klassen entered the United States in January 1942, he outlined the process at the Canadian customs in Gretna, Manitoba, of "going in, showing our papers, answering a couple of questions and it was finished, we could go." Then, a few kilometres into the US, he had to repeat the process at Neche; that is, of "having to stop once again, showing our papers and all was well." Significantly, too, the US Midwest was represented as a worldly space that must be traversed. Along the way in South Dakota and Iowa, Klassen, for one, marvelled at the "lovely towns," but, as he put it, "nothing could steer us from our destination, we constantly drove farther" south.[82] Sometimes, travellers found moments of refuge from that wider world among the Mennonites along the way. In Meade, Kansas, the Klassens were approached at a service station by a local Mennonite, asking "whether we were from Canada en route to Mexico." The pit stop turned into a two-day rest with a Meade Mennonite family, a time to bathe, dress in clean clothes, and visit in Low German.

Upon arrival at the United States–Mexico border, another round of document scrutiny ensued. The Klassens passed through US Immigration without a problem, but had to return to the US side when Mexican authorities in Juárez rejected Jakob Klassen's travel documents and instructed him to telegraph Mexico City for the correct papers.[83] A final challenge always was the crossing of the Sierra Madre into the Bustillos Valley. Most travel accounts described the obstacles as a series of stone outcroppings, cold mountain streams, and sand traps that occasionally damaged a car's motor and crankcase. The final stretch home from Cuauhtémoc, made by horse and wagon, often added a day, even two, to the trip.[84]

For those who could not afford the visit to Canada, the *Steinbach Post* continued, as it had in the 1920s, to provide a link between the new and old homelands. Hundreds of letters to the *Post* during the second decade of settlement contained kinship information and full-length descriptions of funerals, weddings, and engagement parties, intended for transcultural consumption.[85] Significantly, not only did these letter writers bolster old social networks, they did so with shared vocabulary. Many letters, while written in German, were infused with English-language references, reflecting these Mennonite groups' two-generation history in Canada. The English words "corn," "truck," "tractor," "silo," even "Corn Flakes," were common, interwoven seamlessly into everyday German parlance. Not atypical was a 1942 description of work at a new sawmill, in which a writer announced his intention to haul wooden slabs "mit einem 'autotruck' der einen 'trailer' hat" – that is, with a truck equipped with a trailer – and that it would all start upon the sound of the "siren heulen," the howling siren.[86]

Frequently, writers provided a short quote in English to make a point: "'He has beat the record,'" declared J.J. Fehr in a snippet of English after hearing that a neighbour had captured sixteen rats in one night; "'Time is money,'" declared another, who doubted the value of saving $9 a thousand board feet by hauling lumber himself.[87] Mexico Mennonites even adopted new Canadian terms: in January 1939, A.B. Schmidt of Durango counselled that a first-rate "Bennett Buggy," a car turned into a wagon and named after the depression-era Canadian prime minister, could be acquired for a third of the going price of a regular farm wagon.[88] Ironically, the Mexico Mennonites even used English terms within their German-language letters to translate Spanish terms: when, for example, Cornelius Unger and J. Hildebrandt visited Mexico City in 1942, they reported that they first visited the "General Hospital" and then the "National Museum."[89] Ironically, Mennonite businesses in Mexico sometimes adopted English names: a December 1931 letter, for example, announced the opening of the Mennonite-owned "Mexican Implement and Machine Works" in the village of Osterwick near Cuauhtémoc.[90] Here was a hybridized vocabulary that uniquely linked the new settlement in Mexico with the old in Canada.

Temptations to Return

The continued visits to Canada, close kin ties, knowledge of English, and Canadian passports all made Canada a potential haven in a hostile world. Perhaps for some, the old homeland was a land of social unrest and religious betrayal, but trouble in Mexico in the mid-1930s turned Canada into a country of "peace, order and good government" that seemed to beckon them northward. The strong desire to return was precipitated by a specific series of events: first, a personnel registration directive for all foreigners in Mexico; second, a sharp rise in banditry from disbanded forces of the famed but failed northern Mexico revolutionary Pancho Villa, historically an arch-foe of President Obregón's; and third, the especially troubling closure of the Mennonites' private, church-supervised, German-language schools by Mexican authorities, who cited them as violating the Mexican constitution, which prohibited church-run schools. For many Mennonites, Mexico seemed to have become hostile to their original goals and expectations.

The first serious problem arose in the spring of 1932 when Mennonites received word of a mandatory national registration for all foreigners in Mexico, one complete with photo identification.[91] Both requirements were serious matters for the Mennonites: they recalled a similar national registration in Canada during the First World War that seemed linked to impending universal military conscription; and, historically, they saw photographs as forms of self-aggrandizement that violated the Old Testament teaching against "graven images." At first, the Mennonites held out hope that the registration requirement would be waived for sectarian, pacifist farmers.[92] But then, word came from Chihuahua that no one could be exempted, as the registration was specifically directed at all foreigners and served to retaliate against the US's draconian expulsion policy towards Mexicans.[93] After an official in Chihuahua was quoted as saying that noncompliance "will make it bad for [Mennonite] bishops and colony mayors," Mennonites reluctantly submitted to the registration. In the simple words of one correspondent, "So pictures are being taken,"[94] while another reported more dramatically that "things are quite wild here" with Mennonites resisting the ten- to thirteen-pesos registration fee, "a burden on the wallet," and most balking at the very idea, for "photography causes anxiety."[95]

At this very moment of concern came a second one over a sudden increase in crime directed at Mennonite villagers. The early 1930s marked a wave of banditry said to stem from Pancho Villa's defeated supporters, now sequestered in the mountains overlooking the Mennonite settlements. At first, the references in the *Post* to thievery were prosaic: one November 1931 letter noted that "Mennonites are hiring Mexicans who are less expensive than are the Mennonites, but then after dark the Mexicans return for another 'accounting', this time without the supervision of the owner and when the owner wakes up he discovers that the Mexican workers are not that inexpensive after all."[96] Reports on banditry increased rapidly in the following months.

Some Mennonites even became vigilantes, setting aside their pacifist stance. In December 1931, one writer reported how "at David Klassen's in the Swift [Current] Reserve the Mexicans recently attempted again to steal," but left hurriedly after "Klassen grabbed [the thief's] revolver with one hand and his throat with the other."[97] Another Mennonite victim responded even more violently a few months later in February 1932; when Heinrich Banman, a Mennonite store owner, was shot in the mouth in broad daylight by thieves and his cries for help went unattended, he reportedly picked up his own rifle and shot in the general direction of the fleeing thieves. As the correspondent saw it, not only had a crime occurred, but now the so-called "'quiet in the land' ... who had left Canada" because of "religious and school matters, and who do not want their own children to join the armed forces, grab the pistol as soon as it comes to matters of life and death."[98] Mexico was not offering Mennonites an opportunity to live out non-violent principles, after all.

In the weeks following these thefts, Mennonites began requesting that the government restore order, which it willingly provided.[99] "Through the government and in God we want to have order kept," wrote one correspondent in February 1932, but only if it means that "we do not lose our freedom" of military exemption.[100] In March 1932, amidst reports that "our government cares nothing about the thievery," another contributor applauded the arrival of "soldiers," mounted patrols, who would "try to stop the thefts" from occurring.[101] Another writer recorded that "on 4 March 1932, a group of seventeen soldiers rode through [the Mennonite village of] Neuhorst towards the [the Mexican town of] Rubio, investigating places where the Mexicans had stolen."[102] The dispatch of state-issued mounted patrols changed the exclusive Mennonite world, at the least because of state directives that "soldiers stationed at Rubio, when riding through the villages, must be given sustenance."[103] Still, the Mennonites seemed relieved that "soldiers are cracking down on thieves."[104]

By late 1932, letter writers indicated a sharp decline in thievery. Thefts continued but they became less violent and almost benign. A June 1933 letter described how at "Jakob Thiessens' Mexicans stole a piglet and a barn pail [used] ... to fry the piglet,"[105] while one from October 1933 explained that "at Franz P. Bergens' thieves ... pushed in a window and took Bergen's pants and shirt which he had hung over a chair for the night."[106] The Mennonites' fear of the bandits themselves abated. As one March 1933 writer reported, when food was stolen from the Johann D. Martens family, "Uncles Martin [Martens] and Peter Martens ... assembled several neighbours" to pursue the fugitive and did so "without any sense of fear."[107] By 1934, law and order seemed re-established. Impoverished Mexicans "seek 'relief,'" wrote one Mennonite in May 1934, as "each year at this time" they come "for feed, corn to eat, beans ... buying or begging ... but of theft one no longer hears anything," even though they complain that "we are so rich and they are so poor" and "see our productive gardens as immeasurable kingdoms!"[108] When thefts did occur, they were now met with a speedy dispatch of state force.[109]

Nevertheless, both the mandated photo registration and the thievery of the early 1930s caused many Mennonites to doubt Mexico as a place of order. Some Mennonites began to advocate for a return to Canada, while others suggested relocation to an altogether new site – Paraguay, the United States, Australia, or even some obscure Pacific islands where Mennonites could thrive if they turned to fishing.[110] But loose talk of a new return migration turned into pitched advocacy for it in 1935 when Mexican authorities, without notice, closed Mennonite schools.

The very first accounts of the school closings noted the seriousness of the situation and an unflinching Mennonite resolve to take all necessary action to teach their children in their own ways.[111] On 16 May, regular correspondent Johann Wolf reported in rather matter-of-fact language that "in Manitoba Colony last week several schools were closed by the ... school inspector from Chihuahua." As the Wolf report unfolded, it became apparent that Mennonites were alarmed: "Whether it has been a misunderstanding or whether it was directed by the government is to be investigated; to this end two men from Swift Colony and two from the Manitoba Colony have gone to Chihuahua." If necessary, claimed Wolf, the delegates "will go to Mexico City ... to put this serious situation to rest."[112]

The tone in an anonymous letter just a month later, on 15 June, was even graver: "Despite all the beautiful weather it ... is hard to get friendly faces from the people who are increasingly ... fearful and anxious" about the schools.[113] A July writer was no less apprehensive, noting that the delegates were still in Mexico City, leaving the whole school question unresolved.[114] That summer, numerous other reports were lodged, some inflammatory in their pessimism, others false in their hopefulness. One August letter even declared prematurely, "We can again, following our *Ordnung*, teach in our language and according to our beliefs."[115] Another announced that the delegates had returned from Mexico City without a firm guarantee for school freedom and that, ominously, even they as Mennonites had been "unable to meet with the president," and only received a promise that "a document granting us freedom in schools and church matters is to be sent."[116]

The gravity of the matter now provoked intense talk of return migration. On 20 June, only a month after the first school closure, Abram Wolf initiated a year-long debate. Uncharacteristically, he began by contrasting semi-arid Mexico with well-watered Canada, admitting that one "can hardly contain oneself when people from Canada describe how green it all is there." He then moved to the urgent issue at hand: "Mostly people are speaking about the schools which the government has taken from us, and while much effort is being exerted in this matter, we still do not have the hoped-for answer." Mennonites were prepared to take drastic action, wrote Wolf, nothing less than "a new migration," perhaps "a return to the 'fatherland', in other words, 'back home', where government offers protections." Just what "protections" he had in mind was unclear, but many people were already organizing auction sales, so many that local demands for household wares and farm machinery had reportedly declined rapidly. Some Mennonites were said to be desperate, driving "around amongst the Mexicans, trying to sell all kinds of items as best they can," to earn enough to "leave this country." Wolf admitted that even he was considering leaving. Hoping for school freedoms in northern Alberta, he punned on his surname, wondering "if up there in the Peace River a little hole might be found for the Wolf."[117]

Numerous similar reports were filed during a tension-filled autumn of 1935. A September letter announced that an emigration committee had been elected, and another that bus owner Johan Loewen of Neureinland was standing by to whisk people to Canada and that only 10 percent of Mennonites still had faith in Mexico. A third warned readers that the thousand poor Mennonites who had refused the national registration would face a 500-peso penalty if they wished to leave Mexico.[118] An October letter spoke of a group dubbed the "Peace Party," or "Friedens Partei," which, propelled by "school troubles," is "today once again convening a meeting regarding emigration."[119] Then, in November, writer Isaak F. Dyck put the whole affair in historical perspective with a blunt denunciation of a hypocritical and cruel Mexico: "We have been here in this land for thirteen years and at this time we cannot conduct our schools, even though only 50 percent of their [Mexico's] people can read and write." Mexico, lamented Dyck, "has become our stepmother." Without hinting at the irony of it all, he continued that the community had "selected three persons to see if the

Canadian government will once again take us on as its children and give us freedoms in schools and church matters."[120]

By the spring of 1936, letters reported on the first step towards an organized emigration. "Our delegates left for Canada on February 11 to see if there is a place for us where we can live in peace," wrote H.H. Banman, a prospective returnee. He continued, "Some people here ... are completely ready to travel to Canada. I have to sell everything and then we too are ready; most importantly one needs money to travel."[121] A month later, another letter stated that "most people want to return to Canada but are still waiting for the delegates" to return from Canada.[122] The good news they awaited never materialized, for they soon learned that the Canadian provinces remained committed to the policy of assimilation they had enacted twenty years earlier.

The "Othering" of Canada

A mass return migration to Canada never occurred. If migration were to happen, some Mennonites said, it must be to a province other than Manitoba and Saskatchewan, perhaps even to another country such as Paraguay. Johann Wolf wrote in February 1936 that a Brotherhood meeting at Santa Clara Colony had voted to "migrate to Paraguay as they have not received a satisfactory answer from the Canadian government, while Paraguay has promised all the requested freedoms."[123] But even the move to Paraguay did not materialize, and, over the course of 1936, talk of moving to Canada subsided. By April, a letter mentioned that people "talk little about moving as no one knows where it will be better."[124] By September, another letter claimed that those who had not yet cancelled plans had nevertheless postponed them, and, of the families who had moved north, many were already coming back.[125] A December writer reported that while "many from here have driven to Canada this summer with plans to stay there. ... It seems that Mexico is so basically attractive that people who have settled here cannot simply 'up and leave,'" meaning that those "who do leave, eventually come back," even though it meant a return to a severely weakened financial position.[126] One February 1937 writer went so far as to claim that most of the talk about returning north had simply disappeared.[127]

What caused the emigration fever to die down? Certainly, it mattered that in the winter of 1936, Mexico did an about-face and reopened the schools; in fact, now with a declaration from Mexican President Lázaro Cárdenas that Obregón's 1921 promises to the Mennonites were indeed legitimate.¹²⁸ But the other reason for the change in tone was that Mennonite writers who were inclined to castigate Canada took the upper hand. Even as some doomsayers insisted that the Cárdenas declaration was inadequate and that Mexico could never again be trusted, a much stronger chorus of voices – consisting of entrepreneurs and church elders, women and men, Mennonite and non-Mennonite – arose, citing Canada as the bad "step parent." Mexico, they said, had its "dark" side, but Canada was still the great betrayer. If Mexico was a difficult land, it was still the land to which God had led the Mennonites from an intolerant and godless Canada. Indeed, the suffering that life in Mexico entailed was a small price to pay for ultimate religious freedom.

An especially informed September 1936 writer began by calling upon Mennonites to try to understand the complexity of Mexico and to remember a simple fact about Canada. The letter, seemingly written by a German-speaking non-Mennonite, possibly by German consul Walter Schmiedehaus, lauded Mexico, "a Catholic country with a socialistic educational" policy, for its remarkable overture to the Mennonites, "an isolated, pure German folk group with their own confession of faith." Mennonites should not only celebrate that in 1936 their schools are "once again opened and ... operating according to the old ways," they should empathize with the constitutionally bound government and realize that it "is not easy to regulate something [i.e., private schools] for foreigners, while forbidding it to the native born." They should also realize that the recent crime wave merely reflected northern Mexico's recent history: in "the fourteen years of settlement here [four] revolutionary movements have occurred in this region – 1923 De la Huerta, 1925 Miramontes, 1927 Gutierrez, 1929 La Renovatora," and "one should not be amazed that some of these [violent] events have occurred." Mennonites should also take note that advocates for a return to Canada were "selfish" people who were simply "tired of Mexico," had "no passion for work," and often were impoverished wards of "the colony and church." Finally, the writer invoked the logic and authority of "the Old Colony preachers," one of whom in "a recent conversation ... told me in the clearest of terms, 'if it was right for us to leave Canada in those days, it cannot be right for us to return today.'" Clearly, "the situation that spurred [the Mennonites] to emigrate at that time has not changed," and neither "in essence" have conditions in Canada "since the time we arrived here."¹²⁹ Canada in 1936 was no more benign than it had been in 1916.

Religious principle decided the matter for most Mennonite writers. Indeed, writers argued that privation, and even suffering, in Mexico could be redemptive. In August 1936, when A.B. Schmidt of Durango announced that "yesterday the papers came from the President that we are once again to have our [school] freedoms," he speculated that "98 percent of the people would ... stay in Mexico," even if crime did worsen. Some unrest and suffering, argued Schmidt, might even produce a more religiously committed community. Schmidt gave an example:

> One night as two thieves broke into a house, one was heard saying, "let's shoot the man dead and rape the wife." [Hearing this] the wife ran to the neighbour's, with one of the thieves in close pursuit. Catching up with her [at the neighbour's house], the thief wanted to drag her out, but the woman clung to the neighbouring woman and cried for help. Then the neighbour woman spoke, "let us all fall to our knees and ask God for help." When the thief saw this he was ashamed and fled.

Schmidt concluded, "It is still the almighty God who can help," and then asked rhetorically: "Did the apostles live in this world fearfully or in peace?"[130] In a similar letter dated September 1936, Cornelius Banman also acknowledged suffering in Mexico, especially economic hardship. It is true, he said, that "95 percent of our land has been purchased with Canadian money and the cattle, machinery and house furnishings have been brought from Canada ... and if today every person would be asked how it stands, 90 percent would say, worse than fifteen years ago." But it did not matter, Banman insisted, because it would "be right for us to return to Canada" only if someone "in Canada would show us a place where we could live out our faith"; to date, this had not occurred and so Mennonites might well brace themselves for more privation.[131]

Of these various letters, Johan Knelsen's of December 1936 most directly embraced suffering as a blessing. He recalled the good life in Swift Current, Saskatchewan, in 1918 and 1919 and declared, "If it is there today as it was thirty five years ago, then sure, I would go." But he also recalled that in 1921, as "we gathered to consider the question of immigration to Mexico we listened to Bishop A. Wiebe teach us from Corinthians 6: 1–11," about being willing "to be wronged" and eventually "inheriting the Kingdom of God." Knelsen recalled asking himself, "What is causing the elder such anxiety?" Only today, years after the bishop's death, did Knelsen begin to understand: "Do you think it is horrible when our brothers are robbed, or murdered? I would like to advise you, Friend, read through the large *Martyrs Mirror* and in it you will discover the duty of the Christian in the faith."[132] Just as their Anabaptist forebears had been united in Christ in suffering, so, too, Mennonites would find spiritual wholeness within Mexican adversity.

These voices reflected a majority sentiment among Mexico Mennonites, but they did not totally end speculation that a wide variety of sites in Canada or the United States might offer a better life. Indeed, some writers reported sporadic talk of a migration north even as others claimed it had subsided. A June 1937 letter announced that two men were "leaving to travel through the United States to see what it has to offer, before heading to Peace River where they want to move."[133] A September 1937 note had a different focus, reporting that "last week several delegates traveled to Quebec concerning the emigration," hoping that Mennonites might find their place in that province's religiously determined education system.[134] Then, a March 1938 letter recounted a completely new scheme propelled by a visit by "two men from South Dakota ... inviting us to consider their state" as "their government has two million acres of land" and seems willing to commence "talks concerning schools and religion."[135] A veritable South Dakota fever set in, several visits ensued, some families sold their farms, and Dakota boosters chided those who would even think of "returning to their beloved Canada which has given them so much pain and suffering."[136] A year later, though, the much-hoped-for Dakota scheme fell apart as quickly as it had arisen. A March 1939 writer put it bluntly: "Because of the school laws in the U.S.A., the majority have canceled plans for migration."[137]

Even before giving up on US sites, some Mennonites continued their pitch for places beyond North America. In his March 1939 report from Durango, correspondent A.B. Schmidt reported hearing of "invitations for settlement from Central America, from Africa and Bolivia." He asked, "Who can report on Bolivia; what do the friends in Paraguay who live nearby have to say? Things are too land tight here in Mexico, as we have to keep striving so much. ... Still Mexico is a good land, if only there was order."[138] In the Mennonite mindset, no geographic point of settlement was ever fixed.

Another aspect of this outlook lingered through this time and well into the 1940s as the Second World War raged. Memories of Canada as a land of unmitigated assimilation continued to shape the culture of Mennonites in Latin America. A submission from a "Frau Guenther," published in October 1945, reminded readers that the very thought of Canada could still elicit a passionate response. Guenther reflected back on her life in Hague, Saskatchewan, before the 1922 migration and recalled how her destiny was salvaged by her father's stalwart faith:

> [Father] was often encouraged by the local school board to send his daughter to town [for higher] education. He didn't want to and now I am so thankful to him and to God that he didn't. What would have happened if I had gone? The old fashioned, simple dresses would not have survived, as I would have assimilated the ways of the world. What kind of children would I have had? Boys who joined the army, girls who would have mocked the old ways. The children would not have valued the simple rural life they now live out in Mexico.[139]

No doubt, Guenther was hearing that Canadian Mennonite boys were joining the armed forces in unprecedented numbers, that public schools in Canada were conducting patriotic exercises, and that an increasing number of Canadian Mennonites were leaving the farms for nearby towns and cities. If Canada had been a worldly country after the First World War, it was much more so at the close of the Second.

Conclusion

The end of the settlement era in Mexico and Paraguay did not end the Old Colony, Sommerfelder, Chortitzer, and Bergthaler Mennonites' interaction with other countries or communities in other countries. Large numbers of settlers had returned to Canada, 20 percent from Paraguay, and as many if not more from Mexico. During the 1930s and early 1940s, Canadian Mennonites continued to maintain close ties to the old homeland, with the *Steinbach Post* serving as a central vehicle for nurturing social networks consisting of kin and old acquaintances. But such ties to Canada evolved along different lines for the Paraguayans and the Mexicans. The great distance to Canada simply meant that once fully settled, the Paraguayans did not have the means or the will to return to Canada, while Mexico Mennonites not only corresponded with friends and relatives back home, they often travelled north to visit them. When the economic and social climate in Paraguay became difficult, Mennonites hunkered down, capitalized on their close ties to the country's government, boasted of the transplanted nature of their community, and seemed validated by the coming of Soviet Mennonites and visits from Mennonite leaders from the United States. In Mexico, a less verdant climate, a series of thefts, nationalist school closings, and certainly more tenuous ties to government encouraged continued thought of returning to the old homeland.

Indeed, throughout this time period, 1930–1945, Canada maintained its mythical hold on the migrant Mennonite imagination. Both Paraguay and Mexico Mennonites experienced typical nostalgia for their birthplace, the Heimat, and spoke emotionally of having lost contact with loved ones. But in Mexico, Mennonites also engaged in a bitter debate on the merits of a return to Canada in more general terms. When trouble brewed in Mexico, many forgot Canada's culture of anglo-conformity and romanticized the country as a place of peace and order, but many others reminded the diasporic community that Canada had caused the Mennonites a great deal of "suffering" and that any return migration constituted an acquiescence to Canadian hegemony, a militaristic Vaterland. The nostalgia many Mennonites felt for Canada served to bring a cultural coalescence to the scattered community in Latin America, but, ironically, so did a strong antipathy to the old homeland; nostalgia and antipathy together were the underpinning of a common cosmology. Canada was important not only because some settlers pined for it, but also because it was the centre of conversation and debate, it shaped a common vocabulary, demanded an emotional response, and figured large in their religious commitment.

4 Rethinking Time and Space: East Paraguay and Beyond, 1945–1954

In 1948, some 2500 conservative Mennonites from western Canada joined their kith and kin in Paraguay and northern Mexico.[1] About 1700 of these new settlers, mostly members of the smaller Chortitzer and Sommerfelder congregations from Manitoba, moved to tropical East Paraguay, a region previously unsettled by Canadian Mennonites.[2] The remaining 800, mostly of the small, similarly conservative Kleine Gemeinde Mennonites, settled about one hundred kilometres north of existing Mennonite colonies in Chihuahua, Mexico.[3] The most-often-cited reason for these post-Second World War migrations was straightforward enough. Participants spoke of stemming assimilation into Canadian society, encouraged by urbanization and the patriotism of the Second World War. They believed that time could be stopped; indeed, that it could be turned back. They hoped to replicate the close-knit, anti-modern Mennonite culture of frontier Canada, perhaps even aspects of the Mennonite commonwealth of nineteenth-century Russia.

If the aim of the groups who migrated in the 1940s was similar to that of their forerunners in Latin America in the 1920s, it was made more complicated by the existence of, and interrelationship with, three other groups of Mennonites. One consisted of elderly Mennonites in Latin American settlements since the 1920s, who welcomed the newcomers and called upon co-religionists in the South to stay true to traditional ways. The second included more acculturated Mennonites from Canada who travelled south to visit the settlements in Latin America and publicly cajoled their traditionalist cousins to adopt modern ways. The third group consisted of returning migrants, mostly members of the 1948 migration who vetoed East Paraguay upon arrival and returned to Canada, publicly denouncing the South as unfit for Euro-Canadian farm families. The new migration south in 1948 occurred within the context of these three other groups, that is, within a dynamic, evolving cross-current of disparate Mennonite migrations and the contesting voices within them.

This chapter seeks to shed light on this evolving migrant culture of the 1940s and 1950s by examining the wide variety of texts produced by this increasingly complex migrant story. Those texts reveal another dimension of any transnational story: the multi-dimensional sense of time. Space for these Mennonites, of course, was a linkage of specific localities among several nations. But time was even more complex; for the Mennonite migrants, it was a simultaneous layering of a strong sense of the present, a meaning-filled interpretation of an epochal past, a faith in the forthcoming or eternal, and, finally, an abstract view that sharply contrasted tradition and progress. This perspective on time becomes especially apparent when four specific types of text are compared and contrasted: the personal diary (including the travelogue); the published letter in the German-language immigrant newspaper; the memoir; and the news story in English-language weekly newspapers.

Each of these four immigrant texts divided time and space somewhat differently. The diaries, reflecting a strong sense of the present, isolated the day and compellingly juxtaposed it to yesterday and tomorrow, thus structuring unilinear order on a world in flux.[4] The letters in the *Steinbach Post* announced the important events – those pertaining to life cycle and life-shaping moments – of the immediate past, the week, and the month, but produced for a dispersed, first- and second-generation immigrant readership. The published memoirs spoke of teleological design, revealing an attempt to detach and to evaluate a lifetime lived in more than one country, especially with the idea of eternity in mind. The newspaper reports published in one of two English-language Manitoba Mennonite weeklies – the *Altona Echo* and the *Carillon News* – introduced a new perspective, offering broad strokes of time and promising "objective" analysis of the increasingly complex diaspora, albeit on a trajectory of modernity consistent with progress and achievement. Each medium expressed a particular formulation of time: the diary signalled the day; the letter, the week or month; the memoir, the lifetime and even the eternal; and the newspaper report, the wider epochs of traditionalism and modernity. But these were more than simple demarcations of time; they served to illuminate the complex nature and connectedness of the Mennonite migrants' mid-twentieth-century worlds.

This linkage of time with text, however, was intersected by yet other constructions of time that seemed especially relevant to the mid-twentieth-century Mennonite migrants. New time imperatives evident in the travelogue, for example, reflected a demarcation between agrarian and industrial time, similar in ways to E.P. Thompson's comparison of time when seen as "natural in a farm community" and a different "time-discipline" that is "imposed" by industrial technology.[5] In the Mennonite migrants' narrative of uprooting and transplanting, these two cultures of time were not sequential but interwoven, moving from one to the other, and back to the former. The letters not only described recent events for a diasporic audience, because the letters implicitly sought the response of readers back in Canada, but they reached for a common vocabulary of time, framing it within pre- and the post-migration epochs. The memoirs looked backwards, of course, but, in the parlance of Pierre Bourdieu, they also reflected a sense of the "forthcoming" or the eternal, described by one recent study as a conceptualization of it "not only as a future" but a compelling sense that a life was meaningful only as a collective and teleologically oriented struggle; it helped "people make sense of the current state of affairs" and certainly authenticated the sense of sacrifice that sectarian Mennonites felt they were making in the South.[6] The English-language newspaper reports saw the future in quite another way: as with American newspapers analysed by Robert Schudson, they carried reports that spoke of an "objective" evaluation on "progress," imposing a new, even confrontational, criterion onto an ethno-religious community whose very raison d'être was not achievement but continuity and tradition; indeed, maintaining the old *Ordnung*.[7]

The Diary

The simple diary of the everyday, kept by Mennonites in all their farm communities – in Canada as well as in Mexico and Paraguay – was, as noted in chapter 2, a laboriously documented reference, in Gothic handwriting, to daily work patterns, weather conditions, social networks, and social boundary crossings. The diaries measured time in its most basic of units, the single day, reflecting the rhythm of nature and social interactions within a cohesive, village society. Farmer Johan A. Thiessen, whose diary described everyday life during the year of migration to Mexico in 1922, also kept a diary in Mexico, never missing a day between 1931 and 1951, and ending just three years before

Thiessen died at age seventy-two.[8] Similar to his 1922 diary, the record of his life in Mexico was one without introspection and analysis.

Quotidian concern also shaped the diaries kept during the emigration year, 1948, albeit with references that sharply interrupted familiar agrarian rhythm. One diary, co-written by a middle-aged couple planning to relocate to the Kleine Gemeinde settlement at Los Jagueyes, Chihuahua, Mexico, in 1948, demonstrates the migration's disruption on daily life. Abram and Elisabeth (Kornelsen) Plett, who moved from Blumenort, Manitoba, to Mexico and remained there until the 1960s, kept a diary throughout most of their married life,[9] including 1948. Even for that year, the diary's primary focus was on daily farm life, albeit with those disrupting migration moments that shook the extended family and network of neighbours. The week of 22–29 August 1948, for example, was typical except for Sunday, 22 August, when a farewell service blessed the Kleine Gemeinde Mennonite migrants leaving for Mexico, and for Monday, when the Pletts recorded that "in the evening 100 souls left for Mexico from Niverville, the railroad town." Then, for the next week, the diarists' focus returned to farm work and rural kin. That Sunday, the Pletts attended church and then had lunch with their married daughter Tina and her husband Wilbert Fast. For *Faspa*, the light, late-afternoon meal, the Pletts visited the home of Abram's father, and that evening they spent time with their son and daughter-in-law, Henry and Margaret Plett. On Monday the 23rd, work resumed and Abram wrote, "Jake went to Twin Stone with Plett boys. I and Mama [Elisabeth] went to [Doctor] Kroeker." On Tuesday the 24th, Abram began documenting the annual harvest: "After *Faspa* we threshed wheat; yielded 40 bushels per acre so far." On the 25th, more wheat was harvested, and on the 26th, after the lifting of "some fog," a milestone was reached when "we finished cutting the oats and finished threshing the barley at the well, got 60 bushels to the acre." On the 27th, Abram made other references to the harvest. The diary proceeds month by month, without a self-conscious moment.

Then, on 29 November, a single line demarcated a sharp disruption for the entire household. It was a typical late-November day, clear and sunny, with freshly drifted snow, but atypical in that "we all went to C. R. Pletts' from where our loved ones left at [12:40 p.m.] for Mexico." Just two weeks later, 11 December represented another significant day, one that began with the words "we weren't very busy," but evolved to include a visit "to Klaas R. Pletts' to say goodbye; many others had assembled there to say goodbye." In total, some 600 Kleine Gemeinde

Mennonites, or 15 percent of the Kleine Gemeinde community, moved south in 1948, but the daily diary's snippets of information on the migration only hint at its significance. They also skew its complexity, marking it invariably as unilinear, a single-direction move from the familiar and predictable.

The travelogue added quite another dimension to the mid-century Mennonite migrant's sense of quotidian time. As with travelogues generally, it seemed to introduce a heightened "level of individual consciousness of the succession of social and cultural epoch."[10] Uprooted from daily rhythm in one place, the Mennonite traveller marked movement through space and the fleeting appearance of the unusual and strange along the way, especially as improved technologies and the momentum of travel allowed for closer interaction between those who had stayed in Canada and their relatives in the South. The travelogue of this time, in particular, was a record of the speeding up of life and its inevitable deceleration upon arrival and settlement in the new land, and an increased self-consciousness of people as strangers in foreign lands.

The travelogue of Eva Guenther, an unmarried Mennonite woman from Burns Lake, British Columbia, is illustrative. It recounts her February 1949 visit to relatives in the Mexican settlements, a full generation after they were founded. It is an account of a woman from the North who lived in between two worlds. Her largely Low German-speaking agrarian world in northern British Columbia was framed by an assimilated Mennonite's household in Vancouver and those of traditionalist Mennonites in Mexico. Although Guenther focused especially on movement (by bus, car, and buggy) and stasis (at the border or the scene of an accident), it was during time spent among relatives – both those assimilated in booming Vancouver and those standing their cultural ground in archaic Mexico – that her conscious perception of herself vis-à-vis Mennonite tradition became pronounced.

En route to Mexico, Guenther stopped in Vancouver to see a cousin or friend also named Eva who had married outside the Mennonite ethno-religious group. Guenther wrote that on "Friday we drove to see [Mrs.] G. Markevich, that is, Franz Bergens' Eva. At first I thought that Eva couldn't even speak German anymore; she said she had forgotten it." As Guenther put it, "I couldn't speak ... English, so she [the Eva from Vancouver] quickly remembered how to speak German." No doubt, it was an awkward moment for both Evas, for the rural woman discovering an acculturated, urban relative and for the urban resident reminded brusquely of her humble, ethno-religious roots. Mexico reinforced this tension, although Guenther seemed more at ease in this setting. She encountered familiar faces within a close-knit community, staying with one family briefly before moving on to the next. It was a gendered meeting, visiting with aunts and female cousins in the kitchen, and with uncles on the buggy as she was driven from one household to another. Perhaps her relatives accepted Guenther, but she seemed bothered by their traditionalism, noting that "it looks very old fashioned ... here with the sort of clothes they wear." She also set herself apart from them; an "engagement party at Gerhard Kroekers," where Guenther knew the bridal couple well – "the Sudermans' son" and "the Kroekers' daughter, who is Isaak Wiebes' grandchild" – was dismissed as an event she "didn't really enjoy ... because it was all too foreign for [her]."[11] The travelogue highlights the differences among dispersed relatives, sharp contrasts of progress and tradition, linked to specific geographic spaces.

Similar images fill the travelogues kept by the Mennonite migrants who moved from Canada to East Paraguay during the late 1940s. Several of these travelogues were published, some by delegates travelling south in 1946, and a dozen or more by the immigrants themselves in 1948. Most appeared in the *Steinbach Post*, although at least one was published in book form.[12] Unlike the stories of the 1920s migration to Paraguay, these accounts speak of settlement in the country's southeastern rainforest. They also illuminate the increasing complexity of the Mennonites' emigration culture, and do so especially with their emphasis on shifting notions of time. The writers seem fixated on variables of speed, by the sequence of "hurry" and "wait," and by the passage of time, the precise day, but also the hour and even the minute.

The first of these two travelogues was recorded by a young married man, a member of a small vanguard of families, chosen to arrive two months before the main corpus of the 1700 settlers. One of their leaders, Abram D. Friesen of Plum Coulee, Manitoba, heading for Sommerfeld Colony in East Paraguay, described a trip of a lifetime, a hurried bus ride from Manitoba to Florida, and then an even more momentous moment, by airplane from Miami to Asunción. Everything seemed rapid, accompanied with a stark uprooting and startling imposition of time imperatives.[13] The diary noted the precise moment of departure; on "15 May 1948 at 5:30 a.m. [from] our parents' place at Plum Coulee." It was a poignant moment as "we waved to the many farms ... allowing our eyes to take in one last glance."

The trip introduced a new social world as an old community of friends and relatives was replaced by a corpus of travelling companions, six families with eleven small children among them.[14] Imposed timelines and deadlines, and imperatives of speed, replaced agrarian time. At precisely 7:50 a.m., the bus departed from Letellier, and at 8:14, it arrived at Emerson, on the Canadian side of the border. After a long night of travel, the party arrived in Kansas City. Then, on Monday, "the second day of Pentecost, which seemed not like a [religious] holiday," the party continued; given that "buses here in the United States travel very fast ... we arrived in St. Louis at 10:00 p.m.," and just thirty-three hours later, at exactly 7:10 a.m., they entered "hot and humid" Miami. Now, time sped up even more, as after a very short night, the party left at 3:00 a.m. for the airport. And here "we left the earth ... for us all a very serious moment"; soon they "were high in the air ... 58 persons" travelling at "205 miles per hour." After two nighttime layovers – in Port of Spain and Rio de Janeiro – the travel sped up even more. On the last leg into Asunción, the party found itself on "the very best plane" to date, this one "wonderfully constructed and modern ... with a speed of 300 miles per hour."

The "happy, joyous" landing in Asunción put a brake on the passage of time. But even the truck trip east to the town of Independencia seemed hurried, and only in the East Paraguay jungle, with the final forty kilometres by ox cart, did time slow down very significantly. Now, Friesen encountered a culture of slowness that even he, as a Mennonite farmer, resisted. Road construction in the area was underway, for example, but it all seemed incomprehensively unhurried. Here, in Paraguay, he explained, "They place a layer of stones on top [of the gravel or clay base], but they do it by hand ... [As] these Spanish people say, *Manjana* [*mañana*]." Friesen's memoir described a return to agrarian time, but with a tension, pitting a Canadian farmer's sense of time against time in economically primitive East Paraguay.

A second travelogue describes the voyage south by ship of a much larger contingent of migrants, but with similar reference to time imperatives. The writer, self-identified as "Frau [Mrs.] Isaac F. Bergen," hailed from a farm near Rosthern, Saskatchewan. Her immediate migrating cohort consisted of her husband and ten children. And, together, they travelled with an amalgam of Saskatchewan Bergthaler and Manitoba Sommerfelder Mennonites, heading east by chartered train to Montreal to meet up with the *Vollendam* (the very ocean liner that, in 1930, had taken the Soviet Mennonite refugees from Europe to Paraguay).

Arriving in Buenos Aires, Bergen's group moved north by riverboat to Asunción, and then east by train, truck, ox cart, and foot into the heart of the East Paraguay rainforest.[15] Here, they joined the pioneer Sommerfeld Colony.

Bergen began her account on 16 June 1948, with these heady words: "Late in the evening, as we had finished packing at our old place, we drove to siblings Johann Klassens' to bid them farewell." After four days of other final goodbyes, Bergen and her family attended a special farewell service at the church. Bergen makes no reference to the sermon (although she mentions the name of the preacher, Rev. Jacob Bergen), but she does highlight one of the hymns, featuring the emotion-laden Old Testament lyrics, "As Lot and Abram Separated." On the 21st, the family took a final "farewell, from our loving parents." En route to the railway station in Saskatoon, they stopped in the town of Rosthern, where the Bergens saw a Canadian dentist "for one last time" and took lunch at the "Isaac Hildebrands'," making Bergen wonder when "next will we all drink so much milk?" Moving on to Saskatoon, they located their train; Father and the boys spent the final night in it, while Mrs. Bergen and her daughters slept in the apartment of Aunt Susie, an unmarried sister working in the city.[16]

At this point, the tightly knit social network that carried the Bergen family from one caring Mennonite family to another took a new turn. Time now suddenly "imposed" itself with a vocabulary of "must" and "need" and "should." Bergen noted the first imperative after breakfast on the 22nd: "Soon we had to pack up" for the "Isaac Hildebrands had already arrived to drive us to the train station." These time imperatives intersected with descriptions of new places and strangers. After taking leave of loved ones gathered at the station, the train departed at 1:00 p.m. sharp. On board, Bergen described the cooking oven and washing facility in each car – replicated domestic spaces – but she was especially impressed by the rapid passage of time and space. Racing eastward, they reached Yorkton, Saskatchewan, by nightfall; Gladstone, Manitoba, at dawn; and Winnipeg at noon. Here, Bergen became "deeply worried" when "Father and *Ohm* Jacob," who had disembarked to purchase food, failed to return by the time the "train was supposed to depart." After being able to reunite at the next station, Bergen relaxed and again saw the train as a cohesive community. Those from Saskatchewan "went over to introduce themselves to the people from Manitoba," and Manitobans returned the courtesy. It was a coalescing community, reconfigured uniquely within the very instrument that hurtled them from their places of birth. Indeed, Bergen seemed most impressed by the speed and the unknown. It could all be rather "frightening, such as the time when another train suddenly and unannounced ... raced by us." And it could be fascinating, as at dawn after a night of "fast travel," when the party arrived at a "city where we could see that the people were French."[17] The memoir highlighted the shift in time and space well before they left Canadian shores.

The ocean voyage brought a similar range of imperatives and strange sights. At the seaport in Quebec, the travellers were told to board only with carry-on items, and thus the Bergens quickly repacked their belongings and each family member donned as much clothing as possible. They were also told to board as a family, and the Bergens complied in orderly fashion – "Father went ahead, then each of the [ten] children, and then, me, at the end" – in marked distinction from "those who forcibly pushed themselves through" to the front of the line. On-board, Bergen again emphasized the disruption of familiar domestic space and time. For night, she, her daughters, and her younger sons were separated from her husband and the "big boys." In the morning, they were summoned precisely at 6:00 a.m. and told to make their beds. Meals could not be taken until the English command "It's time for the second sitting," and even then the constant threat – "Hurry up, eat, or we will remove the food" – was in their ears.[18]

The passage of time and space was also imposed from the loudspeakers. True, the ship afforded moments of contemplation: the Mennonites' daily evening song on deck included Bergen's favourite hymn: "number 383 from the *Alte Gesangbuch*, the last three lines, 'Let me find in this night a peaceful, sweet rest.'" But many of the noteworthy moments were announced to the travellers via the loudspeakers. On 28 June, Bergen wrote that "we are supposed to be adjacent to New York, but land is no longer in sight"; on 9 July, they were told they had "crossed the equator at 1 o'clock." Over the course of the voyage, time was also measured by the fleeting images of strange worlds: on 30 June, Bergen saw groups "of little fish that fly off from the water"; on 3 July in Trinidad, she watched "little negroes" peddling "large oranges, grapefruit and bananas"; on 13 July, a day out of Rio de Janeiro, she counted an unprecedented "13 ships," signalling the nearby South American port. The voyage ended on a Sunday in Buenos Aires, but to Bergen, it "didn't seem like a Sunday." First, the Mennonites were commanded to disembark, then commanded again, under stressful conditions, to board the crude riverboat for the trip up the Paraná River.[19]

Now Bergen began recording a return to communitarian familiarity, albeit in increasingly primitive conditions. She documented the reversal of progress and eventually the return to agrarian time. The riverboat was overcrowded and its toilets and kitchen dank and crude, or, as Bergen put it, "in Low German we would say *prost*." The train from Asunción into the East Paraguay jungle was similarly crude, and the conditions at the immigrant staging area at a sugar warehouse in Villarrica were harsh, even tragic, as "many" children died.

Deep community ties kept the immigrants focused on their destination; Bergen, for one, was comforted on the train by "Aunt Derk Klassen ... a good mother and grandmother." At Villarrica, the twenty to thirty families cooked outdoors, and, during the strangely cold and humid nights, the men took turns standing guard. Another temporary move by truck over rough roads to Colonia Independencia, "which was closer to our land," made life more bearable, as it was a German-speaking community with plenty of fruit and familiar food – "eggs, butter, chicken, and perogies." But problems persisted: the diarrhea was unrelenting and more children died. Bergen noted that "many families just wanted to return to Canada," and many did; "one after the other," they organized auction sales of goods they had just transported to South America. Still, even before seeing their land, the stalwart met to establish the Sommerfeld Colony's first institutions: one day under a large tent, the group chose *"Ohm* Isbrand Friesen" as their Ältester; on another day, the men assembled to divide the land and designate the villages "by number."

A further degree of normalcy returned the day the freight boxes arrived. Able to replicate the domestic hearth, it was the "box with the oven that we opened first, took it out and set it up." By the end of November, the Bergens commenced the final trek inland, by truck to Caaguazu and then a final day and entire night by ox cart and foot, arriving at Sommerfeld Colony at 4:00 a.m., on 18 December 1948. Six hours later, at 10:00 a.m., they arrived by foot at their lot in a village the settlers called Waldheim.[20]

Time slowed down precipitously in Waldheim. Here, at a place with "grass taller than my head" and not far from "clear, wonderful water," Bergen "spread a blanket on the ground" and she and her family had their first lunch. By evening, three tents had been set up and the family retired, "exhausted." Even though the next day was a Sunday, the normal day of rest, the Bergens worked, erecting a crude, tin-roofed dwelling, although later in the afternoon a bit of tradition returned as neighbours came to visit. Monday marked a more expressed return to traditional old rhythms: "It is usually washday," wrote Bergen, "but first food is to be secured" and so "I got up early, before the others, and baked biscuits." Later, Bergen and her daughter "hacked a path through the bush so that we could string up a wash line," while "the boys and father made a fence, and fashioned a barn for the chickens we had purchased in Independencia." It was a busy week: "We had to work very hard so that we could have some peace and rest at Christmas." Only one incident interrupted her efforts to re-establish agrarian normalcy: one day, "as I was getting water three or four half naked Indians walked by me; as I had heard in Canada about the dangerous Morros I was very frightened, but I wonder if these Indians were as shocked as I was"; but just as quickly she returned to the task at hand. The next day, on Christmas day, the Bergens, along with the other eight village families, each carried a bench to Peter Dyck's place, "our designated church place," and "so we had Christmas in the heat of the summer, instead of the cold winter."[21] No matter the new weather pattern, the foundation of Mennonite community had been replicated.

The Letter

The immigrant letter offered a remarkably different notion of time from that of the diary and travelogue. Letters from Latin America, published as always in large numbers in the *Steinbach Post*, now a full-fledged immigrant newspaper, presented time not as measured by the hour and the day, but in the context of the week and the month. Events within this broader context were believed sufficiently significant to be shared with residents of other locales. Indeed, immigrant letters, inherently communitarian in social nature – employing common vocabulary and seeking reassuring responses in an imagined village – also took a communitarian approach to the construction of time.[22] Not only did they speak of weekly and seasonal rhythms of work and social interaction, they placed pre- and post-migration epochs in comparative perspective. In part, they did so because they heralded a particular dialectic: first, among two generations of letter writers (the quite elderly immigrants with roots in the 1920s emigration, and younger Mennonites of the 1940s); and second, among the settlers in various geographic sites, including the Latin American communities, the original western Canadian sending communities, and the colonies in northern Canada of Carrot River (Saskatchewan), La Crete (Alberta), and Burns Lake (BC) founded in the 1930s.

At the most fundamental level, the *Steinbach Post* allowed all writers, both long- and newly settled, to note important events within the week or the month. The newly settled tended to report on disruptions or milestones in the process of settlement. Peter Thiessen of Sommerfeld Colony in East Paraguay took time to write in December 1949 "because it is too hot over noon time to do well digging," but, more importantly, having reached thirty-three of the required thirty-six feet, his multi-day task was almost completed.[23] Mrs. Derk Klassen of the same colony wrote in January 1953 because she had been injured in a fall and now, "after four weeks, still suffering from quite a bit of pain on my back and side," she had the time.[24] The longer settled writers often reported on their own moments of disruption, times of travel, for example, linked to medical help and reconnecting to old homelands. John D. Redekop's letter of December 1952 was written from Hotel Union in Mexico City, to which he had travelled to seek medical attention for cancer.[25] David Wall wrote from Durango, Mexico, in November 1953 to announce that he and his wife had returned home safely after visiting family and friends in British Columbia, Alberta, and Saskatchewan; they arrived several days late, as the Mexican border officials had become suspicious of the elderly David when they discovered that he had been born in Russia.[26]

Most letter writers emphasized events deemed not routine, but unusual. H.C. Penner's November 1951 letter from the newly established Kleine Gemeinde Mennonite colony at Los Jagueyes, Mexico, highlighted events of importance to readers familiar with his specific colony. He reported first that "today, quite unexpectedly, Jake Bartel, son of G.F. Bartel of Morris, Manitoba pulled up into our yard with a load of oats." He also recounted that his neighbour "Peter Dueck told me that their eldest daughter Rosella has pricked her foot with a pitchfork," that the local school inspector "Cornelius L. Friesen visited the schools last week," and that "our colony recently purchased a thousand sheep from the [nearby] Spanish [immigrant colony]."[27] He ended with a note on the weather, an aberration on 20 November, when it had been "8 degrees below zero."[28] The September 1952 letters by a young, single, Sommerfeld, Paraguay, woman, signing D. Klassen, highlighted similar seemingly banal events. In her letter, she reported a welcome spring rainfall, the milling of corn for her pigs, and the death of two horses from a lightning strike. She also detailed a sewing circle meeting, an intimate, social network, filled with "insider" humour:

> As I currently have my quarters at Johann Froeses' I found myself at a sewing circle hour. Present were Mrs. Frank Dueck, her two daughters, Gerhard Wiebe's two daughters and Mrs. Heinrich Dueck. Once the table had been cleared of supper, things began in earnest. One knitted, the other crocheted, and another patched or sewed, so that the needles flashed in the light of the Coleman lantern lit by Froeses' Johann for the first time this evening. In the midst of all this action Mrs. Heinrich Dueck, trying to patch her husband's pants, had the misfortune of accidentally sewing closed one of the legs, although she rectified it without much time lost.[29]

For Klassen, the sewing circle meeting, a bimonthly or monthly event, was newsworthy for at least two reasons: it marked variation in the daily rhythm of farm life, and signalled the replication of Mennonite community.

As noted above, these letters also established the fundamental epochs of time, especially the pre- and post-migration eras. Many post-migration letters referred to pre-migration times in Canada as a matter of course. In his April 1946 letter, Wilhelm Peters of Cuauhtémoc, Mexico, greeted "former neighbor Franz Wieler," who had returned to Canada in 1945; he jokingly asked whether Franz was still the "goose enemy," a reputation established long ago in Canada when neighbours had woken one morning to a loud bang and the sight of Franz "standing bare feet outside in the snow, gun in hand, watching a goose flapping its wings."[30]

Other letter writers used the emigration from Canada as a benchmark of time. A March 1952 letter from Durango, Mexico, signed "Klaas and Katherina Heide," announced an illness and a death, offered advice on a Canadian baby's health, reported on the family's five-acre wheat crop, enquired about a brother in Burns Lake, BC, joked that the brother should send Canadian venison for dinner in Mexico, and then noted "odd weather of the kind I cannot recall, since we arrived here from Canada."[31] The newly settled also referred to symbols associated with pre-migration Canadian culture. The May 1952 letter of Heinrich C. Penner of Los Jagueyes Colony, for example, referenced a Canadian icon when he reported that "in our village, Wiesenheim, it appears as if Eskimos are moving in; Heinrich Thiessens' ... house, although not of snow blocks, is of earthen blocks that are white washed, giving it the appearance of an igloo."[32] Whether stemming from settlers who had spent thirty years in Latin America or from those just in from Canada, memories of the old homeland and its culture anchored reality in the South.

Other, less benign, letters from the 1950s still bitterly referred to pre-migration Canadian betrayal and served to reinforce an old division between the Mennonites in Latin America and those who had remained in Canada. In his March 1950 letter, Johan Peters of Manitoba Colony, Mexico, reported on a sermon by Ältester Isaak Dyck the previous Sunday in which he had spoken about the migration from Canada to Mexico twenty-five years earlier. Judging from Dyck's published writings, the sermon would have highlighted the lure of worldly assimilation in Canada.[33] In similar shorthand, in a March 1952 letter, D.D. Wieler of Campo 24, Mexico, noted skeptically that several neighbours were pondering a return to Canada, claiming that they could qualify under the "1874 Freedoms." Wieler ended the story with a rhetorical "or?" that reminded his readers that those supposed educational "Freedoms" had disappeared in 1916.[34]

A much more elaborate allusion to these epochs came in February 1953 from regular correspondent Mrs. Derk Klassen of East Paraguay. She, too, noted that several families were giving up on Paraguay, citing it as a country "impossible to deal with," but she did more than report, she offered a history lesson. She recalled how her parents had spoken of horrific times in Russia, times of unchecked theft, but still they managed to thrive financially. She also reminded her readers that during the 1870s on the Canadian frontier, "our parents had an even more difficult time getting started than we here" in East Paraguay. Bringing the Russian and Canadian experiences together, Klassen called on her readership to "think what the people in Russia had to endure" following the Russian Revolution, and "be thankful that our parents prevented us from that fate"[35] by migrating in the 1870s. If the history lesson was a little complex, the message was clear: pre-migration epochs in both Russia and Canada showed that perseverance in Paraguay would be rewarded.

The Memoir

The memoir, in contrast to the diary and letter, reveals another concept of time reordering uprooted lives. Usually penned after a generation in the new land, the Mennonite memoirs spoke of a lifetime in teleological perspective. This medium infused the migration – whether primary, secondary, or return – with religious meaning. And it did so by describing specific events in the new land, such as a family tragedy or serious setback, with language of divine guidance or even eternal afterlife. In other words, the "backward glancing" on life occurred with an anticipation of a "forthcoming" of cosmological significance.[36]

Illustrating this point are two memoirs by Mennonites who moved to Paraguay in the 1920s. The first, written by forty-two-year-old Jacob D. Harder of Menno Colony, Paraguay, in 1946, described the historic journeys of 1926 and 1927 for the curious, but attested to its wider, cultural, meaning. Harder began with a justification for writing: "For a long time I've had the idea to write something ... about the migration from Canada to Paraguay. ... My memories go way back, yes to Canada, and begin when I was only 23." But before detailing his life story, Harder gave it religious meaning: "The reason our forefathers allowed themselves to be separated from their homeland [Canada] was this, because of their faith." He then commenced his own story of the 1926 emigration. He described the frigid sleigh ride in a −30 degree snowstorm to the railroad station in Niverville, Manitoba. He recounted the Mennonites' departure from the station with the locomotive whistling "pfiff" and lurching forward in a shower of sparks, and then, with smokestack belching, it went "zisch, zisch, zisch, and ever farther southward." Inside the train cars, the immigrants sat "without any jubilation, just quiet conversation in Low German, amidst a din of the hum of the wheels under the cars." But religious symbolism soon surfaced again in the narrative. Racing "day and night" eastward to New York made Harder mindful of his status "as a worm" in relation to the divine, while vistas of "water and mountains" reminded him "how great God was." Leaving "the Canadian train" in New York marked a solemn moment as "all eyes looked up and there stood the ship of our voyage." The voyage, a time of seasickness, reminded Harder of a flippant English-language adage: "a little sick, but not in the legs, only in the belly." The ocean's frightening expanse, however, turned his mind back to the solemn; that is, to "the biblical stories of the Apostle Paul being shipwrecked on the Mediterranean." Harder continued the account by interweaving the temporal and the sacred until the settlers arrived at their final place of settlement in the Paraguayan Chaco.[37]

The 1959 memoir of Maria Wiebe Toews, an elderly widow, tells a similar story of divine guidance, albeit over a longer time period and in several countries. It focuses especially on the years 1945 to 1954, and more explicitly presents life as a journey to eternity. Her story has two intertwining themes, familial relationship and physical health, both cast in a teleological framework.[38] Even though Toews made three significant migrations in her life – from Manitoba to Saskatchewan as a child in about 1910, from Manitoba to the Paraguayan Chaco as a middle-aged woman in 1927, and then back to Canada as an elderly widow in 1954 – the migrations themselves are given only minimal attention. Significantly, patriarchal religious leaders and the church receive no mention at all. Instead, Toews focuses on her own experience of migration, specifically her own health problems. The explicit purpose for writing, she declares, is to show how "the Lord has led me through many deep valleys." Writing itself was a religious act for her, for without "a diary of my life ... I just wrote down as God gave me grace."[39]

Toews's memoir begins with her childhood in Manitoba and Saskatchewan. It progresses quickly from the day her future husband, Heinrich Toews of Manitoba, came courting, to the day the young married couple left for Paraguay. The account of the migration itself emphasizes the lifelong familial separation and Heinrich's ill health, with nary a mention of the schools question or the search for agrarian simplicity. Indeed, the voyage south is given short shrift, and a third of it describes a life-threatening hemorrhage Maria experiences. The family's arrival at Puerto Casado on the Paraguay River on 15 May 1927 is presented as a joyous reunion with relatives who, after five months of hardship, "all looked so tanned ... had lost so much weight." For the 1930s and 1940s, Toews similarly focuses on family, especially on the eventual marriages of each of her children.

Still, Toews's memoir is inherently religious. Her own health, especially her decade-long struggle from 1945 to 1954 with cancer of the tongue, is presented but usually with reference to its religious significance. On 3 September 1945, Maria and Heinrich left on a lengthy trip from the Chaco to Buenos Aires to seek help for her painful illness. Toews recalls the specific date when "we left home and traveled by buggy to the end station," the rail terminus at Kilometer 145, and when they arrived in Argentina. She describes her painful "radium treatment" and the November return to Menno Colony, and she thanks "our dear God ... for our safe journey." Another trip the next fall invokes a similar vocabulary: "I felt so lonely in that big, strange city," but "the Lord is close to those who in earnestness call upon Him." A third trip in 1948 brought another round of radium needles, and another revelation that "Jesus accepts and especially looks out for the sick." A fourth trip in February 1952 was made easier by air travel and treatment in Asunción, but, because the "cancer had spread," times were more difficult as Toews required surgery that left her face disfigured. Recalling this event, Toews empathizes with the hemorrhaging woman healed by Jesus in Matthew 9:20 and knows that "through such prolonged suffering our God and Savior wants to train us in patience." The 1952 surgery was successful but her suffering continued. In a cruel coincidence in March 1953, just three days before planning to fly to Asunción for a final visit to the doctor, Heinrich suffered a heart attack at age sixty-four and, in the Mennonite hospital in Filadelfia, he "stretched his hands out to me and died in my arms."[40]

This theme of suffering continues seamlessly in the context of her widowhood and eventual return to Canada during the 1950s. In reflecting on her life, Toews concluded that God's "kindness has led me by my hand and has been with me in my youth." Her only prayer was that God "not forsake me in my old age, when my hair turns grey. Let your grace ... accompany me until the day of death!"[41] Hindsight allowed her to see more clearly life's purpose, comforting her at the end of her migrant journeys.

The Newspaper Report

Representing the fourth concept of time were regular newspaper reports filed by journalists in two English-language weeklies, the *Altona Echo* and the *Carillon News*, based in the Mennonite towns of Altona and Steinbach, Manitoba, respectively. The very birth of these English-language booster papers in this post-war period reflected the nascent belief among Canadian Mennonites in progress and the exorable march of modernity. These viewpoints shaped the English-speaking Mennonite journalists' interactions with their interviewees, whether post-Second World War emigrants to Latin America, returnees from those very colonies, or acculturated Mennonites who visited those colonies. The viewpoints all imposed a progressive understanding on the traditionalist Mennonite societies in the South even as they claimed to provide so-called objective analysis.

The English-language reporters were well aware that the emigrants of the 1940s were stepping outside the trajectory of progress. A January 1948 report in the *Carillon News* on the planned emigration of 180 families from southeastern Manitoba to East Paraguay faithfully listed their goals: the "non resistance tenets of their faith; freedom to control their own schools, in their own language; freedom to live a simple and secluded life within their own community, something quite impossible in the hustling, bustling twentieth century in Canada." The report was noteworthy for more than its thoroughness; it was cast in starkly detached language. The newspaper reporter described the emigrants as a people who "fully realize the hardships into which they are heading ... believing that the full life they enjoy here [in Canada] is no contribution to their spiritual welfare, but rather makes them forget their Deity, and centers thoughts on themselves and material goods."[42] The Mennonite immigrants were so out-of-step with progress, they may as well have been members of an unknown world religion.

In similar fashion, a November 1948 piece in the *Altona Echo* reported on a visit to Manitoba by Rev. Johan Loeppky, the Old Colony Mennonite minister of Osler, Saskatchewan, who had led the historic delegation to Mexico in 1921, but who ultimately had chosen not to join the move. In 1948, however, he was en route south again, this time leading some twenty-five families to Mexico, where he hoped to establish an Old Colony settlement at Los Jagueyes, Chihuahua. With no hint of derision, the *Altona Echo* reporter noted that Loeppky, referred to with the English nomenclature "John Loeppky," believed that Mexico afforded the chance for them "as old-fashioned Mennonites" to be undisturbed "in their way of life." In fact, in Mexico, the migrants would be immune from "drought in Saskatchewan," for "in western Chihuahua ... two cows keep an average family well supplied with the necessities of life."[43] Significantly, the report diverged sharply from the bold advertisements and buoyant farm reports in the *Echo* that championed specialization and commercialization in all sectors of agriculture, including dairying.

Not surprisingly, any signs of progress in the South, as well as any evidence of weakness in the 1948 experiment in traditionalism, were fodder for news in the *Carillon News* and the *Altona Echo*. The newspapers seemed especially interested in the return of about 600 of the original 1700 migrants to East Paraguay, and issued reports on the returnees with apparent objectivity. A May 1949 account in the *Echo* carried a crisp headline, "Back from Paraguay," and announced the return of "Mr. and Mrs. Peter K. Hildebrand and five of their children" who "traveled by plane as far as New York." It reported that the Hildebrands had been "among the group of Mennonites who left Canada in June of last year for Paraguay where they hoped to make the dense forest. ... into fertile farms."[44]

But most articles focused on the specific setbacks in Paraguay. An August 1949 article in the *Carillon* reported on "Aaron Falk, formerly of Schoenthal, who returned with wife and family from Paraguay," and quoted him as saying that "progress is slow" in the new East Paraguay colonies where the villages "are laid out in a similar fashion to those ... formed in southern Manitoba" in the 1870s, with land divided into narrow strips. As Falk saw it, "Clearing the dense forest presents the greatest obstacle to the colonist. It requires a significant amount of back breaking labour to rid even a small area of the almost impregnable undergrowth." He also suggested that "unstable economic conditions [that] are retarding the development of the settlement [are] causing many setters to return to Canada."[45] Primitivism and a lack of progress had caused the return to Canada.

Reports in the English-language weeklies, often by representatives of the North American aid agency, the Mennonite Central Committee (MCC), working in the Paraguayan Chaco, were especially loaded with the language of progress. A typical article reported on MCC representative and Winnipeg entrepreneur Cornelius DeFehr's speech to an audience of 500 in Steinbach in February 1949. DeFehr spoke about a lack of progress arising from a "severe drought" in Paraguay, followed by a grasshopper infestation and then a locust plague; these colonists, he said, had experienced a real "licking."[46] A month later, William Enns reported to a large gathering in Altona on his trip to the Chaco; he registered his concern that at Menno Colony, the "commercial life of the settler is primitive," based as it was on a single colony-wide cooperative that depended on the pre-modern barter system. Then, too, Enns criticized the "absence of industries [which] hampers the orderly progress of settlement."[47]

Using the same vocabulary, other reports heralded progress in the South. In December 1950, the *Carillon* carried the headline "MCC Outlines Progress of South American Mennonites." It quoted MCC representative J.J. Thiessen as predicting a "turn toward eventual prosperity and success" among these Mennonites, even in Paraguay, a country that, in the past, had experienced a monumental "moral and economic decline" through "disastrous wars."[48] Other reports on progress followed. In a June 1953 story, the *Echo* described a Mennonite experimental farm in the Chaco and its introduction of a new cotton seed, ACA–14–42, "a variety introduced with the aid of Ed Peters," a noted and highly successful Mennonite cotton producer of Wasco,

California.⁴⁹ The following year, the *Echo* reported that Robert G. Unruh of Bloomfield, Montana, was managing a MCC-supported experimental farm and overseeing a "nursery stock consisting of several varieties of trees and grapes from California," specifically "seven varieties of grapes ... sent by a Reedley [California] church."⁵⁰

Similar reports observing progress in the South highlighted the Mexico colonies. In one such account in January 1954, J.P. Zacharias from Altona, Manitoba, reported on a month-long visit to Mexico. He had seen "definite progress in the past seven years despite the drought." Where "only a few farmers owned tractors seven years ago," he said, now many more did. The farmers had also exchanged their old Canadian-based farming practices with "more diversified farming," including "corn and beans as well as grain crops." Zacharias had even "seen some apples grown in the Mennonite colonies which looked delicious and sold for prices similar to those in Canada." Then, too, in Cuauhtémoc, an ever-expanding city, a number of "friendly and eager" Mennonite merchants have "opened up business [with] ... goods ... attractively displayed," and if one is not able to speak "Spanish or German, English will do the trick anywhere."⁵¹

Progress was also measured by the growing evangelical fervour that encouraged mission work among indigenous peoples, including their integration into a modern economy. Even leaders at Menno Colony, staunchly communitarian in ethos, issued reports in support of evangelicalism. The 1952 review in the *Carillon* of Rev. Martin Friesen's new history on Menno Colony highlighted the author's description of "adjustments to a new climate," his honesty about the "struggles ... with human nature," and his own spirituality that saw in Menno Colony's history "guidance from God." But, significantly, Friesen's book presented Menno Colony's divine purpose not in terms of an escape from assimilationist or patriotic Canada, but rather as an embrace of evangelical missions, specifically the work of "furthering of God's kingdom among the natives about them" in South America.⁵² In the same vein, a January 1955 issue of the *Carillon News* announced that "The Thorny Chaco and Its Delicate Souls" was "the theme of Missionary Geo Sukkau's address to the Winkler Mennonite Brethren Church." Sukkau was able not only to show "the progress the new settlers have made there" but also to declare, "In Paraguay a believing [Mennonite] congregation has been placed in the midst of the heathen Indians so that these natives see how Christian people live together."⁵³

Good Mennonites in this narrative were mission-oriented settlers; that is, Mennonites who embraced a progressive, forward-moving view of history.

Although the *Echo* and *Carillon* stories envisaged a northern readership, some of the 1948 immigrants in Latin America continued to subscribe to the English-language newspapers. Oftentimes, the migrants used these media, as they used the German-language *Steinbach Post*, to reach out to friends and relatives in the North. But the old and the new media differed significantly. The *Steinbach Post* published letters from the South recounting old ties; the *Echo* and *Carillon* published regular news columns by writers in Latin America who shared the idea of progress undergirding the two papers. Illustrative is a *Carillon* column written by a young woman, Martha Friesen of Bergthal Colony, East Paraguay. Beginning in 1951 when she was only twenty-one, Friesen continued the column for twenty-eight years until 1979. In commenting on the nature of the column, Friesen later wrote that although the reason for the 1948 migration was to "lead a quiet life," unobtrusively and self-sufficiently, "we were young and carefree at the time and didn't see the things older people saw; rumours of war ... the big schools coming and so forth."[54]

Despite her location in the traditionalist Bergthal Colony, the text of her English-language column from her first submission signalled nothing of an anti-modern community. Her first entry, dated 29 March 1951, outlined the unique world in a rainforest, with reports of "malaria fever which gets many people from time to time," of newly planted orchards of "bananas ... orange trees, date trees and grapefruit trees," and of exotic animals, the "tapirs ... traveling along the riverbank" and the "tigers [that] again killed a cow in Silberfeld."[55] Her second report from 1 June 1951 announced marks of progress at Bergthal: "The sawmill is getting to be quite up-to-date"; John Peters's new "brick factory ... has quite a start to date"; and "street improvements are being made in Hochfeld and Rosenfeld."[56] It acknowledged that in comparison to progress in East Paraguay, "everything is better" in the most established Chaco colonies, but asserted, "With the years, I suppose we will get there too." Friesen's third and final entry for 1951, one from 16 November, presented the Bergthal colonists as inherently modern, for they were purchasing, driving, and repairing modern, motorized trucks. The curiously old-fashioned folks in her narrative were not the Mennonites but the Paraguayans, even the urban dwellers in the capital, Asunción. Friesen offered a "funny" incident observed by "Mr. William

Hildebrant" while visiting Asunción: a Paraguayan "woman coming along with a donkey ... stopped in front of the hotel ... and milked the donkey right there and then," then sold the milk to a man from the hotel. Friesen joked, "What do you think folks? Isn't that a handy way to transport milk to town?"[57] Bergthal Colony, in Friesen's estimation, was an island of progress in an exotic and primitive country. The message from Bergthal seemed to be determined by the medium in which it was presented.

Conclusion

The world of Canadian Low German Mennonites in the post-Second World War era was complex. Not only did it link Mennonites in Canada with those in Mexico and Paraguay, it now brought together a variety of Low German Mennonite groups from five different Canadian provinces, two Mexican states, and two Paraguayan regions. It also involved different categories of migrants: first-generation migrants in East Paraguay and northern Chihuahua, and second-generation folk in Mexico's Chihuahua and Durango states and the Paraguayan Chaco. The post-Second World War migrants also came from each of the five different Mennonite church groups: the largest groups now were the Kleine Gemeinde, Chortitzer, and Sommerfelder Mennonites; the smallest, the Old Colonist and Saskatchewan Bergthaler groups. Then, at a direct cross-current to these emigrants from Canada were return migrants, especially from East Paraguay, heading back north. Overlaid on this constellation of coming and going were acculturated North American development workers and missionaries, unwavering in their commitment to economic and social progress.

The complexity of this mid-century world is illuminated by varying, intersecting, and multi-layered concepts of time, as illustrated in a variety of media. The rural diarists saw the migrations as momentary disruptions in the daily need to yield to nature's cycles, while the keepers of travelogues considered the imposition of new, technologically driven imperatives on daily life. The writers of public letters revealed awareness of significant weekly or monthly events, but, as they communicated over vast geographical space, they also employed the vocabulary of sweeping epochs, especially of pre- and post-migration times. The memoirists, on the other hand, created narratives of a lifetime or a series of life-altering events, cast in teleological language, giving them cosmological and even eternal meaning. The newspaper reporters gazed south through a modernizing lens and measured community success in terms of progress, oftentimes in direct contradiction to the Latin American communities' very raison d'être.

The differing concepts of time illustrate how the Mennonite migrants gave meaning to a life lived in nature, across space and in a changing world. In this sense, time, for even the traditionalist Mennonites, was relative. Certainly, ideas differed, depending on the particular manner in which life was considered and on the specific text used to interpret the flux of their world. Importantly, ideas of time reflected the fundamental difference between the immigrant and non-immigrant. Different media of communication produced diverse perspectives, and these, in turn, consolidated a feature of the complex world of the Mennonite migrant, that is, the multi-dimensional sense of time.

5 Meeting the Outside Gaze: New Life in British Honduras and Bolivia, 1954–1972

In the 1950s and 1960s, after a long generation in Mexico and Paraguay, a large number of Mennonites from both countries were on the move again. Many of these migrants seemed ever prepared to make secondary and even tertiary migrations, reflecting the long-held idea that all settlement was ultimately impermanent. Unlike other Mennonite migrations at this time, this mid-century move was not a "return" northward to Canada, but a migration mostly southward, across the boundaries of Central or South American countries. And, significantly, the majority of these migrants were ultra-traditionalists, so-called "horse and buggy" Mennonites, who sought in these southern locations greater degrees of isolation from the wider society and from their more accommodating co-religionists.

This migration within the South consisted of four, distinctive, sub-migrations. The first, in 1956, was but a short move, a relocation of settlers from Menno Colony in the Paraguayan Chaco to the Santa Cruz *departmento* (state) in Bolivia where they established Colonia Canadiense; this colony was bolstered in 1963 by the establishment nearby of Bergthal and Las Pavas colonies by other traditionalist families from Paraguay and Canada. The second migration, beginning in 1958, was a larger and longer one in which Mennonites from Chihuahua state, Mexico, moved south to British Honduras, the tiny country on the Caribbean just south of Mexico, where three colonies – Blue Creek, Shipyard, and Spanish Lookout – were founded.[1] The third and by far the largest migration began in 1967 and entailed a relocation of the most traditionalist of the Old Colony Mennonites (and some Sommerfelders) from Mexico, who settled just south of Santa Cruz, Bolivia, establishing Riva Palacios, Swift Current, Santa Rita, and Sommerfeld colonies. A final notable migration, stemming from Canada, had its genesis in 1968 when a group of Old Colony Mennonites from northern Alberta and British Columbia founded Colonia Las Piedras, north of Santa Cruz. Other migrations during these years were more sporadic and unorganized – from Canada to British Honduras, from British Honduras to Bolivia, and, of course, some return migration to the originating points – and they were smaller in scope than the four outlined above.

Even more than in previous decades, the migrants now travelled within a constellation of nations: some remembered, others encountered; some pushing, others pulling. For the southward-looking migrants, the broader backdrop always was Canada, the old homeland that still presented itself as the hostile, assimilative, modernizing country it had been in the 1920s. Even now in the 1950s and 1960s, old Canada stood threatening. Its acculturated Mennonite communities sent service workers to Mexico and Paraguay, seeking to reform the migrants, and its economy lured thousands of Mexico and Paraguay Mennonites northward, away from old roots, with promises of wage labour and small-town comforts. At the same time, encroaching modernity in the second-generation Mexico and Paraguay communities sent Mennonite traditionalists casting about for a geographic space to sustain their anti-modern, agrarian, and village way of life. The Mexican government's intrusive new social security program, the Seguro Sociale, sent migrants to British Honduras, while the pitfalls of modernization in Chihuahua, Mexico – rubber-tired tractors, motorized trucks, and state-produced electricity – sent many more to Bolivia. The small numbers of Paraguay Mennonites who migrated to Bolivia in the 1950s and 1960s cited the dangers of farm commercialization and mechanization, while the Canadians who moved south in the 1960s named public-school consolidation, town life, and even apocalyptic worries of "end times" and a heinous United Nations.

Enabling these migrations southward was an implicit contract with the British Honduran and Bolivian governments in which the Mennonites "promised" to advance their respective national economic policies, while the host governments offered guarantees of cultural independence to the newcomers. The governments of both British Honduras and Bolivia passed specific laws, in 1957 and 1962, respectively, to exempt Mennonites from military service, state schools, modern welfare programs, participation in municipal government, and national inheritance laws. Both countries expected the Mennonites to help globalize national economies and boost international trade, an expectation spurred on by development programs of the United Nations and even those of the United States. The Mennonite migrations were an integral part of these national agendas, meant to create modern farm economies to end the nations' reliance on food imports by attracting foreign farm immigrants.

Despite the nature of these relatively recent Mennonite migrations, special circumstances make them more difficult to document than those of the 1920s and 1940s. First, as the most conservative of the Mennonites, these migrants were a quiescent people, moving primarily to depart from the company of other, more modern, Mennonite communities in Mexico. As a result, they simply did not reach out to other Mennonites with as many autobiographies or letters as the earlier migrants. Second, the large migration to Bolivia coincided with the 1967 cessation of the publication of the popular old *Steinbach Post*, and occurred during a period in which no newspaper succeeded the *Post*. Although the *Post* prior to 1967 carried some letters from British Honduras, a comparative history of the migration of Canadian Mennonites from Mexico to British Honduras and Bolivia, based on parallel sources, necessitates the location of other caches of information.

Two sources do allow for such a comparative history. However, unlike primary sources used elsewhere in this book, they were generated by non-Mennonite observers. In the first instance, national journalists in the two new homelands filed reports on the newcomers. Because the Mennonites' entry into British Honduras and Bolivia caused quite a stir, the national media of both countries sent reporters to interview the newcomers, and facilitated debates on their virtues and shortcomings. In the second instance, academic experts from the North – master's, doctoral, and post-doctoral students in economics, geography, and anthropology – took note of the migrations of "Canadian" farmers into the wilderness of the two developing countries. The young academics travelled south from Canada and the United States, and visited the Mennonite communities, building rapport with the traditionalists, interviewing them at length, and writing their reports in ethnographically rich theses.

As they undertook their interviews, the journalists and the academics produced valuable information, but they also helped create the very transnational subject. They perceived the Mennonites not only as curiosities and as subjects of study, but as subjects within a structured relationship. In some respects, they constituted what Michael Foucault once dubbed the "meticulous gaze," beholders within a hierarchy of the observer and the observed. In it, the "sovereign power of the empirical gaze ... turns the ... darkness [of the subject] into light [for the observer]."[2] This particular kind of illumination clarifies intrinsic characteristics of the subject as seen by the outsider, who then also defines those features. Certainly, in their visits to the colonies, the journalists and scholars positioned themselves as authorities; they introduced themselves as experts and interviewed the leaders; they promised to produce useful economic reports and "objective" analyses. Historians have highlighted the difference in tone of the journal article and the academic treatise – the popular press's penchant for nationalistic "half conscious emotions" versus the academic's scientific analysis on "grey pages with no illustrations."[3] Still, given that the national press claimed objectivity and that the young academics openly expressed subjective judgments, the stories presented in these two media were similar in crucial ways: both cast their subjects in transnational terms.

This is not to say that they fabricated identities for the Mennonites; certainly, the subjects had their dignity and agency. Just what the outsider journalists and academics observed, for example, often depended on what the Mennonite colonists wished to reveal. Certainly, the Mennonites wanted to be known as stalwart traditionalists, but they also wanted outsiders to see them as useful contributors to national economies and as grateful newcomers within welcoming host nations. In both British Honduras and Bolivia, the traditionalist Mennonites made a mark by resisting national policies and social integration, and on this they would not relent, but their own economic self-interest served to assist their respective host nations meet globally defined national agendas. In British Honduras and Bolivia, as in Mexico and Paraguay, the Mennonites showed themselves to outside observers as a people willing to wander among the nations, settling for a time and then, if necessary, moving on.

The *Times*, the *Billboard*, and the "Hardy Farmer" in British Honduras

The national journalists who interviewed the Mennonite immigrants saw them as unique newcomers. In British Honduras, reporters from the leading, and competing, daily newspapers, the *Belize Times* owned by the ruling People's United Party and the independent *Belize Billboard*, interviewed the Mennonite newcomers and debated their desirability. Oftentimes, the newspapers gushed with enthusiasm, explaining why governments opened the national doors to these peculiar people in the first instance. Sometimes, the journalists addressed national apprehensions. But usually, after speaking with the Mennonites, the journalists produced positive text, even cast in the emotional language of nationalism. Ironically, they defended these foreigners even as the immigrants patently voiced their intention not to assimilate to the culture of their new homes.

This varied tone can be seen in the way journalists reported on the 1958 migration of Mennonites to British Honduras. The first newspaper references to the vanguard of Mexico Mennonite land scouts visiting British Honduras in 1957, for example, addressed the benefit of the Mennonites to the tiny country, often referred to simply as "B.H." In an August 1957 article in the *Belize Times* titled "How Will the Mennonites Help Us," John A. Watler of the newly elected People's United Party (PUP) listed the concerns he had heard about the newcomers: "The Mennonites will not be one with our community; they will naturally only employ [their own] ...; they will have their own religions; they will handle their own affairs; they ... [will have nowhere to] sell their produce; [they] will ... get free lands." But Watler rebutted each of these concerns: the Mennonites would, in fact, eventually "employ [British] Hondurans," and any idea that they "will obtain free lands is ridiculous." But his main argument was made in global language: the Mennonites "will enable us to stop importing what we are now forced to import and thus conserve the dollars we need for other things and eventually buy our own food more cheaply." As Watler saw it, "Let's give the Mennonites a try and see what will be the first results of this experiment[al] immigration to our Country."[4]

British Honduras newspapers in 1957 also provided the context of the Mennonite welcome in general. A June editorial in the *Belize Times* noted a common refrain: "The economic backbone of any country are the small peasant farmers who grow food for themselves and for their fellow citizens." It continued by saying that the centrist Prime Minister George Price's powerful, newly elected PUP government, controlling every seat of the Legislative Assembly, must be committed to "small farmers and working people, while at the same time pledged ... to create a favourable climate for investment."[5] Other reports that year expanded the argument. An October article in the *Times* called for an agricultural college that "would train young men to be farmers – not experts – but men who had a Christian training and who understood the honourable vocation of being a farmer."[6] Another October *Times* editorial passionately heralded ancient times when tens of thousands of Mayan people "lived ... a goodly li[f]e, decent and prosperous," a golden age of food self-sufficiency. The writer continued, "[Let's] use modern methods by all means, fertilize, etc., but for heaven's sake produce what can be produced. ... And use the money which would otherwise ... be wasted by the agricultural department to assist conscientious farmers."[7] The Canadian-descendant Mennonites fit this bill perfectly.

By the fall of 1957, the various newspapers assumed their readers' familiarity with the Mennonites. In October, the *Belize Billboard* carried a bold headline announcing that "Mennonites Now Seeking More than 100,000 Acres of British Honduras Land."[8] The *Billboard* proudly explained that the Mennonite newcomers were no ordinary immigrants. It made this assertion in the context of a long-standing claim of Guatemala to British Honduras territory and Guatemala's protest that "a large body of Mexican workers has settled on Guatemala territory of Belize with the consent of the British authorities." The *Billboard* pointed out that "the news is not true ... [as] it is not Mexican workers but a group of Mennonites of German origin whose ancestors left Russia in 1874" and who "in 1922 ... migrated to the state of Chihuahua in Mexico."[9] It mattered that the Mennonites were not acculturated Spanish-descendant Mexicans, but skilled German-speaking farmers. The following week, the *Billboard* carried another bold headline announcing with apparent approval that a "Nine-Man Mennonite Delegation Here to Clinch Immigration Deal with Govt [Government]." They had come "to sign and seal an agreement [to] ... secure the land they require for their agricultural projects," one that would secure hundreds more Mennonite families for B.H. The story concluded that the government was more than enthusiastic about the coming of these skilled farmers.[10]

Then, just three days later, on 13 December 1957, came the *Billboard*'s most detailed and personalized story to date. It focused on a lengthy interview with "Mr. Peter Wiebe," the so-named Mennonite "delegation guide and interpreter." Through Wiebe, the *Billboard* almost became expert on the internal dynamics of Mennonites, divided into three church groups: "the Keinland [Reinländer] Church (which has about 20,000 souls under its custody) and the Klein Gemeinole [Kleine Gemeinde] Church, which means Little Community Church (which has about 1200 souls under its custody). The other church is the Sommer [Sommerfelder] Church."[11] The *Billboard* even named each of the delegates, the leader Peter Wiebe, but also "Heinrick [Heinrich] Wiebe, Johann Wolf, Franz Rempel and Jacob Weibe [Wiebe] ... Cornelius Reimer and Peter Reimer."

The newspaper quoted the men with obvious respect. From them, the *Billboard* learned that, typically, each Mennonite family "has its own farm and each member of the family ... his own garden," meaning that each girl who learns "gardening from the ... youngest years ... takes pride in her garden." Not only did the Mennonites present themselves as expert farmers, they were small, democratically oriented, rural householders. While "some families have large farms ... other families have smaller farms, 12 acres or more perhaps," but "nowhere is there dire poverty." The Mennonites were also hardy, determined, and hardworking farmers. In Mexico, "the soil was bad" and "water was scarce," but the Mennonites had stubbornly farmed the land, "at first with their bare hands, until they were able to build a thriving community." The communities they built might be isolated, but they would complement, rather than distract from, national goals. They would not, for example, "swamp the market," but would "build up the B.H. export trade in agricultural products. ..."[12] The newcomers were well on their way to making themselves welcome in the new country.

The Mennonite settlers' self-representation did not go uncontested. A July 1958 issue of the *Billboard* featured an open letter by James Meighan of the opposition National Independence Party to the Honourable Louis Sylvester of the PUP. Meighan raised the concern that he had heard that in addition to military exemption, German-language schools, and easy border crossing, the Mennonites were now requesting "exemption forever from payment of estate duty in return for a pledge from the community that never will any Mennonite be allowed to become a public charge." Meighan's criticism was cast in racial terms: "Whites all, the [Mennonites] never vote and never seek political office. [Only] the PUP thinks they are ideal persons to have." Making matters even worse, the privileges the PUP extended to the Mennonites it refused to Caribbean people interested in immigration. Apparently, the government "believe[s] that West Indians are unsavory, barefoot people."[13]

Other negative reports followed. In July 1958, the *Billboard* announced it had learned that the "Mennonites want TH [Tower Hill] lands," causing local milpero leaseholders great anxiety. Readers were also reminded that at "Spanish Lookout, farmers and their families who had been cultivating the land for years on lease, were given $50 and told to get off the land."[14] That the Spanish Lookout Mennonites had purchased the land from a private owner made no difference to some Belizean nationalists; the Mennonites still were foreigners acquiring a national asset.

Overall, however, the Mennonites received positive, even sympathetic, press. The outbreak of polio and typhoid on some of the colonies, for example, might have cast aspersion on the Mennonites as disease carriers, but the stories excused the newcomers. In June 1958, for example, the *Billboard* charged that infected Mennonites at Spanish Lookout had introduced polio into Belize, a fact "government authorities ... have been trying to keep ... a secret."[15] But then, as quickly, the *Billboard* changed the tone of the story, accepting government reports that the Mennonites probably "came in contact with the viruses in B.H." and succumbed to it only because they were a highly hygienic people not immune to polio.[16] When a serious dysentery outbreak in the northern Blue Creek Colony killed twenty-eight Mennonite infants, the *Billboard* again was overtly sympathetic. It reported that the Mennonites themselves linked the problem with the drinking of "polluted rain water," itself arising from their "incomplete shelter accommodation, the heavy rains and the continual arrivals from Chihuahua." The newspaper lauded the Mennonites as a "cheerful and confident" people who were committed to fixing the problem as soon as the heavy rains subsided.[17]

The newspapers' mostly positive interpretation of the Mennonite newcomers corresponded to a broader cultural and political context. Both the *Times* and the *Billboard* presented an image of an economically prosperous and orderly, new, globalized nation. The papers seemed to embrace the place of the country within the British Commonwealth. Indeed, the very year the Mennonites arrived, the tiny Caribbean country hosted the first-ever Royal Family visit. In May 1958, the *Belize Times* reported how "Princess Margaret, resplendent in a pink dress," had alighted in B.H. and embraced the "warmth of [its] welcome"; the *Times* further gushed "that the British Commonwealth was a large and happy family of people."[18] Mennonite settlers, known for their lingering nostalgia for the British monarchy in Canada, no doubt approved. Later that year, the *Times* sponsored a full-page ad that exhibited a strikingly handsome, well-dressed, young Prime Minister Price, whom the Mennonite delegates had met personally in 1957. The ad, featuring the PUP's "Manifesto for Belize Country," was overtly capitalist and continentalist in orientation; it vowed to work against "International

Communism" and "federation with British West Indies," and "accept our natural place on the Central American continent." Again, the Mennonites would have approved, especially of the party's advocacy for "suitable immigrants under a system of selection and control."[19] Despite its strangeness, British Honduras, as presented by the newspapers, was the kind of home in which the Canadian-descendant newcomers could thrive.

La Presencia, *El Diario*, and the Mennonite "National Asset" in Bolivia

Given Bolivia's much larger size, its Mennonite immigrant community received considerably less national attention than in British Honduras. The Mennonites' arrival from Mexico in the mid-1960s, for example, seems to have been virtually ignored by the regional papers of Santa Cruz, the departmento that came to be home to some 10,000 Mennonites in the late 1960s. Evidently, Santa Cruz's *El Deber*, *El Comercio*, *La Crónica*, and *Diario del Oriente* saw the arrival of the Mennonites as a national and not a regional story. Local historian Luis Enrique Rivero Coimbra explains that the reason for the apparent omission lay in the Mennonites' "special status of residence, their conservative religion and, perhaps, the distant and inaccessible places in which they settled." The regional newspapers, writes Rivero, were focused on "everyday problems proper to this city" and on the "important events taking place in the country – Che Guevara's guerrilla war, Teoponte's guerrilla war, continuous coup d'etats against presidents Paz Estenssoro, Ovando and Torres, and Banzer's military putsch from 1971 until 1978."[20] In the context of a volatile regional political culture, the coming of foreign sectarians did not make headlines.

The national newspapers based in La Paz, where the Mennonites from Mexico entering Bolivia first landed in large numbers, did carry some stories of the Mennonite newcomers. And, as in British Honduras, the immigrants were referenced to a broader national project. A May 1967 story in *La Presencia* titled "Colonization in the Santa Cruz Region" reported that the "colonization of eastern Bolivia is one of the tasks being undertaken successfully with the support of brave countrymen from the [Andes] mountain valley and from the altiplano," and also by foreigners, specifically the "Japanese people and by a group of the Mennonite sect."[21] In a similar article in September 1968, *La Presencia* heralded the Santa Cruz region as the "Vital Nerve of Work and

Progress in the Heart of America," and reported that "approximately seven thousand people are colonizing the extensive rich lands" in the Santa Cruz region. It spoke in general terms of "hundreds of foreign families – Japanese, Canadian, German and other nationalities – who have transformed Bolivia at Santa Cruz into their second homeland" and, in the process, gave "a dynamic life" to the region and the wider national economy.[22] The Mennonites – Canadian descendant and German speaking – from this perspective became a national asset upon arrival.

The few times specific Mennonites were named in the national newspapers, they received similarly positive billing. A January 1970 piece in *La Presencia* featured a photograph of a young Mennonite couple, a husband and wife, working at a table saw, most likely in Colonia Canadiense. The story noted that "since Mennonite settlers arrived in this departmento, their work ... has exceeded those of other colonies. The Mennonites have invested approximately half a million dollars and the residence projects (three in this departmento) have been built following the characteristics of modern construction methods."[23] The upbeat story announced that the settlement had "government approval." Newspaper stories also highlighted Mennonite problems in a sympathetic tone. In April 1970, for example, *La Presencia* reported how "a letter addressed to Abraham Loewen, member of the Mennonite colony, and containing a 400 dollar cheque has been taken from the postal office's Certified Letters section of this city by someone forging his signature." Reportedly, police were investigating the crime, although they had not "discounted the possibility that the forger might be a member of the same colony."[24] No matter the origin of the criminal, that this scam had hurt a Mennonite farmer was newsworthy in the national media.

The lengthiest of the various articles on the Mennonites revealed a searing debate over the admission of pacifist, German-speaking, and isolationist immigrants. In an April 1968 op-ed piece in La Paz's *El Diario,* Roberto Lemaitre F. de Córdova, once a high-ranking military official and now seemingly the head of the country's immigration branch, tried to answer a headlined question: "Of what Benefit are the Mennonite Immigrants?"[25] He addressed persistent skepticism and asked, "What does it matter that they use their own language (while learning ours), that they use their own kind of clothing, or even that they appear unsociable and do not assimilate completely with the local society? The important thing is that they work and make our land produce." The Mennonites fit well Bolivia's national and even military strategy, argued Córdova, acknowledging that "it perhaps seems strange that I ... a military man ... [argue that] the Mennonites are a military asset." He offered the following explanation:

> Given the conditions of modern warfare, a country cannot be strong militarily unless it is first rich economically. ... In order to have a powerful army capable of commanding respect for our sovereignty and of regaining [territory] taken from us, we must first overcome our present state of poverty and underdevelopment. ... So when we verify ... that there are immigrants willing not only to invest their foreign capital (thereby stimulating the national economy), but more important[ly] ... till our uncleared lands, populating them and making them produce, there can be no justification for refusing such a group.

Evidently, the Mennonites had presented themselves well to the national leaders; their very penchant for peaceful, isolated existence outside the nation's cultural core could still serve to strengthen that very core.

In a final section of his defence of the Mennonites, Córdova employed transnational language to make his argument. Their origins, he wrote, were "mainly German, Russian and Dutch," and, as importantly, "a large number of them live in the United States, Canada, and Paraguay." Each of these countries had benefited from the Mennonite presence. From time to time, these countries had all "demonstrated their military strength," a might that had never "been diminished because of the Mennonites in their country." Quite to the contrary, the pacifist, agrarian Mennonites had been of military benefit, for if it "is true that armies need soldiers, it is just as true that these soldiers have to eat." In seeming reference to the disastrous 1935 military defeat of Bolivia at the hands of Paraguay, Córdova concluded he was confident that this was "the reasoning that influenced the Paraguayan civil and military authorities to encourage Mennonite colonization in the Chaco" in the 1920s.

Mennonites were not merely immigrants, they were anchored in an international world, and now, in the 1960s, had come to boost Bolivia's place in that wider world. They had convinced national leaders of their usefulness and, in the process, reinforced an identity that Mennonites themselves had honed since they had left Canada in 1922. They were travellers able to integrate into new countries at will and on their own terms.

Foreign Farmers and Visiting Experts

The academics who visited the Mennonite settlers in British Honduras and Bolivia between the late 1950s and early 1970s assembled rich ethnographies on the newcomers. In this instance, the outsider observers were themselves foreigners, young American and Canadian graduate and post-graduate social scientists, most in their late twenties. They travelled south specifically to speak with the Mennonite farmers, and thus to analyse and interpret this migration of northerners to the South.

In British Honduras, they included three geographers, each apparently unfamiliar with the other, but each of whom lived for periods of time with the Mennonites. The first of these visitors was Allan D. Bushong, a twenty-seven-year-old University of Florida doctoral student in geography whose 1961 dissertation, "Agricultural Settlement in British Honduras: A Geographic Interpretation of Its Development," presented the Mennonite newcomers as an example of "agricultural enterprise" in British Honduras.[26] The second was a post-doctoral student from Berkeley University, Harry Leonard Sawatzky, who had just completed a dissertation on the Mennonite migration from Canada to Mexico, and then, in 1969, undertaken a separate study of the Mennonites of British Honduras. A Canadian citizen and a Mennonite by descent, after completing his PhD in 1967, he was hired by Berkeley with funding from the United States Office of Naval Research (ONR), purportedly to provide an analysis to the US navy of British Honduras's "cultural assets," that is, the nature of this Central American society and its potential alignment to US interests. A third geographer, also a Canadian, was Jerry A. Hall, a doctoral student from Clark University in the United States. He descended on British Honduras to search for successful examples of the "Green Revolution" in developing countries, and covered Spanish Lookout Colony with his 1970 doctoral dissertation, "Mennonite Agriculture in a Tropical Environment."[27]

The three social science students who visited Bolivia in the 1960s and 1970s comprised a more disparate group of analysts. The first was an agricultural economist, Kelso Lee Wessel from Cornell University, who, in 1968, defended a doctoral dissertation titled "An Economic Assessment of Pioneer Settlement in the Bolivian Highlands." From a farm in Indiana and an alumnus of the International Farm Youth Exchange Program, Wessel had a natural interest in agriculture and visited Bolivia for thirteen months of field research in 1965 and 1966, a visit that included Mennonites among various farm groups. A second student, James W. Lanning of Texas A&M University, focused his master's thesis in anthropology on field research he conducted in 1969; it was an account of "the way of life" of Old Colony Mennonites from Mexico who had settled to the south of Santa Cruz.[28] In 1969 as well, a Canadian graduate student, Edward W. Van Dyck, studied quite a different group, a community of Old Colony Mennonites who had just arrived from northern Canada and settled to the north of Santa Cruz.[29] Van Dyck's University of Alberta doctoral dissertation, titled "Bluemenort [Blumenort]: A Study of Persistence in a Sect," had initially focused on a community near Fort Vermillion in northern Alberta, but had followed a traditionalist subgroup of the community to Bolivia. In varying ways, each of these young scholars interviewed Mennonites to hear their expressed aims of cultural "persistence" in eastern Bolivia.

Importantly, all six researchers established rapport with the Mennonite settlers. Of the six, Sawatzky alone spoke Low German, but the others found English speakers among the Mennonite settlers, the oldest of whom had been young adults when they left Canada in 1922. Hall and Van Dyck both focused on recently transplanted groups from Canada whose members were reportedly eager to speak with members from the old homeland. Wessel, in Bolivia, seems to have gained entry into his Mennonite community through the company of US Mennonite Central Committee (MCC) worker Daniel Gingrich, who spent more than a year at Colonia Canadiense. For "a closed society," wrote Wessel, he found the Mennonites "very friendly and most willing to talk about their lives and farming, both in Bolivia and previously." In fact, "almost without exception," he noted, "we would be invited into their homes for coffee or the mate gourd would be passed around in the yard."[30] Ironically, Lanning, who visited the most exclusive of the settlements – the Mexico Old Colony groups south of Santa Cruz – spoke most warmly of his relationships with his hosts. Lanning travelled to Bolivia four times between 1968 and 1971, and during each of these two-week-long trips he resided with a family, eight families in total.[31] He even spent an overnight with the family of Jacob Wiebe, a preacher in the Old Colony Church, who was reportedly "most cordial and hospitable."[32]

Just how the various Mennonite communities responded to this situation can mostly be deduced from the young Canadian and American researchers' reports.[33] It seems that the Mennonite interviewees emphasized their unique cultures. They also seem to have highlighted both their ties to various countries and their cultural separation within the new host societies. The Mennonites impressed the researchers in various ways, and also were analysed in a variety of ways, depending on the specific academic discipline of the researcher. But a common feature in the six reports was the description of how the Mennonites' cultural aims were conditioned by a wider world, and a feature in most of the theses was how those aims corresponded to the host societies' globally oriented economic pursuits.

Settlement Blueprints of Blue Creek and Shipyard

The first of these various studies examined the British Honduras colonies and emphasized the unique combination of international linkage and national isolation. While Allan Bushong from Florida determined that the Mennonite newcomers' "agrarian activities" made them "worthy of being singled out ... for special study,"[34] he framed their success with reference to a narrative that linked them to a wider world. He highlighted their global wanderings, enabled in part by their agrarian acumen that had "caused kings, queens and heads of government to welcome them for the purpose of opening agricultural lands."[35] He also spoke of their complicated relationship to the country of their most recent sojourn; indeed, their migration from Mexico had occurred because "native Mexicans refused to sell them more land," because the Mennonites would not "accept the Mexican social security system," and because they worried "that it would be only a matter of time before the Mexican government would cease to honor the promises made in 1921."[36] In the meantime, though, the three B.H. colonies maintained close ties to the sending colonies in Chihuahua, which had offered generous financial support in their bid to settle the rainforest and seemed ever ready to welcome home any disgruntled return migrant.[37] Bushong seemed especially eager to describe overtures of acculturated Mennonites in the United States to B.H. Mennonites. He highlighted how MCC, based in Akron, Pennsylvania, had offered the B.H. Mennonites $4800 in aid in 1960, and, even more impressively, sent them "three air shipments of [pure] bred Holstein heifers, valued at US $7000."[38] Past, present, and developing international ties contributed to their self-identity.

If Bushong was impressed by the Mennonites' internationalism, he was similarly positive about the self-sufficiency of the Mennonites, and especially those at Blue Creek and Shipyard. They had chosen settlement sites well away from the nation's central areas. In fact, getting to Blue Creek Colony required a half-hour trip by car from Orange Walk and then a four-and-a-half-hour trip by "motorized doray [dory]" on the river. A road being built by the government to "provide the Mennonites with easier access to the rest of British Honduras" could not be completed quickly enough.[39] The clearing of the impenetrable jungle was tedious but, again, impressive. They had had to adapt quickly, as the "new and unfamiliar humid tropical environment of British Honduras contrasts sharply with their familiar upland and semi-arid setting in Chihuahua."[40] And they had succeeded. In his visit to Blue Creek in August 1959, Bushong reported that "the land everywhere ... bore the blackened scars of the clearing ritual. No sooner is the land swept free of much of the impeding vegetation ... than construction of [a one- or two-storey] farm home begins ... amidst the recently fired fields."[41] Those fields had begun yielding in short time. By August 1959, half of the 617 acres of cleared land at Shipyard had been planted to corn, while plans for the 650 acres of cleared land at Blue Creek included not only corn, but 2000 citrus and 1500 coconut trees.[42]

A second visiting geographer, Harry Leonard Sawatzky, also emphasized the isolation of Blue Creek and Shipyard. But he noted not so much a temporary frontier isolation as an intentional, religiously informed one, and one he overtly criticized. He cited Shipyard Colony in particular for its "isolation, denigration of learning," with a troubling consequence of "cultural impoverishment." In fact, the Old Colonists could be blamed for the government's rising "impatience with the 'alien' Mennonites' aloof and 'privileged' status."[43]

The newcomers at Shipyard, stated Sawatzky, had made several miscalculations because of lack of outside information. Their mistaken "initial assessment of the verdant jungle growth ... was that it must spring from soil of exceptional fertility."[44] They had failed to make a quick transition from Mexico-based crops of beans and corn to the rice and citrus fruit suited to the tropics. In ignorance, they had purchased seeds of sorghum halepense, a fast-growing grass that turned out to be a weed, invading the "new land as fast as the forest is cleared."[45] They made "grave errors of judgement" when they dismissed the indigenous hardwood trees as impossibly hard and thus burned them, rather than learning to turn them into valuable lumber.[46] Indeed, they had ignored both the advice of the government-sponsored Orange Walk Agricultural Station and "copious evidence of former Maya acceptance of the region," and, hence, had not learned the basic steps by "which the Maya milpero determines and regulates his clearing, burning and planting."[47]

Instead of adapting to a new land, the Shipyard settlers' primary goal had been to transplant old ways developed in Canada and Mexico. The Shipyard colonists' insistence on horse-and-buggy travel and steel-wheeled traction was unmovable, based as it was on an old Canadian narrative of mythical proportion. The Old Colonists could not forget a 1916 vow in which church "leaders in Manitoba and Saskatchewan agreed to ban the automobile forever and to arrest technological innovation in agricultural machinery at the then-existing stage." The ultra-modern, small, family-friendly, steel-wheeled farm tractor of 1916 could be tolerated, but the later rubber-tired tractors of the 1940s and 1950s would be deemed to be virtual cars and thus forbidden. Sawatzky was critical of the practice as rubber tires simply "have considerable advantages of traction and flotation [and] ... fuel economy ... on the difficult soils of British Honduras."[48] The Old Colonists' reliance on horses for travel was equally short-sighted, as horses in the Central American "heat and humidity" were lethargic, especially without high-energy rations of oats. These old practices, Sawatzky scolded, had left "much of the arable *Altkolonier* [Old Colonist] land ... in a very indifferent state of cultivation."[49] Moreover, they had deeply divided the colonists; Blue Creek farmers who embraced new technologies had been "threatened with excommunication," and when they ignored the threats, the "ultra conservatives" left, crowding into the smaller, more traditional, nearby Shipyard Colony, further impoverishing it.[50] The Old Colonist traditionalists certainly had convinced Sawatzky of their commitment to isolation and anti-modernity, even if they had not convinced him of the value of such an outlook.

Speaking of Success at Spanish Lookout Colony

A third colony in British Honduras, Spanish Lookout, settled by somewhat more progressive Kleine Gemeinde Mennonites, did inspire the visiting foreign investigator. Located in the western highlands of the country, some one hundred kilometres to the southwest of Blue Creek and Shipyard,[51] Spanish Lookout was the singular focus of Canadian geographer Jerry Alan Hall in 1970. Hall saw Spanish Lookout Colony's agricultural accomplishments as an example of what British Honduras must do as a country to catch "up in the Green Revolution," stop the self-destructive practice of importing more than "70 percent of its food requirements," and move beyond the British logging colony it still was.[52] The Spanish Lookout Mennonites, to Hall's reckoning, had successfully transplanted mechanized farming systems from the mid-latitude regions of North America.[53]

Spanish Lookout appeared as a model farm to an international audience. In his two extended stays on the colony, Hall observed that the jungle had been cleared and land surveyed in orderly fashion, strictly following cardinal directions and divided into square fields, no matter the very hilly landscape and the parallelogram-shaped tract of land. The colony itself featured a "neat arrangement among the main roads of Canadian-style houses, surrounded by hedge, lawn, and flower beds," all quite "out of place when compared to the ... yards of the ... scattered Mayan or Creole farms."[54] Despite the "Canadian" characteristics, the Spanish Lookout settlers were Kleine Gemeinde Mennonites who emphasized a "tradition of isolation" and "an agrarian 'way of life' based on hard manual labor, nonmonetary goals and the dominance of God."[55] But this philosophy of life did not translate into economic primitivism. Indeed, at every turn, the colony stood out because of sophisticated farming techniques, in contrast to the "under-developed nation of slash and burn migrant peasants."[56]

Importantly, the Spanish Lookout settlers had maintained international ties, especially with kin in Canada whom they left in 1948.[57] They also embraced a fruit-growing project headed up by an Ontario entrepreneur. And they had successfully transplanted aspects of the "poultry industry" common in Manitoba, a province promoting agricultural specialization. A 300,000-bird hatchery established at Spanish Lookout during the very first year of settlement, now augmented by "day-old chicks ... air freighted to the colony from the U.S.,"[58] was especially impressive.

As the international expert, Hall was frank in his analysis. Perhaps the colony population was "in good physical health and show[ed] no apparent signs of inbreeding," but the women, said Hall, seemed "somewhat underweight and anaemic." Perhaps a school system had been established, but "basic reading, writing and arithmetic," he said, were "learned by rote ... rather than by understanding concepts," leaving children much less educated than their Canadian-taught parents.[59] Perhaps new sources of land existed, but, as land prices rose and the first families' children reached the age of marriage, Hall worried that the "classless Mennonite society may become divided into a land rich ... and a landless class." In this case, warned Hall, the

Mennonites might well have to consider yet another extensive migration.[60] Then, too, their limited friendships among the B.H. populace could come to haunt them. Already, reports had surfaced that nationals were "becoming jealous of their country's limited land resources," and that the Mennonites were "not viewed as [fellow] nationals or citizens by the locals," an especially serious charge as most Mennonites, in fact, had not pursued citizenship.[61] In the end, Hall identified two main culprits. The British Honduras government had more or less ignored the Mennonites' transplanted farm methods, "which apparently do work in the tropics," and had done so because of myopic "nationalistic feelings." But the Mennonites also had failed "to sense the ramifications of their presence and actions."[62] They would do well to recognize their own foreignness within B.H.

The British Honduras Mennonites readily shared their successes and failures with the three visiting foreign geographers. The Mennonites might not have fully appreciated or even known that US and Canadian government-based organizations and public universities interested in the economic development of Central America funded the visitors. It is unlikely they knew that at least one North American scholar was visiting each of the three colonies. What is important for this study is that, despite strikingly different conclusions drawn about the three colonies, the Mennonites of Blue Creek, Shipyard, and Spanish Lookout presented themselves as immigrant farmers who avoided integration into any one host society, and as those who maintained economic and even social ties to Mennonites in other lands.

Remoulding Bolivia at Colonia Canadiense

The Mennonites who came to either Bolivia or British Honduras chose between two starkly different countries. Bolivia was a large, landlocked, Spanish-speaking country, shaped by a series of nineteenth- and twentieth-century wars with its neighbours, Chile and Paraguay;[63] British Honduras was a tiny British colony, carved into the Central American coastline claimed by Honduras. Bolivia consisted of mountain plateaus in the west and an extensive, fertile woodland in the east, its Oriente lowland; British Honduras featured a rainforest by the sea and higher ground in its West. Still, the two places offered traditionalist, Canadian-descendant Mennonites in the 1950s and 1960s similar hopes for isolated and self-sufficient agrarian colonies, which, nevertheless, would play important roles in national economic policies. Mennonites were small minorities in both countries, but ones with some swagger, aware of their status as skilled agriculturalists. The three scholars who visited Colonia Canadiense, Riva Palacios, and Las Piedras in the late 1960s and early 1970s highlighted the unique transnational nature of their subjects. They were foreign farmers, possessed of skills honed over four centuries of migration, now serving national agendas determined by a globalized economy.

The first of the three visiting North American scholars, Kelso Lee Wessel of Cornell University, emphasized the political context that enabled the immigration of foreign farmers like the Mennonites. Indeed, the newcomers marked a necessary component of the government's development plan for the Santa Cruz departmento in the country's eastern lowlands. This development was crucial for Bolivia, and made it "the second country in Latin America to initiate a comprehensive agrarian reform" after the Second World War. The aim had been nothing less than "to remold the semi-feudalistic society into a modern agricultural system." From a global perspective, it mattered that in 1952, 99 percent of Bolivia's exports were minerals (mostly tin, following the depletion of its silver mines), an emphasis that not only left its economy extremely vulnerable to hyperinflation, but also made it a net food importer.[64] A central feature of this reform was the settlement of the rich soils in the eastern lowlands, the Oriente. It was a sparsely populated, sweeping, semi-tropical place, with adequate annual rainfall and rich, undulating soils. It stretched in the shape of a massive boomerang, west from the Brazil border to Santa Cruz city, then south to the town of Yucuiba just north of the Argentine border. Wessel described it as a region given to very hot summer days, but cool evenings. It was, in every respect, "one of the few really promising areas for new agricultural development left in the Americas."[65] As such, it could also meet Bolivia's various needs, its requirement for agricultural self-sufficiency, and a correction to a demographic concentration in the western highland regions.[66]

This was the context in which Mennonite settlers were drawn to Bolivia. At first, the government had hoped to encourage the relocation of highlanders from the Andes Altiplano to the fertile Oriente. But another way to develop this region, and, indeed, to set an example for native farmers, was to invite foreign settlement, and thus, wrote Wessel, "special concessions have been granted to groups from other nations who were interested in re-establishing in virgin territory."[67] Following the costly national revolution of 1952 and spurred on by the US agricultural productivity Point IV Program, Bolivia introduced a plan to bring in skilled, foreign agriculturalists. The successful policy resulted in the arrival of some 8500 newcomers in the Santa Cruz departmento between 1954 and 1966.[68]

Among the earliest of these migrants were about a hundred Mennonites from Paraguay, a majority of whom were of Canadian descent.[69] The Mennonites' history in Bolivia began on 15 January 1954 when a group of six scouts arrived from the progressive Soviet-Mennonite colony of Fernheim in Paraguay. The settlement they would establish at Tres Palmes was on cotton-growing land offered to them by the Compañia Algondonera Bolivana.[70] Within three years, Canadian-descendant conservative Mennonites from Menno Colony in Paraguay followed, citing as a reason for migration Menno Colony's "enforced membership in [its] cooperative organization." This 1957 founding of Colonia Canadiense was followed in 1963 by the even larger Bergthal and Las Pavas colonies, established by more Canadian Mennonite migrants from Paraguay or directly by conservative Mennonites from Canada. Consisting of fifty-four families, or about 300 persons, the migrants also came to escape modernity, citing "the religious and educational trends" with "too much secularity" in the schools.[71] The latter groups seemed especially cohesive; their colony land was purchased by "a central committee and then resold to farmers" who could resell it only to fellow Mennonites. And, while content with Bolivia's superior climatic and economic promise, they insisted that they were first and foremost "religiously motivated."[72] They may have been skilled farmers, but they were pacifist sectarians using the global migration paths for religious pursuit.

Still, like the Mennonites in British Honduras, the colonists in Bolivia readily opened themselves up to a foreign scholar's scrutiny. Wessel's conclusions were uniformly positive, with Colonia Canadiense earning his praise as a colony of "spectacular success." The Mennonites were an independent-minded people of virtue, hoping for little more than a chance to be tillers of the earth. They were skilled, small farmers "able to thrive in areas" other farmers had avoided, all the while in tune with market demands.[73] Although located on the semi-arid northern fringes of the Bolivian lowland, they were able to turn the rolling plains of grassland into fertile fields, especially by introducing technologized agriculture.[74] By 1965, the Mennonites, with farms averaging 38 hectares, had cultivated more than half of their 6170 hectares, the balance of which was pasture or fallow lands set aside for future immigrants.[75] The Mennonites had experimented unsuccessfully with their old ally, wheat, but adapted successfully to the commodities of the Bolivian lowland – castor beans, cotton, corn, and peanuts – as well as the hog-feed staple of yucca.[76] They had even mastered dairy and swine production, signalling that they would become "major producers of these products in the Santa Cruz areas within a few years."[77] The Mennonites' success was especially noteworthy: in "comparison with the other colonists in Bolivia – both national and foreign," wrote Wessel, "the Mennonites are much better off."[78] Foreign Mennonites in Bolivia had been given top marks by a US economist.

Romancing the Frontier at Colonia Riva Palacios

The great majority of the first Mennonite immigrants to Bolivia were traditionalist, so-called "horse and buggy" Old Colonists from the Mennonite colonies in Chihuahua, Mexico.[79] The vanguard of what would become an enduring multi-decade migration arrived in 1967 and 1968. The first and largest Mexico Mennonite colony was Riva Palacios, a 40,400-hectare colony of some 2000 immigrants, mostly from Ojo de le Yegua or Nord Kolonie (also known from time to time as Rivas Palacios), a subcolony just north of Manitoba Colony in Chihuahua. In addition, three smaller colonies were founded in Bolivia in 1968, each from a different Mexico colony and together numbering only some 800 residents on about 10,000 hectares.[80] The first two of these smaller colonies – Swift Current and Santa Rita (or Paurito) – also consisted of Old Colony Mennonites and were named after parent colonies in Mexico, while Sommerfeld consisted of somewhat more progressive Sommerfelder Mennonites from Santa Clara in Mexico.[81]

Given their land base and overt cultural intention, it is not surprising that the Old Colony Mennonite colonies became the subject of academic attention almost at once. With only five or six of the envisaged twenty-two villages completed in 1970, James Lanning of Texas A&M University visited Riva Palacios and interviewed the colonists, who seemed eager to speak with him. They presented themselves as religiously motivated migrants, global wanderers, seeking a life of Christian simplicity. The very purpose of their emigration from Mexico, the "base of their decision to move," lay in a searing schism that had sent the stalwart on a migration path to preserve "their traditional religious-based subculture," indeed, hoping that "the old ways could be restored."[82] That culture had been threatened in the rapidly modernizing Mexico colonies, intersected by a paved highway and widely accepting of the "rubber tired tractors as a mode of travel."[83] Bolivia was attractive not only for its thousands of hectares of potential farmland, but for its distance from the "increasingly sophisticated" Mennonites of Mexico and, hence, was a way of halting the encroachment of modernity and maintaining the church's *Ordnung* (sacred order). In Bolivia, the most contested "orders" of religious simplicity – the steel-wheeled tractor, horse-and-buggy mode of transportation, and life without electricity – could stand a chance of being obeyed.

The newcomers in Bolivia emphasized this sharp separation from the Mexico colonies. Unlike their migration from Canada in the 1920s, this move of over 7000 kilometres was a "journey of no return"; most families had sold "their land in Mexico in order to obtain adequate capital to finance the journey." The trip itself was momentous. Lanning's interviewees emphasized the trip by airplane from Mexico City, this "a frequent topic of conversation among the colonists, especially since in virtually all cases it was their first ride in an airplane."[84] Although some of the settlers came by sea, including a small contingent led by their Ältester, Bernard F. Peters, sea travel became reserved for the transportation of farm equipment and household wares, sent to port cities in Chile or Brazil and then by rail to La Paz and Santa Cruz. Only the final leg of the trip from Santa Cruz city to the colonies, about fifty kilometres distant, could be taken by rented motorized trucks.[85]

Despite the arduous migration, the Riva Palacios settlers seemed confident in farming the new frontier. They spoke of an agricultural culture, of ancient ways of interacting with nature, of skills passed down through the generations. They had even learned what not to do; the 1920s move by their parents from Canada to Mexico had left them at a distinct financial disadvantage, for they had exchanged low-priced good land in Canada for high-priced semi-arid land in Mexico; this time around, the migrants to Bolivia had "sold land in Mexico for high prices and bought 100,000 acres for .65 cents an acre."[86] They spoke with confidence of knowing how to develop frontiers. One settler claimed the advantage of having a father who "as a young man moved to Mexico and built a fine farm" and then "moved two additional times in Mexico to underdeveloped satellite [colonies] and now he is building a new farm in Bolivia."[87] There was, thus, nothing primitive or helter-skelter about the founding of Riva Palacios. In fact, "the settlement pattern of the colony as a whole was deliberately planned and surveyed in advance." The settlers even chose the specific location relative to Santa Cruz city with care, intentionally building their colony along a fifty-kilometre-long road constructed by Gulf Oil Corporation, thus securing a link to the markets of Santa Cruz, then a city of 80,000.[88]

Part of the colonists' optimism was the colony's confident standing with the national government. They may have arrived shortly after the famed 1964 coup, in which Vice-President General René Barrientos Ortuño deposed President Victor Paz Estenssoro, the democratically elected signator to the Mennonites' 1962 *Privilegium*, Law 6030. They may even have come in the year of Barrientos's own mysterious death in 1967, and established themselves during the succeeding four tumultuous years of political instability with insurrections brewing in Santa Cruz itself. But the Mennonites at Riva Palacios seemed surprisingly secure in their place in Bolivia,[89] anchored by their *Privilegium*'s "broad religious and education and political concessions."[90] Certainly, the left-centrist Estenssoro government had had its own national agenda in inviting foreign farmers to Bolivia after the 1952 revolution: "the abolition of huge land estates, commercialization of agriculture and the integration of the secessionist prone Oriente regions ...: with the rest of the country."[91] But the Mennonites were especially heartened by the Bolivian government's apparent respect for them, shown in its willingness in 1962 to duplicate almost word for word the promises made by Paraguay to its Mennonites in 1921. And it was on the Paraguay Mennonites' "record of competency that the Old Colony church leaders approached the Bolivian authorities in the fall of 1966," leading to the agreement "that the colonists could enter Bolivia under the auspices" of the 1962 law.[92]

Of special importance were the law's provisions for military exemption and private schools. But other elements were important. Certainly, it mattered to them that the law had been issued at the "governmental palace in the city of La Paz" and bore the signature of the national president.[93] It mattered, too, that the agreement gave them permission to "settle down in any territory of the country" so long as they would "dedicate themselves to ... agricultural labours."[94] Lanning, for one, found it noteworthy that a provision added after the arrival of the Old Colonists – Article 10, requiring Mennonites to "engage teachers for learning Spanish" – was simply being ignored at Riva Palacios.[95] The "basic point of the document," for the Old Colonists, was that it "granted a certain degree of autonomy from the host government of Bolivia."[96] Governments, it seemed, could change, but the law, they somehow believed, was sacrosanct.

Even the rigours of settlement did not seem to deter the Mennonites. The setting of Riva Palacios, they emphasized, lay in a "sea of green," a "shocking contrast to the barren wind-blown prairie" of northern Mexico.[97] Lanning described the settlement, located on the west bank of Bolivia's Rio Grande River, as subtropical, covered in hardwood and softwood trees, many ten metres in height. Certainly, families faced "trials and tribulations" as they forged their new homes in the bush with tiny clearings at first and then the bulldozing of larger swathes of arable land.[98] The task dictated "that each member of the family work from early morning until late in the evening, sometimes by the light of lantern to clear this vegetative barrier."[99] These rigours, Lanning observed, enhanced familial cohesion, especially close father–son relationships, and produced healthy bodies. Certainly, frontier life was primitive, as the typical young family lived in small, one-and-a-half-storey, 18 × 44-foot houses, often with earthen floor bedrooms, and a simple set of first-floor rooms: a kitchen, a bedroom, a roomy pantry, and a place for storage. Still, the Mennonites survived and thrived; in fact, as Lanning put it, the "striking feature of the home was its orderliness and cleanliness."[100]

Riva Palacios's wilderness location did not spell complete isolation. The settlers adjusted quickly to the economy and geography of Bolivia. Discovering Bolivia's complete lack of a "taste for cheese," they de-emphasized dairy farming and turned to "corn, kaffir sorghum, potatoes, peanuts, beans, peas, sunflowers, papayas, melons, cabbage, peppers, squash, radishes, carrots and many other" new crops.[101] They also pursued economic links beyond Bolivia. One settler "with a wife and eleven children explained that in order to obtain $2000 for air passage his entire family went to Canada and worked on a produce farm for six months to earn the necessary money for fares."[102] Another told Lanning that because of an "acute need of ... colonists for farm machinery," the colony sent one of its best entrepreneurs, "Mr. Klassen," by airplane on a "commercial trip to the United States," with "money orders totaling in excess of $3000."[103] Other colonists related how an inflation in local horse prices sent them to nearby Argentina to buy their draught animals.[104] Even in their everyday lives, especially after supper, the Mennonites seemed eager to talk to Lanning about world events – Peru's earthquake of 1970 or US astronaut Alan Shepard's biography – they had read about in the German-language *Reader's Digest*.[105]

The Mennonites' ironic connection to the wider world was also evident in their own culture, stories and artefacts that spoke of world travel. For one, given "the building materials in Bolivia ... they wasted no time in reproducing the design" of the wooden-framed, two-storey house they had left in Canada in the 1920s.[106] For their furniture, they hired Bolivian woodworkers and asked them to reproduce "traditional ancestral furniture found in Mexico."[107] Several families owned Russian clocks brought to Canada by their grandparents in the 1870s.[108] And their collective memory outlined a sequence of changes from one country to another: in Russia, Mennonites had adopted the scythe from non-Mennonites and spoke of it as "a great improvement over the sickle"; in Canada, "the binder was borrowed from Canadian farmers," an improvement over the reaper; and in Bolivia, they might just stop using the steel-wheeled tractor, even though the preachers called such a change "evil."[109]

The Old Colonists also related stories they had heard of life in Canada and the United States, some of them a little far-fetched perhaps, but bearing a semblance of truth, nevertheless. One member claimed to have heard of "dying houses," "places in the United States where families send their elders" to die, presumably senior citizen nursing homes. Another had heard that "all children in Canada wear glasses ... [because] all the children in Canada watch television." A third recalled hearing that "someone was trying to build a machine in Canada that could pull words from the sky," no matter if they had been spoken "eons ago."[110] Their isolation would protect them from a wider world gone askew, one in which wealth and technology were producing a host of social ills.

Certainly, the Old Colonists under Lanning's academic gaze were not without want. Lanning questioned "the doctrine of refraining from artificial birth control" that left the colony with an astoundingly high birth rate. He was repulsed by hearing them utter racial expressions such as "nigger." He questioned the wisdom of their strict dress codes in a land of extreme heat, and described with less than flattering words an Old Colony woman with her dark, heavy, long-sleeved dress, walking through heat-drenched Santa Cruz. He thought the Old Colony members sometimes seemed gullible.[111]

Still, the sum of Lanning's report was that the Old Colony Mennonites appeared to be an example of social well-being. In terms of their health, they gave "the appearance of being sturdy, healthy ... people who responded physically to the rigors of pioneer life." He further described the men as "tall, sinewy and erect" and the women as "robust [with] peasant-type bone structure."[112] Socially, the ancient agrarian way of life lent "a degree of solidarity, in that members interact in a casual and easy manner," dropping by for short visits, "aware of the activities of every one else in the village."[113] Family life was close-knit, with parents and children working side by side and developing "a genuine feeling of togetherness and common purpose."[114] The "mealtimes were a time of physical enjoyment for the whole family as a bountiful table was common," and gratitude was apparent as the Mennonites "bow their heads before [and after] eating for a short, silent prayer."[115] Old age was accorded deep respect, with members boasting "of their tradition of taking care of their own" elderly and with "the younger generation ... consult[ing] their elders for advice when making decisions." Lanning even observed how grandparents were playful with grandchildren, with mutual "reverence" and "mutual love."[116] It all seemed rather utopian.

Even their sombre church and institutional life bore positive results. Their religious teachings, for example, allowed them to negotiate life without being "fearful of death." And, in other respects, the Old Colonists found peace in trusting the divine. To "the God-fearing Old Colonist," wrote Lanning, "the success of the present colonization effort is at the mercy of his Creator."[117] Education was rudimentary, but it was emphasized and sensible; the schoolhouse, for example, was among the first structures in every village, and children with physical disabilities were paid special attention.[118] Politically, the village was profoundly democratic; the village and colony mayors were elected from among village farmers for two-year terms without the option of succeeding themselves in office (at least more than once or twice). Conflicts were resolved by the village mayor, who stepped into such affairs as a mediator, sometimes sending a matter for resolution to "the village council under his direction." Only occasionally, when a situation got out of hand, did the village mayor send it up to the clergy, the occupiers of "the higher echelon of ... rule making in each" colony.[119]

When the Riva Palacios Old Colonists were asked about the future, some doubted the long-term viability of the old ways. Some predicted the eventual acceptance of the pickup truck, just as the steel-wheeled tractor had already justified the ownership of massive modern bulldozers to clear the dense bushland.[120] What could be presumed, concluded Lanning, was that, based on family fertility and community social health, the "contingent in Bolivia may one day replace the mother colony in Mexico as the citadel of Old Colony faith."[121] Bolivia had won its place in Mennonite history.

Old Colony Mennonite minister Johann P. Wall, one of several delegates to South America in 1919 and Mexico in 1920, and a negotiator with the Mexican government during the 1935 school closures. *Die Mennonitische Post.*

Farmer Abram Wolfe and four of his children – from left to right: Maria, Eva, Elisabeth, and Isaak – stopping in Minneapolis in 1922 en route to Mexico. The Minneapolis daily that published this photo described the migrants as leaving "the richest farming district of Manitoba." Note Mr. Wolfe's missing left arm; Mennonite leaders insisted that community members with disabilities be allowed into Mexico. Prof. Rudolf J. Vecoli, University of Minnesota.

Old Colony Mennonite farmers celebrating their first crop of oats in the Bustillos Valley in 1923 near the village of Kronsthal, Manitoba Colony, Chihuahua, Mexico. *Preservings* 28 (2008).

Paraguay Emigration. Nov. 23, 1926.

The steam-driven, crowded riverboat that took the 1926 immigrants north on the Paraguay River, heading from Asunción to Puerto Casado, into the heart of the Paraguayan Chaco. Quiring, *Im Schweisse Deines Angesichts*.

Johann and Tina Peters and their children on board the chartered train from Saskatoon to Montreal in 1948, en route to East Paraguay. The original photo caption reads "Trip into the unknown." Quiring, *Im Schweisse Deines Angesichts*.

Breaking the land after clearing the forest in East Paraguay shortly after the founding of Bergthal and Sommerfeld colonies in 1948. Warkentin, *Pilgrims and Strangers*.

Schoolgirls celebrating their younger siblings in Manitoba Colony near Cuauhtémoc, Mexico, in June 1951. *Mennonite Life* (January 1952).

An Old Colony woman retrieving water in Manitoba Colony near Cuauhtémoc, Mexico, in June 1951. *Mennonite Life* (January 1952).

Leaving for British Honduras by bus from Chihuahua, Mexico, in search of new homes in April 1958. *Mennonite Life* (October 1958).

A new home at Shipyard Colony, British Honduras, one of the first to be constructed in 1958. Note the stilt foundation of the house, an adaptation to a rainforest climate. Warkentin, *Pilgrims and Strangers*.

An auction sale at Riva Palacios, Bolivia, some time after its founding in 1967. The auction sale was a common social event preceding any migration to a new land or a return migration to Canada. *Die Mennonitische Post.*

The schoolhouse at Colonia Canadiense in Bolivia. The colony was founded in 1956 by Canadian-descendant "Chortitzer" Mennonites from Paraguay. Warkentin, *Pilgrims and Strangers*.

Paraguay president Alfredo Stroessner (second from the right) and other government and military officials helping to celebrate Menno Colony's fiftieth anniversary in June 1977. At the far right is colony mayor (*Oberschulze*) Jacob N. Giesbrecht, and third from the right is Kornelius Walde, president of the Comite Social Económico Mennonita. Warkentin, *Pilgrims and Strangers*.

The son or grandson of Abram Friesen, Rosenort, Campo 62, Cuauhtémoc, Mexico, exhibiting a small chest, a replica of those brought along from Russia to Canada. Photo from the 1970s or 1980s. Warkentin, *Pilgrims and Strangers*.

Abe Warkentin (right), founding editor of *Die Mennonitische Post*, in about 1980, with *Post* subscriber Isaak Dyck (left) of Cuauhtémoc, Mexico. The *Post* was a Canadian-based newspaper, launched in 1977, facilitating a flow of ethno-religious information throughout the Low German Mennonite communities in the Americas. *Die Mennonitische Post*.

Two of the daughters of colony mayor (*Vorsteher*) Jakob Friesen in January 2004, of Colonia Ojo de lad Yegua (also Nordkolonie) in Chihuahua, a moderately conservative "Old Colony" Mennonite colony. The floral patterns in the girls' dresses are common throughout the diaspora, but the more modern fashions and bare heads designate a relatively progressive people. Royden Loewen.

The new Mennonite Credit Union building just north of Cuauhtémoc, Chihuahua, in January 2004, on the four-lane highway to Ciudad Obregón that cuts through Manitoba Colony. The Credit Union is a sign of recent rural commercialization and a departure from older systems of credit. Royden Loewen.

The boys of Sabinal Colony on a Sunday afternoon in January 2004, crowding around a truck carrying visiting Canadians. Sabinal is the last "horse and buggy" colony in northern Mexico, located on an arid plain an hour north of Nuevo Casas Grandes. Royden Loewen.

Mexico Mennonite homes in Aylmer, Ontario, a comfortable, new, working-class world for many, but a place of unfamiliar uprootedness for others. *Die Mennonitische Post*.

A Rocky Path at Colonia Las Piedras

If international migration could resolve conflict, it could also exacerbate it. In 1970, a group of about 200 Old Colony Mennonites from Fort Vermillion in northern Alberta moved to Bolivia and established Colonia Las Piedras, where they sought the continuity of old ways. They spoke of being migrants in search of isolation. In the 1930s, their parents, who had decided not to migrate to Mexico in the 1920s, had moved to La Crete and Fort Vermillion in northern Alberta for that very purpose. The province's school laws had made room for their private schools, and the vast, northern, boreal forests had shielded them from the wider world. It was a perfect place to procure "cultural persistence," the topic that graduate student Edward Van Dyck of Edmonton went north to study in 1969. By coincidence, at the very time he began his anthropological research among Old Colonists, a segment of the Fort Vermillion community decided that "cultural persistence" could not be secured in Canada. The migration south presented Van Dyck with a unique opportunity to study a migration in process. In 1970, he followed the group to Bolivia to document their success in reinventing tradition in the South.

According to the migrants, threats to traditionalism in northern Alberta came from several directions – regional, national, and international. The greatest immediate concern was the 1969 regionalization or "consolidation" of public education; the Old Colonists saw this "centralized schooling" as an "imposition of alien schooling," made worse with "sex education."[122] Linked to this concern was the encroachment of missionary-oriented, evangelical Mennonites into the Old Colony community, with an increasing number of conversions to the more modern and individualized faith.[123] The temptation to join more evangelical churches was increasing rapidly. After all, the evangelicals made fewer demands on dress, jewellery, education, and vocation (although more on tobacco use and alcohol consumption), and emphasized personal joyfulness through open talk of "assurance of salvation" and musically accompanied, hearty singings. All this threatened the old communitarian approach to faith.

The migrants also objected in general to life in Canada. They were worried about transformative changes in technology that affected religious morals in this northern community. This worry focused on the car and the pickup truck, which were taking young people from subsistence farming in one of two directions: to a life of wage labour in town for the poor, or to a life of commercialized or capitalistic agriculture for the landed.[124] Moreover, the "mobile privacy" of the car turned a tacitly accepted time of youthful "sowing wild oats" into an uncontrolled time of "sexual experimentation" with common "premarital intercourse," not uncommon "pregnancy before marriage," and increasing marriage to non-Mennonites.[125] And they were worried about the Canadian political scene under the prime ministership of Pierre Elliot Trudeau, who had begun his legacy of liberalizing Canadian society. Amidst talk of bilingualism, sexual freedom, socialism, and the metric system were rumours of a coming evil, internationalized world seemingly prophesied in the biblical book of Revelation. This fear was based specifically on a 1969 message originating with a rabidly anticommunist, US lieutenant general, Pablo Del Valle, and disseminated by the Old Colonists' neighbouring Holdeman Mennonites' newspaper, the *Messenger of Truth*. The apocalyptic idea was that a World Tribunal would soon replace the United Nations and thus subvert Canadian sovereignty with a godless world government. Its first step would introduce a "new currency" available only to those who would "renege upon commitment to their ... [religious] beliefs."[126] The only way to avoid ruin under this "world government" was to seek new places of isolation in the far reaches of the earth.

Freedom for the Alberta Old Colonists lay in Bolivia. Indeed, it promised to be not only a place of persistence, but a return to former times. One immigrant put it this way: "Going to Bolivia will let us have the opportunity of ridding the community of worldly things. In Bolivia we will use horses and wagons again as it was in the early days here. We can have our own ... schools again and our children will have a chance to grow up in our way, speaking Low German instead of English."[127] There were other hopes. In the event of the introduction of a World Tribunal and "its 'new money' ... Bolivia, being a warm country, would be more suitable for ... a subsistence economy."[128] In the South, cash could be replaced by barter, and the market could be made irrelevant through simple living and food self-sufficiency. Then, too, if land could be found "which was isolated ... the young people [would] ... not have ready access to ... towns or cities."[129] Bolivia appeared to have all the answers.

The migrants of 1969 found this specific requirement near a new settlement established by a vanguard of Alberta Old Colony Mennonites in 1967. The earlier group had attempted settlement at an isolated spot at San Ignacio, 250 kilometres northeast of Santa Cruz. Finding it unsuitable for farming, they had relocated after a year to Santa Rosa, 160 kilometres northwest of Santa Cruz, an area of tropical rainforest. It was here, just next to this group at Santa Rosa, that the 1969 group of 200 residents settled.

They had, indeed, selected a supremely isolated spot. To visit them in 1970, Van Dyck had to travel "sixty miles of very narrow, paved highway ... from Santa Cruz to Buena Vista," then on a "one-lane dirt road ... passable only during dry weather," fifty-six kilometres to the indigenous village of Santa Rosa, ending in a "wagon trail and foot path ... to the Old Colony villages."[130] Here, in the wilderness, time was turned back. Traditional village patterns transplanted from Russia to Canada in the 1870s were resumed on lots measuring 125 metres by 1000 metres (12.5 hectares per farm). At the centre of the farm village were two lots – one across the road from the other – designated for the church and for the school, reminding all of the centrality of faith in the community. Reinforcing the isolation, and signalling a recommitted traditionalism, "one of the first rules laid down by the *Bruderschaft* [Brotherhood]" was that tractors, allowed here with rubber tires, were "only to be used for business, not for visiting or personal transportation and no cars or trucks are to enter the community."[131] Bolivia had secured the Mennonites' hope for traditionalism.

The immigrant community, however, proved not to be a place of tranquility. For many in the group, Bolivia turned out to be nothing but a ruse that covered up the very evils the community opposed. To their minds, the very move was filled with hypocrisy. Immigration leaders may have boasted that a Bolivian coup of 1970 was of no concern to them; after all, "most of the South American countries are run by military governments." Nevertheless, rumours suggested that they had "secretly deposited a substantial amount of cash in bank accounts in High Level (Alberta) so that in case of an emergency, they could pay for their fare back to Canada."[132] Migrants may have hoped for increased "mutual love," but the migration itself increased divisions, as some migrants felt "ridiculed" by those who "remained in Alberta," being told even before they left that they were "outside of God's will."[133] Division seemed rampant: between the latecomers from Fort Vermillion and the original San Ignacio settlers; between the Alberta Mennonites at San Ignacio and the even more conservative Mexico Old Colonists at Riva Palacios; between the Mennonites and their native Bolivian neighbours who claimed "that most Old Colonists considered themselves better than the native population"; and between the generations, with parents complaining that "it was impossible to keep the children at home in the new village" and that unregulated liquor trade led to "pronounced abuse of alcohol by young people" sometimes no older than age ten.[134]

The most hurtful division became evident in the conflict between the religious leaders and those who openly began to question the Bolivia option. Making matters worse, village life in Bolivia had increased the power of the leaders, who could now more easily excommunicate the errant and more effectively invoke communal shunning. In Bolivia, the dreaded "*Donnadach* [the traditional Thursday disciplinary church meeting of the ministerial] again became a weekly occurrence and, as a result, deviance in the congregation was regularly confronted by religious authorities."[135] Some members began complaining that the very layout of the farm village compromised privacy, and many longed for their "own quarter section of land" where they would not be watched by neighbours.[136] Ironically, the migrants had come to Bolivia to rediscover "traditional community," but, having done so, many found it repressive.[137] Some went so far as to complain that "you can ... stab your neighbour in the back ... and nobody will chastise you. But break one of their little rules and you've had it."[138] The same folks even complained of increasing class division between the wealthy and the poor, with a concentration of wealth in the hands of "the most influential minister and a few members of his family."[139] Perhaps the elders had denounced wealth accumulation in Alberta, but most adult males seemed engaged in a fierce competition for wealth. As Van Dyck concluded, in Bolivia, more so than in Alberta, religious leadership was coupled with wealth, and this nexus marked "the ultimate course of prestige for the adult Old Colony man."[140] The simple life in Bolivia was proving to be elusive.

In this context, all things Canadian suddenly became romanticized. When Van Dyck arrived in February 1970, he noted that many settlers "asked for something from Canada – even a piece of 'English' newspaper."[141] They seemed to long for Canadian individualism. One immigrant revealed a treasured old copy of the Canadian farm newspaper, the *Western Producer*, and, more specifically, a sermon in it by a British-Canadian minister arguing that "each person has his own mind and soul, and lives his life according to his own inner light. ... Every person is a child of God."[142] This Protestant understanding stood in stark contrast to the Old Colony worldview.

When plans to return to Canada ensued shortly after Van Dyck's arrival, religious leaders rigorously opposed them. The migrants were told that a return to Canada would lead to "increased worldliness" and, consequently, a contravention of the "'true tradition of the fathers'."[143] The leaders even "invoked shunning against the group" planning to return, and when this sanction failed, they "decreed stringent economic sanctions."[144] The leaders added other warnings: "Canada has been taken over by hippies; there is rising inflation in Canada; Canada ... is now a military dictatorship."[145] And then, in sermons, the religious leaders pleaded with the returnees: "The Old Colony were God's chosen people ... [and] as the chosen ones of God, the Old Colony were obligated to be totally separated from the rest of the world" and be like "Christ's disciples," simple people "with little or no education."[146] For the naysayers, the message fell on deaf ears.

By April 1970, some eighty-five persons had returned to Canada. They arrived back home as a defeated people, for in "deciding to return to Canada, all individuals belonging to the pro-Canadian faction fully realized that such a return constituted an admission that they had been wrong."[147] For the return migrants, Bolivia had proved to be the very opposite to a place of "persistence." The failed experiment, in fact, dislodged some returnees from old ways entirely; some embraced a middle-class Canadian world upon arrival, at once accepting electricity, telephones, and even old-age pensions from government.[148] Van Dyck, of course, did not become close to those who stayed in Bolivia. But, in his position as confidant of the malcontented progressives, he cast his study in a particular way. His subjects were as transcultural in orientation as were Lanning's; it was just that the phenomenon had starkly different implications for the progressives who returned to Canada from the implications it had for the traditionalists who remained in Bolivia. For the returnees, life outside the nation spelled failure and bitterness; for the persisters, such a life held the promise that no one nation could impose its programs and policies on its inhabitants.

Conclusion

The traditionalist Mennonites who settled in British Honduras and Bolivia in the 1950s and 1960s lived in a transnational world. They negotiated with governments for specific privileges to stand outside national cultures, ironically, a request that corresponded to the governments' aim for economic development and integration into global capitalism. And they thought of themselves as sojourners, and presented their story in these terms to both national journalists and international scholars. By speaking to these outsiders, the Mennonites reinforced their foreignness, their peculiar mission in Central and South America, and their participation in the economic transformation of the South.

Both the journalists and visiting scholars variously exhibited exuberance for, and opposition to, the newcomers, and reported on the full range of the Mennonites' social problems, state of health, and internecine jealousies. The conversations the Mennonite newcomers had in English with the visiting young North American academics in particular produced specific, recorded, detailed information about their colonies. Unlike several earlier North American social scientific studies of Paraguay and Mexico Mennonites – by US Mennonite scholars Winfield Fretz, Calvin Redekop, and Harold S. Bender, in particular – these outsider works bore a patently non-Mennonite perspective, and most were non-German-speaking doctoral and master's students. Their reports thus were characterized by a particular dialectic, one placing worldly-wise academics in conversation with typically quiescent sectarians. The academics introduced the Mennonite newcomers in British Honduras and Bolivia to an international academic world, but, in these works, the self-aware Mennonites presented themselves in their own ways, thus articulating a specific version of their cultural identity. Part of this story was always personal, as many of the settlers came to trust the English-speaking academics as acquaintances, and even as friends. The intruders meant no harm, of course, but they came as experts and authorities, and, as such, they narrativized the migrations, they judged the settlement efforts and the economic achievements, and they critiqued the newcomers' attempts to stop the modern world. Usually, they offered explanations of the Mennonites' social behaviour, their religious impulse, way of life, gender relations, or intra-group conflict.

Both the journalists and the academics could be overtly negative, criticizing a lack of economic progress, the refusal to modernize, or even power relations within the colonies. They could, as well, be laudatory, sometimes praising those colonies that did commercialize or sometimes the most traditionalist for keeping to old ideals and cohesive social interaction. The young scholars seemed especially interested in showing how these exclusive Mennonites fit the national agendas of the respective countries in which they settled and the ways in which they related to the international world – Mexico, Canada, the United States – including the goals of the United Nations. In the process, they ironically reinforced the image of a people beyond any one nation. It was an image the traditionalist Mennonites were eager to embrace.

6 Crystallizing Memory: The "Return" of the Kanadier, 1951–1979

During the very time that many Mennonites within Latin America were moving ever farther southward, pursuing old ways in British Honduras and Bolivia, thousands of others headed in the opposite direction, back to the old homeland of Canada. The vast majority of these migrants northward were from Mexico, given its proximity to Canada, although hundreds also came from Paraguay's Menno, Bergthal, and Sommerfeld colonies.

No matter their origin, these migrations to Canada differed from the church-ordered group migration southward and within the South. The move northward was a haphazard, economically driven and individually ordered, chain migration. Especially for the Mexico Mennonites, the migration north was a relatively simple affair. It usually entailed a four-day road trip by truck or car, through the American Midwest, an entry into Canada made easy with a readily accessible Canadian passport, and a simple slide into low-paying, non-skilled farm or factory jobs. Shelter was most often a rented house and, however dilapidated, it often marked the beginning of a slow move upward to ownership of a house and roomy yard in a small town. Social problems, the inevitable bane of migrants everywhere, were addressed by a liberalizing post-war Canadian welfare state and by rigorous aid programs run by such organizations as the MCC Canada and, for a time, its Kanadier Concerns Committee.

This migration northward, however, was more difficult than the migration southward in another respect, for it entailed a sharp break with the very goals of the first emigrants from Canada in the 1920s. It marked an abandonment of the dreams of the migrants' parents and grandparents. Mid-century, heady Canada marked a new frontier, not one of forest or prairie sod, but of wage labour, religious pluralism,

English schools, and lives in featureless bungalows well removed from the homes of other migrants; life here was strange and often socially alienating. The move, after all, spelled a sharp separation from family networks and close-knit church life in the South, sometimes made frighteningly clear when the church reacted to the relocation with excommunication and subsequent shunning. Often, the migration was driven by stark poverty, and constituted a desperate dash northward to Canada, away from socially debilitating landlessness in the Mexico and Paraguay colonies and those countries' fragile economies.

Because most of the migrants had but a single economic strategy – manual wage labour by both parents and all adolescent and adult children – their best opportunity often was not in the old, somewhat familiar, western homelands of Manitoba and Saskatchewan. Certainly many did return, the Mexico migrants especially to the region around Winkler, Manitoba, and the Paraguay Mennonites to Steinbach, Manitoba. But the majority chose strange central Canada, specifically Ontario, to work in its numerous small factories and on its intensive vegetable and tobacco farms. True, Ontario was already home to tens of thousands of Mennonites, but they were the unrelated Swiss and Russländer Mennonites, all well established and conversant in English. Thus, although the long-settled Mennonites in Canada provided aid, they did not constitute a cultural beachhead for the wave of Low German-speaking, elementary school-educated, Mexico Mennonite newcomers in Ontario. In fact, the newcomers from Mexico were often dubbed the "Kanadier," literally, the "Canadians," the poor descendants of the 1870s migrants from Russia to Manitoba. In Ontario, the Kanadier seemed even more noticeable than they would have been in western Canada. Perhaps the Kanadier were a people still possessing Canadian passports, but in Latin America they had missed out on two generations of progress, upward mobility, and cultural "refinement." They knew their place at the bottom of a Mennonite vertical mosaic.

The story of the Kanadier migrants from Mexico in Ontario can be told using a variety of sources, including the *Steinbach Post*, which, until 1967, featured myriad letters not only from Latin America, but also from Ontario. As did immigration letters elsewhere, they reported on good jobs and housing in Canada. Crucially, they laid out the most efficient road to central Canada: north, following the well-worn road that Mennonite visitors to Manitoba and Saskatchewan had taken since the 1920s, highway #54 from El Paso to Wichita, but then veering off to the northeast, on strange interstate highways, through Kansas City, gigantic Chicago, and dynamic Detroit, into the temperate lakeside country of rural southern Ontario. Many other stories appeared in the English-language rural newspapers, such as Manitoba's *Altona Echo* and the *Carillon News*, which, as noted in chapter 4, often cast the returnees as a beleaguered and defeated people requiring aid from North American agencies such as the MCC.[1]

The newspaper, however, is only one of several sources of information on this migration. Another, given the recent nature of the migration north, is oral history. And because the language of heart and hearth for the Mennonites from Mexico was still the dialect of Low German, "Plautdietsch," the stories they remembered required no formal filtering into the written medium of High German or English. Indeed, Low German, or "Dietsch," as the immigrants simply called it, had expressed an ethnic Mennonitism in nineteenth-century Russia and western Canada, and still did so in late twentieth-century Mexico.[2] It was the medium in which the migrants from Mexico expressed the most heartfelt fears, hopes, and dreams, making oral conversation in Low German a fundamentally important text for them.

This chapter examines the interviews with fourteen men and women conducted mostly in Low German during the summer of 1979.[3] The focus of this oral history project was on the Mennonites from Mexico, the Kanadier, but it was initiated by Conrad Grebel College, a Mennonite liberal arts college located on the campus of the University of Waterloo in Ontario.[4] Funded by the Multicultural Society of Ontario, the oral history project was carried out by Ronald Sawatsky, a young Canadian graduate student in religious history. Because Sawatsky was able to converse in Low German, his interviews moved beyond the rudimentary topics of weather, kinship lines, and jobs, even past issues of gender, ethnicity, and politics, to the basic story of immigration, with a special focus on religion. Sawatsky was especially interested in the beginnings of the Old Colony and Sommerfeld immigrant churches in southern Ontario. If one of the weaknesses of the project was a list of four or so prescribed questions, it was also its strength, for it seemed to move to the core of the immigrants' worlds and produced stories of passion, betrayal, and hope.

The interview replicated the well-known cultural moment of the Sunday afternoon conversation in the living or dining room. Most of the interviews occurred within the immigrant's home, and thus the recordings captured the sounds of doors opening and closing, of children laughing and crying, of parents placating them, and of telephones ringing. The informants included the elderly who had been born in Canada before the migration to Mexico in 1922 and the more youthful, those born in Mexico in the 1940s. Sawatsky invited the interviewees to recount the reasons for the migration north in the 1950s and 1960s, the beginnings of the Low German Mennonite community in Ontario, and the challenge of rebuilding a religious community without sanctioned religious leadership. Mostly, he asked for the articulation of individual and corporate memory, the underlying cultural artefact of group identity.

Sawatsky's questioning technique echoes the thoughts of Arjun Appadurai and Carol Breckenridge, who write, "Diasporas always leave a trail of collective memory about another place and time, and create new maps of desire and attachment."[5] The interviewees readily recalled Mexico, using its images to anchor a trajectory that naturally took them back to Canada. Their collective memory of a "return" to Canada often included not just one move, but several, most often failed attempts to reintegrate into Mexico, overlaid with a "desire" for Canada.

More specifically, their memory making corresponds to Jan Assmann's theories of "communicative" (everyday) and "cultural" (pomp and ceremony) memory, with the Mennonites from Mexico seemingly engaging in more of the former and not the latter. Indeed, unlike the producers of "cultural" memory, the Low German migrants had not sought the interviews, not lobbied for them, and usually had no intention of publicly celebrating their own return. Moreover, it was a memory in the making in which the migrants "conceive[d] a unity and peculiarity through a common image of their past."[6] Sawatsky's work revealed that the immigrants to Ontario were in the process of creating a "collective memory," building a common narrative to help negotiate "times of uncertainty."[7] These memories focused on migration from and into Canada, on travels within the three North American nations, on negotiating the cultural labyrinth of sending and receiving societies in complex ways, and on religion, through which they struggled to provide shape and meaning to these disparate pathways. The memories gave expression to an emerging identity: the Low German-speaking migrant from Mexico in southern Ontario.

Childhood Memory

The more elderly of the migrants who returned north in the 1950s had been away long enough to feel only distantly Canadian. Still, each had vivid childhood memories of Canada and of their parents' stories about

Canada. Almost always, these memories were family-centred. Heinrich and Maria Voth, born in 1913 near Swift Current (Saskatchewan) and in 1910 near Didsbury (Alberta), respectively, both recalled family lore of late nineteenth-century life in "Russia," although without knowledge of just where in the Russian Empire their ancestors had lived.[8] Both also recalled childhood moves to and from Alberta: Heinrich remembered his father's employment with the "Peter Burns Beef Company" and his family's "own small ranch ... ranching beef." Maria, who was thirteen when her young, widowed mother moved to Mexico in 1923, had many memories, including living near Didsbury, a location her parents rejected on account of its English-language school.[9] Anna and Cornelius Peters also recalled childhood moves.[10] Anna, born in 1915 and age seven when her parents relocated to Mexico in 1922, "remembered well" accompanying her father when he hauled wheat from their farm to nearby Gretna, Manitoba. Cornelius, born in 1913 near Hague in central Saskatchewan, and a young boy when his parents migrated in 1922, recalled his family's repeated moves, required because his father taught school: a few years in Hague, then in Reinland and Neuhorst in Manitoba, then back again to Saskatchewan.

Other old-timers recalled bitter moments of loss and separation. Anna and Heinrich Banman were both born in 1912 near Swift Current, Saskatchewan.[11] Anna was fifteen when her family joined the migration in 1927. She had a highly developed sense of "home," and a closely knit nuclear family as well as an extensive network of relatives:

> When I remember "home" it's always [southwestern] Saskatchewan. ... We lived on a farm. Had four neighbors; my father's sister and her family, the Henry Friesens, lived nearby. And my father's brother's family, the Abram Klassens and Peter Klassens, and then there were my parents, John Klassens. ... All my siblings were born there. ... With me it's ten [children].

Anna Banman's family had not "actually planned to move" to Mexico, but then, one day, they realized that "the preachers and everyone had left. ... [and] all [my parents'] brothers and sisters had moved to Mexico. ... [Suddenly] the *Dietsche* living around us were gone." And even though Anna's relatives remained in the "Old West" north of Saskatoon, their close Swift Current acquaintances moved, and "that's why [we] ... did too." Heinrich's memory of loss in Mexico was especially vivid: "I remember my mother dying when I was six years old; my father was a widower for a while and then ... we [a family of ten] had a stepmother." When Heinrich was fourteen, his stepmother died and his father married a third time, to a Mrs. Krahn, who had her own ten children. Shortly thereafter, in a desperate response to poverty, his father and new stepmother left Heinrich and a number of his siblings with relatives in Mexico and returned to Canada. The family had become transnational in the wake of its disintegration.[12]

Given the dislocation of family and friends, it is not surprising, perhaps, that a common childhood memory of the 1920s migration was of animals. Indeed, the animals – dogs, horses, and cows – were prominent in almost all these childhood memories. Peter Giesbrecht, born in 1917 near Gretna, Manitoba, and age six when his family moved in 1923, had a single memory of Canada: how "my uncles rode on a sleigh pulled by dogs in winter."[13] His memory of the 1923 train trip through the American Midwest also involved animals: "I and my father went into the livestock cars and attended to the animals. [We] had our dogs along" and they "tried to jump from the train; some ran back" to Manitoba; in fact, "I heard that they made it back to Manitoba."[14] Anna Peters had a single child-centred memory when she was seven of the "the last evening in Manitoba when we were waiting for the train," that being that "I was very thirsty; I'll never forget that." But her memory broadened for the trip itself to include how she "with my father ... tended to the animals ... [in] the livestock car."[15] Heinrich Voth's most vivid memory at age nine of arriving in Mexico consisted of several dynamic animal stories; the first was of "one family's horses ... big horses for those days," bolting when they were unloaded from the train, breaking "the halters and the rope" and galloping "east ... [so] glad to get off that train."[16] Then there were the dogs: arriving on the open fields of the Bastillos Valley was "difficult for my parents" but for "my cousin and me, once we were off the train, we both had a dog ... and we played with them, walking barefoot on that dry Mexican grass. Oi-yoi-yoi."[17] For the child of a large family, the farm animal was the constant in a world in flux.

Each of the old-timers also recalled hearing about the reasons for the move; often, they were the memories conveyed by their parents or stories from the street. Cornelius Peters remembered that when he was eight, "they were saying that we would have to go to school under the flag. ... I was still quite young then [but] I picked up that our beliefs were being taken away." Other memories seemed filtered by what parents told them later. Heinrich Voth knew that the move was a response to "district schools [that] were coming in and [my parents] didn't want that; they wanted to keep the German. ... They wanted to remain unattached. ... They were expected to serve in the military, they didn't want that, they wanted to be the 'quiet in the land.'" In similar vein, Anna Peters recounted her own parents' recollections: how the "church, the preachers ... were committed to running their own schools, in our own language. That's why they believed we needed to move ... to Mexico." Anna Banman's memory was infused with mixed feelings: she had been "brought up to believe that attending English school was entirely contradictory to what we believed. Even after everyone had left [for Mexico] we couldn't attend the English school and by that time we really wanted to."

The remembered world of the child migrant reveals the unique perspective of the powerless in the community: the migration involved friends, animals, and motion. But even then, they understood snippets of the broader reason for the move, an intentionally religious migration, speaking to the very culture of their parents' worlds among the nations.

Leaving Mexico

Recollections of the return migration to Canada, thirty to forty years later, were cast in very different language. Now it was an escape, not from a hostile government, but from a variety of social conditions: abject poverty, conservative religiousness, physical violence, or simply a seemingly alien culture.

Poverty was at the root of the return migration for many. The thirty-year interval between the 1922 arrival in Mexico and the exodus of the 1950s marked rising wealth for some, but unrelenting poverty for most. Anna and Cornelius Peters recalled how, after their wedding in the 1930s, they had "a very modest beginning." With a small 700-peso inheritance from Anna's family, they began by renting "a small patch of land" and continued by earning "an extremely low" salary of a peso a day, "working together cutting corn." John Banman, born in 1939, noted that "as far as I can remember back ... my parents [were] poor. ... Some years were very poor, other years they were not, not quite so poor." John's father, Heinrich, summed it up in ironically fatalistic language: there was a "large gap between the rich and the poor; the poor were used to being poor and the rich were used to being rich. The poor didn't know what the life of the rich entailed and the rich didn't know what life was like for the poor. It worked well!" For those with some means of travel, migration to Canada spelled relief. Abe Loewen, born in 1938, recalled that in Mexico, "my parents were always poor ... [but] Canada was a rich land, so we heard. My father had always wanted to return to Canada."

True, the 1940s had marked economic improvement in Mexico. Peter Giesbrecht, for example, recalled that in about 1946, he and his family moved to a new colony, Nord Colony or Ojo de la Yegua, where "the church bought some land ... and so I was able to buy a piece." Heinrich Voth remembered his early years at Santa Clara, where "we were poor, poor, poor," and "the poor and the laborers simply couldn't make it." But these years were followed by better times: in 1935, he bought a small piece of land, and then, in the late 1940s, receiving "help from the boys," he farmed land rented from Mexicans in La Dama, some distance from the colony. Similarly, Corny Friesen recalled that "the Depression years," when "we ate a lot of corn and tortillas," were followed by the early 1940s, when "my father did very well" with "very good harvests," meaning "we bought new equipment, all of it, [including] new tractors."

A terrible drought in the early 1950s, however, reversed fortunes for many. Anna and Heinrich Banman, for example, returned to Canada in 1952 for a simple economic reason – "there was a crop failure one year" – so the Banmans hung "onto the livestock for another year," and then the banks "convinced me to borrow money" for yet another year. ... [Then] the third year we also had crop failure, but by now I had a big debt and the cattle sold for a very low price." The family was destitute.

Canada spelled promise for other reasons. Those forced to seek a livelihood outside the comfortable social boundaries of the Mennonite colony feared social integration with their Mexican neighbours. Peter Giesbrecht, who made a relatively good living farming rented land some ninety kilometres from the main Mennonite colonies, headed to Canada in 1955 because "as the children were getting older we didn't want to be living among Mexicans, didn't want our children to get accustomed to Mexican mores; they were growing older ... so we sold [everything] and moved to Manitoba." Corny Friesen, who had done well with lumber and rented land, returned to Canada in 1956 because of violence, referring vaguely to an event "with the Mexicans" that "terrorized us." After six months of being fearful, "my wife and kids thought it might be a good idea to leave because ... they didn't want to experience something like that again." Canada was seen as the land of safety.

Others pointed to the conservative Old Colony Mennonite church leadership in Mexico. Anna Peters recalled that when they moved to Canada in 1954, "the biggest reason was the church." Cornelius "couldn't get along with" the Old Colony leaders; "he didn't care for how things were developing in the church." And when the couple "started attending the [small] Holdeman [Mennonite] church quite a bit," attracted by their more progressive "beautiful singing" and evangelically oriented offers of friendship, the Old Colony leadership became openly resistant to the couple. Then, when Cornelius, who to that point had travelled with "only horse and buggy," purchased a motorcycle, he was excommunicated and put under the ban. The Peters family left for Canada and then, when, after "two summers and a winter," they returned south "with a truck with all our belongings," Cornelius was banned a second time: "We had decided we wouldn't use the truck [in Mexico], we'd just use it to bring our stuff there. But that wasn't allowed. ... They excommunicated him right away. ... [and] people looked at us askance ['from the side on'] because we had been to Canada. We stayed [in Mexico for only] seven months."

A similar account of trouble with religious leaders came from Nettie (Klassen) Banman, who recalled her parents' arrival in Canada in 1951: "My Dad was sick and tired of farming, first of all, and ... he didn't like the ... Old Colony Mennonites because of all the do's and don'ts." And, although in Canada, "he didn't make headways in the financial area. ... he really enjoyed being free."

The narrative of the exodus from Mexico was that of leaving a land of repression. For some, the migration began to address thirty years of economic hardship; for others, it marked a rejection of conservative cultural values. For the migrants north, Canada was a Canaan that spelled relief from both a haunting poverty and a closed community.

Border Crossings

A third section in this oral migration narrative was the trip back to the old homeland. The immigrants who, in 1979, recalled the move spoke of an excitement that swept through the Mexican villages in the early 1950s. For many, the idea of a return to Canada seemed a matter of birthright, even though they had rejected Canada in the 1920s. In fact, the border crossing presented strikingly little concern.

The only border Anna Peters recalled having crossed in 1954 was the Mexico–United States border. Her travelling party of two young families, each with many children, on the back of a large, tarp-covered truck stopped abruptly for several days in the "outskirts of Juárez." Here, the women and children "waited under the trees [as the] men went into the city, to ... Immigration [offices], to sort it out." Although they had their passports and exit visas in order, "the other families didn't and we had to wait until everything was looked after." Anna Banman also recalled crossing the Mexico–US border in her family's trip north in 1965; more precisely, she recounted the feeling of fear for her family's legal status when, for five months, they sojourned illegally in California to work the fruit harvest to finance their trip. Anna's brother had found work – for husband Heinrich and their four grown sons – with "the English," English-speaking Americans, who "we knew ... were eager to get workers from Mexico" and happy to do "it under the table." The problem was clear, for although the border control "let things be" if there were no complaints, periodic clampdowns occurred:

> [One day] we received a letter ... saying that everyone had to leave. ... I was ... firmly convinced that we would be sent out, they knew exactly where we were. ... Henry said we needn't have left ... but I ... said we had to leave, which we did. It wasn't right that we left without giving notice [to the employers] but if we had we wouldn't have been able to leave. [Later] we got the letter from Mexico – they had deported everyone.

The US–Mexico border zone seemed fraught with danger and uncertainty.

In contrast, the Canadian border was but a small inconvenience. Abe Loewen recalled that, in 1951, his parents felt the right of citizenship "as soon as we entered Canada." He emphasized the idea that "my parents were coming home; my parents were born in Canada." He contrasted his family's experience with a later one in the 1970s, when "younger people who were born in Mexico ... want[ed] to return to Canada" on their own, without their parents' supporting documents, or, even more problematically, those "many who have Mexican-born parents and are themselves born in Mexico." As Loewen recalled it, "Our only problem was that we couldn't speak English," which itself wasn't insurmountable as "our driver could speak English; he was 'Kjleen Jemeensch,'" the Low German phrase for a member of the Kleine Gemeinde. As such, he had migrated south only three years earlier, in 1948, and hence "was well acquainted with driving ... through the States [and with] English. He could manage."

In fact, the only concern seemed to be with the legal status of some of the children. Corny Friesen recalled that the Canadian border presented no problem for him and his wife, as "we were both coming home." Still, "we ran into some difficulty getting all the documents for our children," specifically "those who were born between 1944 and 1948." For some reason, "Mexico insisted that any children born during those years were Mexican." Anna and Heinrich Banman recalled their family's 1965 entry as having "worked very smoothly"; as Anna put it, "We had our citizenship; we were both Canadian." Their only problem was that "our children's status wasn't alright," as, in Mexico, "we registered our marriage only after several of our children were born. That caused problems on the applications of our children," because, for a time, they were "considered illegitimate." But in the end, "it wasn't a problem for coming into Canada." Heinrich Banman even took advantage of the fact that "we had never brought a car in before," meaning that "all I had to do was buy Canadian registration and it was a Canadian car."

The memory of even the migrants who had been born in Mexico attests to an abiding sense of right of entry into Canada. Aron Wall, born in 1940 and resident of La Honda Colony in Zacatecas state in the 1960s, knew the system: "I got my Canadian citizenship in [the] Chihuahua [Mennonite community] through. ... a Mr. Joseph Knelsen who was [providing that service] at that time. He went to Chihuahua [City] and got my Canadian citizenship papers"; simple enough, as Aron's parents had their "Canadian birth certificates." It was a similar story with Aron's wife: "Her parents were also born in Canada; they were actually married" in Canada, and "four of their children were born" in Canada. Thus, it was simply a matter of waiting "a while; probably six months" until her document arrived. Even the trip north was uneventful, for a social network was already in the making: "We came [by car] with an Aron Schroeder ... the son of Isaak Schroeder. ... We crossed at Detroit" with "no trouble at all." In Ontario, the Walls drove right over to "Peter Zachariases' ... at Leamington; I had gotten to know him as a young school boy."

The memories offered by the return migrants created two geographic poles: the originating country of Mexico, and the ultimate receiving society of Canada. Mexico's incipient economic hostility and continued cultural strangeness, the amorphous space of the United States in between, and Canada's native welcome were recalled in order of appearance. But the sequence and tenor of the memories crystallized a narrative of "coming home." Indeed, the part of the narrative that seemed "unnatural" was not the crossing back into Canada per se, but the specific crossing into Ontario.

The interviewees emphasized the process by which they replaced Manitoba as the "natural" point of return with that of southern Ontario, a new site for Old Colony and Sommerfelder Mennonites, a place that came to be associated with the words "more money." Peter Giesbrecht recalled that the drought years of the early 1950s generated "a lot of talk" about Manitoba: "People were beginning to come [to Canada] ... in '51, '52. Many Mennonites were moving then. People we knew, friends started going to Manitoba." But, almost at once, talk arose that "there was even more money to be made in Ontario." In a short time, Ontario fever set in. Abe Loewen echoed those words: he recalled how his parents believed "there was more money to be earned in Ontario doing manual labor." Nettie (Klassen) Banman remembered that part of the reason for Ontario fever was her uncle William Reimer's 1954 poem about it. Although he himself had never visited Ontario, "he was a great one for making up ... poems and really decorating them with words. ... It was a long poem, about two or three pages long and had. ... the nicest words about Ontario." Presumably, it, too, spoke of opportunity in Ontario, for, as Nettie recalled it, the "poem sort of helped a lot of people to come to Ontario. ... It was passed around on the colonies in Mexico." By the time Aron Wall and his wife left La Honda Colony in Zacatecas state in about 1967, it was assumed they were going to Ontario. Aron's wife "had a brother here with whom we corresponded. He told us there was money to be earned here [in Ontario]. ... No one ever talked about going to work in Manitoba or Saskatchewan."

The process by which the first Old Colony Mennonites to arrive in Ontario in 1951 rejected Manitoba and Saskatchewan was part of several of the migration narratives. Abe Loewen recalled that the Jacob Fehr family, the very first Mexico Mennonites in Ontario, sojourned in Manitoba for three years before moving to Ontario. Abe recalled how, in 1951, his parents followed suit, travelling first to Manitoba, where "my parents got to know" the Fehrs, who "sang the praises of Ontario." Thus, in the summer of 1952, after a short sojourn in Manitoba, "my father bought a ... 1931 Model A" and the family headed east to Ontario. It was a memorable trip: "The car was full, it was July, very hot. Driving was terrible. The top speed was 30 [to] 32 miles per hour. ... We drove through the U.S. We came through Chicago. ... My father knew about three words of English." Peter Giesbrecht also recalled the trip from Mexico to Ontario via Manitoba: he and his family travelled in the back of a tarped truck with another family, that of "David Klassen, my wife's brother [who] had a truck." They lived in Manitoba for "one winter and two summers," hoeing beets and looking "after cattle on a farm," but "by then people were moving again ... [saying] there was even more money to be made in Ontario."

The story of the very first direct trip from Mexico to Ontario in 1954 was also the most poignant, a remarkable Steinbeck-esque account of treachery, uprootedness, and alienation, even deceit and villainy. Anna Peters recalled that the trip occurred in the most primitive of conditions in the back of a truck owned by a Peter Fehr, the son of Jacob Fehr, who had settled near Aylmer in 1951. Anna recalled, "It was a truck with a tarp tied over top. We were more than forty people, five families, each with seven or eight children. ... The truck box was completely full, from corner to corner." The trip itself and the crossing into Canada are given short shrift: "That's how we drove through the States. ... Twelve days, I think."

Locating "home" in Ontario was the most difficult, according to Anna Peters. Having crossed the border at Detroit, Fehr took the families to a particular house in the countryside and told them they "could all live in it until we found our own places." The problem was that "when we arrived we ... found it all boarded up and locked. No one was allowed to live in it. It wasn't theirs, they had only rented it." Fehr then took the group to Avon, near Tillsonburg, to another place with "a house on the yard, lots of bush next to the road [but] ... that house too was locked up, no one could live there. We spent three days there, living behind the bush." One night when it rained heavily, the Fehr family moved into their truck; the Peters family and the three other families needed to find their own shelter, and that night, they "went into the house which was off limits. ... to make beds [on the floor, in the dark] for everyone so we could sleep. ... When it cleared up we lived outside again." After several days, the men "found a big ... brick house with a second storey. We all moved into there. Five families ... more than forty [people]. ... We set something up outside and that's where we cooked. None of us had anything."[18]

For many migrants, Ontario became a permanent home only after a period of cross-border jostling. "More money" might be made in Ontario, but the province could prove alienating in a cultural sense, compelling a return to Mexico, itself often disappointing for religious reasons. Corny Friesen recalled how, in 1956, he and his wife "had an auction, sold everything and moved" to Ontario, arriving on "December 3, 1956."[19] But it was a short stay: "We were here for two years, but didn't feel at home so we returned for the winter, but [in Mexico] I had so much trouble with the Old Colony church, the ministers, they wanted to excommunicate me immediately, put me under the ban, so my wife said, 'why should we bother with this, we have a home in Canada' ... so [in 1956] we had an auction again." Corny recalls this moment as the most difficult, for it required giving up their lease on 500 acres of rented land close to Los Jagueyes.[20] Similarly, Nettie (Klassen) Banman recalled a short-lived sojourn of only "a couple of years" after her family moved to Ontario in 1954. Nettie's father decided to return to Mexico because, in Canada, "we girls were getting too rebellious. We wanted to keep our money when we earned money and we engaged in worldly things as [Father] called it. And he decided ... we got to go back to Mexico." In Mexico, Nettie, however, outmanoeuvred her father by dating John, a boy she had met in Canada "at a party at my parents' place; [we were] great ones for having parties and dancing." In March 1960, she and John, accompanied by a chaperone, left Mexico and "came to Canada to get married." Her own parents then followed them back to Canada in 1963.[21]

Memories of economic uncertainty and religious differences in Mexico reinforced the idea among the immigrants that Canada was their homeland. If the border crossing into Canada seemed easy, the entry into strange Ontario was treacherous. But Mexico itself was remembered with ambivalence: at once the familiar homeland and the repelling land of cultural restriction.

Settling in Ontario

The oral history narrative of settling in Ontario, for the immigrants in this account, is ultimately a story of survival, even success. A hard beginning was followed by support from good people who intervened to help out, even to confront villainy and exploitation. This was followed by bumps along the way, excruciating physical work, and, finally, a modicum of upward mobility. Financial success was measured most readily by ownership of a modest house, or, better still, a rural lot with house and small farm. Failures and disappointments occurred, but the 1979 interviewees made little reference to the domestic violence or substance abuse recorded in other texts pertaining to Mexico Mennonite immigrants or in the stories told in other uprooted communities. The major disappointments related to failed farming attempts among these deeply agrarian people, who often found the prospect of long-term wage labour humiliating.

The narrative of settlement in Ontario made early reference to vital social networks for fundamentally dislocated immigrants. Indeed, the strangeness of Ontario was made manageable only through a nascent, transplanted, social network. The moment one family put down roots, another could follow. Abe Loewen recalled how, in July 1952, his family made their way to that first Mexico Mennonite family in Ontario, "the Jacob Fehrs" of Aylmer.[22] Loewen remembered that "my father had the address of Jacob Fehrs. It took us half a day to find them, but we found them eventually. Once we were here they could help us out." Within a very short time, with the Fehrs' help, members of the Loewen family found work "on a farm ... thinning out tobacco plants. The Fehrs had done it several times already. ... You could earn a lot of money doing that."[23] If the Fehrs helped out the Loewens, they in turn helped out others. Early in 1953, their in-laws, "the David Klassens" arrived, and then, in 1954, both couples gave assistance to Anna and Cornelius Peters and family.

Long-established Ontario Mennonites, no matter their cultural distance from the Kanadier, also had their place in the narrative. Anna Peters recalled how her family's destitution after long travel on the back of a tarped truck and life in boarded-up houses ended when fellow Mexico Mennonite Abram Loewen Sr. appealed to the more established and progressive Ontario Russländer Mennonites for help. He made them "aware of our situation, our living situation and that we had nothing," and soon, "a few filled-up trucks, came to that old brick house ... [with] stoves and clothing, bed frames, food. They brought it to us." The Ontarians also intervened to free the Peters family from an oppressive financial bind to the owner of the truck: "The man we came with, was [also] the foreman; he oversaw the large fields of beets, we were his labourers. ... We got paid just enough to buy bread. ... He said we were so poor that bread and jam, bread and butter was good enough for us. We weren't supposed to buy meat. He paid us two dollars per day." Anna recalled that "the Jacob Petkaus" in particular came to their aid; when "they found out ... that we had such a difficult time making ends meet they ... helped us three families move to Port Rowan and we worked there for the [established] 'Russlända' [Mennonites] for forty cents an hour. ... [We] thought things were really going well here. We kept everything we earned."[24] Unrelated Mennonites had come to their aid.

The early years of wage labour were difficult. Almost always, they marked a hard time of seasonal contracts and back-breaking labour in the fields. Cornelius Peters recalled the difficult work during that summer of 1954: "We were working on the soy bean field at that time, pulling [soybean plants]," the time just "before tobacco season and also before tomato season." He recounted that it was a little easier in the tobacco season: "Anna was leaf handler" and he "used horses to transport the tobacco from ... the field," dragging "the bolts [the final distance] to the door [of the drying sheds] with the tractor." The seasonal labour never really ended; it only changed in nature. During the winter, the couple gleaned corn: "We had bought ourselves a one ton truck. ... We crawled onto it and gleaned corn," the kernels "left over ... after the picker," which they then sold. It was a very difficult first winter: Cornelius recalled that Anna "wanted only to return to Mexico," and the couple even borrowed money to enable them to return. But they stayed in Canada that spring and the seasonal round began anew.[25]

Perhaps the most difficult aspect of settling in Ontario was the feeling of discrimination arising from their low status as Mexico-origin immigrants. Heinrich Banman recalled his feeling when he discovered that the "Canadian Mennonites look[ed] down on Mennonites from Mexico," and "when I worked in the factory ... they would say 'you Mexican' to me." For Banman, these were strongly pejorative terms: from his experience, most Canadians considered Mexicans to be "thieves" and people who "weren't trustworthy." It was an important moment for Banman when "the English" came to know the "'Dietsche' from Mexico" and discovered that they "were honest people."[26]

Wage labour had its pitfalls, but when an entire family's wages were pooled, a household could survive. Indeed, one of the first tasks of the newcomers from Mexico was to procure jobs for the children as well as for the parents. Peter Giesbrecht recalled that, in 1955, the youngest "children started school right way," but "not the oldest two," as "they could work on the same farm I was." As Peter saw it, "Sure, wages were low then, but together [the boys made] ... sixty-five cents an hour. ... My daughter could start work right away [too] and the second winter the next son would start. Our sons have all worked in the tobacco processing plant."[27] Corny and Katherine Friesen and their twelve children were among the first families from Mexico in the Leamington area; when they arrived in 1956, they made wages a primary concern. Corny was grateful for his first farm job with the acculturated Mennonite Brethren people, as they still "all spoke German." But he also realized that "they weren't paying enough [at] ... sixty cents an hour," and so he went to work for "the 'English' [who] recruited me by offering a dollar [an hour] so I worked there." But even then, the household relied on wages made by "my wife and kids [who] picked tomatoes."[28]

No matter how meagre a household income, it was enough to procure at least rudimentary shelter, seen in hindsight as the first step towards property ownership. Abe Loewen recalled that, in the very first years, "we rented," but already in 1953, when "we moved to St. Catharines ... my parents bought a house right away. ... They are now [in 1979] living in their third house here. ... Never a new house, but they've always owned modest, older houses here."[29] Peter Giesbrecht recalled "looking for a house to rent" within days of arriving in Ontario in 1955, then "renting for four years," until "I bought a place and we lived there for four years. Sold that and bought another. We lived there for four, five years and then we bought this house ... in '69."[30]

For many of the traditionally agrarian Mennonites, an urgent goal was not only to obtain property but to procure a small farm or at least a rural lot that allowed for some measure of replicated self-sufficiency. Cornelius Peters outlined his enviable story: during their first winter in 1954, they "lived on a bit of a farm" looking "after the livestock and got milk in exchange; had chickens as well." Then, during the first summer, they rented a house in Vienna, close to the canneries at Aylmer: "Just before winter [that year] ... we bought [our first] property by Copenhagen, five acres of land, with a building" that allowed them to keep "a few cows and pigs."[31]

Farming of any kind, however, was virtually impossible for the vast majority of the Mexico Mennonites. Even Corny Friesen, who had managed financially in Mexico and who in 1963 "bought a farm in Aylmer, not ... expensive," could not succeed. He calculated that "I wouldn't be able to live long enough to make a go out of it. The interest rates were so high. ... [We raised] corn, oats. I also had forty cows." His strategy was simple enough: "Sold the farm and bought a house and then went into construction," a world in which "when we work, we work!" and "don't have any time to talk."[32] Ultimately, their status as newcomers lay in their work ethic and small properties, not – as in the worlds of their parents – in farms owned.

Re-establishing the Church

Each one of the fourteen interviewees highlighted the importance of religion in mapping the new life in Ontario. The move north often entailed a sharp break with the Old Colony or Sommerfelder Mennonite churches in Mexico. The church leadership there disapproved strongly of a return to the land the Mennonites had left in the 1920s, and consequent excommunications were not uncommon. Even though most of the newcomers could not conceive of community life without a church at its centre, religious leaders were not among the first immigrants in Ontario. This leadership vacuum allowed several, sharply competing, narratives to form. An evangelically oriented account derided the communitarian Old Colony church as irrelevant in Canada and suggested that only a more personalized evangelical faith mattered. The other, more traditionalist, account proposed that the communitarian church of the Old Colonists, perhaps reformed from the strict Mexico ways, could very well be adapted to Canada. It seemed as if the common nature of the migration and settlement narrative evaporated when it came to religion; memories of religion recalled bitter conflict and produced two complex and competing church identities.[33] Perhaps, as Steven Vertovec has observed for immigrants generally, the Mexico Mennonites in Ontario shared a "trail of collective memory about another place," but the "new maps of desire and attachment" in the new land diverged significantly.[34]

The first families recalled attending the "strange" churches of the Canadian Mennonites, but without spiritual or social satisfaction. Abe Loewen remembered that, in 1953, when his family lived for a time in Elmira, Ontario, his parents "attended a Pennsylvania Dutch church" belonging to a Mennonite "group that drives ... black cars [with] black bumpers," the Weaverland Mennonites. The problem here was simple: "My parents didn't feel at home there." Then, when his family moved to St. Catharines to work in the orchards of the Niagara Peninsula, they "attended a [progressive] General Conference church," a place where Abe "attended Sunday school ... [and] became a little bit more familiar with the gospel." Again, his parents "weren't able to feel comfortable there."[35] Anna Peters also recalled an early association with existing Canadian churches, with the "'Russlända' ... Mennonites in Port Rowan ... [who] came to our area and held a service under the trees" with "a separate session for the children." The Peters family attended this church for three years. Anna especially recalled the pastor, a

"Mr. [Jacob] Braun; we were really impressed with him. ... He often came to our place ... and entertained the children with all kinds of things. ... It was very foreign for us to see a minister interact with children like that." But again, there were problems. At some point, Braun and his companions offended the immigrants, especially "three women, their husbands as well," by saying that "God kept his eye ... not on what was outside, but what was inside us" and that "God wasn't concerned about ... what kind of clothes we wear." It contradicted what "we were accustomed to from Mexico."[36]

The strangeness of these churches increased early support for a reconstituted Old Colony church in Ontario, a dream that came true in 1958. Anna Peters recalled in detail how "we [Old Colonists] agreed amongst ourselves that we needed a church." Perhaps most of her immediate migrating "group had had enough of the Old Colony," but "there were those who definitely wanted to stay Old Colony." Knowing that the traditionalist leadership in Mexico had opposed the migration northward and would not assist them, the group wrote "to the Old Colony church in Manitoba to find out whether or not something could be organized here." Peters recalled that, in 1958, when Rev. Jakob Neudorf of Manitoba came "this way to buy a car in Toronto," he took the time to "stop in here to visit with ... this group."

Peters remembered the visit as nothing short of the miraculous. She recalled how "we met in the evening at Jakob Harders'," he being a man with physical disabilities who lived in a tiny two-room dwelling:

> [It was] completely full, all Mennonites from Mexico ... [Neudorf] preached there; it was a sermon ... that really moved us. Big William Fehr was there, David Klassen as well; [for a long time] they didn't get along at all! But [David] said, that evening it hadn't even crossed his mind that ... [William] was his enemy. The sermon had been that powerful, for everyone. We also sang "Altkolonier Wiesen" [the slow, chant-like melodies], just like in Mexico. ... We also sang "Sole Wiesen" [faster melodies] ... hearty singing.[37]

Events unfolded rapidly. Neudorf "reported back to the 'Ältester' in Manitoba" and he sent Rev. Jakob J. Froese "here to start the church," with a "spring service ['Farjoasche Koakj']," followed by a baptism for the youth (one in which Anna and Cornelius Peters's eldest son Ben was baptized), and then a communion service.

Quickly, a leadership structure was established. The Manitoba leaders dispatched Rev. Peter Harder, a one-time teacher in Mexico who had first been elected preacher some twenty years earlier (but for some reason had never been ordained), to become the Ontario Old Colony church's permanent minister.[38] Ministers, deacons, and song leaders were chosen in short order. Corny Friesen recalled the process by which he was chosen as a song leader: "When we arrived," the leaders informed him that they "were missing ... a song leader"; as he had been a "song leader for six years" in Mexico, for a time even "the lead song leader," he should be their "new song leader"; Friesen reluctantly agreed and the old cadence of "Langwiese" Old Colony singing was fully restored.[39] Anna Peters's recollection of the first church's architecture – that is, the old school at Port Burwell "remodeled" and "surrounded by big trees" – filled out the narrative of the reconstituted church.

The tranquil times of the first year or two soon dissipated. The fact was that the Old Colony church was bombarded from both the left and the right, from both progressive and traditionalist forces. Sawatsky's 1979 interviewees differed sharply on what happened, although most agreed that part of the problem was the influence of the Mexico Old Colony leadership. As Anna Peters put it, "a lot" of Mexico Mennonite immigrants refused to attend the reconstituted Old Colony church because they believed that, in Canada, it was not "doing things in the right way, they sing differently and ... there are [other] differences." Another problem was that, for a long time, "if an Old Colony person from Mexico comes here and then attends here and joins ... he is banned over in Mexico."[40]

Then, too, the early leaders of the Ontario Old Colony church were said to have undermined their own members by condemning life in small-town Ontario. One interviewee recalled that in about 1961, Peter Harder, the new Ältester in Ontario, supported by a conservative "group basically ... from Durango [Mexico]," decreed that every Old Colonist "should leave this area" to farm in Rainy River, in far-off northwestern Ontario.[41] Most members refused and invited Manitoba leaders back to Ontario to conduct another round of elections.[42] Other Old Colonists who shared the fear of "worldly" Ontario left for secluded East Paraguay, as "things were going too far here." In addition, there were recollections of how Leamington's Old Colony Ältester Henry Reimer "abandoned us" with a hastily conceived plan to establish an agrarian settlement in Seminole, Texas; it all happened "too quickly ... nothing was properly taken care of," and the result was "very destructive. ... It caused a real upheaval."⁴³ Old ideals of agrarian simplicity died hard.

If the interviewees agreed that these cross-border directives undermined the Old Colony church, they differed sharply on whether the old church deserved support in the first instance. Conservative Mennonites saw the old church as a place of tranquility. Church trustee (Vorsteher) Aron Wall noted the ease of raising money: they would simply "calculate what our costs are per month and then divide it among the group, among all those who are here"; everyone paid readily.⁴⁴ The broader Old Colony network by 1979 was complex enough, with different congregations in Kitchener, Aylmer, or Leamington, but, as Wall saw it, "it is all one group." Peter Giesbrecht, another conservative voice, spoke with pride of the church's effort to maintain knowledge of German among the youth, especially his church's Sunday School "extension" building where eighty to one hundred children attended German classes in 1979.⁴⁵

Heinrich Voth, who helped form another conservative church, the Sommerfelder, in Ontario in 1968, similarly spoke of the ease with which church life was re-established: "There was a small group of people," Old Colonists from Chihuahua, "who ... wanted to become Sommerfelder" and "approached us about starting a Sommerfelder church." As "we'd always been Sommerfelder ... we said, why not?" So, "the Sommerfelder 'Ältester' in Manitoba," John Friesen, was invited to Ontario. "He was very helpful. He came here" and continued to do so, twice a year, for the "Springtime Church" to see "if there are any young people [desiring baptism] and then again in the fall for the Communion service."⁴⁶ The only concern was that the Sommerfelder in Mexico would not associate with the Ontario Sommerfelder, as "they believe that Canada is a heathen place." As Voth saw it from Ontario, it made no difference "whether Mexico or here, it's the same." Both groups used "exactly the same books," and had the same open view on motorized vehicles. Voth had even heard that the founding Ältester of the Sommerfelder congregation in Manitoba in the 1890s, Abraham Doerksen, had transported a Model T by train when he moved to Mexico in the 1920s.⁴⁷ No matter these similarities, Mexico and Canada produced two, significantly different, types of religious community.

The evangelicals who left the Old Colony held a different perspective of faith. They saw in the old church a stagnant church, unable to meet the spiritual needs of immigrants in Ontario. Corny Friesen recalled that even Rev. Jakob Neudorf, the Old Colony preacher who helped establish the Ontario Old Colony, was dismissed in about 1962 when he accepted an evangelical vocabulary, preaching about "being saved." The Old Colonists had traditionally considered such language prideful and unable to articulate the need to "yield" to God. However, when Friesen and some others in Ontario welcomed Neudorf's new vocabulary and invited him to conduct church service, conservatives in the church "locked the door." Friesen was dismayed that Old Colony preachers could read sermons "about a second birth" but insist that it is too prideful "to claim that you *have* to be born again."[48]

Other evangelicals reared in Old Colony ways spoke of similar conflict. John and Nettie Banman recalled searching for a "true faith" within the Old Colony church after they were married in 1960, but, as "we didn't feel that there was anything that the church had to offer us ... we just drifted away." Everything changed for the Banmans in 1968 when their four-year-old son Michael was killed in a car accident. John recalled, "It was that same night that we realized our need for spiritual things. ... It was that night that we gave our hearts to the Lord." Nettie recalled an even more emotional time:

> I realized then that I would never see my son again. ... I knew he was with the Lord but where would I be? [One night] I was so down ... I screamed out to the Lord ... to forgive me and to save me and I wanted to be with my son [in eternity]. ... We'd always been taught that Christ had come to this earth to die for us but we'd never been taught to accept the salvation part. So about 4 o'clock at night ... [a] sort of warmth came over me. ... [and] I got the assurance ... I'm going to ... see my son again and going to see Christ.[49]

It was a powerful vision, infused with both Old Colony and evangelical teaching, amidst a personal crisis. It was enough to break old ties.

Many of the more evangelical immigrants now began to join Canadian-based Mennonite churches that used the Low German dialect in their services and were linked through some kinship tie to the Mennonites from Mexico. John and Nettie Banman, strongly disliking aspects of the Old Colony church – the "filth" of smoking, the avoidance of "scripture reading," the determination to "keep to [old] ways" – denounced their leaders as not knowing "what they were doing because they had been in Satan's darkness," and then promised to "pray for them." In 1968, the Banmans left the old church and joined the Evangelical Mennonite Mission Church (EMMC).[50] Here, they felt spiritual nurture and the freedom to express their evangelical faith in church groups that met to study the Bible. The popularity of the EMMC, however, soon produced its own set of problems. By 1979, Nettie was concerned that "they're catering too much to the people that are coming from Mexico and not enough to the people that ... are raised here" in an English milieu. Then, too, John worried about non-Mennonite influences in the church, such as the "doctrine ... on eternal security and ... immersion baptism," teachings that seemed to de-emphasize a disciplined lifestyle.

At the same time, new alliances did form, such as the 1977 understanding between the EMMC and a similar body, the Evangelical Mennonite Conference (EMC), when it also moved in to begin a church for Mexico Mennonite immigrants. John welcomed the EMC, recounting how it was a conservative Sommerfelder Church member, his brother-in-law Peter Dyck, who "started to preach the gospel clear" and invited "the EMC from Manitoba." At first, "we didn't feel that this would further the work of the Lord. ... but after a meeting [of] ... about three hours ... we ... agree[d] that ... we would ... work together instead of working against each other."[51] The joint forces of the EMMC and EMC offered the migrants an evangelistic alternative to the more communitarian Old Colony and Sommerfelder churches.

Conclusion

The "return" of the Kanadier Mennonites was often not an actual return of particular migrants, but a migration to the land of their grandparents. Neither was it a return to old places, for by far the largest number of these migrants settled not in familiar western Canada, but in the unproven territory of highly industrialized southern Ontario. The region served well the interests of impoverished, Low German-speaking immigrants with an elementary school education: small factories and intensive vegetable farming provided a livelihood for families with many hands. If a measure of economic security awaited them, Ontario was disconcerting in many other ways, for it was fundamentally different from the insular, agrarian communities of Latin America. In the shadow of Canada's largest city, Toronto, it signalled everything the traditionalist Mennonites from the South were not.

Ronald Sawatsky's 1979 oral history project revealed that these Mennonite immigrants were adapting quickly, not only by finding work and shelter, but also by developing a collective memory of the sojourn in the South and integration into Canada. The immigrants from

Mexico he chose to interview seemed to think of the migration north in the 1950s and 1960s as a sort of coming home; Canada seemed to welcome them, and its economy seemed to afford them a predictable, if hard, route to a relative economic security. The only feature of the story on which their narratives disagreed was the matter of religion. Many observed that valuable religious ties to Mexico still existed, others were determined to break with Mexico but replicate a reformed version of the old ways, and others again saw the old ways as harmful in every respect. What they did agree on was that the memory of religious life in Mexico – attracting or repelling – mattered as they negotiated their way in Canada.

The Kanadier immigrants in Canada were a diasporic people, and, as such, they told stories of the old homeland as they knew it and shared their mental maps of the new place as they desired it. In the process, they created a narrative that anchored them in new realities as they experienced them. It was their own transnational story. What distinguished these immigrants from so many others was that their collective memory reminded them of their right as Kanadier to Canadian citizenship. It was a legal right and, with the stories they told of re-immigration, of hard work, and of honest, church-based, family life, it seemed to become for them also a cultural right. The narratives still separated them from the nation's cultural mainstream, but it placed them comfortably within the complex social makeup of Canada.

7 Imagining a Pan-American Village: Reading *Die Mennonitische Post*, 1977–1996

The grandchildren of the migrants who left Canada in the 1920s, the so-called "third generation," established their lives as adults in the last quarter of the twentieth century. Like their parents, they did so as transnational subjects, albeit in quite a different world; they seemed to move more often, stayed in closer contact with dispersed kin, and migrated into ever-new regions. During these years, for example, Low German-speaking Mennonites from the South claimed Texas, Oklahoma, and Kansas as their homes, as well as Nova Scotia in Canada, La Pampa in Argentina, Tarija in far southern Bolivia, and Campeche in far southern Mexico. They travelled by jet plane and used inexpensive forms of communication, including cell phones and the Internet. In the process, they increasingly cultivated a new ethno-religious identity as Low German-speaking Mennonites of the Americas, often simply the *Dietsche*, a word with a particular meaning in majoritarian Spanish- or English-speaking host societies. They knew their place within that subgroup of Mennonites possessing a shared history in the early twentieth-century emigration from Canada, still using Low German for family discourse, and cultivating a corporate memory of sojourn in one or more of the Central or South American countries. This consciousness was especially apparent in the pages of a new newspaper, *Die Mennonitische Post*, launched in 1977.

Die Post, more than any other cultural tool, gave expression to a Low German Mennonite world. It consisted of the nations the immigrants knew, some more favourably predisposed to their ethno-religious goals than others, some more accessible than others. More importantly, it was a world imagined as a village of fellow Low German-speaking Mennonites superimposed on this constellation of nations.

Different from Benedict Anderson's watershed idea of nation as "imagined community" propelled by print capitalism and secularism, these Mennonites created their own sort of "imagined village." Following Anderson's template, the Mennonites too "lived the image of their communion," for the fact is that "all communities larger than primordial villages of face-to-face contact ... are imagined."[1] But the Mennonites' imagined pan-American village had no linkage to state, no power, no sense of destiny or progress; it was imbued with nostalgia, religion, and cosmology to pull them not into a nation but apart from one. For the Mennonites, the imagined ethno-religious village, spread out from Canada to Argentina, linked people within several nations, turning villagers into transnational subjects. Reflecting Canadian scholar Daphne Winland's observation of ethnic groups "in a postmodern world," the Low German Mennonites were "increasingly drawn into an ever-expanding and often perplexing array of networks and linkages, many of which defy the familiar lines between 'here' and 'there.'"[2] They linked to places within several countries, connected as imagined residents of a village consisting of hundreds of points among the nations.

Many "move to Canada or to the United States," others "look more to the South"

In some ways, *Die Post* was similar to any booster paper, telling stories of "making good," of material success, meant to inspire the community at large. Certainly, many of the Canadian-descendant Mennonite settlements of Mexico and Paraguay flourished in the late decades of the twentieth century and had good reason for a bit of triumphalism. Northern Mexico's well-rooted Manitoba, Swift, and Durango colonies, as well as Menno Colony in the Paraguayan Chaco, each founded in the 1920s, had evolved into highly productive and technologized rural districts and towns. In Mexico, a twenty-kilometre-long industrial and commercial strip on a four-lane highway cut through the middle of historic Manitoba Colony, north from Cuauhtémoc to Ciudad Obregón.[3] In Paraguay, the town of Loma Plata at Menno Colony, eventually linked to the country's hydroelectricity and fibre-optic grid, was a thriving commercial centre, producing a large percentage of the country's dairy and beef products.[4] Both places also sustained a rich network of social institutions, including high school, and even college and university education, offered bilingually in German and Spanish. Specific communities within the Chihuahua and Chaco colonies supported senior citizens' complexes, clinics and hospitals, bookstores, credit unions, and even museums and archives. An increasing religious diversity, although usually within the wider Mennonite fold, was testimony to religious vibrancy.

Similar trends described the settlements founded in the 1940s and 1950s. Los Jagueyes in northern Mexico was now an important farm-service centre, while Bergthal and Sommerfeld in East Paraguay represented commercialized soybean production regions, each with a full set of institutions, the latter eventually boasting two hospitals. The British Honduras (Belize after 1982) colonies dominated their country's dairy and poultry sectors, while the first Bolivian colonies had successfully experimented with a wide variety of new commodities, including soybeans and corn, had found a ready market for dairy products, and had given economic vibrancy to Santa Cruz state.[5] From the 1970s to the 1990s, Mennonites celebrated these accomplishments at elaborate fiftieth-, sixtieth-, and seventy-fifth-anniversary festivities, often graced by visiting governors and even some national leaders.[6]

This image of thriving communities, however, obscures a cultural reality obvious in the pages of the new *Mennonitische Post*. Low German-speaking Mennonites, many claiming Canadian citizenship, were on the move, spreading centrifugally. They created heart-wrenching stories of separation and dispersion, of siblings and parents and children moving in opposite directions, but also stories of reunion and well-being in new lands. Some stories were of cultural loss, of immigrants losing their way, their collective identity, and their place in religiously defined community. Other stories told of individuals finding a mooring in religion, some in Low German-based evangelical churches of the North, others in the old-order "horse and buggy" communities of the South. But they shared a commonality: they were part of a Low German Mennonite diaspora whose members were criss-crossing the Americas, often passing by one another. A typical observation in the *Post* was an October 1996 report from northern Mexico that noted that "most people from Cuauhtémoc move to Canada or the United States ... but the residents of Nuevo Casas Grandes region ... look less to the north and look more to the south," especially to Bolivia.[7]

The continuing diaspora was indeed complex. Numerous internal migrations grew out of the earlier moves of the 1950s and 1960s, when Chihuahua Mennonites had expanded to nearby Ojo de la Yegua and to the somewhat more distant colonies near Nuevo Casas Grandes,[8] while

Durango Mennonites had founded La Honda Colony in Zacatecas state. Now, in the 1970s, 1980s, and 1990s, other forays occurred; in Mexico, north to Las Virgénias Colony on the US border and east to Tamaulipas state on the Gulf of Mexico. In Belize, Mennonites moved southward within their tiny country, and, in Bolivia, eastward across that country's mighty Rio Grande, tracking towards the Brazilian border. Numerous small groups moved internationally without obvious pattern: undocumented migrants headed for Canada, and Canadian citizens to Texas and Oklahoma. More moves occurred within Central and South America: from Mexico to East Paraguay, from Belize and East Paraguay to Bolivia, from Belize to Costa Rica. The movement was made all the more complex by large numbers of seemingly perpetual migrants, most often travelling between Mexico and Canada; they were sojourners whose lives were determined by seasonal jobs, family exigency, employers' whims, and uncertain documentation.

Despite these many variations, the majority of migrants fit the two-pronged diasporic model, southward for the most traditional, and northward for the more accommodating. And it was a set of migrations roughly following an ideological divide, oftentimes announced in intense debate, often within family circles. Both the northward- and southward-bound Mennonite migrants believed they were breaking from some kind of traditionalist shackle of repression – economic or cultural – by overcoming the very forces that seemed to restrict their freedom. The southward-bound migrants spoke in old communitarian language of refusing to "conform to the ways of worldly" capitalism and consumer culture in Mexico, while the northward-bound migrants found in wage labour and the promise of upward mobility a way to critique and even reject an archaic and arcane agrarian simplicity in Mexico and Paraguay.

Yet, against this religious divide was a fundamental cultural unity. It was a linkage apparent in the pages of *Die Mennonitische Post*, consisting of news stories, editorials, and a steady flow of letters by ordinary readers. Less than an array of good or bad news stories, these reports and letters describe the very contours of the Low German Mennonites' imagined world spread over the entire western hemisphere. The reports and letters spoke of wide travel, social networks independent of national cultures, and pragmatic relationships with the wider society. They repeated old Anabaptist teachings of "being strangers and pilgrims" amidst worldly temptation and economic uncertainty. They revealed a constant reconnaissance for economic opportunity, whether based on good land in the South or stable jobs in the North. The writers remembered the stories of their grandparents' migration. They articulated a particular view of the meaning of good citizenship, one demonstrated by the exercise of skill and a strong work ethic, rarely by patriotism or nationalism. Most importantly, this collection of letters reveals an imagined geography, a constellation of disparate places in seven different countries.

"Our 'Dietsche' Mennonites ... need this paper"

Die Mennonitische Post was a unique literary medium. While based in many ways on the old *Steinbach Post*, it was not a privately owned newspaper but one supported by the church-based service agency, Mennonite Central Committee Canada (MCC Canada), an organization shaped by the most progressive and urbanized of Mennonite churches. In the 1970s, MCC Canada, concerned with the economic and cultural well-being of the dispersed Low German immigrants in the South, and especially of the impoverished Kanadier returnees to Canada, established a Kanadier Concerns Committee. The committee's vision was to use a new newspaper, *Die Mennonitische Post*, to help facilitate social networks and a common identity among the Low German Mennonite migrants. Soon after it began publication in 1977, the *Post* began attracting thousands of letters from farm and labouring families, exhibiting what a student of the *Post* describes as "shared religious beliefs, common history and ethnicity, mutual acquaintances and relatives," but, perhaps most importantly, "a migratory, pilgrimage lifestyle," all within an "imaginary Mennonite village."[9]

The success of the *Post* was immediate. Letters flowed in from the far corners of the Americas as Low German Mennonites seized on a new opportunity of connecting with loved ones. Upon receiving his first issue in April 1977, one writer recalled his boyhood when his mother had read the *Steinbach Post* to the entire family gathered around her; he now endorsed the new effort to reach "our *Dietsche* Mennonites spread throughout the world," for they desperately "need this paper for their unity and brotherhood."[10] Other readers welcomed the democratic nature of the *Post*. In September 1977, A.G. Janzen wrote to "welcome *Die Post* in our home," for, "handled in democratic fashion, here everyone can express himself; what one doesn't like, one can ignore."[11] The paper, in his estimation, would sustain a strong sense of peoplehood. Among the few reservations recorded was one from

"Mrs. Peter Boschman" of Winkler, Manitoba, who protested that she "would now have to learn to write in Latin orthography, as I always wrote with German [Gothic] orthography in the *Steinbach Post*."[12] The modern orthography evidently bothered few readers, for the newspaper quickly became immensely popular. In fact, by 1983, the senior editor, Abe Warkentin, the former editor of the English-language *Carillon News*, reported that *Die Post* had received no less than 8000 letters in its first six and a half years.[13] Fifteen years after its founding, in 1992, MCC Canada described a subscription base of 5100 in eight countries, and announced its willingness to subsidize the newspaper for readers in the economically volatile South at a cost of $100,000 per year.[14]

In part, *Die Post* created a transnational identity; more apparently, it gave expression to one that already existed, revealing the contours of an intentional Low German Mennonite diaspora in the Americas. Both the editors and letter writers spoke of it. Among many early references to the remarkable scattering, editor Warkentin noted in November 1977, "Travel always becomes easier; today one can be in Canada, tomorrow in South America, Africa or Europe. … One thing is certain, more and more people are traveling, even between Winnipeg and Asunción. While waiting in airports one can often hear Low German spoken … as many Mennonites go abroad to visit relatives."[15] Warkentin sometimes gently chided the ethnocentricity of this social network. In 1989, he announced for his readership the upcoming Twelfth Mennonite World Conference, to be held in Winnipeg, one that would culminate in a worship service in the city's 30,000-seat football stadium. Warkentin emphasized that the conference would attract hundreds of Mennonites from Asia and Africa, oftentimes the children of early twentieth-century converts to Christianity: "I don't know [if all Mennonites] will be able to appreciate this" meeting, wrote Warkentin, for "there are still those among us who have never seen a black Mennonite, or believe that Mennonitism was ever meant for anyone other than one just like us," Low German folks.[16]

Myriad letters and travelogues suggested that Warkentin was at least partially correct. It seemed that an imagined, pan-American, Low German-speaking village shaped the thinking of *Die Post* readers. In an October 1982 issue, a letter, signed "Peter und Elisabeth Wiebe" of Hague, Saskatchewan, provided German-language lyrics to be sung to the tune of the well-known American revival chorus "What a Friend We Have in Jesus." The first of eleven stanzas set the theme: "Dearest, widely scattered readers / scattered far throughout the world / mostly seen through foggy glasses / one can but imagine you / where have all the loved ones settled / these the people we once knew / traveled far, where have they settled? / where are you, and in which land?"[17]

Even though poetry and hymn writing was common among Low German Mennonites, and especially in *Die Post*, most writers spoke about this diaspora in more ordinary forms. One popular early feature in *Die Post* was the travelogue, describing extensive trips by air and car to visit long-lost relatives in the South or the North. In one June 1977 report, Johann and Katherina Banman of New Bothwell, Manitoba, opened with a familiar refrain: "As we had so many acquaintances in Paraguay, we agreed, to visit them all." Then came quotidian detail, interlaced with emotion, of meeting family and friends they "had not seen in twenty-eight years." At the home of Rev. David Klippenstein in Bergthal Colony, East Paraguay, "it didn't take long and the chicken noodle soup was on the table and with many [relatives] at the table we did much visiting there, just like the old times." The next day, "we were at my schoolmate's, Tina Fehr, today at Mrs. Johann Doerksen's," and, in the end, the visits were "too short, as many years have flown by." After days of visiting on the colony, the Banmans embraced an even wider diasporic geography: they visited the Asunción business of "friend Heinrich H."; they despaired that a planned visit to the Chaco was cancelled due to wet roads and irregular airplane traffic; and, sadly, "we also did not get to Bolivia," a place where "we also have friends."[18] The travelogue told readers about a visit, and also reminded them of the imagined outer margins of the diaspora.

By 1980, the travelogue had become so popular that the usually generous *Post* editor intervened bluntly. In his opinion, the travel accounts were too numerous and, inevitably, they were also "far too long, with the writer emphasizing all the wrong things, exactly what time one has left the yard, with whom, with whom they had supper, which airline they took, how long they drove." Rather, counselled the editor, "write about matters of interest to others!"[19]

What did interest letter writers was the wide variety of geographical places and climates that had become home to Low German Mennonites. The travelogues often alluded to stark physical gradations. In one May 1982 account, Johan Neudorf described a 15,000-kilometre round trip by road from Coaldale, Alberta, to Belize. As he put it, it was a trip from Canada where it was "cold, to the USA, not so cold, to Mexico, warmer, to Belize, still warmer."[20] Some writers even suggested a link between weather patterns and cultural differences: an August 1993 contributor spoke of how at "+3 it is cold in Paraguay and at −30 it is cold in

Canada." Subsequently, he noted, people drink "*Yerba* [tea] at home in Paraguay, Black Tea at Pizza Hut or McDonalds in Canada," and even store attendants in "North and South America look completely differently," a sour look in the South, a sweet smile in the North, for "when it is cooler than +45 one can quite easily look friendly."[21] Talk of weather may have seemed banal to some readers, but it was just another way of speaking about the Mennonite diaspora.

The far-reaching nature of the diaspora was also articulated by references to specific locations, the writer's and those of loved ones scattered in the Americas. The approximately fifty letters in each biweekly issue of *Die Mennonitische Post* followed the familiar pattern of letters in the old *Steinbach Post*: they spoke of weather, health, and market, and sent greetings to friends and relatives. What was new about the greetings in *Die Mennonitische Post* was how frequently they were addressed to people in three, and sometimes four or five, countries. In a not atypical December 1982 letter from Wheatley, Ontario, Anna Dyck hailed a convalescing David Wolf of Manitoba, Canada, and greeted "all the cousins" in Alberta and Saskatchewan, after which she shifted to the common parlance of imaginary travel: "Then to Bolivia to siblings Herman Dycks ... then I have to go to Mexico and greet all the siblings and the parents. Yes, then also to Texas where Franz Martens live. ... So then I have almost gone out throughout the world." Having done so, the writer circled back home to Ontario to describe "the store we have set up here ... the Etcetera Shop ... where I also work one evening a week."[22]

The *Post* also drew writers from every cultural and social sector of the Low German world. Moderately conservative Low German Mennonites in Canada used *Die Post* to greet their kin spread across North America, while traditionalist "horse and buggy" Old Colony Mennonites in Latin America used it to greet theirs spread from Bolivia to Mexico. And both sets of writers used it to follow kin lines across strict church borders. The *Post* also drew women as well as men, welcomed both those who wrote to celebrate and to lament, and gave space to both the humorous and moralistic.

Anyone wishing to connect with loved ones was able to do so. In his December 1982 letter, D. Penner wrote from the "horse and buggy" colony at Rio Verde, East Paraguay: he "praised God" for good health and expressed gratitude for good soybean-planting weather, but he also complained that his siblings in Mexico never wrote: "Where have the Bernard Penners stayed? ... Can brother Johan Penner. ... please write a long letter to *Die Post*, of how you are faring in the beautiful old homeland" of Mexico?[23] In her October 1992 letter, Susanna Klassen of the "horse and buggy" colony at Sabinal (northern Mexico) responded to a request for information from a friend in Campeche (southern Mexico), and did so by joking that when her married brother from Zacatecas (central Mexico) had come north to help construct a house, he learned to wash his own clothes, albeit by using the construction site's cement mixer. The story no doubt reflected "Mennonite" gender roles, but it also revealed a social network across the far reaches of Mexico. Like so many writers in the North or the South, moderate or traditionalist, Klassen concluded with greetings to "members of our kinship group which is huge and scattered through the whole world."[24] Both Rio Verde and Sabinal were isolated "horse and buggy" communities, one 300 kilometres northeast of Asunción, the other 300 kilometres northwest of Chihuahua City, but the writers from both places identified with an imagined village stretching 15,000 kilometres from northern Alberta to central La Pampa.

Die Post even had a children's section that told a similar story, one in which children were encouraged to express their own diasporic imaginations. Perhaps the section's editor encouraged a rather radical reimagining of the Low German Mennonite diaspora, with stories of missionary children, and serialized stories of world traveller Michael, imagining *The Big Trip* to visit "Bombo the African youth ... Tuktu the Eskimo and many other children in the wide world."[25] The Mennonite children, however, wrote of another world: everyday life on the farm. A typical issue from 1981 featured a letter from twelve-year-old Margaret from Las Piedras Colony, Bolivia, who wrote that "we have ten orange trees and another four plum trees" and that she herself had "planted a few strawberries,"[26] and one from thirteen-year-old Heinrich from Cuauhtémoc, Mexico, who reported on his family's crops, then added that "I have planted some maize and beans for myself."[27]

These children's imagined world invariably followed old friends into new countries and greeted relatives in the Mennonite diaspora. A 1982 letter by ten-year-old Elisabeth Martens of Nuevo Ideal, Durango, employed familiar parlance to ask about former neighbours: "To Paraguay, to Johann Klassens, what work are you doing? We often think of you." She added that her younger sister "Agatha often asks where the family is that had an Aganetha and a Susanna, and I tell her that they have moved far away."[28] The letters not only revealed an imagined social network but also spoke of a child-centred yearning.

A 1987 letter by eleven-year-old Tina Banman of Las Piedras, Bolivia, announced that she had spent the day washing dolls' clothing, but then thanked her Aunt Margaretha and Uncle David, presumably from Ontario, for a photo they had sent, adding, "It looks very good, and I never tire of looking at it."[29] A children's network, linking Canada, Mexico, Paraguay, and Bolivia, existed within a similar adult network.

"A photo of my parents ... who moved ... in 1927"

By the late 1970s, historical memory and the abundant sharing of those memories also reinforced this imagined Mennonite village. This decade marked the sixth since the first wave of migrants southward in the 1920s. Those who were elderly in the 1970s had been born in Canada and now revelled in youthful memories of the 1920s-era migration. Not surprisingly, *Die Post*'s very existence seemed to generate letters recalling old times. Several came with photographs of parents: one in 1978 shared "a photo of my parents ... who moved after their parents on both sides decided in 1927 to join the migration to Paraguay"; another in 1980 came with a photograph of the 1921 delegation to Mexico; one in 1981 attached an image of his parents before their turn-of-the-century wedding.[30] Others located their parents in the epic saga of the past in different ways: "If I am right," wrote Jacob N. Friesen of Durango, Mexico, in June 1985, "then my parents and the Cornelius H. Ungers of Warman, Saskatchewan are ... the very last two couples from the first emigration of 1925 to [Durango] Mexico who are still alive, that is, couples whose marriage has not been broken through death." And then, to explain the significance of his observations, Friesen added, "Father is quite ill and lies in Rosthern, Saskatchewan in the hospital."[31]

Despite the strictly patriarchal nature of most congregations in the diaspora, women readily told their stories in *Die Post*. Their accounts seem especially self-reflexive, with the author at the centre of the migration story, and the passage of time precisely recorded as it affected them personally. Written from Canada in October 1977, and recounting her family's arrival in Paraguay in 1927, Susan Sawatsky's letter held both these elements: "It is today 50 years since my parents, one sister and I, arrived in Paraguay at Puerto Casado. We were part of a group of 100 souls. We left on August 23 from Canada by train and arrived at Puerto Casado on the 23rd of September, early in the morning." She recounted specific moments of hardships: "On the 15th of October my sister died and on the 15th of November my mother died; the 19th of November my father died. We had not been there for more than two months." And she connected the story to recent times: "When we returned [to Canada] in 1965 we made the same trip in 24 hours by air. We have children, grandchildren and in-laws in the Chaco."[32] It was the story of a young girl in Paraguay, but cast over the course of a lifetime, and linked to a return migration to the old homeland.

In her lengthy letter from Mexico in December 1978, Helena Woelke was even more self-reflexive and time-conscious. She similarly placed herself in the flow of history: "As I am so alone ... I have much time to write, think and read, so I will try to write my life's journey." A remarkable array of precise moments followed. She recalled the 22 March 1922 arrival in Mexico on the second chartered train and encampment at Rosenhof "by the lake," then the first nights in a tent torn by strong winds. She remembered the erection of the first wooden schoolhouse, also serving as immigration shelter. She recounted precise social encounters of yesteryear: as a restless child in church when she had to "sit perfectly still by mother"; as a student when she had "mastered everything the teacher gave us to learn"; as a girl at play when she "outran everyone at school." Memories of food were especially vivid: one year's harvest yielded ninety sacks of potatoes; another year brought Mexican soldiers demanding boiled eggs; overall, the twelve children survived on ground corn; a baby sibling's birth introduced "an earthly pilgrim who also wanted to be fed." She remembered misfortune on the farm: the time her father was forced to euthanize their four lovely but seriously ill horses; the time she almost drowned when the hay wagon tipped over into a brook; the time she injured a leg "chasing the bulls." She recalled the moments of her own household formation, her marriage at age nineteen to Heinrich S. Woelke of Gruenfeld, her many pregnancies and her life at middle age. Then, quite suddenly, the narration ended, abruptly and unexplained. Helena's concluding remarks referenced her grandmother's death, a "woman so full of love, always giving us goodies and always standing by her door until she saw we were safely home. ... She had flown away as the owl into the long long night." Thus, Helena signed off, having shared a life rooted in family, stitched across the generations.[33]

Other women memoirists focused on the specific moments of emotion; that is, of humiliation in strange lands, or of peace within familiar circles. "Frau" Klaas Banman of Chihuahua, writing in November 1985, recalled a 1933 trip with her family of nine children and parents to visit relatives in Canada, a trip that left her feeling alienated. In a matter of just ten years, Canada had become a foreign place: "It seemed to us that the Mennonites who had not moved to Mexico were very high minded. They wore different clothes and ... spoke English well. ... They made fun of us. ... On Sunday we attended their church and I dressed in clothes of my relatives in order to better fit in."[34] Margaretha Siemens of Clear Creek, Ontario, writing in April 1986, seemed overwhelmed by nostalgia for the church life of her youth in Mexico: "[I] think back to ... the time when we in Chihuahua were united with the Durango church ... in one love-filled congregational fellowship. Many of the elderly will well recall the good old times, yes? Often one thought to oneself: 'What will the preachers ... tell us that is new?' Yes, the old and always the new 'good news' is this, 'repent and believe in the gospel and do not rely on your own understanding' and 'love your neighbor.'"[35] It was a simple religious message, and one that reached back emotionally to old places.

Men, too, added their voice to this memorializing, albeit more often, it seems, with moralistic reflections that focused on other men.[36] A writer in February 1978 recalled reading *Robinson Crusoe* when he was a youth and contrasted it to "the Mennonite story that is no fiction." The latter story involved "my father who ... spent his energy in the pioneer years in the wilderness" and died with a "deep-seated yearning" in his old age "to once again see his previous homeland."[37] Another writer publishing in that same month reprinted an article titled "A Moses of the Latin American Mennonite Migration," and recalled the life and death of Rev. Johan Wall, the 1920s-era immigrant leader. The writer added, "Modern Mennonites will not perhaps understand why anyone, who lived in a democratic land, free and in landed prosperity would choose to ... migrate into poverty and primitive conditions." But he added that Wall's life could "show us something of the validity of early Anabaptist Christianity and awaken in us the preparedness to be Christian in our time."[38] A history of border crossings was also a history of instruction.

Men also seemed more willing than women to express bitter doubts about the wisdom of leaving Canada in the first instance. In his August 1977 reflection, Jacob W. Falk of Paraguay spoke of his deep yearning for Canada: "I and my wife were born in Canada, fifty years ago. ... Today I cannot understand why we live in Paraguay for we have had it very hard ... we have gone through hunger, heat ... and sickness. For what? I cannot today answer that question."[39] A fifty-year retrospective suggested the migration might have been for naught. In his October 1977 letter, Jacob P.D. Wiebe of Paraguay recalled how in "the first years

... in about 1929 my uncle Peter E. Pries ... bid farewell to his [married] children as he desperately wanted to return to Canada." The only reason Pries had changed his mind was that "when he said his farewell, his eldest granddaughter cried inconsolably, distressed that she would never again see her grandfather." Pries's decision was not based on religious ideals, nor on Chaco's climate, but simply on family bonds.

In their letters to *Die Post* in the 1970s and 1980s, the elderly who lived dispersed among the nations of the Americas found space to recall memories of migration. Those memories undergirded the cultural unity of the scattered Low German community.

"Permission to remain in Canada"

At the foundation of the diasporic imagination was a particular meaning attributed to the word "citizenship," a frequently discussed issue in *Die Post*. Letter writers to the *Post* seemed on an almost unending quest for official immigration papers, and the *Post*'s news reports similarly addressed this quest. The fact was that most grandchildren of the 1920s migrants qualified for Canadian citizenship. Their status was based on the Canadian immigration department's liberal interpretation of various citizenship acts that allowed the grandchildren of those born in Canada to obtain citizenship, at one time with the proviso that the grandchild live in Canada for a year before his or her twenty-eighth birthday.[40] This provision explained in part the strong northward impulse, one that gathered force during the 1970s and 1980s, reaching 35,000 Latin America Mennonites in Canada by the mid-1990s.[41] Still, uncertainty about the third generation's status generated frequent appeals to government as well as debates about who might or might not qualify under what circumstances.

Both the letters and the reports in *Die Post* depicted a somewhat contradictory view of government. A distant and faceless force, on the one hand, government was also a highly personalized social organism consisting of revered state leaders who could be approached, indeed beseeched, in person. But, arguably, the two views were two parts of the same viewpoint that saw a national government as a legal tool in the Mennonites' quest for a pacifist and separate social existence. In this equation, citizenship entailed being a law-abiding, peaceable, and self-reliant person, but not one strongly identifying with a particular nation-state. The former view of citizenship was a biblically ordained duty; the latter was a problematic nationalism, a mental and potentially militaristic "conformity to this world." Legal citizenship was a necessity in this world, social citizenship guaranteeing social aid might be justified, but cultural citizenship having to do with heart and loyalty could not be tolerated.[42] If a form of cultural citizenship existed, it was linked to the congregation or the colony, and certainly to that imagined village, the Low German-speaking Mennonite diaspora in the Americas.

Usually, references to the Canadian government by northbound return migrants regarded their "legal" citizenship. *Die Post* was filled with stories on the process of obtaining this right of belonging. A 1977 report described the joy of obtaining passports through the help of such organizations as MCC Canada and in difficult circumstances: "Last month seventy-six persons from fourteen families, all Mennonites from Mexico, ended their long wait, as they finally all received their citizenship papers." The story reported that as "cucumber, tomato and tobacco" workers in southern Ontario, the recipients were "young families seeking to make a home in Canada" who, because of "the intervention from various people [obtained] permission to remain in Canada."[43] Heart-wrenching accounts of being refused entry to Canada put this story into context. A 1988 example told of "a large family from Mexico seeking entry to Canada at Emerson, Manitoba." Unfortunately, the family had "been denied entry," as its members "were not Canadian citizens nor did they have 'landed immigrant status'; all they had were 'clarification of status' letters stating that they once had been Canadian citizens who had lost their right to citizenship on their 24th birthday."[44] Other reports noted the high cost of obtaining correct documentation. One from 1995 warned of the need for an "inordinate sum of money to obtain all the documents," $1750 if a Canadian spouse "wishes to sponsor one's partner," plus $100 for each child under the age of nineteen, "plus the costs of a medical examination."[45] The community was preoccupied with the question of just how legal permission to stay in Canada could be obtained.

The problem with this pragmatic view of citizenship was that it could be misused, and the editorial staff at *Die Post* saw it as their duty to address the issue. Of special concern was the possible misuse of Canada's social safety net and questions of the moral right of Mennonites from Latin America to partake of state-funded medical services. Letters did report on visitors from the South coming to Canada for medical treatment, although usually without reference to its Medicare program.[46] Still, in a September 1983 issue, the *Post* editor scolded Mennonites who "unlawfully deal with various government programs" and "benefit from programs to which they have never paid into." The editor concluded, "I think at one time the name Mennonite meant more than it does today." A year later, the editor chided "Mennonites who receive Canadian and American family allowances when they live in Mexico," and concluded that "I don't know if many or only a few are doing this, but it is sad ... for our obligation should be to build up the country, not to use it."[47] As the editor saw it, Mennonites had a duty to uphold the law, and this also meant sending their children to school. A 1990 report told of "school officials ... seeking to get the children of Mexico Mennonites to attend school," and solicited a chiding from the *Post* editor: perhaps it was difficult for Mennonite children to attend school "in a strange land with a strange language," but parents should realize that "it is lawfully required that children must attend school, the importance of which is something they do not fully understand."[48]

A much more serious disregard for Canadian law was reported in a 1992 national news story in which the Canadian CTV network turned Mexico Mennonite involvement in the drug trade into a nationally televised story. *Die Post* reported the story with the startling headline "TV Program on Drug Smuggling Shocks Mennonites in Canada." It told of a *Fifth Estate* investigation into a Mennonite drug ring set in Cuauhtémoc and reaching into southern Ontario and Manitoba, resulting in the imprisonment of twenty-four Mexico Mennonites in Chihuahua, Texas, and Ontario. The program named Abraham Harms, previously of Wheatley, Ontario, now of Mexico, as a "key person in the 'Mennonite Mob' involved in bringing drugs from Mexico to Ontario." Authorities estimated that a network of some one hundred Mennonites controlled 20 percent of the marijuana smuggled into Ontario. Most concerning for *Die Post* was the assault on the Mennonites' reputation. The story explained that "customs officers who were interviewed by *Fifth Estate* were shocked that a group who they believed to be a strong religious community would be involved in criminal activity." Especially concerning was the TV program's suggestion that the Old Colony church in Canada was "protecting these people accused of drug smuggling." The TV program explained that Cornelius Banman of Plum Coulee, Manitoba, accused of drug running and out on bail of $120,000, apparently frequented an Old Colony church in Winkler. The sad consequence was that officials on both borders no longer saw "conservatively dressed Mennonites who come over ... from the USA to Canada" with generosity and trust.[49] Clearly, some Mennonites had developed an extreme view of detached citizenship.

If *Die Post* emphasized respect for Canadian law, it also portrayed Canada as a welcoming place for Low German Mennonites from the South. When the immigrants faced instances of discrimination from long-settled Canadians, the *Post* editor did not hesitate to intervene with a sharp rebuke: "We in Canada ... discriminate not only against other races, but also against Mennonite return migrants," wrote the editor in 1979. The reason for this discrimination, he said, was twofold: first, because of greed, as "[we] worry that the arrival of other people may mean that we will get less"; and second, and more seriously, because Canadian Mennonites "have become high minded," holding "high rank in universities and businesses, and even in government we find our Penners, Friesens, Hieberts and Funks ... [and] we have become rich and we think it is because that we are so valuable or intelligent and that God has blessed us."[50] Ironically, the most generous voices of welcome came from numerous German-language ads in *Die Post* from the Canadian government itself. These messages, specifically from Canada's Minister of State for Multiculturalism, "welcomed" the migrants to Canada in German: one from 1980 featured a map of Canada and the message, "You Belong to Canada, and Canada Belongs to You."[51]

But other, more subtle, notes featured a welcoming Canadian government. A 1984 report on a small migration, this one of Belize Mennonites to the picturesque Kennetcook region (more precisely, Northfield) of Nova Scotia, was cast in the language of yesteryear. It described an effort by a dozen Kleine Gemeinde Mennonite families to establish an orderly farming community on 2600 acres of land. The community reportedly had a leader in Jacob C. Penner, was awaiting a minister in Martin R. Penner, and had inhabited "six farm houses, three barns, one church building and one community hall." But the article also noted that the Belize newcomers were assured of a welcome in central Nova Scotia, as "the government is seeking hard working farmers to settle unused farm land."[52] A 1996 MCC report applauded the founding of a rapidly growing Old Colonist church at Vauxhall, Alberta, and the welcome that locals had provided for 167 families from Mexico within the previous year. But it especially emphasized how administrators from the public "schools in the area were concerned to obtain a better understanding of the Mennonites" and that many adults now were eager to "learn more about the country [of Canada] and the language."[53]

With the creation of these communities came a self-confidence that not only was Canada their rightful home, but that the newcomers were welcome to express their particular Low German or even Latin Americanized culture in Canada. In November 1987, a *Post* writer explained that many returnees were settling in Winkler, Manitoba, because it lay in a region from which "their parents or grandparents at one time emigrated and in which one can still speak Low German." Indeed, in regional factories bearing such names as Monarch Industries, Lode King, and Triple E, newcomers could "find work with no need to speak English."[54] Then, too, Winkler was home to a chapter of "the Old Colony Church ... that offers a traditional spiritual fellowship for ... these return immigrants." A report two years later explained that those unable to integrate well could tune into a Low German-language radio program, hosted by Rev. Cornie Loewen, every Monday night at 9:30 p.m. on local radio CFAM. Loewen explained that many of his "listeners were recently immigrated Mennonites from Latin America, who are not yet very familiar with the English language." He reported that his sermons emphasized "holy living within a healthy family milieu" and that they tackled issues prevalent among the immigrant community, including "tobacco, strong drink, marriage, depression."[55] Southern Manitoba presented itself well as home to the newcomers.

The self-confidence of the immigrant was especially apparent in festive newcomer celebrations. During its first decades of publication, *Die Post* reported, in upbeat fashion, on annual "Treffen Days" (literally, "Meeting Days"). Held at various points across Canada, the Treffen Days assembled thousands of Low German-speaking Mennonites from Latin America. An August 1978 report, for example, described a recent gathering at Centennial Park in Clearbrook, British Columbia, featuring a Vancouver musical group and highlighting guests from "many different countries," but especially from Paraguay and its culturally divergent "Menno, Neuland and Fernheim colonies."[56] In time, specific Treffen Days developed for Canadian-descendant immigrants to Latin America, days appropriately dubbed "Kanadiertreffen" Days. One such event, held in 1991 at Stanley Park near the town of Morden, Manitoba, drew 600 to 700 people, all speaking "the mother tongue – Low German – happily with a bag of sunflower seeds," a snack food that had come to be associated with Manitoba Mennonites. The afternoon took a serious note with the singing of "Christian songs in High German, Low German and English" and an hour-long history lesson by popular radio speaker Gerhard Ens. In his talk, titled "The Mennonites in Russia: Yesterday and Today," Ens emphasized that "through their faith in God our ancestors were able to leave behind their goods ... and make a practical new beginning in a strange land. ... They feared no pain and trouble when religious freedom was within reach."[57] For a descendant of these migrations, it was a reassuring narrative.

The primary identity of the newcomers lay in their own history of migration. Canadian citizenship was less a cultural identity than a legal right allowing for the building of the Mennonite community. Mexico and Paraguay Mennonites had returned to Canada to find jobs, but they still thought of themselves as members of a broader community. The return had been an economic necessity, but in Canada one could still be steadfastly a Low German Mennonite of the Americas.

"The very type of people that built up the [American] West"

Citizenship for the Low German Mennonites in other parts of the Americas bore a somewhat different meaning from citizenship in Canada. For Mennonites who made their homes in long-settled communities in Mexico, Paraguay, Belize, and Bolivia, and those in the most recent settlements in these countries, and now, too, in Argentina and the United States, citizenship per se was less important than land ownership and the legal permission to reside in a particular country. Canada was a place to which migrants "returned" to claim a birthright, but other countries in the Americas were more often seen as sites of sojourn; if citizenship was required to stay in the country, so be it, but if other means could be found, that, too, was fine.

The United States, a new place of settlement for the Low German Mennonites during these last decades, marked such a site. It was a country their grandparents had passed through on the way to Mexico and Paraguay, and, from time to time, had been seen as a welcoming land. In the 1970s, however, it became more than a fleeting land, and by the end of 1995, MCC Canada estimated that 10,000 Mexico Mennonites had settled in the US. They had established farm settlements and compact trailer villages in Seminole (Texas) and Boley (Oklahoma), but eventually had also moved farther north. They could be found in large numbers in the Liberal and Copeland regions in southwestern Kansas, and in smaller numbers in Iowa, Colorado, California, and Nebraska, often to seek work in meat-packing plants.[58] And, although these places provided a steady, working-class wage, the Mennonites faced the constant concern of the right to remain in these places.

The first sizable group of Low German Mennonites from Mexico arrived in the US in early 1977 without a firm guarantee of this permission; indeed, they came with but a vague assurance from real-estate agents that citizenship would be forthcoming. *Die Post* reported at length on their coming: some 500 Mennonites had settled in the western Texas district of Seminole, a mere day's drive north from the historic Chihuahua settlements; another 50 Mexico Mennonites had found homes in Boley, Oklahoma. Most arrived with capital to purchase farmland, the expressed intention of starting a farm community, and the belief that land ownership would secure the required legal status.[59]

The Mennonites, however, soon discovered that they had been duped about obtaining that status, and found themselves in legal limbo. In June 1977, their story gained national notoriety, and, in an unusual step, *Die Post* reproduced a story from the major US news magazine *Newsweek*. This account reported that near Seminole, Texas, "Old Colonists of Mexico have made a down payment on 7500 acres of land" valued at $4,000,000. It further reported, "It is possible that another 15,000 acres will be purchased ... and that 125 families have moved to the Seminole region, and that more were coming." And not only were Mexico Mennonites coming, they also were coming south from Canada after sojourns in Ontario, most on sixty-day tourist visas, hoping to obtain citizenship documents later.[60]

Other sources highlighted the Mennonites' two basic problems: the immigrants had been duped into believing that US citizenship would come with landownership, but also, most of the ranchland they had purchased had no water rights, an absolute requirement to irrigate the semi-arid land and produce sustainable cotton crops.[61] This lack of water rights eventually caused the newcomers to default on their loan repayments and lose their down payments on land. Because the land had been severely overvalued, they were forced to find wage labour in the town of Seminole. *Die Post* picked up the story in subsequent issues, reporting in August 1977 that the whole settlement was failing, as the "Mennonites have been unable to obtain immigration visas." The story quoted an unequivocal "Charles Perez, director of the Immigration and Naturalization Service [INS] for this district," who said that "land ownership alone is not enough, to become [a] citizen." Perez had also announced that a convoy of trucks carrying the personal belongings of Old Colonist Mennonite migrants had been stopped at the US border in El Paso and would have to "turn around and return" to Mexico.[62]

The Mennonites had one significant advantage: their reputation as honest, hard-working people. The *Newsweek* story from June had reported that American businessmen in Seminole were delighted with the Mexico Mennonites, whom they declared to be "the very type of people that built up the West in the very first years."[63] Many locals apparently had benefited from Mennonite purchases of mobile homes and other goods. This goodwill did not solve the central problem of the west Texas Mennonite community's illegal status.

But by November 1977, a solution to the crisis seemed to be in the offing when high-profile Senator Lloyd Bentsen of Texas agreed to personally intervene and managed to postpone the INS order of deportation. Bentsen's pitch was enough, reported *Die Post*, to ensure that the "Mennonites, who came from Mexico and Canada, will receive permission to stay in this land."[64] Over the next two years, *Die Post* followed the account of Bentsen's private bill in the United States Senate to allow most of the Mennonites in Seminole (as well as in Boley, Oklahoma) to become citizens. It noted the active assistance from MCC offices in Washington and Akron, Pennsylvania. It recounted Bentsen's selflessness, because he was running the risk of appearing racist in fighting for Caucasian Mennonites while ignoring illegal Latino migrants from Mexico.[65] In the end, President Jimmy Carter signed Bill 707 into law, granting citizenship under unusual circumstances to 683 specifically named Mennonites.[66]

The Mexico Mennonites who stayed in the US experienced both the good and the bad. The small settlement of Mennonite settlers at Boley, Oklahoma, for example, fared relatively well, and although also named on the Bentsen bill, they did not experience the same social upheaval as the Seminole Mennonites. Perhaps they found their new setting in Boley strange in that it was both English-speaking and predominantly African American, but then it also lay near Corn, Oklahoma, an historic US Mennonite place. Most importantly, the Boley Mennonites were on a strong financial footing. Picking up a report from a US Mennonite newspaper, *Die Post* reported in December 1977 that nine families were living in mobile homes near the Canadian River and working 1500 acres as a community, with plans to divide the land and build separate farmsteads. They were also planning to build a small hospital, as they were awaiting other families from Mexico. In the meantime, they had established an English-language school of sixteen students with a teacher who had an education from Canada. The group members even reported an excellent first harvest of one hundred bushels of milo per acre and good returns on wheat and soybeans.[67]

The vanguard of Texas Mennonites had a more checkered time and found economic integration more difficult. In fact, most of those who stayed in Texas simply could not pay the land tax and lost most of their land in April 1979. Over the next few years, stable families reportedly paid off their debts, but others remained unsettled, unsure of where to turn. A March 1982 letter by Cornelius Loeppky, who had left Texas in 1979, reported that "we also bought land there, but we lost everything, along with all of those who had purchased land there," and added that "many of those in Seminole have moved away, although as we have heard, many have again moved there."[68] Other reports from the same year were just slightly more positive. A July 1982 letter noted that most newcomers "work on farms and in factories and are appreciated by their employers, although this accommodation is different than the one they had originally planned."[69]

But the US remained an uneasy place for many Mexico Mennonites. Reports continued of comings and goings, a perpetual restlessness, especially among so-called undocumented newcomers. In a March 1987 letter, Gerhard Knelsen of Seminole wrote to say that the family of his brother Joseph had arrived from Mexico, "also to earn something," but that another brother, Abram in Mexico, was considering Bolivia; in the meantime, he wrote, in the Isaac Fehr household, "the wife has travelled to Mexico and her husband is here completely alone ... and his siblings send him no letters; he is poor."[70] Other reports spoke of undocumented families moving far inland to find work at meat-packing plants. A March 1991 letter described families from Seminole, and also some directly from Mexico, arriving in the town of Storm Lake, Iowa, to join 1300 labourers at the giant Iowa Beef Packers plant. According to *Die Post*, the "employers are determined to hire Mennonites as they have heard that they are hard workers and reliable," and thus they "recruited" the Mennonites "to this region." Storm Lake, reported *Die Post*, was "the most recent place where one can find 'Kanadier' Mennonites."[71]

Increasingly, it seems, these wage workers simply ignored legal requirements for citizenship. A 1995 report noted that because many Mexico Mennonites no longer had Canadian citizenship, it had become easier for them to even consider travelling to the United States as illegal immigrants. As *Die Post* noted, it "is very difficult, if not impossible, to estimate the number of Mennonites from Mexico now in the U.S. ... [They] move with great frequency from one place to another, and many do not have the correct immigration papers and work illegally. ... Today one can find these Mennonites in Texas, Oklahoma, Kansas, Colorado and California," as well as in Iowa and Nebraska. The report suggested that Mennonites might continue to enter the US indefinitely to find work. Although the very largest concentration, 4000 strong, was still at Seminole, "a Mennonite minister in Liberal, Kansas reported 45 [new] families ... in the last year," making for a total of "250 families in southwestern Kansas." In addition, half a dozen Mexico Mennonite families lived in Adams, Oklahoma, while "east of Newton, Kansas, where earlier there was a single family, there are now six."[72]

Ironically, perhaps, the Mexico Mennonites who failed to obtain legal citizenship showed inordinate signs of seeking cultural assimilation. Reports from each of the US settlements described Old Colony Mennonites joining more evangelical churches that allowed them to discard telltale traditional dress, abandon old hairstyles, and partake of American consumer culture. A May 1987 letter reported the profound concern of Old Colony member Elisabeth Teichrob of Seminole, Texas, who wrote that she "longed so much for her children and grandchildren. ... When I think of all my children in a row, how they live so scattered about, then I have such longing it produces many tears." She was grateful that her children were making a good livelihood, "able to provide for a very fine table," but she worried that they were being assimilated. Teichrob was concerned that, among her children and grandchildren, "only English is being spoken," and wondered "how long before there won't be any German church." She worried about the evangelical missionaries who "these days seek to spin one's head" with a very personalized faith that encouraged prayer that addressed God with the informal word "Father." Teichrob was indignant: "Hasn't Jesus taught us to pray [more formally] 'Our Father in heaven' and told us not to babble like the heathen. And don't we read in the [Old] Songbook, 'Dearest Jesus, we are here in order to obey you and your Word ... so that the hearts in this world may move to where you are.' Why don't the other churches leave us [Old Colonist Mennonites] in our peace. ... I wish to write no more than what the Holy Scriptures say."[73] Evidently, her interpretation of these scriptures contradicted mainstream American evangelicalism.

Certainly, some old ways continued. The Old Colony founded German-language churches and even the evangelical missionaries worked in Low German. By 1991, the Mennonites at Storm Lake, Iowa, for example, had been organized by the Canadian-based Evangelical Mennonite Conference (EMC) with rented facilities from an Evangelical Free Church and an attendance at a Low German service of fifty to sixty people. Already, a baptismal service, a communion service, and a wedding had been planned.[74] A June 1994 report from Seminole, Texas, even announced that a local Low German-speaking Mennonite had become a missionary to Mexico's Old Colony communities: the specific report was that "Rev Dietrich Harms and family of Seminole, Texas, and the musicians, Eduard and Christine Klassen of Ontario, Canada, were in [Cuauhtémoc] region from June 12 ... to hold evangelical services."[75] The overall theme in the United States seemed to be that legal citizenship was treasured if and when it was available, but what mattered most were secure jobs and a religious faith that was at once meaningful and enabled an easy integration. The Mennonites from Mexico to the United States had learned, though, that an old view of citizenship tied to the ownership of farmland was possible for only a select few.

"We never hear ... complain[ts] about the President"

This view of citizenship had shaped the historic settlements of the Low German Mennonites in Mexico and Paraguay. Making no promises of patriotism, their main strategy was to earn the right to belong in any given nation by showing their worth as hard workers and law-abiding residents. Always this strategy included appeals to the highest authorities, whether state governors or federal leaders, in times of trouble. Even as the century came to a close, the old idea of *Privilegium* shaped the approach of Mennonites to government in the original Latin American communities in Chihuahua, Durango, and the Chaco.

Stories about Mexico in *Die Post* still presented the nation indirectly as a Mennonite "home." Affection for landscape, village life, and even Mexican cuisine was expressed, but rarely were the Spanish language, Mexican literature, or the Mexican nation-state celebrated. Mennonites in Mexico were not Mexican at heart. A January 1989 account in *Die Post* of about one hundred draft-age Mennonite men in Chihuahua, Mexico, signing up for "Pre-Cartilla" military cards, is illustrative. The article noted that while "no Mennonite needs to 'march'" – that is, engage in military service or even alternative community service – the registration "is undertaken in order that the [young men] can ... obtain Mexican passports and with those they can secure Canadian passports."[76] Ironically, Mennonites were willing to become "Mexican" if it guaranteed them the right to leave Mexico.

Mennonites were also happy to honour Mexican authorities, especially for their efforts to guarantee them separate status within the nation-state. In May 1990, *Die Post* reported on an unusual event in the Chihuahua Mennonite community, the visit of a Mexican president. President Carlos Salinas de Gortari's historic visit to Manitoba Colony, near Cuauhtémoc, was said to be the first by a Mexican president since the 1920s. Significantly, 10,000 Mennonites came out to see him and 500 students from twelve villages lined the street of the village of Blumenort. But significantly, too, the children sang, "Welcome here, Dear Friend" in German, and Salinas's five-minute speech was translated into Low German. And, while he honoured the Mennonites by visiting five different private homes, and took *Faspa*, the traditional late-afternoon lunch, at the "Peters residence," *Die Post* especially emphasized Salinas's promise "to honour the 'Privilegium' signed by President Obregón in 1921."[77] It was a document guaranteeing the Mennonites the right to remain outside the national culture.

The issue of Mennonite responsibility to Mexico was specifically raised in a lengthy and insightful article in April 1993 by successful entrepreneur and community leader Peter Rempel of Manitoba Colony, Chihuahua. Titled "1922–1992, 70 Years of Mennonites in Mexico," Rempel's article heralded the Mennonite achievements in Mexico, but suggested that they could be better citizens. President Salinas had declared "that Mexican laws were pluralistic enough to accommodate particular interest groups, if they in other ways were valuable to the country, and thus privileges would be preserved." The problem, according to Rempel, was that the Mennonites had become apathetic. They seemed unwilling to "speak to our children about the Anabaptist teachings of our ancestors," and lacked in "virtues, sincerity, contentedness, the [commitment to] mutual benefit and working for others" required of good citizens. Many even seemed to disregard Mexican law, openly charging "exorbitant interest rates," engaging in "embezzlement, or simply not paying taxes," and participating, "as often, and as much as possible, in the corrupt importation of goods," and this, stated Rempel, was "just to mention a few things."[78] Mennonites were not even making plans to obey Mexico's new law on compulsory secondary education, or to adjust to the new North American Free Trade Agreement. Rempel called for Mennonites to work together, to maintain their identity as an Anabaptist people, pacifist and nonresistant, but also to be model citizens in other respects. Significantly, though, Rempel's call to good citizenship and deference to Mexican authorities did not entail assimilation to the Mexican nation, the abandonment of the German language, or traditional Anabaptist pacifism. Good citizenship was still on Mennonite terms.

Reports from Paraguay emphasized a similar approach to citizenship. Often, dignitaries who visited the Canadian-descendant Mennonites seemed to reaffirm their minority status in a foreign country. A 1977 story reported that the Canadian ambassador to Argentina and his wife, "Mr. Bissonnet and Mrs. Bissonnet," visited Menno Colony in Paraguay on 2 July. The report noted with some pride and a hint of irony that Bissonnet was the "first Canadian official to visit Menno Colony, founded by Canadian Mennonites because of [1916] school laws in Manitoba."[79] In January 1988, the high-profile Canadian Member of Parliament, Jake Epp, and wife Lydia, evangelical Mennonites from southeastern Manitoba, also visited Menno Colony. It was a weighty visit, as the Epps arrived with an entourage that included the Canadian ambassador to Chile and other officials from Canada. Epp's aim, according to *Die Post*, was to get to "know the Mennonite colonies of the Chaco, and especially the Canadian [descendant] colonies, more fully."[80] The Kanadier of the Chaco were still Canadian fifty years after leaving the old homeland.

Mennonites in Paraguay, as elsewhere in the Americas, continued the long-standing Anabaptist "two-kingdom" theology that taught a disengagement from the nation-state. In seeming contradiction, these pacifists simultaneously considered themselves separate from the state, subject to government, and, within Mennonite circles, capable of judging a government's success. Especially, the state's record on law and order and its economic management were fair game. A May 1982 letter from the newly settled "horse and buggy" Durango Colony in East Paraguay related how these colonists had left Mexico because of unchecked violence. The letter, signed "Franz and Margaretha Friesen," offered a glowing and somewhat racialized report on the social aspects of East Paraguay, the Friesens' home now for four years: "I can say truthfully, we do not want to return to Mexico, even though it was a big change for us. The government [here] is very good. ... Only occasionally does one hear of a murder. ... Anyone involved in the marijuana trade is unmercifully dealt with. Also, it is said, that anyone who lets on that he has a communistic outlook. ... is sought out, and given a 'free' [airplane] ride, albeit, one out onto the lake. Also we never hear the native Paraguayans complaining about the president."[81] Certainly, not all Mennonites would have shared this cavalier approach to politics, but the implicit view that good citizens were a grateful, deferential, and law-abiding people did reflect a majority perspective.

Ironically, perhaps, Mennonite migrants held a particular respect for orderly government. In 1989, when Paraguay's strongman President Alfredo Stroessner was overthrown in a coup d'état, *Die Post* recalled the particular affection that Paraguayan Mennonites had had for him: "For the 23,000 Mennonites life continues as before the coup" even though many Mennonites "openly appreciated [Stroessner] as he left their colonies undisturbed ... and no Paraguayan Mennonite has had to serve in the military." Indeed, the "Mennonites were often honoured by visits from the president," who "was often openly proud of the colonists' achievements, especially in the dry, isolated Chaco region, which until the establishment of the Mennonite colonies was considered an uninhabitable and fruitless region."[82]

This paternalistic relationship with government continued well past Stroessner's time. In 1993, when Menno Colony mayor Cornelius Sawatsky visited Canada, he addressed a gathering of business leaders in Steinbach, Manitoba, and quoted the new president, General Andrés Rodríguez Pedotti, as stating that the "Mennonites were an example to Paraguayans." Sawatsky spoke of an implicit and abiding pact: the Mennonites "had kept their word" to the country's leadership, for even though they paid a heavy cost in pioneering, with 10 percent of the settlers dying in their first year in Paraguay, they had "made the Chaco fertile." The Paraguayan government, for its part, rewarded the Mennonites "with a charter of privileges, their own schools in German, military exemption, self-governance, their own inheritance system, etc."[83]

"In this world we are never fully at home"

More recently settled Mennonites in Bolivia and Argentina shared this deference to governments that granted the privileges of military exemption, private schools, and local autonomy. But as the majority of these southerners were traditionalist "horse and buggy" Old Colony Mennonites, they were also the most insistent on minimal identification with a state or nation.

The specific nature of the Bolivian Mennonite community's relationship to its host society was variously outlined in *Die Post* shortly after it was launched. In July 1977, J.J. Driedger of Las Piedras Colony answered the question, "Are we fully at home here?," with a short rebuke: "In this world we are never fully at home. We are all on a journey to the greatest homeland and cannot make our home here."[84] Six months later, Driedger added to his view on being at "home" in any one nation-state: "The world is large, and one can live anywhere one wants to, as long as no one tells us where we have to live."[85] For Driedger, ultimate citizenship lay in heaven, and any citizenship in this life must yield to the primacy of religious ideals.

Making the same point, but now by contrasting the Bolivian and Canadian Mennonites, a writer in September 1977 recounted how he had lived in Canada from 1947 to 1969. There, he had encountered Mennonites who, having attended English-language schools, were "ashamed to be identified as Mennonites." The Canadian Mennonites, declared the writer, had trampled on the very birthright offered by "our great-grandparents and grandparents and mothers and parents, who moved from Germany to Russia, from Russia to Canada and Mexico and so forth."[86] Canadian Mennonites suffered from a lack of "steadfastness" and had given in to the lure of patriotism and assimilation. Appropriately, the anonymous writer signed off as "the searching pilgrim."

Bolivia was a godsend to so-called "pilgrims," but even they could never separate themselves from government totally. Moreover, because national policies affected the Mennonite colonists, they felt it within their right to readily judge governments, their economic performance, and their efforts to maintain order. Mennonites might not vote but they had their opinions, which they shared in *Die Post*, especially during the tumultuous years of hyperinflation in Bolivia during the 1980s.

A letter written from Valle Esperenza Colony noted in May 1982 that President Celso Torrelio, a military leader who would be deposed that July, had declared on TV and radio (two media not allowed to most Mennonites in the South) that his government would "hold the value of the 'peso' [the Mennonite term for the boliviano] to 44 per [US] dollar until December." The writer was indignant, as "it is not two months since then and already money merchants on the street are paying 80 [bolivianos per dollar]. For flour and other essentials the prices are to be frozen so that it is cheap to obtain and still every week the prices rise."[87]

Ten months later, another letter criticized the government, now democratically elected and headed by President Hernán Siles Zuazo, although in more oblique language: "About Bolivia not much good can be reported. Now one pays 540 'pesos' for one U.S. dollar. Soon we will look at the 'peso' with skepticism and think, 'you are worthless.' I have a huge stack of money and can't purchase anything with it. How do things look like in the North?"[88] The letter writer was inviting transnational comment on national fiscal policy.

Letters from Bolivia expressed another common idea among the Low German Mennonites. While government must be respected, the Mennonites' teaching of separation from the world forbade close association even with its local representatives, especially gun-toting police. An April 1983 story reported that the Mennonite colonies of Swift Current, Sommerfeld, and Riva Palacios near Santa Cruz had been "hit by thieves using armed force." According to the story, "police are investigating the cause of this problem, which has existed for well over a year, according to statements by [two Mennonite colonists] Abraham Rempel and Bernard Peter Rempel." The crime had been serious, as "as three men came to a store, took the owner prisoner and stole 20,000 'pesos', about forty US dollars." The victims' response was to "record the license number of the thieves' car and hand the information over to officials in Santa Cruz." The two Rempel colonists seemed quite displeased, though, that their Mennonite leaders were unwilling to do more. They were overtly critical: the "police is willing to establish patrols in this region, but Mennonites don't want the police in their region."[89] The leaders would rather suffer indignation than rely on local government agencies.

Still, the pre-modern idea that national governments could aid the Mennonite settlers in their ethno-religious quest survived. In June 1990, *Die Post* reported that four Bolivia Mennonites – Bernard Wall, Abram Neufeld, and Heinrich Giesbrecht from Valle Esperanza Colony, and Jacob Rempel from San Jose de Chiquitos Colony – had been arrested and sent to Palma Sola prison, where they "find themselves imprisoned on account of debt" incurred after a "harvest failure." The problem, however, did not seem insurmountable, as, it was noted, "the government is intervening."[90] A March 1992 report outlined another long-standing issue solved by government intervention. At Sommerfeld Colony, indigenous Bolivians were taking over parts of the colony, claiming ownership of it. *Die Post* described this as a "land problem that the colony mayors have been struggling with for a long time." Significantly, the story announced that the "land problem" had been solved with an appeal to the national government in La Paz. Apparently, the Sommerfeld leaders and "the Indian leaders, both of whom claimed the land, traveled to the capital of La Paz and there signed an agreement, according to which the Indians will move off the land; only one man remains on the land, demanding more money."[91] Mennonites would not mix with local government, but they readily appealed to it at the national level.

Old ideas of citizenship were evident also in Argentina, the most recent host country for Low German-speaking Mennonites moving south from Mexico. Numerous reports in *Die Post* outlined the process of settlement, but, clearly, what mattered most to the Argentine-bound Mennonites were military exemption and permission to run their own affairs according to their idea of *Privilegium*. A December 1989 account reported on attempts by the Old Colony Mennonite community of Capulin in Chihuahua, Mexico, to settle in Argentina. It noted that four emigration "delegates – two colony mayors, one preacher and one deacon – who went to Argentina have come back with favourable reports." It spoke about their "friendly" reception near Santa Rosa, La Pampa province, and their sense that the "climate there is suitable for crop and cattle farming, similar to what they know from Mexico." The foundations for a replicated farm community were clearly present. But, the report continued, a 22 August "Brotherhood meeting, attended by those interested in emigration," had been informed that no recommendation could be made, as "first the question of the 'Privilegium' must be ruled on" by the Argentine government.[92] The reality in Argentina was that Mennonite requests contradicted the country's constitution, yet local interests demanded an accommodation for the Mennonites.

Late in 1989, Capulin delegates joined yet another Mexico Mennonite delegation, one from La Honda Colony in Zacatecas, in seeking a personal audience with the Argentine president, Carlos Menem. According to La Honda delegates Johan Fehr and Jacob Penner, the trip "had been unsuccessful," as they had hoped to "speak with the president" in person, but he had not "had time for them" during their time in Buenos Aires. Then, when in late November, "they were supposed to have another chance" to see him, "it turned out to be too long a wait" to correspond to their travel plans, and they left Argentina for Paraguay, a previously planned stopover on their return north. Nevertheless, the delegates were heartened by the fact that they "had been well received by the president's officials," who had said "that it was not impossible to obtain a 'Privilegium.'"[93] Fertile land and friendly hosts were less important than a national guarantee of separation from military service and patriotic schooling.

Conclusion

The tens of thousands of Canadian-descendant Low German Mennonites who travelled among the Americas in the late twentieth century imagined a particular geography. Their identity was first and foremost that of a religious minority that viewed migration as a way to counter social, cultural, or economic problems of a hostile modern world. Their sense of homeland always entailed the idea of pilgrimage through this world to the next, to their ultimate homeland, which they knew as eternal life in heaven. The migrants certainly used the word "homeland" to denote places in this world, but it was a relative term, the place from which their grandparents had come, Canada, or more recent points of origin, increasingly Mexico or Paraguay. In any case, "homeland" did not constitute a national identity, and migration to another country readily occurred if it advanced the interests of community or family. Consequently, Mennonites undertook new and more treacherous migrations, to the United States, where many settled as undocumented migrants, and to Argentina, where old privileges seemed tenuously granted.

Perhaps the Mennonite diaspora in the Americas was expressed in a fundamental divide, separating those heading up to the United States from those moving down to Argentina, or those moving to Canada from those setting out for Bolivia. Despite their differences, the northward and southward migrants shared the imagined geography expressed in *Die Mennonitische Post*. The editors of *Die Post* regularly guided the discussion, explaining the social dynamics around specific migrations, reporting on the ever-widening circle of settlements, and offering counsel on how to adapt to different settings. Still, the dominant voice in *Die Post* always was the ordinary letter writer from any one of hundreds of villages and townsites spread across the western hemisphere. These letter writers seemed to see the countries of North and South America not as nation-states with which to affiliate or as entities that possessed impenetrable borders. They were countries with specific places of promise. Many writers hoped that the economic and social structures of a revitalized, imagined, supranational village could be secured by crossing national boundaries. They were overseeing the construction of a Mennonite village that knew no national boundary in the cultural sense of the word. In this respect, migration and a diasporic culture continued to be the very underpinning of group survival.

8 Homing in on the Transnational World: Women Migrants in Ontario, 1985–2006

In a sense, nothing orderly or certain characterized the turn of the twenty-first-century, Canadian-descendant, Mennonite diaspora in the Americas. The vast network of communities stretching from Canada to Argentina was dynamic, even messy. Most children were taught traditional ways incongruent with modernity, couples struggled with large families, householders jostled for space to thrive, and the elderly pondered yesteryear's sacrifices. People continued to move; enabled by inexpensive air travel and modern highway systems, many moved several times, and some seemed in perpetual movement, always searching for better livelihoods and reconnections with loved ones. Church life diverged on either the communitarian or evangelical pathways; deeply competitive in their own ways, both traditions published books, instructed youth, and preached about morality and the hereafter. Agriculture was tested in the perennial search for new land and better crops, hopes for adequate precipitation, and concerns about volatile world markets. Questions of citizenship in Bolivia, Canada, the United States, and elsewhere raised questions about the long-term viability of Low German-speaking Mennonite communities within each of these nations.

Still, by 2006, when research for this final chapter began, the basic shape of a Low German Mennonite transnational "village" was apparent, most prominently in the three, highly identifiable, settlement nodes, each with at least 50,000 residents – eastern Bolivia, northern Mexico, and southern Ontario[1] – but also in a hundred other places in western Canada, the United States, Belize, Paraguay, southern Mexico, and Argentina. The variation of life and challenges within this hemispheric village was remarkable, but common assumptions undergirded it. To understand it would require travels to the ends of the Americas: from southern Bolivia to northern Alberta, from central Nova Scotia to southwestern Kansas, and many places in between.

And to know these places would require meeting the people at work, in the hayfields of eastern Canada, the forest camps of northern Alberta, the giant abattoirs of western Kansas, the cotton fields of southern Bolivia. It would lead to the red brick or grey adobe church and school buildings of the majority Old Colony group, as well as to the white wood-framed or stately brick buildings of the smaller, usually more evangelistic, churches. It would mean listening in on the voices analysed in previous chapters: sermons on suffering and purity; debates on land acquisitions; cries of nostalgia for an old homeland; multi-layered ideas on space and time; curt exchanges with curious outsiders; deliberations on issues of citizenship; disagreements on matters of faith.

This story has been complex and dynamic, indeed, one increasingly so over the course of three generations. In a sense, chapter 7 was the natural conclusion in this account, one with broad strokes, linking a scattered people in the various corners of the Americas. And yet, as numerous scholars have asserted, the full range of transnationalism cannot be understood only by surveying its farthest reaches. It also requires a focus on the local, the place from which ordinary members of the diaspora hone lives in global context. Arjun Appadurai observes that for migrants, in both the old homeland and in the new, "even the most localized of ... worlds ... [have] become inflected, even afflicted, by cosmopolitan scripts."[2] Households or communities are never just transplanted, but "reconstituted" as "global ethnospaces" in the context of multiple migrations and stories of the old homeland that give meaning to an uprooted world.[3] A close look at these ethnospaces reveals the ordinary person's life-world, "sites of selfhood," to employ a concept by anthropologist Michael Jackson. His focus on the subjective "I" and its relationship to a broader world highlights "one's strategic struggle to sustain and synthesize oneself as a subject in a world that simultaneously subjugates one to other ends."[4] To listen to the migrant voices from "the most localized" of spaces is to discover "the human need to imagine that one's life belongs to a matrix greater than oneself, and that within this sphere of greater being one's own actions and words matter and make a difference."[5] To see this larger matrix, this "cosmopolitan script," with any degree of clarity is to find those members who did not lead, make the official pronouncements, or negotiate with the presidents of the nations, and perhaps never wrote letters to newspapers or were interviewed by them.

Counterintuitive perhaps, this book thus ends by coming full circle, back to where it began with a specific set of bounded, regionalized locations in a single one of the various countries. Similar to the first chapter, this final chapter presents a gendered story, one in which action was shaped by the local community's expectations of typical female and male behaviour. It also focuses on how location in one place was conditioned by imagined life in another. But, unlike the first chapter, this final one moves into the very recesses of the local, that is, the household set within the local economy and neighbourhood congregation. It focuses on the worlds of six, ordinary, immigrant women who moved between Mexico and Ontario in the 1980s and 1990s. It seeks in their narratives an understanding of how transnationalism was experienced in the most circumscribed of migrant worlds.[6]

The six women were interviewed in 2006 by Kerry Fast, at the time a Low German-speaking doctoral student of religion at the University of Toronto, whose own parents and grandparents had lived in Mexico for a time.[7] The women seemed to speak with ease, some in English and others in Low German, about their migrant experiences. They outlined their youthful pasts in Mexico, the times of their family's repeat migrations between Canada and Mexico, their intricate kinship networks, their relationships with husbands and children, the stories they told their children, the memory of Mexico that shaped their links to new localities. They highlighted local quandaries faced upon arrival in the North, their uprootedness, and how they came to choose the one country over the other. They gave voice to the importance of gender, the inherited cultural patterns from Mexico, and the changing relations in working- and middle-class society in Canada. They articulated destabilizing, vulnerable social contexts on the one hand, and strengthening family bonds and comforting, face-to-face, congregational encounters on the other. In the process, they illuminated the inner core of this diasporic Mennonite community.

The women were historical and gendered subjects who possessed a common commitment to household and family within a common continental labour market, citizenship regime, and patriarchal ethno-religious world. But their stories differed, depending on how they arrived in Canada – as young girls, young women, or mothers, as married or single, as communitarian or evangelical – and as each one placed herself at the centre of a transnational story. By doing so, each of the women, introduced by pseudonyms below, gave voice to a fundamental characteristic of such a story. The most localized of ethnospaces – that is, the family and household – was also linked ineradicably to the most expansive of immigrant spaces.

208   Village among Nations

Two Girls and Transnational Childhoods

The first two interviewees, girls when they arrived in Ontario from Mexico in the mid-1980s, illustrate the thinking of children growing up in a migrant community. Nettie Wiebe was the youngest of nine children, who, at age nine, migrated from Chihuahua state to Ontario.[8] Here, she married a fellow Old Colony Mennonite and worked with him for a time in greenhouses, but, with the birth of her three daughters, focused her energies on homemaking. The second interviewee, Elisabeth Rempel, the eldest in her family, also arrived in Ontario in about 1985 at age seven, albeit from La Honda Colony in Zacatecas state.[9] At age eighteen, after twelve years in Canada, Rempel returned with her family to Mexico, where she married a fellow Old Colony Mennonite, but then embarked on a series of repeat migrations between Zacatecas and Ontario. Both Wiebe and Rempel experienced the transnational from within family. To employ the words of historian Marlene Epp, both experienced the migration as an historical moment in which "mental place was culturally encoded in familial relationships and domestic spaces," even while they experienced the ambivalence of "individually 'looking back' ... [and] collectively 'moving forward.'"[10]

For Nettie Wiebe, the migration north certainly occurred within the context of expanding kinship networks. Wiebe had stark memories of grinding poverty in Mexico: "We were always very poor," eating "mostly potatoes and beans and bread with coffee, black coffee," and very occasionally, on Sunday, they had meat. She recalled how her own father "wasn't able to work that much" and that her older brothers, who "helped my uncles on the fields, planting and picking up the crops" or "worked at the apple factory," didn't earn much. Wiebe recalled with bitterness her more well-to-do uncles and aunts in Mexico, "but it always seemed like they wanted to keep stuff for themselves," leaving the "ones behind with nothing." Local kinship ties seemed to offer little hope.

Thus, her family looked beyond Mexico, hoping to find more generous relatives elsewhere. She recalled a failed attempt by her family to join relatives in Bolivia; unfortunately, after many days in the back of a decrepit camper truck, she and her family were forced back by a "small war," likely in Guatemala. Upon their return to Mexico, Nettie's father and her three brothers found work on a cattle ranch near the border city of Juárez, far from any Mennonite community. Hope of rescue from debilitating poverty, however, came from stories of relatives in Canada. Wiebe recalled that, from a child's perspective, it seemed as if in Canada, "they picked money from trees"; at the very least, "we wouldn't have to be hungry a lot, we'd be eating healthy." The lifeline in Ontario came from relatives – uncles, aunts, and a couple of brothers and a sister – familiar people who "sent somebody down to get us and ... to help us with our passports." Thus, her parents sold their meagre belongings and "went straight here and stayed here."

In Ontario, the Wiebes followed the familiar lines of the distended clan. They headed to a relative's house, Wiebe's aunt's in Aylmer, where they lived "for a couple of weeks and [then] moved into our own." Her aunt also arranged jobs: it was work for the whole family, including for young Nettie, "picking strawberries and cucumbers ... [not] the best jobs." Life outside this kinship network seemed frightening. Wiebe recalled her family's sequence of moves, from Aylmer to Blenheim to Chatham to Pain Court, "always field work." During the winter months, Wiebe was able to attend school but she found it "scary," as she didn't know any English; after "a couple of months ... we were able to get along with everybody," but it remained an unfamiliar territory.

A sense of agency for Wiebe came from within the household and church community, no matter their official patriarchal natures. Wiebe's account of beginning her own family places her at its centre. Only by dropping out of school at about fourteen was she able to gain control of her life within a strictly Mennonite network. She was determined to marry a particular Mennonite boy; earlier boyfriends she had "dumped before they did me," but when she first met her future husband, she thought at once, "Maybe we could have something here," and they began dating. Then, when he "tried breaking up" with her, she simply decided not to "let him go," and six months later they were married. Her self-effacing conclusion was that "life works in mysterious ways."

After marriage, life within the Old Colony congregation took on new importance for Wiebe. In fact, she began teaching in its German Sunday School, in part because "they had a hard time [getting] teachers there" and her "husband said, 'whatever, just do it.'" But she also felt a duty: "There is lots of German kids that don't speak German [and] we're supposed to keep the language that mom speaks; that's [the language of] our religion that we're supposed to keep."

From this vantage point, Wiebe felt secure enough to partake of the offerings of the Canadian welfare state that citizenship allowed. In fact, she was implicitly critical of the traditional self-sufficiency of the Mexico Mennonites. Her own Canadian citizenship status was important, and Wiebe spoke of the need to "'re-intention' ... before my 28th birthday,"[11] to declare her desire for citizenship as a child of Canadians born abroad.

It was an important enough step for her to drive to the "passport office" in Toronto, a place with "just crazy drivers." Citizenship was crucial, for she recalled how, before her father-in-law's 2004 death, he "didn't have any papers, any health cards or nothing, so he was always afraid of going to the hospital and doctors because it was so expensive." Then, too, his income without a government pension was limited to the remittances of his two unmarried daughters, or, as Wiebe put it, with only "two girls working for them." The incident underscored her own desire for security as a Canadian citizen.

Memories of her childhood in Mexico remained etched in her mind even as she began having her own family in Canada. But they were ambivalent recollections. She enjoyed telling her daughters of childhood in Mexico, in such colour that they themselves "want to see the animals and go horseback riding." One of her favourite stories placed an incident in Mexico as the foundation of her parents' union:

> There had been this one other single guy that knew my mom. Well, my dad, he knew her kind of too . ... And this other guy he wanted my dad to take him [to her place, on his] ... buggy and horse. ... My dad ... had no intention. ... [to allow his friend] to go there by himself or to be with my mom. [As] soon as [my dad] got there he figured, no, my friend he can't have her. I want her. And he brought the other guy to some place else. ... There had been this other lady who had really wanted to get married to my dad, but my dad didn't want her, so he brought this guy to that lady and he came back to my mom.

The stories about Mexico that shaped Wiebe's life, however, were also hard-luck accounts: "If I tell [my children] they'll get sad. I tell them they are lucky not to live in a world that we lived in. [I] tell them that Grandma and Grandpa ... were always very sad that life was so hard, [but] that it wasn't their fault." An antithetical Mexico figured prominently in Wiebe's new Ontario world.

Elisabeth Rempel's account of moving from Mexico emphasized less the broad family network important in Wiebe's life and rather her own nuclear family's movement. Rempel's family left La Honda Colony in Zacatecas in stages: in about 1985, they first came to Canada as seasonal workers, stayed "just past that Christmas and then they went back [to Mexico] ... had an auction there ... sold everything, and ... came back [to Canada] for good." Here, as a young teenager, Rempel began working in apple orchards and packing houses, "all the variety, except picking cucumbers." Then, abruptly when she turned eighteen, her parents decided to return to Mexico, and Rempel and her siblings grudgingly accompanied them.

Back in La Honda, Rempel worked at odd jobs; most memorably, in the difficult annual pinto bean harvest. Just a year or so after returning, she married, fully expecting to have her family in Mexico. But life was unsettled and emigration seemed to be the panacea. Even within La Honda, she and her husband moved four times in quick succession, from her parents' place to a farm temporarily vacated by friends who had gone to Canada, then to the husband's parents' spacious house, and finally to a small house, purchased for them by her parents-in-law. All the while, the young couple survived on milk sales from their three cows, each identified by English names according to Canadian custom dating to the 1920s – Liz, the wedding gift from her parents; Black, from his parents; and Spots, their own purchase. When the milk cheques proved insufficient during the drought years of the late 1990s, the couple and their baby moved back to Canada, a place Rempel recalled with fondness.

This time, the distended family network factored in the move north. The young couple connected with Rempel's brother, who had defied his parents and stayed in Canada as a teenager in 1998. As Rempel recalled it, boys were able to "work around and kind of grab the parents and push them in one direction." Despite this kinship tie, Rempel was unsettled in Canada, and just eight months later, she and her husband returned to Mexico. Her reasoning for the decision was straightforward: "My parents were down there [and] ... I had relatives there." After another eight-month period, it became evident that Mexico could not sustain her young family. Thus, they moved again, this time to Kansas, where they lived as undocumented migrants for two years, her husband working "on a farm with livestock." From Rempel's perspective as a young mother, these moves were all "very hard, very hard," for no sooner had they "settled down and got familiarized ... and then ... [they] were uprooted ... and then settle[d] for a new place."

Longing for legal status, "somewhere where you're able to do things and not fear that you'll be deported," and "a permanent place for our kids to grow up," the small family returned to Canada. It was the place with the extended family, but it also provided a legal footing in an amorphous world and it provided social services and health care, on which Rempel came to rely as a young mother. In fact, without explanation, Rempel's narrative included Canadian health-care providers as an authoritative force in her life. After the birth of four children, for example, she defied old church teachings against fertility control and had a tubal ligation; as she put it curtly, "The doctor wanted us to be done." Within her evolving world, Canada provided a trustworthy security shield.

In contrast, Mexico reminded her of a soulless, repressive place. The move back to Mexico as a teenager had been "terrible," a place to which it was "just so hard trying to adjust." Rempel thought, "If my parents had moved when I was younger, it would have been easier, but we just really felt out of place there." Her plan at the time, to stay in Canada with a friend, failed: "My mother found out [and] she wouldn't have any of it. ... She's like, 'no way, you're coming with us; you're not of age yet ... you have to stay with us until you're at least 20.'" Even then, Rempel knew her parents were after an elusive goal: they wanted to return to Mexico to teach the children traditional ways, "a little bit more farm life and. ... none of [the] stuff that was going on [in Canada]." This also entailed embracing the traditionalist "dress code" for girls, one that called for "those solid, like a band type of thing" around their waists, and aprons, which "they wore all the time." Given her teenaged frame of mind, cultural conflict was in the offing. She and her sisters simply "didn't change much of our [Canadian] clothing" and "mom didn't enforce" the colony's dress codes. In fact, when the colony ministers, worried that "the world was changing too much ... came out one day and really gave [Mother] some talking to," Rempel's mother stood up for her daughters. She was even "kind of really angry, or sad about" the visit from the ministers, although later "she said if that's the only reason they come by here, then it's enough to laugh about."

Rempel's childhood memories in Mexico shaped her life in Canada. Her husband, for one, had his own difficult memories. As the second youngest of eight children in a home where his mother had died when he was eleven, he could not forget a difficult family life in which his widowed father became "pretty depressed and turned to alcohol." Rempel's own memories were similarly disconcerting. True, Mexico had elements of the bucolic rural childhood; it was "fun ... when you were younger," a place with stories of being chased by an angry ewe protecting her "awfully cute" little lambs and of Mother confronting a "nasty" billy goat by "grabb[ing] his horns" and seating "herself on his back ... rode and rode on him. ... It was so funny!" But her overwhelming memories of being a young adult in Mexico recounted another set of realities – arduous work, poverty, drought, and cultural conflict. When her brothers and sisters from Chihuahua and Zacatecas went north to Canada for visits, they had no temptation to return.

A Mother of Teenagers and Stories of Suffering

A similar flow of ideas and values, but marked by deeper tragedy and gendered division, describes the life of Aganetha Thiessen.[12] Thiessen was in her early thirties and a mother of nine when she left Durango, Mexico, for Ontario in the mid-1980s and eventually made a home in rural Norfolk-Haldimand County. The arrival followed the tragic death in Mexico of her mother-in-law, killed when a truck rammed into their horse-drawn buggy at dusk. Only a premonition by Thiessen's husband kept them from travelling on that buggy that night and saved them from a worse fate. But the accident caused them intense grief, plus bitter dislocation. The remarriage of her father-in-law pressured Thiessen and her husband to leave his father's "very nice" family house. Multiple moves, from one rented place to another, followed; it was a life of poverty, one "without a farm, without cattle, without much income." She and her husband eked out survival on the earnings from a small printing press.

Employing the social resources of the kinship network reaching north to Canada seemed to be the only solution to their troubles. The emigration experience, however, proved extremely difficult: when "we began to travel to Canada ... it was very crude. ... I had to be in the back [of the pickup truck] with the nine children. In the front were my husband and the driver, and perhaps a child in between." The trip was made emotionally difficult because Thiessen's mother "did not want us to go to Canada." Once in Ontario, Thiessen's family made its way to her husband's sister Trien's place. Even this connection was "so unpleasant; we had these nine children underfoot. [Fortunately] our children were all so good, well good enough, at least they had a TV they could watch." But soon, they were reminded of the limits of kinship kindness. Just two weeks after their arrival, sister-in-law Trien became "afraid that the landlord would come in, and suddenly announce, this isn't your own place, this isn't a motel. Well yes, then we had to seek to get out of there." After a brief stay with another Mennonite family, the Thiessens finally found their own place, a "house with three very small rooms ... and it wasn't even a house that had been insulated and dry walled. But it was better, we weren't living with others."

Canada remained a strange and even hostile land. True, they found work, "I and my husband, cutting asparagus," but "it was only a few hours a day that we could earn money; together I and my husband could earn only about 200 dollars a week." Then, too, it was work that separated Thiessen from her young children: "The children were at home, having to fend for themselves. It was such a terrible time for me." She was compelled to ask her "eldest daughter, who was only twelve" to babysit, knowing "that she was actually too young ... but we couldn't [afford] a babysitter. We were completely at the bottom, completely without money." One day, to Thiessen's horror, the twelve-year-old phoned the farm to say that while she was trying to do the family's laundry, little Annie had become badly scalded, an accident ultimately requiring the young girl to be hospitalized for two weeks. Thiessen's overwhelming concern at the time was "Oh, what should we do? What would have happened if someone [in the family welfare agency] had ... found out? We just had to keep earning."

Indeed, the concern that they meet the approval of the Canadian boss and the authorities was ever-present. As the summer turned to fall, the work became that of picking peppers and then Thiessen became pregnant with her tenth child. "I recall how hard I worked, picking those peppers, and then suddenly I was bending over in those branches, and vomited and vomited. I looked up [terrified]; had someone seen me, 'nope,' I continued picking fast." Canada was not a land of potential allies for an impoverished family.

After their first summer in Canada, the family returned to Mexico. Thiessen was relieved to be back "home," and she and her husband started up their old printing business. She was determined to remain in Mexico: "I thought, and actually said it too, no one will take me alive from here back to Canada, so horrible had it all been. However, once it was summer again, the dollars were so desperately needed ... so we raced off again [to Canada] with our herd of children ... in a single car." Then, for the winter, they returned again to Mexico. "We were so happy; we had a nice house there. But just to live in that house, that was of no use. My husband had borrowed so much money he was worried we would not be able to feed the children." So, for the third consecutive summer, they headed north, "to see if we could pay the debt that we had outstanding." It was to be the Thiessens' final move from Mexico, forced because "my husband always worked as long as he could, and always nicely brought home the 'food'. ... But he was always insistent that the children must have a good life." Again, Thiessen's mother objected to the move north: "She believed that our people had once left Canada because [the authorities] ... had closed their [Mennonite] schools, and I think, they hadn't been able to have such good church services [in Canada] as they now have. And she thought it was still so. ... And it was almost impossible to convince her, that things could be much more traditional here [in Canada in the 1990s] than in the past."

Thus, Canada became home to the family of twelve. In 1995, the Thiessens were able to purchase their own house and, over time, the children grew into teenagers. But that life stage introduced a new era with its own set of troubles for the uprooted family: "The children simply don't listen to you as they grow up. First always, when they were small, it was so hard for me ... and I would say to my mother, if only the children could be big enough to help me. 'Oh,' she said, 'when they are small they squeeze the lap, when they are big [they tear at] the heart'. ... Well, I have discovered just that; it's certainly difficult."

A heart-wrenching tragedy illustrated her point. It was the story of "our son Jakob who was killed ... in a car accident," his second serious accident incurred after embarking on a reckless life in which he often "no longer came home for night." Thiessen recalled in minutiae her response upon first hearing of each of Jakob's accidents. In the first instance, the police startled her at her door, and in the second, she received an eerie phone call from a sister-in-law who had been at the scene of the accident. After the first accident, Jakob was sent home to recuperate, and Thiessen put all aside to assist him, but he coldly refused his mother's aid. He suffered depression and spoke of suicide. He spent most of his time holed up in his room with a television, watching questionable movies, or with his girlfriend behind a closed door, coming out only after Thiessen had herself gone to bed. She hardly knew what to do, "as I treasured him so much." Her only comfort before his tragic death was that he had once told her, "I am no longer as wicked as you think, I no longer drink that much or do drugs," and "when he didn't come home" for a night, he insisted "he was at the Zachariases'; they all liked him so much. ... And okay, that gave me some rest."

After Jakob's second accident, the one leading to his death, she found similar comfort. The police reported that, even though he had been at a party, he had not been drinking, and that the accident had been the result of icy roads. And then, when she saw his corpse, his right hand was raised, "as if he had begged for help" just before his death; "that is how it appeared to me, and from that moment it was easier." Thiessen became satisfied that Jakob had made his peace with God at the last moment, even though he had earlier spurned the Old Colony church. She found comfort in hearing that his ex-girlfriend had given birth to his child; "I would love to raise that child, but it is hers after all; so long as she is nice to it."

Thiessen said that life was easier with the other children: "Two of our girls work, and they also give us some money. ... And in the summer the school children will also go to work, if nothing else they will grade asparagus." Another factor that made life bearable was her Old Colony congregation. In fact, Thiessen was convinced that it was a more effective congregation than the one they had left in Durango: in Canada, "they are more clear in their preaching, or articulate just what the situation is ... so that the youth can better understand it all. They use more [the familiar] Low German here than High German."

Similar to the experience of the other women in this study, Mexico eventually became a place of ambivalent memory for Thiessen. True, it marked a tranquil rural world, but one of economic hardship. Perhaps "in Mexico ... things were not as handy as here; I often had to carry water a long distance to wash. ... On the other hand, I could work much harder than I can now ... I just no longer have the same spirit." Even the act of birthing was easier and more genuine in Mexico: "I was always among Mennonites. ... I was always able to discuss everything in Low German. ... There, they let me walk about until it was time ... able to tend to the house, doing the laundry before hand." In Canada, "they fasten me up on a bench or table, my nerves almost didn't let me do it." Then, too, she recalled how easy it was to raise children in Mexico. She could only hope that in Canada they "would all nicely go to church each Sunday, and to try to learn the Bible as best they can. Then I would be very happy."

Still, on balance, Mexico was a place of bitter disappointments: "It was completely different there ... I didn't like it. There was quite a practice there of [the men] going to the city. I had to stay home, and the man drove to the city; he had 'friends' there, and he drank, and perhaps, too often. ... For that reason I just don't want to return." Thiessen noted that when one "has so many things go through one's head, one loses the spirit of life." An economically solid base in Ontario, undergirded by the teachings of the Old Colony church, made life bearable. Thiessen's deepest concern was with the spiritual and economic well-being of her children and her husband. In the end, Canada seemed to offer more than Mexico.

Two Young Mothers and the Canadian Soul

Justina Krahn[13] of Swift Colony and Lisa Klippenstein of Los Jagueyes Colony, both located in Chihuahua state, arrived in Canada in the mid-1990s, ten years after the three women above. Krahn was single at age twenty-three, and Klippenstein, age twenty-seven, was newly married.[14] It was a later decade in which the Mexico Mennonites seemed more comfortable in an urbanizing Ontario. The two young women's lives differed in some ways: Krahn came directly to Ontario with her parents and joined an Old Colony church; Klippenstein, of Kleine Gemeinde Mennonite background, first came to Manitoba and then resettled in southern Ontario, where she joined the relatively more progressive Evangelical Mennonite Church (EMC). Still, both Krahn and Klippenstein negotiated similarly reconfigured kinship networks and church congregations.

As in most other cases, Justina Krahn's first memory of arriving in Ontario related to an encounter with relatives. After entering Canada, her family made straightaway for her uncle and aunt's house in Chatham. Krahn's first memory of entering the house near midnight was not one of familiarity but of strangeness associated with industrialized society: "The first thing I smelled when I opened the door was bleach. Bleach water people drink here! My aunt was sitting there feeding her baby and I'm like, 'what are you doing with bleach in the middle of the night?'. ... But I [drank] the water, then I [knew] what it was. The smell!" This encounter was followed by disquiet as her family of nine seemed to overfill the small house. Krahn recalled vividly that those first few days were "not good ... but once we were in our own place it was okay." The work was similarly unsettling. Krahn's assignment was in the fields, picking cucumbers and tomatoes, making for "the hardest summer of my life." The family lived near the field, so "[we] were there when the sun came up and we were there when the sun went down, so we had a long day. That was hard work, but we made it."

Like many other Mennonites in Ontario, the Krahns returned to Mexico for the winter, but then, the next year, they went north for good. The work on an asparagus farm and a vegetable-processing plant in Wellington and then at Langton, where they "worked in tobacco," was very difficult. But memories of poverty in Mexico kept them in Ontario. Krahn recalled how, during the first years in Canada, "we ate a lot" and constantly reminded ourselves how "in Mexico, we didn't have much food" other than *"nudlen jebrot* [fried noodles]." Her working-class status – a paycheque and access to consumer goods – gave her a sense of security in Ontario: "I ... felt more free, ... people weren't always looking down on you, I guess because they didn't know how you grew up, being poor and beaten down ... I guess that made it feel more like home. You felt safer."

Even her marriage to a fellow Mexico Mennonite was set against memories of old ways in Mexico. She met her future husband one Sunday while she was boarding at her uncle and aunt's, during a time when she worked in the tobacco fields. As Krahn recalled it, the marriage seemed predestined. At first sight, she liked the young man; in fact, "I saw him turn red, so I turned red," and a year later they began dating; "I had had boyfriends before but ... for the first time I felt loved." She knew he respected her when he didn't bring "either whiskey or beer," nor did he try "to make you drink. ... When he first came [to visit me] ... I went outside to him; he asked me, do you want a beer, and I said no. So he never brought it in. ... If he's willing to leave that behind for me that means he loves me." She also respected him as a "good guy," and easily listed the reasons: "He had a job and had been working there for seven years when we met. He had his own apartment and he had a beautiful truck ... [And] he had to do it all on his own ... [as] his parents died when he was young. ... He was his own cook, cleaning and did laundry and everything." Seven months after their first date, they married and, over time, she gave birth to six children.

Although Krahn distanced herself from Mexican memories, she attempted to replicate as much of the old ways as possible in Ontario. She spoke with gratitude that her husband had obtained a good job as a welder at a car-parts factory, a vocation in metalworks not dissimilar to the available jobs in Mexico. Krahn recalled fondly that they moved from the town of Delhi with its tiny lots and rented a house in the countryside, with a yard large enough for the children to ride their bikes and for her to have a large garden. Life was difficult, to be sure: Krahn worked for five weeks in the fields each summer with her older children, and "worked until midnight, every day ... doing laundry, cleaning, baking." But family life was cohesive and infused with reciprocity: "Sometimes my husband ... [would] just go home and do some cleaning, cooking. ... We had a great life!"

Krahn especially appreciated the opportunity of raising her family within old social patterns. She willingly undertook summer fieldwork to earn enough for private Mennonite school tuition and drove the children the nineteen-kilometre distance to the school each morning. As she put it, "If we sent the children to a public school, we could use that money for a house, we could do that. But I think having them in a private school is worth the money." At first, the children attended the Glen Meyer Mennonite School, a privately owned, conservative Mennonite, English-language school with a strong religious curriculum. Later they attended Walsingham Private School, also a Mennonite school, but church-owned and -operated. Both Glen Meyer and Walsingham embodied the conservative ways of the Mexico Old Colonists that Krahn valued: the schools "don't have a TV ... and [no] Halloween parties and all that. That's not something we teach our children. We want them to learn more out of the Bible than just out of the world. ... Our girls wear dresses at school. Every girl has a dress on."

These old values were also ones Krahn emphasized at home: "Even my great-grandmother, she always told us never to wear men's clothing. So we try to keep it in our family, so the [children] will know what their ancestors were like." In fact, Krahn emphasized this training almost daily and treasured the moments when "my husband would take the Low German [New] Testament and read it to them; when he does that ... it may sound funny, but it kind of looks like 'a hen with chickens all around' ... all so eager to listen." The German-language Old Colony Mennonite church remained important to Krahn: unlike the times in Mexico, in Canada, "We always go to church; we hardly miss a Sunday." The children, she said, attended German Sunday School from age "five to twelve and after twelve they're going to church." In church, she felt drawn to "just hearing the gospel ... [and] different things that the Bible says. ... Praying and everything."

Mexico remained an important place in Krahn's memories. At first, "I always said, I'm going back very soon and I meant it, and I did, we all did," at least to visit. Then, after her best friend Margaret's death in Mexico and the emigration of most of her and her husband's siblings, Mexico lost its appeal. Temptations to return remained: "Sometimes it comes into your head," but then she would "hear things about it, 'naa,' I don't want to." The apprehension built on images of Mexico as a place of poverty, violence, and drug abuse. Memories of her family's old, red-clay brick house in Mexico were off-putting; it was built well enough and it was warm in wintertime, but it was "so ugly ... from the outside it looked so old." She was similarly apprehensive of the youth culture on the colonies: "At first when our children were growing up, we were thinking ... about where ... we want to raise them, where do we want to send them to school?" As she saw it, in Canada, the youth "have more respect for the law. ... After hearing all the things that go on in Mexico among the youth you don't want to move there." Mostly, Mexico represented a place of endless work for Krahn, who, during the interview, turned from English to Low German to describe the work: "Picking apples, cutting corn and pulling beans ... most of it was apple picking for about three months a year." Still, when her curious children asked about Mexico, she told "them everything, how we grew up, how we had to work, and what we had to eat," and then also of the "times that we climbed mountains ... [and] just [drank] out of the spring water ... laying on our stomachs and drink[ing]; that was good water!" Ironically, Canada with its "bleach" water proved to be a haven that Mexico with its clear mountain water could not be.

For Lisa Klippenstein, Mexico itself was a place where Canadian Mennonite missionaries had introduced new religious emphases. Her parents, having left the traditionalist Old Colony church, now affiliated with the somewhat more progressive Kleine Gemeinde at Los Jagueyes Colony. As a young woman, she herself felt drawn to the even more open Canadian-based mission church, the EMC, situated just outside the colony. These missionaries, hoping to steer youth from a pastime of "go out and drink," had introduced the local young people to a common Canadian church youth practice of Thursday-night volleyball. Here, Lisa met her future husband, and adopted the romantic language of modern culture. Because his parents travelled to work summers in Ontario, he was gone a lot, and so "it took a while to get together again." But when they did, she "had more joy, the love, it felt like real love, I never cared so much to keep anybody. ... I always prayed a lot; I wanted the right one."

Despite Klippenstein's relatively progressive Mexican past, she experienced the move she and her husband made to Canada a year and a half after their wedding as a sharp break. Even though her parents decided to accompany the young couple when they discovered that Klippenstein was pregnant with her first child, she was unsettled. She worried that Canada was an assimilative and materialistic place, and that they were simply moving for the money. As she recalled it, "I never heard much good things about Canada until I got here, well, besides the money ... I heard many times [people] say that in Canada you do whatever you want. There's no God; God won't see you there." The rumours seemed to stem from "the people when they want to come back for the winter to Mexico; they ... have to shave off their [worldly] moustache and the girls have to get rid of their clothes because it's a sin in Mexico. That's maybe where it came from, saying ... there's no shame in Canada."

In time, Klippenstein came to see a different Canada, one with a soul. It had "always sounded like there were ... no caring people until I got to Canada, and I was surprised that I actually found real Christians. Yah!" She even "found some good friends and some church people. ... They took me out for breakfast ... [and] came over to visit," and invited her to their "Mornings out for Moms." She began adapting quickly to a modern, evangelical, Mennonite church. "I [wore] a [black] kerchief for the first couple of months; and I only had it because our church ... in Mexico ... that was their thing, that's what they did. I knew that [the black kerchief] wouldn't get me to heaven." One of the reasons she "felt comfortable right away" in the church was that "I knew some people who had come here ... from Mexico; and some of those, they can understand you better."

Klippenstein distanced herself from other aspects of Mexico. When her young family moved from Manitoba to Ontario, they obtained a spacious, five-bedroom house and built a solidly middle-class life. They sent their children to the large, local, public school, where "they enjoy it, and they do good too, good grades so far." When she considered their future, she thought in terms of middle-class ideals: "My youngest one will be an artist or secretary. ... my oldest one ... she's a sports girl. My little one loves skating ... and she loves dancing as well; they both like ballet. ... On TV ... I watched the [Olympic] champions ... for skaters and there was [the Mennonite speed skater] Cindy Klassen. ... I thought, oh, I wouldn't mind if that would be my girl." Even a doubly tragic year, one in which her brother was killed in Mexico and her eldest daughter contracted leukemia, was set in language that made Mexico seem distant and Canada a natural home. As she put it: "In the middle of that time [of my daughter's illness] my brother got killed in Mexico, so we went to his funeral, taking our sick child with. And then she got so bad there and we had to come back and leave her in London [at the hospital]. A hard time, but I managed. ... Just prayed and asked God for help." Canada had become a trusted haven.

In Canada, Klippenstein also found a reconfigured gendered world. She found work outside the home, including a part-time job in Leamington at a "daycare at the gym, just to get my membership," allowing her to exercise there "three days a week," a much less expensive endeavour than to do it at "Curves in Tilbury." In addition to this income, Klippenstein sewed wedding gowns or plain dresses, some for as much as $200. Customers came by word of mouth: "They'll find you if it's cheaper; good Mennonites will find you." But she was mindful that her first duty was to her small children: "It's not fair for the kids if you make yourself too busy with sewing."

Mexico came to hold little cultural promise for Klippenstein. In fact, when she returned for visits, "I have my T-shirts, my capris, my hair the way I want to, and I don't take off my ring. ... It took me awhile to let them know that I'm still the same person ... it's not that I'm too *grootsch* [big-wig] for them too." Once, "one of my sisters came here [from Mexico] and they went to our church and ... their experience was too [that] there is more loving people out here than they actually thought." Mexico came to represent a repressive conservatism, a place with "no sports" and, if they engage in sports, "then they have their preachers there right away. ... When you're an Old Colony [person] you're scared [of] your preacher." Klippenstein was convinced that Canada had more soul and love than Mexico, ironically, more in tune with traditional Mennonite cultural values. In addition, Canada certainly had more money and greater promise of upward mobility.

A Single Woman's Self-Sufficiency

Another feature of the gendered domestic world is illustrated in the life of Anna Bartsch, who arrived in Leamington, Ontario, from Swift Colony in Chihuahua in 1995 as a single, twenty-six-year-old woman.[15] Like so many other migration pathways, hers was a chain migration; she arrived with her married brother, his wife, and a sister, and was joined just a little later by two brothers. Similarly, the reason for her move was financial. As the eldest children in a family of eight, Bartsch and two of her siblings came to Canada after "my parents actually sent us here. ... It was very dry there [in Mexico] and we had a big debt to pay and we couldn't pay it." The family's strategy was simple: "We send money to Mexico so our family could live there." Bartsch agreed wholeheartedly to the plan. She recalled insisting that just as soon as they would get "a phone call from Mrs. Philip Dueck [who] ... is working with papers, like with citizen[ship]" and they had their "citizen[ship] I am gone to Canada because we hardly had food on the table in Mexico."

Like the other immigrants, Bartsch and her siblings navigated a kinship network. In Ontario, they found work in greenhouses through "the children of Abram Neufelds, Mam's cousins who work in greenhouses."

As it did for the other women, Canada represented a strange land in numerous ways. First, they had to procure a social insurance number, a surprise, as "we hadn't even known that such a thing existed." Then, "right away we had to work Sundays, that was also something we weren't used to." But, as Bartsch noted, the work brought "pretty good money" and, after returning to Mexico for the winter of 1995–96, "we came, the whole family; then we lived here."

This sense of hardship and survival in Canada reflects the accounts of the other five married women but, as a single woman, Bartsch honed a particular sense of self. As anthropologist Doreen Klassen argues, the small minority of single Mennonite women in Mexico places special value in "being able to stand alone," a stance that "characterizes their ideal of the personal development, self-definition, and responsible connection with their community."[16] Canada allowed Bartsch an even greater independence: "Over here we get our paycheques, usually regularly." She liked the fact that "when one asks, 'can we purchase this?'" one doesn't have to say "nope, we have no money." The time she moved from a greenhouse to a plastics factory was a moment of importance, for the latter was a better paying job and, as a machine operator, it was also physically easier. And, although she worked mostly with other Low German speakers, she liked "the 'English' people too" – that is, the non-Mennonites – and saw the factory as a place for satisfying social encounters. The work allowed her, as an unmarried woman, to "have my house; I like that very much. Not everything fits here, but I like that, and I like yard work."

Other aspects of her life in Canada enhanced her feeling of independence. The bilingual EMC church she attended "makes me feel at home; going to church, it feels like family members." She usually attended both the English and the German services. Although she knew that no one specific "church will take one to heaven," she liked hers in particular for allowing women to have uncovered hair in worship, but also to keep other familiar practices, such as the German language. She also gained satisfaction from assisting her parents in Mexico: "My father had been a little too brave [heady], he built large granaries, and then he got into too much debt, and now we could no longer pay for them. And there were many others in a similar situation. ... And then when I came here, then I [helped him get] out of that debt." Finally, she especially liked the fact that, in Canada, "the government seems to offer more protection than in Mexico."

Perhaps because of her self-sufficient status in Ontario, Bartsch seemed especially generous towards Mexico, stating that she "liked everything about Mexico." True, she recalled that going without sufficient food "was very depressing; I was depressed ... perhaps for an entire year, as my parents were no longer that spry." And she did not like the dry, windy winters or the old earthen houses. Still, she remembered resisting the first trip to Canada, as "I liked to live in Mexico when we lived there." She thought fondly of the Spanish and English lessons she took in adult evening classes in the Kleine Gemeinde Mennonite church. But she also enjoyed memories of the farm: "From age 11 till 15, perhaps till 20, we had this herd of [twenty-four] cows to milk; I always had to milk, or I could work choring the calves and hogs, that was good." And she recalled familial cohesiveness: "Almost all of Mom's siblings lived there, and most of my Dad's.... And I always thought, that is how I would live too, all at one place, not with one moving here, and the other there. ... Oh, I would have liked it," if everyone lived nearby. But for single women, and "there are many," Mexico simply offered little choice and only the promise of loneliness.

Bartsch had a special sense of family history anchored in three different countries. Her place in the female lineage was important to her: "My grandma was [named] Anna and my Mom and me." She even had a photograph of her great-grandmother, taken in Canada before the emigration of 1922. She was not sure, but believed that her maternal "grandmother was born in Canada, that's what allowed *Mamme* to obtain her citizenship, and that is what allowed us [children] to obtain ours in Mexico." Bartsch recalled her other grandmother's explanation that what the Old Colonists had "disliked about the schools [in Canada] was that they all had to learn English."

Her grandmother had sometimes spoken about the original migration south. She spoke of the time they "came from ... Canada to Mexico," how "they took cows and horses and everything with them, and en route they had to stop to milk!" And she recalled stories of family lineage, how "we came from Russia and then we came from Canada. I wish I could still recount all of that exactly." Fortunately, her grandmother had inherited "a Russian clock, a tall one, completely reaching the floor." It had become a family heirloom: one day "some Mexican [who] knew about it.... was there for a whole day, wanting to buy it and my grandmother said 'no'!" Bartsch could be assured that, despite her feeling of permanence in Canada, at least one treasured material artefact still tied her world to that of her grandparents and great-grandparents in nineteenth-century Russia, pre-1922 Canada, and, more recently, Mexico. Her world was grounded in an intergenerational, imagined village located across immense space.

Conclusion

The worlds of these early twenty-first century, Ontario, Low German-speaking Mennonite women spanned two countries, Canada and Mexico. But, as in the worlds of most immigrants, the migratory pathway did not primarily link two nations as much as two particular geographic sites.[17] The nature of this outlook was shaped by a set of even smaller social spaces; that is, the household, the kinship network, and the congregation. In turn, these localized spaces were affected by transnational ties and images. Indeed, the local and the international stood in a dialectic tension.

A globalized commodity-based economy, for example, pushed Mennonites from Mexico, and a global labour market and relatively liberal citizenship laws pulled them north to Canada. Moreover, the migration northward was rarely a singular, unilinear move, but one of several migrations; some of the women moved first to Bolivia or the United States, and most experienced repeat migrations between Mexico and Canada. But each of the women migrated along established networks, usually shaped by kinship ties. Those ties also carried the flows of information that cast Canada alternatively as a place where "money grows on trees," as a country with a superior social safety net, as a cold and heartless place, as a place of moral licence, or as a place of vibrant faith. After homes were established in Ontario, old homes in Mexico mattered: memories of poverty or religious conservatism in the South squelched anxieties of uprootedness in the North; recollections of romantic rural life and close-knit kin groups in the South fed nostalgia for the old homeland. Even though Canada was the favoured of the two places for these particular women, memories and ties to the other shaped life in it.

This chapter has told only one version of the relationship between the local and the transnational. Women not interviewed in this oral history project – that is, those who still moved between the two countries seasonally, or those who had returned to Mexico for good – would, no doubt, have had their own versions of this experience. So, too, would women seeking old ways within Bolivia or Belize, those who lived in Kansas or Iowa as undocumented migrants, those who survived Mexico's droughts and economic volatility, even those in southern Alberta or southern Manitoba. But their households, too, would have been informed by ties to localities in other lands, and the wider diaspora would have had its effect on the most private and intimate of social ties.

The women interviewed here certainly highlighted these "local" ties. They spoke of their roles as mothers and wives and daughters within patriarchal structures, in both the household and the church. The mothers emphasized a life of protecting, raising, and vying for their children in a new land, some planting them within a refashioned Old Colony church community, others encouraging integration into Canada's middle class, some hoping for both. The wives inevitably referenced their worlds to those of their husbands, their jobs and skills, or their support for the family. Most of the married women also associated strongly with the male-ordered Mennonite congregation, the Old Colony women donning the religiously significant black kerchief, the more evangelical Mennonite women participating in church programs heralding heterosexual marriages and family life. The one unmarried woman in this study was first and foremost a daughter, duty-bound to parents, in particular to a father in debt, and then, as she gained her independence, she also identified strongly as a member of a male-led evangelical church consisting mostly of Mexico Mennonites.

These women's own stories, however, volunteered to a Canadian university-educated ethnographer, placed themselves at the centre of a transnational and gendered world. They outlined their specific "sites of selfhood" that linked their domestic and wider worlds in particular fashion. In remarkable ways, these female narratives rode roughshod over the officially patriarchal contours of their worlds. Several of the married women suggested that they had initiated the formation of their families, while others cast the various migrations as their own idea, to feed their families or enhance kinship networks. Each spoke of the religious meaning they themselves obtained in their congregations; none highlighted the significance of specific male leaders. Several noted the idea of mutuality in marriage and child rearing; the only veiled criticism of their men referred to careless living outside the women's purview.

The storytelling in this 2006 oral history project gave these six women a moment in which to ponder the transnational elements of their lives. Their narratives were infused with personal accounts of hardship and sacrifice as women, but also with stories of women who survived and gained sufficiency within their families and transplanted communities. Their world among the nations was a world experienced by them in the most intense, face-to-face, daily encounters of the domestic and the local.

Conclusion

The transnational story of the Low German Mennonites did not end at the turn of the twentieth century. The three people who were introduced at the beginning of this book – Jakob Wall of Ontario, Maria Penner of Nova Scotia, and Isaak Goertzen of Alberta – represent but a few variations of the diasporic story of these Canadian-descendant Mennonites in the Americas. However dissimilar their stories, the term "transnational" for these Mennonites is much more than an abstraction, more than a vague restructuring of the world, a vast global economy, a revolution in communication, an enhanced program of multiculturalism. For them, a world "among the nations" marks a shared, lived reality.

This reality was made clear to me in conversations with Mennonite migrants with homes in Canada, but also with dozens of other migrants scattered throughout the Americas, whether the moderately conservative Mennonites in northern Mexico and the Paraguayan Chaco, or with the most traditionalist so-called "horse and buggy" Old Colonists in Bolivia or East Paraguay. Their worlds were dynamic, compelled by family loyalty and religious conviction, characterized by international migration and flows of information, and shaped by never-ending religious debate, economic imperative, and citizenship concerns. These stories continue to this day, reflecting the very arguments in this book.

Meet seven more of these transnational people, each encountered along the way between 2004 and 2012.[1] They offer testimonials to a world consisting of a constellation of villages set beyond any single nation-state. They demonstrate how a people of the rural and the local has engaged the wider world, in a variety of ways, some predictable, others ironic, most multifarious.

Hein Heide takes me in as a visitor to his home in Los Jagueyes Colony (Quellenkolonie), in Chihuahua state, in January 2004. He tells me his story in perfect English. Born in Mexico to impoverished Old Colony Mennonite parents, he and his family lived for a time with exiled Spanish revolutionaries near Los Jagueyes. Sadly, the young Heide children were abandoned here by their parents and forced to find shelter at Los Jagueyes, where the Duecks adopted Hein as a foster son. As a teenager, he rejoined his birth family in British Columbia, but returned to marry in Mexico and work as a farmer and machinist. He relates a long and bitter story of a tractor deal in which a well-to-do and pious, but unscrupulous, Mennonite neighbour shortchanged him in importing a tractor for him from Texas. The Chihuahua Mennonites might have learned to navigate US markets judiciously, but, to Hein's mind, they should be more judicious about importing its values of accumulation and self-interest.

Maria Neufeld, of Cupisei Colony near Santa Cruz, Bolivia, is a petite, friendly woman, married to the colony mayor, Johan. Wearing the telltale floral-patterned print dress and black kerchief of a traditionalist Low German Mennonite woman, Maria is surprised to discover during my visit in March 2004 that my children once attended Elmdale Elementary School in Steinbach, Manitoba, a school Maria herself attended as a girl in the mid-1950s when her family sojourned in Canada after economic setbacks in Belize. She vividly recalls her teacher, Mr. Melvin Toews, who also taught my daughter forty years later. Still able to read in English, Maria asks me to send her a copy of Canadian novelist Miriam Toews's "best seller" *Swing Low*, recounting Melvin's tragic death by suicide. Perhaps Canada's assimilative culture has driven Maria's family to the South, but her childhood in the North and even her beloved public schoolteacher cannot be forgotten.

Martin Klippenstein is a ten-year-old boy from a village in Riva Palacios Colony near Santa Cruz, Bolivia. When, in March 2004, Dick Braun – my MCC host, originally of Osler, Saskatchewan – and I overshoot the Klippensteins' driveway in our red Toyota 4x4, stop and back up to the driveway, there is young Martin, dressed in black overalls, long-sleeved shirt, and cowboy hat. He exclaims, "You were completely lost; hurry, Mame already wants to eat." We park behind the barn to avoid too much attention on this "horse and buggy" colony. Later, Martin's grandfather reflects on the family's financial state; his unmarried adult daughter, now in Ontario against church wishes, has sent money to purchase eight head of cattle, and he shares the farm's limited earnings with his married son. But he worries about little Martin and the other grandchildren's futures in Bolivia and muses about jobs in Canada – a profitable option but one that would make it impossible to keep the old ways.

Levi Hiebert and his wife Rosalie meet me at the Asunción airport in March 2004 and then, the next morning, we speed along the Trans Chaco highway, five hours northwest into the vast Chaco region to Menno Colony. We spend several days touring it and visit the massive colony dairy and abattoir cooperative, the local archives, and, of course, a "fence" (a word borrowed from the English that has evolved into their Low German word for "ranch") of beef cattle. Levi shows me the historic spot where the Mennonite settlers first camped on the trek inland from Puerto Casado in 1927. A former schoolteacher who has studied in Germany and Canada, Levi now writes a Chaco-based, nature studies curriculum for an outside agency. On the day we leave the colony, we notice at the highway that the last strand of fibre-optic cable has just been laid, thus irrevocably connecting Menno Colony to the outside world. The Paraguayan Mennonites can now connect to the old homeland at will.

Lydia Froese, her husband Isaac, and their children meet my wife and me on the parking lot of the Wal-Mart in picturesque Zacatecas City in central Mexico in December 2008. We know the Froeses from a 2007 road trip they took across Canada and the US, visiting relatives along the way. We now follow the Froeses a hundred kilometres north from Zacatecas, past the colossal Corona beer brewery, to La Honda Colony. Here the Froeses show me their thriving lumberyard business, a state-of-the-art dairy farm, but also the original 1964 red-clay houses, still home to the colony poor. After dinner, the Froeses' daughter and the daughter of Lydia's cousin Julia fête our visit with Spanish gospel songs. The next day, on Sunday, I get up at sunrise to attend the traditionalist Old Colony church where the minister laments the tragic death of a little boy the day before, but also decries "the many computers and TVs" on the colony, which, "if collected and burned at one place," he says, "would produce a very large bonfire." The wider world beckons even in Mexico's rural interior.

Cornelius Fehr (a pseudonym) is an Old Colony bishop in East Paraguay whose congregation in July 2009 seems to be in open rebellion. He is a thin, quiet, and pleasant man, wearing a cowboy hat and black overalls, but also the black shirt of the head minister. He is grateful for his simple farm world, for his loving family and a wife who "is good to him." But he is also troubled, for he has preached against the car and truck, but to little avail, for even the Brotherhood's agreement to reserve Sunday for only horse-and-buggy travel is eroding. He asks about the 6000 Mennonites from Asia, Africa, Europe, and the Americas, meeting at the Mennonite World Conference in Asunción, a conference my travel companion, Prof. Paul Redekop of Winnipeg, and I have been attending in July 2009. But modern ways spook him, and he seriously wonders if a move to southern Bolivia may be necessary, for there the Geschwister (the church brothers and sisters) still practise the old ways.

Margaretha Bergen, a widow in her mid sixties, steps out of her Manitoba Colony house into the hot Bolivian sun, when Ramont Schrock and I drop by for an unannounced visit in February 2012. She invites us to disembark and we visit; she recalls fondly my graduate student Karen Warkentin's visit in 2009. She also recalls her own visits to Canada with her late husband, Franz, for three consecutive years in 2005, 2006, and 2007, working for a time in Ontario, then purchasing second-hand combine harvesters in Manitoba and shipping them in large containers to Bolivia. She has earlier visited her siblings in Paraguay, Belize, and Mexico; the latter is her birthplace. She tells us that with the exception of one child in Canada, her eleven children live in Bolivia. Of these, ten are members of the Old Colony church, and she is grateful that her one son who has left Manitoba Colony has found a good Bolivian Campa woman and religious faith in a non-Mennonite church. But, having seen the wider world, she is content in her "horse and buggy" Manitoba Colony, following "the way we have been taught."

These people, all Canadian citizens or the adult children of Canadian citizens, are in the process of making a transnational village. It is not a village in the literal sense of the term, not even an "imagined community," as Benedict Anderson uses it in his much-cited work on nationalism.[2] This community has no geographic boundary; rather, it is far-flung over vast distances. Neither is it powerful or sovereign in any way, able to reshape identity, erode old languages, and fashion a new cosmology. Instead, it has the trappings of an agrarian community, consisting of an inherited vocabulary, deeply rooted history, and common ethno-religious understandings that generate a lasting sense of village, even though it is an imagined one superimposed over an entire hemisphere.

This "village" consists of tens of thousands of individuals who have never met. Today, it links a hundred places, stretching from La Crete (Alberta) in the north, to Guatrache in the Argentine Pampa in the south; from Northfield (Nova Scotia) and Bergthal (East Paraguay) in the east, to Liberal (Kansas) and Santa Cruz (Bolivia) in the west. In between lie communities in half a dozen countries – Canada, the United States, Mexico, Belize, Paraguay, Bolivia, and Argentina – and in various regions in each. And, every year, new Low German settlements are grounded, most recently near Swift Current and Yorkton in Saskatchewan, in Quintana Roo and San Luis Potosi states in southern Mexico, and in Beni and Xiama states in northern Bolivia. Mennonites in these places are well aware of one another.

They are connected by both genealogy and church membership, in the Old Colony Mennonite church or another relatively conservative congregation. Almost always, they are fluent in *Plautdietsch* (Low German), and many read the same ethno-religious newspapers. They are all socialized in Mennonite ways, practising or aware of the religious teaching on nonconformity, simplicity, non-violence, and separation from the "world." They worry that unchecked middle-class consumption, upward mobility, and, of course, nationalism, will undermine old ways.

This very religious and ethnic identity hints at yet another way in which this transnational community is a "village," indeed, a village within a village. Most of these Low German Mennonites live day-to-day in what Anderson describes as "primordial villages of face-to-face contact" rather than in a broad national community.[3] Theirs are "closed" and rural places rather than "open" urban societies, to employ terms from classical sociology.[4] Most of these people build close relationships based on corporate memory and compelling ascription, not on professional linkages or common national identity. Most avoid college or even high school education, and most are farm householders or work with their hands, in the crafts, or trade in craft-based products. Church life for most is simple, with much emphasis on obedience and community cohesiveness, and on lives of love, service, and simplicity. At the foundation, they are members of real villages, places in which life is held together by kinship networks, common codes of conduct, folklore, even gossip, and shared ways of making a livelihood. Their Mennonite "village," thus, is both a real face-to-face community and a transnational constellation of hundreds of small places within an immense geography.

Despite the conservative culture of both the face-to-face and the imagined pan-American village, it is not a culture based on unchanging ways or a sterile habit of mind. It is dynamic in myriad ways, reinventing what is traditional, contesting much of what is modern, and always debating what must be kept and what adopted.[5] The most progressive members of the wider village have de-emphasized attempts to remain a visibly simple people, and their understanding of "nonconformity" is to avoid personal vices, keep close to their Low German kin groups, and find salvation in the teaching in evangelical churches. The most traditionalist add new codes of conduct: the black overalls that men wear, first seen in the US Midwest in the 1920s, have become a symbol of humility; the steel-wheeled tractor, the hallmark of innovation in the 1920s, has been frozen in time to represent nonconformity; the broad-rimmed hat decked with brilliant ribbon that women adopted from Mexican culture is readily used to cover their faces from the invasive cameras aimed at them by curious outsiders. The more progressive and the more traditionalist share the cultural repertoire of diaspora in their ethno-religious quests. They have taken the biblical image of "scattered among the nations" and turned it on its head; to be scattered is not a curse, but reflective of the virtue of being "pilgrims and strangers" in this world. The estimated 250,000 descendants of the original emigrants from Manitoba and Saskatchewan in the 1920s and 1940s are usually deferential to local and state or national authority, but most embrace transnational linkages as natural, and consider it virtuous to cultivate village loyalties beyond the nation and among the nations.

The seven Low German Mennonites introduced above – Hein, Maria, Martin, Levi, Lydia, Cornelius, and Margaretha – are scattered in the Americas; they live apart from one another in several countries and disparate regions within them. They all have strong connections to other countries, many have resided in more than one, all have close acquaintances or family members in two or more, and all have strong transborder religious connections. Canada is a common reference point for them; it is the birthplace of the grandparents, a place to visit, an economic refuge, a country of peace and order, one of several homes in a sequence of sojourns, the issuer of passports. Canada exists for them, even though its official culture or selected tradition excludes them from its national narrative. The problem is that most of the subjects in this book do not have a place within the broad themes of Canadian history: colony to nation, liberal ascendancy, refugee centre of the world, or multicultural nation.

Yet, their story illuminates what Canada was in past decades: in the 1920s, a confident young "dominion" flexing its cultural muscle; in the 1930s, a desperate place of economic depression; in the 1940s, a burgeoning urbanized country and "middle power"; in the 1950s, a beacon of economic hope and full industrialization; in the 1960s, a country erecting an inclusive social safety net; in the 1970s, a multicultural nation welcoming minorities speaking foreign tongues; in the 1980s, a country building an enhanced manufacture-based export economy in evolving free trade zones; in the 1990s, a place indelibly intertwined in a global community through technological advances. The seven Mennonites above self-identify as Mennonites, residents of insular places in the far corners of the Americas. Nevertheless, they all live with some aspect of Canada, some through collective memory, others affected directly by its economic policies and citizenship laws.

Transnational societies in the past were complex, and in its eight chapters, this book has attempted to uncover that complexity in various ways. In the first instance, it mattered that such communities were informed by particular mindsets – religious, political, or ethnic – that could variably persist, become dormant, or be reawakened by community leaders. Significantly, too, these communities often considered the local in terms quite outside a sanctioned national discourse, their fields and the villages belonging first and foremost to the people who inhabited them. Far from Canada, they shared a diasporic mindset, unfixed residences, and nostalgia for the lost homeland. Later migrations occurred within a cultural cross-current of long-settled migrants, "echo" migrants, return migrants, repeat migrants, and in a context, too, of shifting notions of time and space. In time, they attracted the gaze of outsiders, government officials certainly, but also members of national media and international academics, shaping the way they saw themselves. When many "returned" to Canada, images of homelands were reformulated, old migration paths "remembered," and narratives of migration prepared for grandchildren. At the close of the twentieth century, as they scattered over an ever-broader geography, they maintained their transnational village, employing new media, including newly formed newspapers, to hone a common identity rooted in shared vocabulary and history. In the final analysis, their transnational world still affected the most localized of their worlds, the domestic unit in small communities, and the most personal and gendered of identities.

This book has focused on the way a transnational world evolved over time. It has considered how religious belief, environmental interaction, gender, memory making, and ethnic identity infused the process of migration and settlement. Another goal, no less, has been to explain through the story of the Low German-speaking Mennonites scattered across the Americas just how transnationalism manifests itself in the everyday life of migrant peoples. Residence in more than one country, repeat migrations, an imagined ethno-religious village, and flows of information created common bonds. But, in the end, the most important goal was simply to tell the remarkable story of a Canadian-descendant people who moved among the nations of the Americas to contest and implicitly critique a nation-centric world. Ultimately, theirs was a village charted beyond any one nation.

Notes

Introduction

1 Field notes, by author, January 2007.
2 Ibid., July 2005.
3 Ibid., August 2004.
4 Thomas Faist, "Transnationalism in International Migration: Implications for the Study of Citizenship and Culture," *Ethnic and Racial Studies* 23, 2 (2000): 189.
5 See Dirk Hoerder, "Transcultural States, Nations, and People," in *The Historical Practice of Diversity. Transcultural Interactions from the Early Modern Mediterranean to the Postcolonial World*, ed. Dirk Hoerder, with Christiane Harzig and Adrian Schubert (New York: Berghahn Books, 2003); Luann Good Gingrich and Kerry Preibisch, "Migration as Preservation and Loss: The Paradox of Transnational Living for Low German Mennonite Women," *Journal of Ethnic and Migration Studies* 36 (2010): 1499–1518; John Eicher, "'Wise as Serpents, Innocent as Doves': Mennonite Migrations, 1870–1943," PhD diss. proposal, University of Iowa, 2012, who employs the term "national indifference" as used in recent works by James Bjork, Tara Zahra, and others; Lorenzo Cañás Bottos. "Transformations of Old Colony Mennonites: The Making of a Trans-statal Community," *Global Networks* 8 (2009): 214–231.
6 Lloyd L. Wong, "Transnationalism, Active Citizenship and Belonging in Canada," *International Journal* 63 (2007–8): 87.
7 See Dhiru Patel, "The Maple Neem Nexus: Transnational Links of South Asian Canadians," in *Transnational Identities and Practices in Canada*, ed. Vic Satzewich and Lloyd Wong (Vancouver: University of British Columbia Press, 2006), 155, who writes of South Asians abroad whose "diverse social,

cultural, religious and ethnic environments of their original homelands ... prepared them" to navigate a wider world based on "the traditional 'selective engagement' developed by their ancestors." See also Jeremy Stolow, "Transnationalism and the New Religio-politics: Reflections on a Jewish Orthodox Case," *Theory, Culture and Society* 21 (2004): 110, 121. He writes of anti-Zionist Orthodox Jews whose history shatters "much of the conventional wisdom about the nation-state as the locus classicus of identity formation," but historically also "worked within a deterritorialized frame of reference that was not bound to any one nation-state." I am indebted to Susie Fisher Stoesz for pointing out this insightful article to me.

8 See Kelly L. Hedges, "'Plautdietsch' and 'Huuchdietsch' in Chihuahua: Language, Literacy and Identity among the Old Colony Mennonites in Northern Mexico," PhD diss., Yale University, 1996.

9 See James Urry, *None but Saints: The Transformation of Mennonite Life in Russia, 1789–1889* (Winnipeg: Hyperion, 1989); Frank H. Epp, *Mennonites in Canada, 1786–1920: The History of a Separate People* (Toronto: Macmillan, 1974); E.K. Francis, *In Search of Utopia: The Mennonites of Manitoba* (Altona, MB: D.W. Friesen and Sons, 1955).

10 See Romans 12:2 and I Peter 2:11 (New International Version). For a full discussion of this idea, see Adolf Ens, *Subjects or Citizens? The Mennonite Experience in Canada, 1970–1925* (Ottawa: University of Ottawa Press, 1994). For a more popular depiction of this idea, see Abe Warkentin, *Gäste und Fremdlinge: Hebräer 11:13; Strangers and Pilgrims: Hebrews 11:13* (Steinbach, MB: *Mennonitische Post*, 1987).

11 See James 1:1 in the New Testament and Ezekiel 36:19 in the Old Testament.

12 Ann Curthoys and Marilyn Lake, "Introduction," in *Connected Worlds: History in Transnational Perspective*; http://epress.anu.edu.au/cw/mobile_devices/index.html, accessed 13 August 2010. Also informing the ideas in this chapter are the following works: Nancy Foner, "Second Generation Transnationalism: Then and Now," in *The Changing Face of Home*, ed. Peggy Levitt and Mary C. Waters (New York: Russell Sage, 2002), 242–54; Nina Glick Schiller and Linda Bash, "From Immigrant to Transmigrant: Theorizing Transnational Migration," *Anthropological Quarterly* 68 (1995): 48–63; Donna R. Gabaccia, "Is Everywhere Nowhere? Nomads, Nations and the Immigrant Paradigm of United States History," *Journal of American History* 86 (1999): 1115–34; Dirk Hoerder, "Historians and Their Data: The Complex Shift from Nation-State Approaches to the Study of People's Transcultural Lives," *Journal of American Ethnic Studies* 25 (2006): 85–96; Christine Harzig and Dirk Hoerder with Donna Gabaccia, *What Is Migration History* (Malden, MA: Polity, 2009).

13 Steven Vertovec, *Transnationalism* (New York: Routledge, 2009), 21.
14 C.A. Bayly, Sven Beckert, Matthew Connelly, Isabel Hofmeyr, Wendy Kozol, and Patricia Seed, "AHR Conversation: On Transnational History," *American Historical Review* 111, 5 (2006): 1444.
15 Ewa Morawska, "'Diaspora' Diasporas' Representations of their Homelands: Exploring the Polymorphs," *Ethnic & Racial Studies* 34, 6 (2011): 1031; Dirk Hoerder, "Historians and Their Data"; Christine Harzig and Dirk Hoerder, "Transnationalism and the Age of Mass Migration, 1880s–1920," in *Transnational Identities and Practices in Canada*, ed. Vic Satzewich and Lloyd Wong, 37; Bayly et al., "AHR Conversation," 1448.
16 Among the hundreds of congregational histories and those of the main Mennonite denominations – Mennonite Church, Mennonite Brethren, Evangelical Mennonite, Brethren-in-Christ, Old Order Mennonite – most focus on experiences of one nation or one region in one nation. See, for one example, Adolf Ens, *Becoming a National Church: A History of the Conference of Mennonites in Canada* (Winnipeg: CMU Press, 2004).
17 For the *Mennonite Experience in America* series, see Richard K. MacMaster, *Land, Piety, Peoplehood: The Establishment of Mennonite Communities in America 1683–1790* (Scottdale, PA: Herald Press, 1985); Theron F. Schlabach, *Peace, Faith, Nation: Mennonites and Amish in Nineteenth-century America* (Scottdale, PA: Herald Press, 1988); James C. Juhnke, *Vision, Doctrine, War: Mennonite Identity and Organization in America, 1890–1930* (Scottdale, PA: Herald Press, 1989); Paul Toews, *Mennonites in American Society, 1930–1970: Modernity and the Persistence of Religious Community* (Scottdale, PA: Herald Press, 1996). For the *Mennonites in Canada* series, see Frank H. Epp, *Mennonites in Canada, 1786–1920: The History of a Separate People* (Toronto: Macmillan, 1974); *Mennonites in Canada, 1920–1940: A People's Struggle for Survival* (Toronto: Macmillan, 1982); T.D. Regehr, *Mennonites in Canada, 1939–1970: A People Transformed* (Toronto: University of Toronto Press, 1996).
18 See, as an example among an especially rich historiography on the Amish or Old Order Mennonites, Isaac Horst, *A Separate People: An Insider's View of Old Order Mennonite Customs and Traditions* (Kitchener: Herald Press, 2000); Donald B. Kraybill and Carl F. Bowman, *On the Backroad to Heaven: Old Order Hutterites, Mennonites, Amish, and Brethren* (Baltimore: Johns Hopkins University Press, 2001); Charles E. Hurst and David L. McConnell, *An Amish Paradox: Diversity and Change in the World's Largest Amish Community* (Baltimore: Johns Hopkins University Press, 2010).
19 See Ens, *Subjects or Citizens?*; and William Janzen, *Limits on Liberty: The Experience of Mennonite, Hutterite and Doukhobor Communities in Canada* (Toronto: University of Toronto Press, 1990), on the conditions leading up

to the Mennonite emigration from Canada in the 1920s. See H. Leonard Sawatzky, *They Sought a Country: Mennonite Colonization in Mexico* (Berkeley: University of California Press, 1971) for an historical geography of the migration and settlement in Mexico. See Calvin Wall Redekop, *The Old Colony Mennonites in Mexico: Dilemmas of Ethnic Minority Life* (Baltimore: Johns Hopkins University Press, 1969), and J. Winfield Fretz, *Pilgrims in Paraguay: The Story of Mennonite Colonization in South America* (Scottdale, PA: Herald Press, 1953) for two sociological studies on Mexico and Paraguay, respectively. For an analysis of these sociological studies, see Ben Nobbs-Thiessen, "Mennonites in Unexpected Places: Sociologist and Settlers in Latin America," *Journal of Mennonite Studies* 28 (2010) 203–24. See Anna Sofia Hedberg, *Outside the World: Cohesion and Deviation among Old Colony Mennonites in Bolivia* (Uppsala: ACTA Universitatis Upsaliensis, 2007), and Lorenzo Cañas Bottos, *Old Colony Mennonites in Argentina and Bolivia: Nation Making, Religious Conflict and Imagination of the Future* (Leiden: Brill, 2008), for two anthropological studies on Bolivian and Argentine Mennonites. See Carel Roessingh and Tanja Plasil, eds., *Between Horse & Buggy and Four-Wheel Drive: Change and Diversity among Mennonite Settlements in Belize, Central America* (Amsterdam: VU University Press, 2009). See David Quiring, *The Mennonite Old Colony Vision: Under Seige in Mexico and the Canadian Connection* (Steinbach, MB: Crossway Publications, 2003), and Larry Towell, *The Mennonites: A Biographical Sketch* (London: Phaidon Press, 2000), for two transnational studies linking two nations.

20 See James Urry, *Mennonites, Politics and Peoplehood: Europe, Russia, Canada, 1525–1980* (Winnipeg: University of Manitoba Press, 2006); John J. Friesen, *Building Communities: The Changing Face of Manitoba Mennonites* (Winnipeg: CMU Press, 2007); Kraybill and Bowman, *On the Backroad to Heaven*. They use the terms "conservative," "conserving," and "old order," respectively, to refer to the more traditionalist wing of the Anabaptist community in North America. Because "conservative" is frequently employed to denote fundamentalist or evangelistic groups, which arguably the Low German Mennonites are not, I have elected to employ "traditionalist," which, of course, is problematic in its own way as it implies "changlessness." The term "old order" is problematic as it also serves as the official name of a branch of Swiss-American Mennonites, the Old Order Mennonites, while the term "preserving" has had limited application to date.

21 For histories of these various groups, see Leonard Doell, *The Bergthaler Mennonite Church of Saskatchewan, 1892–1975* (Winnipeg: CMBC Publications, 1987); Friesen, *Building Communities*; Delbert F. Plett, ed., *Old Colony Mennonites in Canada 1875 to 2000* (Steinbach, MB: Crossway

Publications, 2001), and *Saints and Sinners: The Kleine Gemeinde in Imperial Russia, 1812 to 1875* (Steinbach, MB: Crossway Publications, 1999). For a study that places much of this diaspora in a wider context, but covers the various colonies and migrations in cursory fashion, see Jaime Prieto Valladares, *Mission and Migration: Global Mennonite History Series, Latin America* (Intercourse, PA: Good Books, 2010). For another that integrates this story in a general history of Mennonites since the sixteenth century, see Adina Reger and Delbert Plett, *Diese Steine: Die Russlandmennoniten* (Steinbach, MB: Crossway Publications, 2001). For an overview of the migration from central Saskatchewan to Durango in the 1920s, see Jacob G. Guenter, Leonard Doell, Dick Braun, Jacob L. Guenther, Henry A. Friesen, Jacob W. Loeppky, John P. Doell, Peter G. Giesbrecht, Anna Bueckert, and Anna Braun, *Hague-Osler Mennonite Reserve, 1895–1995* (N.p.: Hague-Osler Reserve Book Committee, 1995).

22 Lisa Chilton, "Canada and the British World: Culture, Migration, and Identity," *Canadian Historical Review* 89 (2008): 89–95; Adele Perry, "'Is your Garden in England, Sir': James Douglas's Archive and the Politics of Home," *History Workshop Journal* 70 (2010): 67–85; Sarah Carter, "Transnational Perspectives on the History of Great Plains Women: Gender, Race, Nation, and the Forty-ninth Parallel," *American Review of Canadian Studies* 33 (2003): 565–96; Allan Greer, "National, Transnational, and Hypernational Historiographies: New France Meets Early American History," *Canadian Historical Review* 91 (2010), 695–724; Karen Dubinsky, Adele Perry, and Henry Yu, "Introduction: Canadian History, Transnational History," in *Within and Without the Nation: Canadian History as Transnational History* (Toronto: University of Toronto Press, forthcoming); Henry Yu, "Is Vancouver the Future or the Past? Asian Migrants and White Supremacy," *Pacific History Review* 75 (2006): 307–12.

23 Bayly et al., "AHR Conversation," 1449.

24 See Gerald Friesen, *Citizens and Nation: An Essay on History, Communication, and Canada* (Toronto: University of Toronto Press, 2000).

25 Ivana Caccia, *Managing the Canadian Mosaic in Wartime: Shaping Citizenship Policy, 1939–1945* (Montreal and Kingston: McGill-Queen's University Press, 2010).

26 See Franca Iacovetta, *Gatekeepers: Reshaping Immigrant Lives in Cold War Canada* (Toronto: Between the Lines, 2006); Royden Loewen and Gerald Friesen, *Immigrants in Prairie Cities: Ethnic Diversity in 20th-Century Canada* (Toronto: University of Toronto Press, 2009).

27 See, for example, Jean Burnett, *Coming Canadians: An Introduction to a History of Canada's People* (Toronto: McClelland and Stewart, 1988).

28 See Bruno Ramirez, *On the Move: French Canadian and Italian Migrants in the North Atlantic Economy 1860–1914* (Toronto: McClelland and Stewart, 1991); Randy William Widdis, *With Scarcely a Ripple: Anglo-Canadian Migration into the United States and Western Canada, 1880–1920* (Montreal and Kingston: McGill-Queen's University Press, 1998); Yukari Takai, *Gendered Passages: French-Canadian Migration to Lowell, Massachusetts, 1900–1920* (New York: Peter Lang, 2008).
29 For examples, see Ramirez, *On the Move*; Loewen and Friesen, "Prairie Links in a Transnational Chain," in *Immigrants in Prairie Cities*.
30 Vertovec, *Transnationalism*, 15–16; see also Foner, "Second Generation Transnationalism."
31 Bayly et al., "AHR Conversation," 1450.

Chapter 1

1 For background studies of the context and actual events of the 1916 school legislations, see Alan M. Guenther, "'Barred from Heaven and Cursed Forever': Old Colony Mennonites and the 1908 Commission of Inquiry regarding Public Education," *Preservings* 29 (2009): 4–13; Adolf Ens, *Subjects or Citizens? The Mennonite Experience in Canada, 1970–1925* (Ottawa: University of Ottawa Press, 1994); William Janzen, *Limits on Liberty: The Experience of Mennonite, Hutterite and Doukhobor Communities in Canada* (Toronto: University of Toronto Press, 1990).
2 For context, see Ken Osborne, "One Hundred Years of History Teaching in Manitoba Schools, Part I, 1897–1927," *Manitoba History* 36 (1998): 3–25.
3 Isaak M. Dyck, "Emigration from Canada to Mexico, Year 1922," trans. Robyn Dyck Sneath, 2005 (unpublished manuscript in possession of author). This book was published most recently as Isaak M. Dyck, *Die Auswanderung der Reinlaender Mennoniten Gemeinde von Kanada nach Mexiko* (Cuauhtémoc: Imprenta Colonial, 1993). See also Isaak M. Dyck, *Anfangs Jahre der Mennoniten in Mexiko* (Cuauhtémoc: Heinrich Dyck, 1995); Isaak M. Dyck, *Hinterlassene Schriften vom Ältester Isaak M. Dyck, Blumenfeld, Mexiko* (Cuauhtémoc: Jacob Klassen Fehr, 2000).
4 See Adolf Ens, Jacob E. Peters, and Otto Hamm, *Church, Family and Village: Essays on Mennonite Life on the West Reserve* (Winnipeg: Manitoba Mennonite Historical Society, 2001).
5 Sidonie Smith, *Subjectivity, Identity and the Body: Women's Autobiographical Practices in the Twentieth Century* (Bloomington: Indiana University Press, 1993), 18, 22.

6 Julie Rak, "Introduction, Widening the Field: Auto/biography Theory and Criticism in Canada," in *Auto/biography in Canada: Critical Directions* (Waterloo: Wilfrid Laurier University Press, 2005), 3.
7 Jeremy Stolow, "Transnationalism and the New Religio-politics: Reflections on a Jewish Orthodox Case," *Theory, Culture & Society* 21, 2 (2004): 109–37. http://dx.doi.org/10.1177/0263276404042137. Accessed 1 August 2012.
8 See Carl Berger, *The Sense of Power: Studies in the Ideas of Canadian Imperialism, 1867–1914* (Toronto: University of Toronto Press, 1970), and the recent elaboration of this watershed analysis in Gerald Friesen and Doug Owram, eds., *Thinkers and Dreamers: Historical Essays in Honour of Carl Berger* (Toronto: University of Toronto Press, 2009).
9 For a broad statement of this explanation, see Eric Hobsbawm, *Age of Extremes: The Short Twentieth Century, 1914–1991* (London: Abacus, 1995), 15; for a recent micro-study of it as relating to corporate culture, see William K. Carroll, "From Canadian Corporate Elite to Transnational Capitalist Class: Transitions in the Organization of Corporate Power," *Canadian Review of Sociology and Anthropology*, 44 (2007): 265–88.
10 Dyck, "Emigration from Canada to Mexico."
11 Ibid., 3.
12 Ibid., 2.
13 Ibid., 3.
14 Ibid., 4.
15 Ibid.
16 Ibid.
17 Ibid., 6.
18 See also Johann Wiebe, *Die Auswanderung von Russland nach Kanada, 1875, in Form einer Predigt* (Strassbourgo, Mexico: Strassbourg Platz, n.d.).
19 Dyck, "Emigration from Canada to Mexico," 10.
20 Ibid., 14.
21 Ibid., 19.
22 Ibid., 22.
23 Ibid., 25.
24 Ibid., 19, 20.
25 Ibid., 24, 25.
26 Peter R. Dueck, diary, 1916, transcribed by Henry Loewen, Evangelical Mennonite Conference Archives, Steinbach, MB.
27 Ibid., 9 January 1916, 22, 23, 27.
28 Ibid., 14 February 1916, 10.

29 Ibid., 20 February 1916; 11 March 1916; 26 and 27 December 1916.
30 Ibid., 11 March 1916; 2 April 1916; 2 July 1916.
31 Ibid., 17 September 1916; 3 December 1916.
32 See Frank Epp, *Mennonites in Canada, 1920–1940: A People's Struggle for Survival* (Toronto: Macmillan, 1982), 109–28.
33 Martin W. Friesen, "Eine Neue Heimat in der Chaco Wildness," trans. Herman Rempel (unpublished document in possession of author), 31. See the original: Martin W. Friesen, *Eine Neue Heimat in der Chaco Wildness* (Altona, MB: Published and bound by D.W. Friesen & Sons, 1987). See also Martin W. Friesen, *New Homeland in the Chaco Wilderness*, trans. Jake Balzer (Loma Plata: Historical Committee of the Menno Colony, 2009).
34 David Rempel, diary, 6 August 1919–26 November 1919, Volume 5015, Mennonite Heritage Centre, trans. Jake K. Wiens.
35 David Rempel, letter collection, Volume 4395, Mennonite Heritage Centre, trans. Robyn Dyck Sneath (unpublished manuscript in possession of author, 8 August 1920).
36 Ibid., 20 and 22 August 1919.
37 Ibid., 1 September 1919.
38 Rempel, letter, 22 August 1919.
39 Rempel, diary, 9 September 1919.
40 Ibid., 15 September 1919.
41 Rempel, diary, 28 September 1919.
42 Ibid., 12 October 1919.
43 Ibid., 15 October 1919.
44 Ibid., 15, 26, 28 October 1919.
45 Ibid., 9, 24, 26 November 1919.
46 Johan M. Loeppky, "A Travel Report to Mexico in the Year 1921," trans. Robyn Dyck Sneath (unpublished manuscript in possession of author). For a published translation of the Loeppky diary, see *Preservings* 26 (2006), 37–44. For a biography, see Abram G. Janzen, *Ältester Johan M. Loeppky, 1882–1950: Wie ich Ihm in Errinerung Habe* (Hague, SK: Self-published, ca. 2003).
47 Ibid., 1.
48 Ibid., 2.
49 Ibid.
50 Ibid.
51 Ibid., 3.
52 Ibid.
53 Ibid., 5.
54 Ibid.
55 Ibid., 4.

56 Ibid., 6.
57 Ibid.
58 Ibid., 7 and 8.
59 Ibid., 9.
60 Ibid., 9 and 10.
61 Ibid., 11.
62 Ibid., 15.
63 Ibid.
64 Ibid., 17 and 18.
65 Ibid.
66 Ibid., 19 and 20.
67 Ibid., 21. Unknown to Loeppky at the time, the Reimer family would eventually join the Old Colony Church in Mexico.
68 Ibid., 22.
69 Friesen, "New Homeland in the Wilderness."
70 Bernard Toews, *Reise-Tagebuch des Bernhard Toews, 1921* (Loma Plata, Paraguay: Geschichtsarchiv, Schulverwaltung der Kolonie Menno, 1997).
71 Ibid., 11.
72 Ibid., 20.
73 Ibid., 26.
74 Ibid., 13.
75 H. Hack, "Land Problems in the Paraguayan Chaco," *Boletín de Estudios Latinoamericanos y del Caribe* 34 (1983): 104.
76 Toews, *Reise-Tagebuch*, 28.
77 Ibid.
78 Ibid., 31.
79 Ibid.
80 Ibid., 33.
81 Ibid.
82 Friesen, "New Homeland in the Wilderness," 51.
83 Ibid., 52.
84 Toews, *Reise-Tagebuch*, 37 and 38.
85 Ibid., 39.
86 Ibid., 43.
87 Ibid., 44.
88 Ibid., 72.
89 Ibid., 47.
90 Ibid., 48.
91 Ibid.
92 Friesen, "New Homeland in the Wilderness," 63.
93 Toews, *Reise-Tagebuch*, 51.

94 Friesen, "New Homeland in the Wilderness," 65.
95 Ibid., 66.
96 Toews, *Reise-Tagebuch*, 96.
97 Ibid.
98 Ibid., 98.
99 Ibid.
100 Martina E. Will, "The Old Colony Mennonite Colonization of Chihuahua and the Obregón Administration's Vision for the Nation," MA thesis, University of California, San Diego, 1993. See also Martina E. Will, "The Mennonite Colonization of Chihuahua: Reflections of Competing Visions," *The Americas* 53 (1997): 353–78; Jürgen Buchenau, "Small Numbers, Great Impact: Mexico and Its Immigrants, 1821–1973," *Journal of American Ethnic History* 20 (2001): 23–49.
101 In a cruel coincidence, during the 1920s as 6000 Mennonites were welcomed into Mexico, about 6000 Chinese-Mexicans were expelled on overtly racial grounds. See Grace Peña Degaldo, *Making the Chinese Mexican: Global Migration, Localism, and Exclusion in the US-Mexico Borderlands* (Stanford: Stanford University Press, 2012).
102 Peter P. Klassen, *The Mennonites in Paraguay: Kingdom of God and Kingdom of this World*, trans. Gunther H. Schmitt (Filadefia, Paraguay: Self-published, 2004), 52. For passing reference to a similar perspective, see Kathleen Lowrey, "Ethics, Politics, and Host Space: A Comparative Case Study from the South American Chaco," *Comparative Studies in Society and History* 53 (2011): 898.
103 Winfield Fretz, *Pilgrims in Paraguay: The Story of Mennonite Colonization in South America* (Scottdale, PA: Herald Press, 1953), 15.

Chapter 2

1 Waldemar Janzen, "Geography of Faith," *Still in the Image: Essays in Biblical Theology and Anthropology* (Winnipeg: Self-published, 1982), 148.
2 John C. Weaver, *The Great Land Rush and the Making of the Modern World: 1650–1900* (Montreal and Kingston: McGill-Queen's University Press, 2003). For an exemplary micro-analysis of this idea, see Ryan Eyford, "An Experiment in Immigrant Colonization: Canada and the Icelandic Reserve, 1875–1897," PhD diss., University of Manitoba, 2011. For a comparative study that links land acquisition and ethnic landscape, see Frances Swyripa, *Storied Landscapes: Ethno-Religious Identity and the Canadian Prairies* (Winnipeg: University of Manitoba Press, 2010), and John C. Lehr, *Community and Frontier: A Ukrainian Settlement in the Canadian Parkland* (Winnipeg: University of Manitoba Press, 2011).

3 Weaver, *The Great Land Rush*, 354.
4 See, for examples, Royden Loewen, *From the Inside Out: The Rural Worlds of Mennonite Diarists, 1863–1929* (Winnipeg: University of Manitoba Press, 1999).
5 Johan A. Thiessen, *Tagebuch, 1922–1924*, microfilm 708/709, Mennonite Heritage Centre, Winnipeg.
6 Jakob J. Peters, *Tagebuch, 1919–1924*, microfilm 180, Mennonite Heritage Centre, Winnipeg.
7 Walter Schmiedehaus, *Die Altkolonier-Mennoniten in Mexiko*, trans. notes by Robyn Sneath (Bad Kreuzbach: Pandion Verlag, 1984), 57-58.
8 *Steinbach Post*, 8 March 1922.
9 Ibid., 18 October 1922.
10 Ibid., 3 January 1923.
11 Ibid., 25 May 1924.
12 Ibid., 11 July 1923.
13 Ibid.
14 Ibid., 1 August 1923.
15 Ibid., 9 July 1924.
16 Ibid., 1 August 1923.
17 Ibid., 9 January 1924.
18 Ibid., 29 August 1923.
19 For a fuller discussion of social boundaries between Mennonites and their Mexican neighbours, see Andrea M. Dyck, "'And in Mexico We Found What We Had Lost in Canada': Mennonite Immigrant Perceptions of Mexican Neighbours in a Canadian Newspaper, 1922–1967," MA thesis, University of Winnipeg, 2007.
20 *Steinbach Post*, 9 May 1923. A similar description appears in a 25 February 1925 letter.
21 Ibid., 16 May 1923.
22 See Adolf Ens, *Subjects or Citizens? The Mennonite Experience in Canada, 1970–1925* (Ottawa: University of Ottawa Press, 1994).
23 *Steinbach Post*, 21 May 1924.
24 Ibid., 15 August 1923.
25 Ibid., 7 January 1925.
26 Ibid., 17 December 1924.
27 Ibid., 11 June 1923.
28 Ibid., 15 August 1923.
29 Ibid., 21 February 1923.
30 Ibid., 27 August 1924.
31 Ibid., 26 March 1924; 1 October 1924.
32 Ibid., 7 July 1926.

33 Ibid., 1 September 1926.
34 Ibid., 1 May 1927.
35 Ibid., 27 July 1927.
36 Ibid., 18 May 1927. See Ibid., 22 June 1927, and 25 September 1927.
37 Ibid., 28 September 1927.
38 Ibid., 1 September 1926.
39 Ibid., 1 June 1927.
40 Ibid., 14 December 1927.
41 Ibid., 8 February 1928.
42 Ibid., 14 December 1927.
43 Ibid.
44 Ibid., 21 May 1924; 21 May 1927.
45 For the rich story of the founding of Menno Colony, see especially Martin W. Friesen, *Eine Neue Heimat in der Chaco Wildness* (Altona, MB: Published and bound by D.W. Friesen & Sons, 1987). See also Johann W. Toews, *Unser Leben in Paraguay* (Loma Plata, Paraguay: Self-published, ca. 2002); Jacob A. Braun, *Im Gedenken an jene Zeit: Mitteilungen zuer Entstehungsgeschichte der Kolonie Menno* (Loma Plata: Geschichtskomitee, 2001). For Menno Colony places in the context of the general history of Mennonites in Paraguay, see Peter P. Klassen, *The Mennonites in Paraguay*, Vol. I: *Kingdom of God and Kingdom of this World*, trans. Gunther H. Schmidt (Filadelfia, Paraguay: Self-published, 2004); Gerhard Ratzlaff, *One Body, Many Parts: The Mennonite Churches in Paraguay* (Asunción: Evangelical Mennonite Association of Paraguay, 2001).
46 *Steinbach Post*, 13 June 1927.
47 Ibid., 22 June 1927.
48 Ibid., 14 December 1927.
49 Ibid.
50 Ibid., 24 November 1926.
51 Ibid.
52 Ibid.
53 Ibid., 20 April 1927.
54 Ibid.
55 See Willard H. Smith, "Corporación Paraguaya." Global Anabaptist Mennonite Encyclopedia Online. 1953. http://www.gameo.org/encyclopedia/contents/corporacion_paraguaya. Accessed 2 January 2013.
56 This temperature was recorded in Réaumur, the temperature gauge Mennonites brought with them to Canada from Russia; it marked 42 degrees in Celsius.
57 *Steinbach Post*, 20 April 1927.

58 Ibid., 20 April 1927.
59 A 30 November 1927 letter in the *Steinbach Post* notes that on 3 May, a caravan of nine families left for the Chaco.
60 J. Fretz, *Pilgrims in Paraguay: The Story of Mennonite Colonization in South America* (Scottdale, PA: Herald Press, 1953), 16.
61 *Steinbach Post*, 17 August 1927.
62 Ibid., 4 September 1927.
63 Ibid., 7 December 1927.
64 Ibid., 19 October 1927.
65 Ibid., 30 November 1927.
66 Ibid., 7 December 1927.
67 Ibid., 25 May 1927.
68 Ibid., 12 October 1927.
69 Ibid., 4 September 1927.
70 Ibid., 19 October 27.
71 Ibid., 29 June 1927.
72 Ibid., 1 June 1927.
73 Ibid., 21 August 1929.
74 Ibid., 29 June 1927.
75 Ibid., 17 August 1927.
76 Ibid., 11 September 1929.
77 Ibid., 21 August 1929.
78 Ibid.
79 Ibid., 4 September 1929.
80 Ibid., 21 August 1929.
81 Ibid., 4 September 1929.
82 Calvin Redekop, *Strangers Become Neighbours: Mennonite and Indigenous Relations in the Paraguayan Chaco* (Scottdale, PA: Herald Press, 1980), 95–8. For other accounts of Mennonite – indigenous relations from the perspective of Mennonite scholars, see Edgar Stoesz, *Like a Mustard Seed: Mennonites in Paraguay* (Scottdale, PA: Herald, 2008); Peter P. Klassen, *The Mennonites in Paraguay: Encounter with Indians and Paraguayans*, trans. Gunther H. Schmitt (Kitchener: Pandora, 2002); René D. Harder Horst, *The Stroesner Regime and Indigenous Resistance in Paraguay* (Gainsville: University of Florida Press, 2007).
83 *Steinbach Post*, 31 July 1929.
84 Ibid., 23 October 1929.
85 Regarding concerns with the indigenous people also, see Friesen, "A New Home," 159.
86 *Steinbach Post*, 24 August 1929.

87 Ibid., 21 August 1929; 21 August 1929; 4 September 1929.
88 Ibid., 20 November 1929.

Chapter 3

1. It is difficult to establish just how many Mennonites still lived in Mexico and Paraguay in 1930. Both communities saw large numbers, perhaps as many as 20 percent, return to Canada, but both communities also had very high birth rates, so much so that their populations doubled every seventeen years or so. On Paraguay, Edgar Stoesz, *Like a Mustard Seed: Mennonites in Paraguay* (Scottdale, PA: Herald Press, 2008), 28, writes that the number of Mennonite colonists fell from 1763 to 1257 by April 1928. Statistics published in J. Winfield Fretz, *Pilgrims in Paraguay: The Story of Mennonite Colonization in South America* (Scottdale, PA: Herald Press, 1953), indicate a low of 1309 in 1929, presumably 31 December 1929, and a figure that doubled through natural increase alone to 2560 in 1945.
2. For a thorough description of the physical characteristics of these colonies, see H. Leonard Sawatzky, *They Sought a Country: Mennonite Colonization in Mexico* (Berkeley: University of California Press, 1971).
3. Martin W. Friesen, *Eine Neue Heimat in der Chaco Wildness* (Altona, MB: D.W. Friesen & Sons, 1987). See translated versions in Martin W. Friesen, *New Homeland in the Chaco Wilderness*, trans. by Jake Balzer (Loma Plata, Paraguay: Historical Committee of the Menno Colony, 2009); and Martin W. Friesen, "A New Home in the Chaco Wilderness," ca. 1950, trans. Herman Rempel (unpublished manuscript in possession of author).
4. For a brief history of the *Steinbach Post*, see Abe Warkentin, *Reflections on Our Heritage: A History of Steinbach and Hanover from 1874* (Steinbach, MB: Derksen Printers, 1971), 119–21.
5. Ewa Morawska, "'Diaspora' Diasporas' Representations of their Homelands: Exploring the Polymorphs," *Ethnic & Racial Studies* 34, 6 (2011): 1029, 1031.
6. See John D. Thiesen, *Mennonite and Nazi? Attitudes Among Mennonite Colonists in Latin America, 1933–1945* (Kitchener, ON: Pandora Press, 1998).
7. See Fretz, *Pilgrims in Paraguay*.
8. Robin Cohen, *Global Diasporas: An Introduction* (Seattle: University of Washington Press, 1997).
9. Takeyuki Tsuda, *Diasporic Homecomings: Ethnic Return Migration in Comparative Perspective* (Stanford: Stanford University Press, 2009), 6.
10. Ewa Morawska, "Return Migrations: Theoretical and Research Agenda," in *A Century of European Migrations, 1830–1930*, ed. Rudolph J. Vecoli

and Suzanne Sinke (Urbana and Chicago, University of Illinois Press, 1991), 279, 282, 286. In the same volume, see also Walter Kampenhoefer, "The Volume and Composition of German American Return Migration," 293–314.
11 Charles Tilly, "Contentious Repertoires in Great Britain, 1758–1834," *Social Science History* 17 (1993): 253–80.
12 Quoted in A. Friesen, "A New Home," 206.
13 *Steinbach Post*, 12 March 1930. The letter was originally written on 2 January 1930.
14 Ibid., 29 October 1930.
15 Ibid., 12 March 1930.
16 Ibid., 6 June 1931. Concerning the importation of flour, see also Ibid., 2 August 1931.
17 Ibid., 4 March 1932.
18 Friesen, "A New Home," 331–46.
19 *Mennonite Encyclopedia*, Vol. V, *Menno Colony*.
20 Jake Peters, "Mennonites in Mexico and Paraguay: A Comparative Analysis of the Colony Social System," *Journal of Mennonite Studies* 6 (1988): 204. In 1937, Mennonite Central Committee purchased Corporación Paraguaya for $57,500. The settlers at Menno Colony paid $5 an acre for land originally purchased for $1.25 by Corporación Paraguaya. Fretz, *Pilgrims in Paraguay*, 24.
21 *Steinbach Post*, 12 February 1930.
22 Ibid., 2 August 1931.
23 Ibid., 12 February 1930.
24 Ibid., 28 February 1931.
25 Ibid., 3 June 1931.
26 Ibid., 11 August 1932.
27 Friesen, "A New Home," 272.
28 According to Friesen, "A New Home," 266, the trip took five hours. See also Gerhard Ratzlaff, *The Trans-Chaco Highway: How It Came to Be*, trans. Elizabeth Unruh Leite (N.d., n.p.), 31–2.
29 Friesen, "A New Home," 266ff.
30 *Steinbach Post*, 31 January 1931.
31 Ibid., 4 June 1930.
32 Ibid., 11 June 1930.
33 Ibid., 9 April 1930.
34 Ibid., 15 August 1931.
35 Ibid., 18 October 1933.
36 Ibid., 6 March 1935. See also Ibid., 10 April 1935.

37 See Matthew Hughes, "Logistics and the Chaco War: Bolivia versus Paraguay, 1932–1935," *The Journal of Military History* 69 (2005): 436; Elizabeth Shesko, "Constructing Roads, Washing Feet, and Cutting Cane for the Patria: Building Bolivia with Military Labor, 1900–1975," *International Labor and Working-Class History* 80 (2011): 13.
38 *Steinbach Post*, 9 April 1930.
39 Ibid., 25 August 1932.
40 Ibid., 23 March 1933.
41 Ibid., 4 July 1934.
42 Ibid., 13 September 1933.
43 Ibid., 25 April 1934.
44 Ibid., 23 March 1934.
45 Ibid., 23 March 1933.
46 Ibid., 16 November 1938. See also Ibid., 2 February 1944.
47 Ibid., 18 October 1944.
48 Ibid., 20 September 1933; 1 February 1934.
49 Ibid., 31 December 1931.
50 Ibid., 17 November 1934; 18 March 1936.
51 Ibid., 27 September 1933.
52 Ibid., 19 May 1932.
53 Ibid., 6 April 1933.
54 For a full description of Mennonite–Mexican relations, see Dyck, "And in Mexico We Found What We Had Lost in Canada."
55 *Steinbach Post*, 9 June 1932.
56 Ibid., 1 September 1932.
57 Ibid., 4 May 1933. A 13 June 1934 letter in the *Post* spoke of Mexican workers helping in the construction of B.A. Rempel, Neureinland brick factory.
58 Ibid., 8 November 1936.
59 Ibid., 2 March 1933.
60 Ibid., 3 July 1935.
61 Ibid., 8 July 1936.
62 Ibid., 12 October 1933.
63 Conversations with Carlos Colarado (Winnipeg) and John Reimer (Steinbach), who are descendants of such unions dating from the 1930s and 1940s.
64 *Steinbach Post*, 5 May 1932.
65 Ibid., 2 May 1934.
66 Ibid., 4 May 1933.
67 Ibid., 15 May 1935.
68 See Mae M. Ngai, *Impossible Subjects: Illegal Aliens and the Making of Modern America* (Princeton: Princeton University Press, 2004).

69 *Steinbach Post*, 12 November 1931.
70 Ibid., 31 December 1931.
71 Ibid., 26 November 1931.
72 Ibid., 4 February 1932.
73 Ibid.
74 Ibid., 11 March 1932. Later that spring, when a local Mennonite businessman who had travelled out of Mexico suddenly appeared among the colonies, the letter writer mused that "Butcher Penner who has several businesses here, is back, and seemingly has opened the border [by himself]. It is a wonder that other folks who want to come to Mexico cannot get through and this one can. One can see who is a businessman." Ibid., 5 May 1932. In a 12 October 1933 letter, the writer announced that he "had heard it said that the border is once again open for Canadian immigrants."
75 Ibid., 19 November 1931.
76 Ibid., 2 July 1935.
77 Ibid., 15 June 1938.
78 Occasionally, these later trips brought the travellers face to face with the spectacular, such as the 100-mile-an-hour roller-coaster ride A.W. Peters took while visiting Winnipeg in 1938, a side trip he needed to take to prepare papers for the return to Mexico. Ibid., 7 December 1938.
79 Ibid., 8 December 1937.
80 Ibid., 4 July 1945.
81 Ibid., 14 January 1942.
82 Ibid.
83 Ibid.
84 Ibid., 7 December 1938.
85 In the 10 June 1936 issue, for example, Bernhard Penner began his letter thus: "On the 2nd of March we were at Peter P. Hildebrandt's for an engagement party; their foster daughter Anna Hildebrandt with Abram Hildebrandt, and on the same day Katherina Braun, Heinrich Braun's daughter, [had] an engagement with Jakob Andreas." Ibid., 10 June 1936.
86 Ibid., 15 July 1942.
87 Ibid., 25 May 1933.
88 Ibid., 4 January 1939.
89 Ibid., 27 May 1942.
90 Ibid., 10 December 1931.
91 Surprisingly, the problem of "agritista" squatters reported on by Sawatzky, *They Sought a Country*, seems absent from the letters in the *Steinbach Post*. See also Dyck, "And in Mexico We Found What We Had Lost in Canada."
92 *Steinbach Post*, 12 May 1932; 2 June 1932.

93 Ibid., 1 September 1932. For a full account of the US policies towards Mexican citizens crossing the border during the 1930s, see Ngai, *Impossible Subjects*.
94 *Steinbach Post*, 4 August 1932.
95 Ibid., 11 August 1932.
96 Ibid., 26 November 1931.
97 Ibid., 10 December 1931.
98 Ibid., 17 February 1932.
99 For background to the dispatch of armed soldiers to protect foreign farmers, see Martina E. Will, "The Mennonite Colonization of Chihuahua: Reflections of Competing Visions," *Americas* 53, 3 (1997): 368.
100 *Steinbach Post*, 17 March 1932.
101 Ibid., 31 March 1932.
102 Ibid., 7 April 1932; 31 March 1932.
103 Ibid., 7 April 1932; in July 1932 came a note that "food and feed have been taken to soldiers in Rubio," presumably by Mennonite officials. Ibid., 4 July 1932.
104 Ibid., 2 May 1932; 28 May 1932.
105 Ibid., 12 January 1933.
106 Ibid., 12 October 1933.
107 Ibid., 9 March 1933.
108 Ibid., 9 May 1934.
109 Ibid., 10 June 1934. See also 23 September 1936; 28 July 1937.
110 In 1934, correspondent J.J. Peters reported that England had recently gifted to Australia two small islands 350 kilometres northwest in the "middle of the Pacific," amidst excellent fishing and possessed of a "very healthy climate." Peters speculated that "if Mennonites 15 years ago had begun with these islands, perhaps it would have worked, as at that time only a few strange fishers worked on these islands. But ... I am completely happy here in our ill-reputed Mexico." Ibid., 4 April 1934.
111 For a first-hand account of these negotiations and the conflict within the community as a result, see Johann P. Wall, "Letters to Isaak M. Dyck," trans. with an introduction by John J. Friesen, in *Preservings* 29 (2009): 19–20, 24–7.
112 *Steinbach Post*, 12 June 1935.
113 Ibid., 26 June 1935.
114 Ibid., 17 July 1935.
115 Ibid., 3 July, 14 August 1935.
116 Ibid., 28 August 1935.
117 Ibid., 3 July 1935.
118 Ibid., 2 October 1935.

119 Ibid., 6 November 1935.
120 Ibid., 11 December 1935.
121 Ibid., 11 March 1936.
122 Ibid., 22 April 1936.
123 Ibid., 5 February 1936.
124 Ibid., 29 April 1936. According to the writer, "Freedoms have been offered here if we promise with written signatures to stay here [in Mexico]. But we need more than school freedoms. We need protection for life and property," and then he proceeded to tell how, in broad daylight, Marten Klassen, returning from the city where he had hauled beans, was robbed by three bandits, who took his thirty-five-peso profit, and then was shot in the buttocks, forcing him to be hospitalized. Ibid., 6 May 1936.
125 Ibid., 23 September 1936.
126 Ibid., 16 December 1936.
127 Ibid., 3 February 1937; 24 March 1937.
128 See Will, "The Mennonite Colonization of Chihuahua," 358.
129 *Steinbach Post*, 16 September 1936.
130 Ibid., 5 August 1936.
131 Ibid., 4 November 1936.
132 Ibid., 6 January 1937.
133 Ibid., 30 June 1937.
134 Ibid., 1 September 1937.
135 Ibid., 31 March 1938.
136 Ibid., 8 March 1939; 8 February 1939; 11 May 1938.
137 Ibid., 29 March 1939.
138 Ibid., 22 March 1939.
139 Ibid., 24 October 1945.

Chapter 4

1 Some 1700 Mennonites migrated to East Paraguay, in equal numbers to Bergthal and Sommerfeld colonies; about 800 to northern Mexico, 600 to Los Jagueyes, and 200 to Sommerfeld Colony there. Of the 1700 in Paraguay, some 600 returned in short order.
2 J. Fretz, *Pilgrims in Paraguay: The Story of Mennonite Colonization in South America* (Scottdale, PA: Herald Press, 1953), 48–52. See also Einige Brüder der E.M.C., Geschichtsbildband zum 50jährigen Bestehen der Kolonie Sommerfeld, 1948–1998 (Sommerfeld, Paraguay: Verwaltung der Kolonie Sommerfeld, 1998). The East Paraguay immigrants also included some Saskatchewan Bergthalers.

3 See Arden M. Dueck, Myron P. Loewen, Leslie L. Plett, and Eddy K. Plett, *Quellen Kolonie* (Torreon, Coahuila, Mexico: Impresora Colorama, 1998); Jacob U. Kornelsen, *25 Jahre in Mexico: Beschreibung Von der Quellenkolonie, 1948–1973* (Cuauhtémoc, Mexico: Self-published, 1973) for a history of the Kleine Gemeinde settlement at Los Jagueyes, Chihuahua, also known as Quellenkolonie. A small settlement of Old Colony Mennonites, led by Rev. Johan Loeppky, also established a settlement near Los Jagueyes.
4 See Jacques Derrida's description of "'the present' ... mean[ing] what is 'now' (*das Jetzige*) – which we represent as something within time (*etwas interzeitiges*), the 'now' serving as a phase in the stream of time." Jacques Derrida, *Margins of Philosophy* (Chicago: University of Chicago Press, 1982), 34.
5 E.P. Thompson, "Time, Work-Discipline and Industrial Capitalism," *Past and Present* 38 (1967): 58, 90; for a critique of Thompson's view, see Mark M. Smith, "Old South Time in Comparative Perspective," *American Historical Review* 101 (1996): 1432–69.
6 Quoted from his book *Pascalian Meditations* (Cambridge, 2000) in Anna Sofia Hedberg, *Outside World: Cohesion and Deviation among Old Colony Mennonites in Bolivia* (Uppsala, Sweden: Uppsala Studies in Cultural Anthropology, 2007), 28.
7 For a discussion of modern communication systems and especially how newspapers divided history from cosmology and spread the enlightenment ideas of progress, see Benedict Anderson, *Imagined Communities: Reflections on the Origin and Spread of Nationalism* (London: Versa, 2006), 36, 65. For a discussion of the rise of "objectivity" in post-First World War newspapers in the United States, see Michael Schudson, *Discovering the News: A Social History of American Newspapers* (New York: Basic Books, 1978), and especially Chapter 4, "Objectivity Becomes Ideology: Journalism After World War I," 121–59. I wish to acknowledge Mary Ann Loewen for bringing this work to my attention.
8 Johann A. Thiessen, "Tagebuch," vols. 708 and 709, Mennonite Heritage Centre, Winnipeg.
9 *Abram and Elisabeth (Kornelsen) Plett Daily Diary, Los Jagueyes, Mexico*, trans. Marie Plett (Blumenort, MB: N.d.).
10 See Robert A. Fothergill, *Private Chronicles: A Study of English Diaries* (London: Oxford University Press, 1974), 11, 14.
11 Eva Guenther, travel diary, 1949, vol. 4652, trans. Robyn Sneath, Mennonite Heritage Centre, Winnipeg.
12 *Steinbach Post*, 26 February 1947; 9 June 1948; 6 October 1948; 20 October 1948. Travelogues also exist for some 600 Manitoba Kleine Gemeinde Mennonites who, in 1948, followed their Old Colony cousins who had

settled in northern Mexico in 1922, and can be found as published letters in the *Familienfreund*, Evangelical Mennonite Conference Archives, Steinbach, Manitoba.
13 Abram D. Friesen, "Reisebericht von Abram D. Friesen," *Steinbach Post*, 29 September 1948.
14 The six families are headed by Abram Friesen, J.C. Braun, Jake Friesen, Jacob Hildebrand, John Wiebe, and John Dyck.
15 Frau Isaac F. Bergen, "Reisebericht der Frau Isaak F. Bergen," in *Unsere Reise Nach Paraguay, 1948*, ed. Jacob H. Sawatsky (Sommerfeld, Paraguay: Self-published, 2004): 20–37.
16 Ibid., 21.
17 Ibid., 21, 22.
18 Ibid., 22.
19 Ibid., 23–5.
20 Ibid., 29–30.
21 Ibid., 33–7.
22 Alessandro Portelli's description of oral history as recording that which is "symbolic of a wider epoch, that which attends psychological healing," and that which is "time-marking" and, hence, "meaningful," may also be true for the published immigrant letter. See *The Death of Luigi Trastuli and Other Stories: Form and Meaning in Oral History* (Albano: SUNY, 1991), 26.
23 *Steinbach Post*, 1 February 1950.
24 Ibid., 15 February 1953.
25 Ibid., 3 December 1952.
26 Ibid., 11 November 1953.
27 Ibid., 5 December 1951.
28 Ibid.
29 Ibid., 8 October 1952.
30 Ibid., 11 April 1946.
31 Ibid., 19 March 1952.
32 Ibid., 7 May 1952.
33 Ibid., 22 March 1950.
34 Ibid., 9 April 1952.
35 Ibid., 15 February 1953.
36 For another memoir that emphasizes eternity, see Isaak Dyck, *Das Ungluck Welches den Ehrsamen Diakon Isaak Dyck betraf, 4 April 1944* (Strassbourgo, Mexico: Strassbourg Platz, n.d.).
37 *Steinbach Post*, 7 August 1946.
38 Maria (Wiebe) Toews, *My Recollections of Experiences in Canada and Paraguay*, trans. Victor Janzen (Steinbach, Manitoba: N.p., n.d.).

39 Ibid., 1.
40 Ibid., 59, 63, 65, 67, 70, 71, 78.
41 Ibid., 89, 90, 92, 94, 106.
42 *Carillon News*, 30 January 1948.
43 *Altona Echo*, 24 November 1948.
44 Ibid., 11 May 1949.
45 *Carillon News*, 3 August 1949.
46 Ibid., 9 February 1949.
47 *Altona Echo*, 22 June 1949.
48 *Carillon News*, 13 December 1950.
49 *Altona Echo*, 24 June 1953.
50 Ibid., 19 May 1954.
51 *Carillon News*, 27 January 1954.
52 Ibid., 27 August 1952.
53 Ibid., 12 January 1955.
54 Alan Wiebe, ed., *News from Paraguay by Martha Friesen, Colony Bergthal (1951–1979)* (N.p., n.d.).
55 Ibid., 7–8.
56 Ibid., 9–10.
57 Ibid., 13.

Chapter 5

1 For histories by Mennonites of these various settlements, see Jacob Harms, *Das Hinterlassene Heft vom Verstorbenen Jacob Harms, 1914–1993* (Strassbourgo, Chihuahua: Strassbourg Platz, 2001); G.S. Koop, *Pioneer Jahre in British Honduras (Belize)* (Belize City: Self-published, n.d.); Verna Martens, *Beyond Our Wildest Dream: Beginnings in Blue Creek* (N.p.: Jake Martens, 2007); Royden Loewen, "Reinventing Mennonite Tradition: Old Ways in the Jungles of British Honduras," in *Diaspora in the Countryside: Two Mennonite Communities and Mid-Twentieth Century Rural Disjuncture* (Toronto: University of Toronto Press, 2006), 169–201; Sieghard und Sylvia Schartner, *Bolivien: Zufluschtsort der konservativen Mennoniten* (Santa Cruz, Bolivia: Self-published, 2009).
2 Michel Foucault, *The Archaeology of Knowledge and the Discourse on Language,* trans. A.M. Sheridan Smith (New York: Pantheon, 1972), xiii.
3 Mariana Valverde, *Law and Order: Images, Meanings, Myths* (New Brunswick, NJ: Rutgers, 2006), 2, 5.
4 *Belize Times*, 29 August 1957.
5 Ibid., 22 June 1957.

6 Ibid., 22 October 1957.
7 Ibid., 31 October 1957.
8 *Belize Billboard*, 8 October 1957.
9 Ibid., 4 December 1957.
10 Ibid., 10 December 1957.
11 The correct names are: Reinlaender Mennonite, Kleine Gemeinde Mennonite, and Sommerfelder Mennonite.
12 *Belize Billboard*, 13 December 1957.
13 Ibid., 9 July 1958.
14 Ibid., 17 July 1958.
15 Ibid., 19 June 1958.
16 Ibid., 20 June 1958.
17 Ibid., 22 July 1958.
18 *Belize Times*, 3 May 1958.
19 Ibid., 30 November 1958.
20 E-mail from Luis Enrique Rivero Coimbra to Royden Loewen, 9 February 2010, trans. Gustavo Velasco.
21 *La Presencia*, 7 May 1967, trans. Gustavo Velasco.
22 Ibid., 23 September 1968.
23 Ibid., 15 January 1970.
24 Ibid., 7 April 1970.
25 *El Diario*, 5 April 1968; quotes from translation in James W. Lanning, "The Old Colony Mennonites of Bolivia: A Case Study," MSc thesis, Texas A&M University, 1971, 122–4.
26 A.D. Bushong, "Agricultural Settlement in British Honduras: A Geographical Interpretation," PhD diss., University of Florida, 1961, ii.
27 Jerry Alan Hall, "Mennonite Agriculture in a Tropical Environment: An Analysis of the Development and Productivity of a Mid-Latitude Agricultural System in British Honduras," PhD diss., Clark University, 1970.
28 Lanning, "The Old Colony Mennonites of Bolivia."
29 Edward W. Van Dyck, "Bluemenort [Blumenort]: A Study of Persistence in a Sect," PhD diss., University of Alberta, 1972.
30 Kelso Lee Wessel, "An Economic Assessment of Pioneer Settlement in the Bolivian Highlands," PhD diss., Cornell University, 1968, 68.
31 Lanning, "The Old Colony Mennonites of Bolivia," 43.
32 Ibid., 80.
33 In December 1980, I visited Spanish Lookout colony where Menno Loewen, former colony mayor, recalled the visits by Jerry Hall and H. Leonard Sawatzky with fondness, and cited both men as experts in economic analysis.

34 Bushong, "Agricultural Settlement," 106.
35 Ibid., 107.
36 Ibid., 108.
37 Ibid., 122.
38 Ibid., 124.
39 Ibid., 123.
40 Ibid., 119.
41 Ibid., 111.
42 Ibid., 116.
43 Harry Leonard Sawatzky, *Mennonite Settlement in British Honduras* (Berkeley: University of Berkeley, 1969).
44 Ibid., 13.
45 Ibid., 15.
46 Ibid., 19.
47 Ibid., 41.
48 Ibid., 33 and 34.
49 Ibid., 34.
50 Ibid.
51 Spanish Lookout was the subject of yet another geographer's analysis, which, for the sake of space, is not covered here. See R. Langemann, "The Development of a Model for the Life Cycle of a Closed Agricultural Colony: The Mennonite Colony of Spanish Lookout, British Honduras," MA thesis, Simon Fraser University, 1971.
52 Hall, "Mennonite Agriculture," 9 and 10.
53 Ibid., 19.
54 Ibid., 53.
55 Ibid., 21.
56 Ibid., 65.
57 Ibid., 28.
58 Ibid., 166 and 167.
59 Ibid., 73.
60 Ibid., 6.
61 Ibid., 187.
62 Ibid., 396.
63 See, for example, Ronald Palmer, "Politics and Modernization: The Case of Santa Cruz, Bolivia," PhD diss., ca. 1960, undertaken with the help of MCC in Santa Cruz.
64 Wessel, "An Economic Assessment," 20. Such an inflation occurred between 1950 and 1956 when the price for a US dollar rose from 150 Bolivianos to 11,640.

65 Ibid., 13. "Sugar cane, rice, cotton, maize, coffee and fruits can all be grown in abundance in this area," wrote Wessel. He further described the region as representing "about 9% of Bolivia's total land area; it is bounded by very flat, wet and hot tropics to the north, and flat, desert like Chaco to the east and south." Ibid., 13.
66 Ibid., 2.
67 Ibid., 3 and 4.
68 Ibid., 5.
69 Ibid., 34.
70 Ibid., 57 and 59.
71 Ibid., 58.
72 Ibid.
73 Ibid., 57.
74 Ibid., 59.
75 Ibid.
76 Ibid.
77 Ibid., 60.
78 Ibid., 62. In comparison, the Okiniwas arrived in 1954, after a 1948 attempt by merchants to organize a migration to help peasants flee the aftermath of the Second World War, a 1952 presidential allotment of 10K hectares of national territory, and a ten-year colonization plan. But not until 1956 did they find a permanent settlement of Okinawa Colony east of Montero. Each family was given, free, fifty hectares of bushland. Although up to 90 percent of the cropland was in rice, "since 1960 proportionately less rice and more maize and yucca have been grown each year." Ibid.
79 Lanning, "The Old Colony Mennonites," 39.
80 Technically, Riva Palacios colony purchased the land in acres, 100,000 acres for an average price of $.65 an acre; it had a population of 2172 in 1971. The three different languages represented in these names marked a virtual map of Mennonite migrations: Sommerfeld, meaning "summer field" in German, was a common type of name found among nineteenth-century Mennonites in Russia and was the name of a Mennonite village in Manitoba; Swift Current referred to the town in southwestern Saskatchewan and the colony founded by Mennonites from Saskatchewan in Chihuahua, Mexico, in 1922; Paurido or Santa Rita referred to a Mennonite daughter colony within Chihuahua, located near Mexican villages bearing these names; the name Riva Palacio (without an "s") was the legal name of a land block on which Nord Kolonie or Ojo de la Yegua was founded in Mexico.

81 Unlike the Old Colony "horse and buggy" Mennonites, the Sommerfeld Colony, consisting of Sommerfelder Mennonites, allowed tractors to be equipped with rubber tires.
82 Lanning, "The Old Colony Mennonites," iii.
83 Ibid., 26.
84 Ibid., 30.
85 Ibid. See Bernard F. Peters, *Hinterlassene Schriften von Aeltester Bernard F. Peters* (Santa Cruz, Bolivia: Johan F. Hamm, 2003).
86 Lanning, "The Old Colony Mennonites," 29.
87 Ibid., 32.
88 Ibid.
89 Certainly, their comfort predated the rise of the German-descended Hugo Banzer Suárez as military dictator from 1971 to 1978.
90 Lanning, "The Old Colony Mennonites," iii.
91 Ibid., 16.
92 Ibid., 27.
93 Ibid., 114, 116.
94 Ibid.
95 Ibid.
96 Ibid., 85.
97 Ibid., 48.
98 Ibid., 68.
99 Ibid., 36.
100 Ibid., 67.
101 Ibid., 54.
102 Ibid., 30.
103 Ibid., 47.
104 Ibid., 52.
105 Ibid., 73.
106 Ibid., 97.
107 Ibid., 66.
108 Ibid., 67.
109 Ibid., 90.
110 Ibid., 75 and 84.
111 Ibid., 67 and 97.
112 Ibid., 42.
113 Ibid., 59.
114 Ibid., 69.
115 Ibid., 71.
116 Ibid., 75.
117 Ibid., 77 and 78.

118 Ibid., 83.
119 Ibid., 86.
120 Ibid., 95.
121 Ibid., v.
122 Van Dyck, "Bluemenort [Blumenort]," 99, 115, 116.
123 Ibid., 116.
124 Ibid., 41.
125 Ibid., 57, 58, 115.
126 Ibid., 117 and 123.
127 Ibid., 120.
128 Ibid., 117.
129 Ibid., 111.
130 Ibid., 130.
131 Ibid., 137.
132 Ibid., 125.
133 Ibid., 128.
134 Ibid., 148, 150, 152, 154, 161.
135 Ibid., 155.
136 Ibid., 161.
137 Ibid., 163.
138 Ibid.
139 Ibid., 144.
140 Ibid., 63.
141 Ibid., 157.
142 Ibid., 164.
143 Ibid., 159.
144 Ibid., 165.
145 Ibid., 167.
146 Ibid.
147 Ibid., 171.
148 Ibid., 174.

Chapter 6

1 See William Janzen, "Welcoming the Returning 'Kanadier' Mennonites from Mexico," *Journal of Mennonite Studies* 22 (2004): 11–24; and *Build Up One Another: The Work of MCCO with the Mennonites from Mexico in Ontario, 1977–1997* (Kitchener, ON: Mennonite Central Committee Ontario, 1998). See also Lucille Marr, *The Transforming Power of a Century: Mennonite Central Committee and Its Evolution in Ontario* (Waterloo, ON: Pandora, 2003).

2 See E.K. Francis, "The Mennonite Commonwealth in Russia: A Sociological Interpretation," *Mennonite Quarterly Review* 25 (1951): 173–82; Jack Thiessen, *Mennonite Low German / Mennonitish-Plauttdeutsches Wörterbuch* (Madison: University of Wisconsin-Madison Max Kade Institute for German-American Studies, 2003).
3 In total, forty-eight interviews were conducted; the ones chosen for this project include a representative selection of them, including interviews with both elderly and more junior members, members of the majoritarian Old Colony church, but also members of the Sommerfelder Mennonites, and members of both conservative and evangelical churches. The interviewees did not include Mexico Mennonites unaffiliated with any church, a group identified by historian Bruce Guenther.
4 All interviews are from the "Mennonites from Mexico Oral History Project," organized by Conrad Grebel College, Waterloo, Ontario, funded by the Multicultural History Society of Ontario, deposited at the Mennonite Archives of Ontario (hereafter MAO). The interviewer was Ronald Sawatsky; twelve of the forty-eight interviews quoted in this chapter are from translated and transcribed notes by Kerry Fast, Toronto.
5 Quoted in Steven Vertovec, *Transnationalism* (New York: Routledge, 2009), 6.
6 Jan Assmann and John Czaplicka, "Collective Memory and Cultural Identity," *New German Critique, NGC* 65, 65 (1995): 127. http://dx.doi.org/10.2307/488538.
7 Ibid., 128.
8 Interview #7340 with Henry S. and Maria Voth by Ron Sawatsky, 5 June 1979, in Copenhagen, Ontario; oral recording in MAO; translated from Low German by Kerry Fast; translated typescript in possession of author.
9 Ibid.
10 Interview #7350 with Anna and Cornelius F. Peters by Ron Sawatsky, 16 May 1979, in Aylmer, Ontario; oral recording in MAO; translated from Low German by Kerry Fast; translated typescript in possession of author. See also a photocopy of the diary of Cornelius Peters's father, Jacob Peters, 1915–1934, at MAO.
11 Interview #7348 with Anna and Heinrich Banman by Ron Sawatsky, 16 May 1979, in Aylmer, Ontario; oral recording in MAO; translated from Low German by Kerry Fast; translated typescript in possession of author. See also a photocopy of the diary of Cornelius Peters's father, Jacob Peters, 1915–1934, at MAO.
12 Ibid.
13 Interview #7639 with Peter Giesbrecht by Ron Sawatsky, 20 June 1979, in Aylmer, Ontario; oral recording in MAO; translated from Low German by Kerry Fast; translated transcript in possession of author.

14 Corny Friesen had a similar memory of dogs. Interview #7077 with Corny Friesen, by Ron Sawatsky, 24 August 1979, in Port Rowan, Ontario; oral recording in MAO; translated from Low German by Kerry Fast; translated transcript in possession of author.
15 Interview with Anna and Cornelius F. Peters.
16 Interview with Henry S. and Maria Voth.
17 Ibid.
18 Interview with Anna and Cornelius F. Peters.
19 Interview with Corny Friesen.
20 Ibid.
21 Interview #7343 with Rev. John and Nettie Banman by Ron Sawatsky, 11 June 1979, in London, Ontario; oral recording in MAO; English transcript by Kerry Fast in possession of author.
22 Interview #7351 with Abe Loewen by Ron Sawatsky, 15 May 1979, in Aylmer, Ontario; oral recording in MAO; translated from Low German by Kerry Fast; translated transcript in possession of author.
23 Ibid.
24 Interview with Anna and Cornelius F. Peters.
25 Ibid.
26 Interview with Heinrich Banman.
27 Interview with Peter Giesbrecht.
28 Interview with Corny Friesen.
29 Interview with Abe Loewen.
30 Interview with Peter Giesbrecht.
31 Interview with Anna and Cornelius F. Peters.
32 Interview with Cornelius Friesen.
33 For a history of the Old Colony Mennonite Church in Ontario, see Delbert Plett, ed., *Old Colony Mennonites in Canada 1875 to 2000* (Steinbach, MB: Crossway Publications, 2001). For a history of the Evangelical Mennonite Mission Church, see Jack Heppner, *Search for Renewal: The Story of the Rudnerweider / Evangelical Mennonite Mission Conference, 1937–1987* (Winnipeg: Evangelical Mennonite Mission Conference, 1987).
34 Quoted in Vertovec, *Transnationalism*, 6.
35 Interview with Abe Loewen.
36 Interview with Anna and Cornelius F. Peters.
37 Ibid.
38 Peter Giesbrecht recalled that earlier there had been a minister, Jake "Neudorf from Manitoba," and another minister, Peter Harder, who had been "elected a minister in Manitoba but he hadn't accepted it there."
39 Ibid. These first singers included "Cornelius Enns, another one was Gerhard Wiebe from Port Burwell," later from Tillsonburg.

40 Ibid. John Banman recalled in 1979 that on a recent trip back to Durango, "they are still what our ... Old Colony people in Chihuahua province were 15 years ago or 20 years ago. ... dress[ing] more old fashioned ... and ... a lot of them ... don't drive cars, trucks. ..."; but "they've done away with" excommunications. Nettie Banman recalled that, by 1979, the Old Colony ministers in Mexico "say they release them but they don't excommunicate them," having become "fed up of the excommunicating business," and reflecting the fact that "in the first place they came to Canada" because of strict church regulations. Interview with Rev. John and Nettie Banman.
41 Peter Giesbrecht recalled that Harder led a large migration to Rainy River; when it failed, Harder moved back to Manitoba.
42 Interview with Cornelius Friesen.
43 Interview with Peter Giesbrecht.
44 Interview #7074 with Aron S. Wall by Ron Sawatsky, 30 July 1979, in Elmira, Ontario; oral recording in MAO; translated from Low German by Kerry Fast; translated transcript in possession of author.
45 Ibid.
46 Interview with Heinrich Voth.
47 Ibid.
48 Interview with Corny Friesen.
49 Interview with John and Nettie Banman.
50 John and Nettie, like others, have pieced together the Old Colony story. They began in about 1959 or 1960 in Bayham Township, between Port Burwell and Vienna, renting a little old school. They stayed there for four or five years and then, in 1964 or 1965, they purchased a church in Springfield. Later, Walsingham and Wheatley started, and when the Banmans left, there were some 800 members between Leamington and Springfield. The first bishop was Mr. Henry Reimer of Leamington, elected after the Banmans left. Rev. Jacob Giesbrecht of Nord Kolonie, Mexico, elected preacher in Ontario, was another preacher who "could see that our church was in darkest need." Ibid.
51 Ibid. The EMC had come with Cornelius J. Dyck in late September 1977, the meeting with the EMMC occurred in summer 1977, and Peter Dyck left the Sommerfelder in November 1977.

Chapter 7

1 Benedict Anderson, *Imagined Communities: Reflections on the Origin and Spread of Nationalism* (London: Versa, 1992), 6.

2 Daphne N. Winland, "'Our Home and Native Land'? Canadian Ethnic Scholarship and the Challenge of Transnationalism," *Canadian Review of Sociology and Anthropology* 35 (1998): np/8.
3 On the economic development to the Cuauhtémoc area Mennonites, see the work of Pedro Castro, including his English-language piece, "The 'Return' of the Mennonites from the Cuauhtémoc Region to Canada: A Perspective from Mexico," *Journal of Mennonite Studies* 22 (2004): 25–38.
4 *Die Mennonitische Post*, 20 September 1996. See also Leo-Paul Dana and Teresa E. Dana, "Collective Entrepreneurship in a Mennonite Community in Paraguay," *Latin American Business Review* 8, 4 (2008): 82–96.
5 See J. Valerie Fifer, "The Search for a Series of Small Successes: Frontiers of Settlement in Eastern Bolivia," *Journal of Latin American Studies* 14 (1982): 426–27.
6 See, for example, Martin W. Friesen, ed., *50 Jahre Kolonie Menno, Chaco, Paraguay, 1927–1977: Eine Gedenkschrift zum Fuenfzigjaehrigen Jubilaeum* (Loma Plata, Paraguay: Verwaltung der Kolonie Menno, 1977); *75th Anniversary Celebration of the Mennonites in Mexico, 1922–1997*, a movie produced by Otto Klassen in collaboration with el Comité Pro Archivo Histórico y Museo Mennonita, 1977.
7 *Mennonitische Post*, 4 October 1996.
8 The Nuevo Casas Grandes colonies included Buenos Aires, Capulin, and El Cuervo.
9 Robyn Dyck Sneath, "Imagining a Mennonite Community: The Mennonitische Post and a People of Diaspora," *Journal of Mennonite Studies* 22 (2004): 205–20.
10 *Mennonitische Post*, 19 May 1977.
11 Ibid., 15 September 1977.
12 Ibid., 19 May 1977.
13 Ibid., 19 August 1983.
14 Ibid., 10 June 1992.
15 Ibid., 17 November 1977.
16 Ibid., 18 May 1990.
17 Ibid., 15 October 1982. "Liebe, weit versteute Leser / weit verstreut in aller Welt / In Gedanken wie durch Glaeser / mach man sich so oft ein Bild / wo sind all die vielen Lieben / die wir frueher gut gekant / hingeresit und wo geblieben / Wo sind sie? Im welchem Land?"
18 Ibid., 2 June 1977.
19 Ibid., 18 June 1980.
20 Ibid., 7 May 1982.

266 Notes to pages 182–9

21 Ibid., 6 August 1993.
22 Ibid., 17 December 1982.
23 Ibid., 3 December 1982.
24 Ibid., 4 November 1992.
25 Ibid., 8 January 1982.
26 Ibid., 19 June 1981.
27 Ibid.
28 Ibid., 16 April 1982.
29 Ibid., 20 February 1987.
30 Ibid., 17 February 1978; 18 April 1980; 20 February 1981.
31 Ibid., 18 January 1985.
32 Ibid., 20 October 1977.
33 Ibid., 15 December 1978.
34 Ibid., 15 November 1985.
35 Ibid., 18 April 1986.
36 Ibid., 20 October 1977.
37 Ibid., 17 February 1978.
38 Ibid., 3 February 1978.
39 Ibid., 4 August 1977.
40 In this regard, see the work of William Janzen, including his "Welcoming the Returning 'Kanadier' Mennonites from Mexico," *Journal of Mennonite Studies* 22 (2004): 11–24; *Build Up One Another: The Work of MCCO with the Mennonites from Mexico in Ontario, 1977–1997* (Kitchener, ON: Mennonite Central Committee Ontario, 1998); *Limits on Liberty: The Experience of Mennonite, Hutterite and Doukhobor Communities in Canada* (Toronto: University of Toronto Press, 1990).
41 *Mennonitische Post*, 2 October 1987. The story also quantified the migration north from Menno Colony in Paraguay between 1948 and 1986 as consisting of 502 families, with 150 families returning from Canada to Menno Colony.
42 For a discussion on legal, social, and cultural concepts of citizenship, see T.H. Marshall, *Class, Citizenship, and Social Development: Essays* (Garden City, NY: Doubleday, 1965); Robert Adamoski, Dorothy E. Chunn, and Robert Menzies, *Contesting Canadian Citizenship: Historical Readings* (Peterborough: Broadview, 2002).
43 *Mennonitische Post*, 21 April 1977.
44 Ibid., 18 March 1988.
45 Ibid., 7 April 1995.
46 Ibid., 6 March 1987; 5 June 1987.
47 Ibid., 19 October 1984.

48 Ibid., 1 June 1990.
49 Ibid., 20 March 1992.
50 Ibid., 16 March 1979.
51 Ibid., 17 November 1978; 15 February 1980; 6 November 1981.
52 Ibid., 6 April 1984.
53 Ibid., 20 December 1996.
54 Ibid., 20 November 1987.
55 Ibid., 15 December 1989.
56 Ibid., 18 August 1978.
57 Ibid., 1 August 1991.
58 Ibid., 15 March 1991; 17 November 1995.
59 See John Friesen, *Field of Broken Dreams: Mennonite Settlement in Seminole, West Texas* (Winnipeg: Self-published, 1996).
60 *Mennonitische Post*, 7 July 1977.
61 Friesen, *Field of Broken Dreams*.
62 *Mennonitische Post*, 4 August 1977.
63 Ibid., 7 July 1977.
64 Ibid., 3 November 1977.
65 Ibid., 6 April 1979.
66 Friesen, *Field of Broken Dreams*, 22ff.
67 *Mennonitische Post*, 15 December 1977.
68 Ibid., 5 March 1982.
69 Ibid., 2 July 1982.
70 Ibid., 20 March 1987.
71 Ibid., 15 March 1991.
72 Ibid., 17 November 1995.
73 Ibid., 1 May 1987.
74 Ibid., 15 March 1991.
75 Ibid., 17 June 1994.
76 "All 535, including the Mennonites, are to report to the military [headquarters] in Cuauhtémoc to register for their pre-cartilla. ... Next December they must present themselves to obtain their 'cartilla liberada.'" Ibid., 20 January 1989; 5 February 1988.
77 *Mennonitische Post*, 1 June 1990.
78 Ibid., 16 April 1993.
79 Ibid., 4 August 1977.
80 Ibid., 5 February 1988.
81 Ibid., 7 May 1982. He further noted, "In addition there are no beggars in the villages, and [on] the long trip to Asuncion anyone can see that they live in small houses, huddle in groups drinking Terere and with their few

268   Notes to pages 199–207

acres of mandioca, mais and banana and orange trees ... it looks as if they have nourishment and clothing and are content." They may be a "humble and simple people" but they are a clean and honest people.
82 Ibid., 17 February 1989.
83 Ibid., 5 February 1993.
84 Letter from *Die Mennonitische Post*, 21 July 1977, quoted in Lukas Thiessen, "Land and Heimat: The Concept of Home in the Letters of Low German-Speaking Mennonites from Bolivia in Die Mennonitische Post," unpublished undergraduate essay, University of Winnipeg, 2009.
85 Letter from *Die Mennonitische Post*, 17 February 1978, quoted in Thiessen, "Land and Heimat," 14.
86 *Mennonitische Post*, 4 August 1977.
87 Ibid., 21 May 1982.
88 Ibid., 2 April 1983.
89 Ibid., 15 April 1983.
90 Ibid., 18 June 1990.
91 Ibid., 20 March 1992.
92 Ibid., 15 December 1989.
93 Ibid. See also Ibid., 19 May 1995.

Chapter 8

1 Conversations with Kennert Giesbrecht, editor of *Die Mennonitische Post*. See also William Janzen, *Build Up One Another: The Work of MCCO with the Mennonites from Mexico in Ontario, 1977–1997* (Kitchener, ON: Mennonite Central Committee Ontario, 1998).
2 Arjun Appadurai, "Global Ethnospaces: Notes and Queries for a Transnational Anthropology," in *Recapturing Anthropology*, ed. R. Fox (Santa Fe: School of American Research Press, 1991), 181, 207.
3 Ibid., 181, 207.
4 Michael Jackson, "Introduction," in *Politics of Storytelling: Violence, Transgression and Intersubjectivity* (Copenhagen: Museum Tusculanum, 2002), 13.
5 Ibid., 14.
6 For other studies of Mexico Mennonite women in Ontario, see Marlene Epp, "Pioneers, Refugees, Exiles and Transnationalisms: Gendering Diaspora in an Ethno-Religious Context," *Journal of the Canadian Historical Association* 12 (2001): 137–54; Kerry L. Fast, "Religion, Pain and the Body: Agency in the Life of an Old Colony Woman," *Journal of Mennonite Studies* 22 (2004): 103–40; Luann Good Gingrich and Kerry Preibisch, "Migration

as Preservation and Destruction: The Paradox of Transnational Living for Low German Mennonite Women," *Journal of Ethnic and Migration Studies* 36 (2010): 1499–1518.
7 It is crucial to disclose that the oral histories below came about as an invitation for Low German Mexican Mennonite women to talk about their experiences of moving from Mexico to Ontario. Half the women volunteered to tell their stories after a public invitation; the other half were approached but reminded that they were under no compulsion whatsoever to enter the interview process. Most of the women requested anonymity; even numbers spoke in English and Low German. All were informed that their stories would become public in some fashion. Clearly, the women told their stories for purposes of their own, and they withheld information and recounted facts as they saw them. All interviews were set up, conducted, and transcribed by Kerry L. Fast (University of Toronto), under the supervision of the author in 2006. The original tape recordings are in the possession of Kerry L. Fast; copies of the transcriptions are in the possession the author. The ethical dimensions of the project were adjudicated by the University of Winnipeg Ethics Committee. Translations from Low German are by the author.
8 Interview in English with "Nettie Wiebe," a pseudonym, on 29 May 2006, in Chatham, Ontario, with Kerry Fast. The interviewee moved to Canada in about 1987 from Chihuahua. In 2006, she was twenty-eight years old, married, and mother to three children.
9 Interview in English with "Elisabeth Rempel," a pseudonym, on 23 and 29 May 2006, in Chatham, Ontario, by Kerry Fast; transcript of interview by Kerry Fast in possession of author. In 2006, the interviewee (from Chihuahua and La Honda, Zacatecas) was twenty-eight or twenty-nine years old, married, and mother to four children. She first came to Canada in about 1985.
10 Epp, "Pioneers, Refugees, Exiles and Transnationalisms," 149.
11 A reference to citizenship regulations requiring children of Canadian citizens born abroad to declare their intention to claim Canadian citizenship for themselves.
12 Interview in Low German with "Aganetha Thiessen," a pseudonym, on 7 March 2006, in Frogmore, Ontario, by Kerry Fast; transcript of Low German interview by Kerry Fast in possession of author. The interviewee arrived in Ontario from Blumenort, Durango, sometime in the 1980s; in 2006, she was about fifty years old, married, and mother to thirteen children. Quotes translated into English by author.

13 Interview in English with "Justina Krahn," a pseudonym, on 21 February 2006, in Frogmore, Ontario, by Kerry Fast; transcript of interview by Kerry Fast and in possession of author. The interviewee arrived in Canada in about 1988 from Swift Colony, Chihuahua; in 2006, she was in her early forties, married, and mother to six children.
14 Interview in English with "Lisa Klippenstein," a pseudonym, on 17 June 2006, in Leamington, Ontario, by Kerry Fast; transcript of interview by Kerry Fast in possession of author. In 2006, the interviewee from Campo 69, Mexico, had lived in Canada for ten years; she was in her thirties, was married, and was mother to three daughters.
15 Interview in Low German with "Anna Bartsch," a pseudonym, on 14 July 2006 in Leamington, Ontario, by Kerry Fast, transcript of Low German interview by Kerry Fast in possession of author. In 2006, the interviewee was thirty-seven years old, single, having first come to Canada in 1996 from Campo 111, Swift Colony, Mexico.
16 Doreen Helen Klassen, "'I wanted a life of my own': Creating Singlewoman Mennonite Identity in Mexico," *Journal of Mennonite Studies* 26 (2008): 55.
17 See, for example, Dirk Hoerder, "Transcultural States, Nations, and People," in *The Historical Practice of Diversity. Transcultural Interactions from the Early Modern Mediterranean to the Postcolonial World*, ed. Dirk Hoerder with Christiane Harzig and Adrian Schubert (New York: Berghahn Books, 2003).

Conclusion

1 Field notes by author. The names Martin Klippenstein, Cornelius Fehr, and Margaretha Bergen are pseudonyms.
2 Benedict Anderson, *Imagined Communities: Reflections on the Origin and Spread of Nationalism 1992* (London: Versa, 2006).
3 Ibid., 6.
4 For a discussion of these classical terms, see Robert A. Nisbet, "Community as Typology – Toennies and Weber," in *The Sociological Tradition* (New York: Basic Books, 1966), 71–83.
5 For other studies that link the idea of dynamic cultural reinvention with traditionalist Anabaptist society, see Donald B. Kraybill, *The Riddle of Amish Culture* (Baltimore: Johns Hopkins University Press, 2001).

Glossary

Ältester / Eltesta – the elected head of the Mennonite church, translated as "bishop" (in High and Low German, respectively)

Bergthaler – descendants of "Bergthal" Colony in Russia; literally, "mountain valley"; also members of a congregation by that name

Brandverordnung – fire insurance bureau

Bruderschaft or Bruderrat – a meeting of all baptized males; the Brotherhood assembly

Chortitzer – one of the smaller of the five Mennonite denominations, named after the village of Chortitz, Manitoba, the place of residence of its Ältester and itself named after Chortitza (Khortitsa) Colony in New Russia, and a congregation that settled in Paraguay in 1927 and 1948

Dietsch – technically, "German" in Low German

Dietsche – technically, "Germans" in Low German, but usually synonymous with Low German-speaking Mennonites

Donnadach – literally, "Thursday" in Low German, but with reference to weekly ministerial meetings at the church to which errant members are summoned to account for their actions, or where members approach ministers with their spiritual concerns

Einheimische – indigenous

Faspa – a light, late-afternoon meal

Frau – Mrs. or wife

Gemeinde / Jemeend – congregation (in High and Low German, respectively)

Jenseit – literally, the "other side," used to designate communities that lie on the "other side" of rivers, most often used in Manitoba for members of either the East or West Reserve to designate members from the "other side" of the Red River

Kleine Gemeinde / Kjleen Jemeend – one of the smaller of the five Mennonite denominations, literally meaning "small congregation"; founded in Russia in 1812 (in High and Low German, respectively), and a congregation that settled in Mexico in 1948

Lehrdienst – the council of ordained ministers

Ohm – Mr. or a term of deference to an older man

Onkle – literally, "uncle" but a term of deference to an older man

Ordnung – church-sanctioned "order"

Plautdietsch – West Prussian Low German, infused with Dutch and Russian words; the dialect spoken by the subjects of this book

Privilegium – literally, "privileges" or a "charter of privileges" granted to the diasporic Mennonites by governments; it usually included military exemptions and school freedoms

Russländer / Russlända – post-Russian Revolution Mennonite migrants from the Soviet Union (in High and Low German, respectively)

Schulz / Schult – village mayor (in High and Low German, respectively)

Schulzenbott / Schultebott – the council of all male householders in any given village (in High and Low German, respectively)

Saskatchewan Bergthaler – descendants of "Bergthal" Colony in Russia, but more conservative than the "Bergthaler"; similar to Sommerfelder Mennonites, also known at times as Altbergthaler, and a congregation that settled in Paraguay in 1927

Sommerfelder – one of the smaller of the various Mennonite denominations; named after the village of Sommerfeld, Manitoba, the place of residence of its founding Ältester, and a congregation that settled in Mexico and Paraguay in the 1920s and in East Paraguay in the 1940s

Tante / Taunte – literally, "aunt" but a term of deference to an older woman (in High and Low German, respectively)

Waisenamt – literally, the "orphans bureau" but, more precisely, "inheritance bylaw enforcement office"

Waisenvorsteher – the elected head of the Waisenamt

Vorsteher – colony mayor, elected for specific terms

Bibliography

Manuscripts: Public

Guenter (Ginter), Eva. Travel diary, 1949, Volume 4652, Mennonite Heritage Centre, Winnipeg, translated by Robyn Dyck Sneath.
Mennonite Archives of Ontario.
Mennonite Heritage Centre, Winnipeg.
Peter, Jacob. Diary from Manitoba, Mexico, 1915–1934.
Rempel, David. Letter collection, Volume 4395, Mennonite Heritage Centre, translated by Robyn Dyck Sneath.
Rempel, David. Diary, 6 August 1919–26 November 1919, Volume 5015, translated by Jake K. Wiens.
Thiessen, Johan A. "Tagebuch." Volume 708 and Volume 709.

Newspapers

Belize Billboard
Belize Times
Carillon News
El Diario
Christlicher Familienfreund
La Presencia
Menno Blatt
Mennonitische Post
Steinbach Post
Red River Echo

Oral History Interviews

Interviews by Kerry L. Fast, in "Mexico Mennonite Women of Southern Ontario Oral History Project," funded by Social Sciences and Humanities Research Council grant to author. All names are pseudonyms. Typescript of interviews in possession of author.

> Bartsch, Anna. 14 July 2006, Leamington, Ontario.
> Klippenstein, Lisa (Leena). 17 June 2006, Leamington, Ontario.
> Krahn, Justina. 21 February 2006, Frogmore, Ontario.
> Rempel, Elisabeth. 23 and 29 May 2006, Chatham, Ontario.
> Thiessen, Aganetha. 7 March 2006, Frogmore, Ontario.
> Wiebe, Nettie. 29 May 2006, Chatham, Ontario.

Interviews by Ronald Sawatsky, in "Mennonites from Mexico Oral History Project," organized by Conrad Grebel College, Waterloo, Ontario, funded by the Multicultural History Society of Ontario, deposited at the Mennonite Archives of Ontario [hereafter MAO]. All interviews below were translated from Low German and transcribed by Kerry L. Fast. Paper copies in possession of author.

> Banman, Anna and Heinrich. Interview 7348, 16 May 1979, Aylmer, Ontario.
> Banman, John and Nettie. Interview 7343, 11 June 1979, London, Ontario.
> Friesen, Corny. Interview 7077, 24 August 1979, Port Rowan, Ontario.
> Giesbrecht, Peter. Interview 7639, 20 June 1979, Aylmer, Ontario.
> Loewen, Abe. Interview 7351, 15 May 1979, Aylmer, Ontario.
> Peters, Anna and Cornelius. Interview 7350, 16 May 1979, Aylmer, Ontario.
> Voth, Henry S. and Maria. Interview 7340, 5 June 1979, Copenhagen, Ontario.
> Wall, Aron S. Interview 7074, 30 July 1979, Elmira, Ontario.

Interviews by Royden Loewen. Handwritten field notes in English or translated from Low German into English by author; in possession of author.

> Bartsch, Henry. June 2005, Aylmer, Ontario, Canada.
> Fehr Kehler, Tina. February 2010, Winkler, Manitoba, Canada.
> Froese, Lydia (Plett). December 2008, Colonia La Honda, Zacatecas, Mexico.
> Goertzen, Isaak. August 2004, La Crete, Alberta, Canada.
> Heide, Hein. January 2004, Colonia Los Jagueyes, Chihuahua, Mexico.
> Hiebert, Levi. March 2004, Loma Plata, Paraguay.
> Loewen, Myron. March 2009, St. Agathe, Manitoba, Canada.
> Neufeld, Maria Neufeld. March 2004, Colonia Cupisei, Santa Cruz, Bolivia.

Penner, Maria (Loewen). July 2005, Northfield, Nova Scotia, Canada.
Schmidt, Johan. July 2009, Colonia Rio Verde, Rio Verde, Paraguay.
Thiessen, Aron. March 2004, Colonia Riva Palacios, Santa Cruz, Bolivia.
Wall, Jakob. January 2007, Colonia Durango, Nuevo Ideal, Durango, Mexico.

Primary: Books and Articles

Bender, Harold S. "With the Mennonite Refugee Colonies in Brazil and Paraguay: A Narrative, Personal." *Mennonite Quarterly Review* 13 (1939): 59–70.
Bergen, Frau Isaak F. "Reisebericht der Frau Isaak F.Bergen." In *Unsere Reise Nach Paraguay, 1948*, edited by Jacob H. Sawatsky. Sommerfeld, Paraguay: Self-published, 2004.
Dueck, Menno B. *Rueckerinnerungen an Yermo (Durango): Wie ich es Kennen Lernte als Schullehrer und in Krankheit*. Cuauhémoc: Self-published, ca. 1963.
Dyck, Isaak M. *Anfangs Jahre der Mennoniten in Mexiko*. Cuauhtémoc: Heinrich Dyck, 1995.
– *Die Auswanderung der Reinlaender Mennoniten Gemeinde von Kanada nach Mexiko 1970*. Cuauhtémoc: Imprenta Colonial, 1993.
– *Hinterlassene Schriften vom Aeltester Isaak M. Dyck, Blumenfeld, Mexiko*. Cuauhtémoc: Jacob Klassen Fehr, 2000.
– "*Das Ungluck Welches den Ehrsamen Diakon Isaak Dyck betraf, 4 April 1944*." Strassbourgo, Mexico: *Strassbourg Platz*, n.d.
Einige Brüder der E.M.C. *Geschichtsbildband zum 50jährigen Bestehen der Kolonie Sommerfeld, 1948–1998*. Sommerfeld, Paraguay: Verwaltung der Kolonie Sommerfeld, 1998.
Fretz, J. *Pilgrims in Paraguay: The Story of Mennonite Colonization in South America*. Scottdale, PA: Herald Press, 1953.
– *Mennonite Colonization in Mexico*. Akron: Mennonite Central Committee, 1945.
Friesen, Abram. "Reisebericht von Abram D. Friesen." *Steinbach Post*, 29 September 1948.
Friesen, Martin W. *Eine Neue Heimat in der Chaco Wildness*. Altona, MB: Published and bound by D.W. Friesen & Sons, 1987.
– *New Homeland in the Chaco Wilderness*, translated by Jake Balzer. Loma Plata, Paraguay: Historical Committee of the Menno Colony, 2009.
– ed. *50 Jahre Kolonie Menno, Chaco, Paraguay, 1927–1977: Eine Gedenkschrift zum Fuenfzigjaehrigen Jubilaeum*. Loma Plata, Paraguay: Verwaltung der Kolonie Menno, 1977.
Friesen, Uwe. *Unter der Heizen Sonne des Suedens*. Loma Plata, Paraguay: Geschichtskomitee der Kolonie Menno, 2002.

Harder, David. *Schule und Gemeinschaft Errinerungen des Dorfschllehrers, 1969.* Cuauhtémoc: Strassbourg Platz, 2006.

Harms, Jacob. *Das Hinterlassene Heft vom Verstorbenen Jacob Harms, 1914–1993.* Strassbourgo, Chihuahua: Strassbourg Platz, 2001.

Kliewer, Friedrich. "Mennonite Young People's Work in the Paraguayan Chaco." *Mennonite Quarterly Review* 11 (1937): 119–30.

Peters, Bernard. *Eine Lehrreiche Ermahnung.* Santa Cruz, Bolivia: Johann F. Hamm, 2003.

Romero, Genaro. *Colonización Mennonita.* Asunción: Imprenta Nacional, 1933.

Toews, Bernhard. *Reise-Tagebuch des Bernhard Toews, 1921.* Loma Plata, Paraguay: Geschichtsarchiv, Schulverwaltung der Kolonie Menno, 1997.

Toews, Johann W. *Unser Leben in Paraguay.* Loma Plata, Paraguay: Self-published, ca. 2002.

Toews, Maria (Wiebe). "My Recollections of Experiences in Canada and Paraguay, 1959," translated by Victor Janzen. Steinbach, MB: N.p., n.d.

Verwatlung der Kolonie Menno. *Mennonitische Kolonisation im Paraguayischen Chaco unter Gestz Nr. 514.* N.p.: 1984.

Wall, Johann P. "Letters to Isaak M. Dyck," translated with an introduction by John J. Friesen. *Preservings* 29 (2009): 19–20, 24–7.

Wiebe, Alan, ed. *News from Paraguay by Martha Friesen, Colony Bergthal, 1951–1979.* N.p., n.d.

Wiebe, Johann. "*Die Auswanderung von Russland nach Kanada, 1875, in Form einer Predigt.*" Strassbourgo, Mexico: Strassbourg Platz, n.d.

Secondary: Books and Articles

Adamoski, Robert, Dorothy E. Chunn, and Robert Menzies. *Contesting Canadian Citizenship: Historical Readings.* Peterborough: Broadview, 2002.

Althusser, Louis. "Ideology and Ideological State Apparatuses." In *Lenin and Philosophy, and Other Essays,* translated by Ben Brewster. London: New Left Books, 1971.

Anderson, Benedict. *Imagined Communities: Reflections on the Origin and Spread of Nationalism, 1992.* London: Versa, 2006.

Appadurai, Arjun. "Global Ethnospaces: Notes and Queries for a Transnational Anthropology." In *Recapturing Anthropology,* edited by R. Fox. Santa Fe: School of American Research Press, 1991.

Assmann, Jan, and John Czaplicka. "Collective Memory and Cultural Identity." *New German Critique,* NGC 65, 65 (1995): 125–33. http://dx.doi.org/10.2307/488538.

Almeida, Barney. "La colonización menonita en Chihuahua." *Estudios Americanos (Servilla, Spain)* 5 (1953): 581–8.
Bayly, C.A., Sven Beckert, Matthew Connelly, Isabel Hofmeyr, Wendy Kozol, and Patricia Seed. "AHR Conversation: On Transnational History." *American Historical Review* 111, 5 (2006): 1441–64. http://dx.doi.org/10.1086/ahr.111.5.1441.
Bennion, Janet. *Desert Patriarchy: Mormon and Mennonite Communities in the Chihuahua Valley*. Tucson: University of Arizona Press, 2004.
Berger, Carl. *The Sense of Power: Studies in the Ideas of Canadian Imperialism, 1867–1914*. Toronto: University of Toronto Press, 1970.
Bjerg, Maria. *Historias de la Immigración en la Argentina*. Buenos Aires: Edhasa, 2009.
Bourdieu, Pierre. "Structures, *Habitus*, Practices." In *The Logic of Practice*. Stanford: Stanford University Press, 1990.
Bowen, Dawn S. "To Bolivia and Back: Migration and its Impact on La Crete, Alberta." *Journal of Mennonite Studies* 22 (2004): 59–82.
Braun, Jacob A. *Im Gedenken an jene Zeit: Mitteilungen zuer Entstehungsgeschichte der Kolonie Menno*. Loma Plata: Geschichtskomitee, 2001.
Buchenau, Jürgen. "Small Numbers, Great Impact: Mexico and Its Immigrants, 1821–1973." *Journal of American Ethnic History* 20 (2001): 23–49.
Burnett, Jean. *Coming Canadians: An Introduction to a History of Canada's People*. Toronto: McClelland and Stewart, 1988.
Caccia, Ivana. *Managing the Canadian Mosaic in Wartime: Shaping Citizenship Policy, 1939–1945*. Montreal, Kingston: McGill-Queen's University Press, 2010.
Cancian, Sonia. *Families, Lovers and their Letters: Italian Postwar Migration to Canada*. Winnipeg: University of Manitoba Press, 2010.
Cañas Bottos, Lorenzo. *Old Colony Mennonites in Argentina and Bolivia: Nation Making, Religious Conflict and Imagination of the Future*. Leiden: Brill, 2008. http://dx.doi.org/10.1163/ej.9789004160958.i-216.
– "Transformations of Old Colony Mennonites: The Making of a Trans-statal Community." *Global Networks* 8 (2009): 214–31.
Carafa, R., and J. Carlos. "Distribucion especial e immigracion extranjera." In *La poblacion*. La Paz, Bolivia: Instituto Latinamericano de Investigaciones Sociales, 1988.
Carter, Sarah. "Transnational Perspectives on the History of Great Plains Women: Gender, Race, Nation, and the Forty-ninth Parallel." *American Review of Canadian Studies* 33, 4 (2003): 565–96. http://dx.doi.org/10.1080/02722010309481367.

Castro, Pedro. "The 'Return' of the Mennonites from Cuauhtémoc to Canada: A Perspective from Mexico." *Journal of Mennonite Studies* 22 (2004): 25–38.

Chasteen, John Charles. *Born in Blood and Fire: A Concise History of Latin America*. New York: W.W. Norton, 2008.

Chilton, Lisa. "Canada and the British Empire: A Review Essay." *Canadian Historical Review* 89, 1 (2008): 89–95. http://dx.doi.org/10.3138/chr.89.1.89.

Cohen, Robin. *Global Diasporas: An Introduction*. Seattle: University of Washington Press, 1997. http://dx.doi.org/10.4324/9780203228920.

Curthoys, Ann, and Marilyn Lake. "Introduction." In *Connected Worlds: History in Transnational Perspective*, edited by Ann Curthoys and Marilyn Lake. Canberra: Australian National University, 2006. http://epress.anu.edu.au/wp-content/uploads/2011/06/cw_whole_book.pdf. Accessed 13 August 2010.

Dana, Leo-Paul, and Teresa E. Dana. "Collective Entrepreneurship in a Mennonite Community in Paraguay." *Latin American Business Review* 8, 4 (2008): 82–96. http://dx.doi.org/10.1080/10978520802114730.

Derrida, Jacques. *Margins of Philosophy*. Chicago: University of Chicago Press, 1982.

Doell, Leonard. *The Bergthaler Mennonite Church of Saskatchewan, 1892–1975*. Winnipeg: CMBC Publications, 1987.

de Drachenberg, Pidoux. "Immigracion ye colonizacion en el Paraguay, 1870–1970." *Revista Paraguaya de Sociologia* 34 (1975): 65–123.

Dubinsky, Karen, Adele Perry, and Henry Yu, eds. "Introduction: Canadian History, Transnational History." In *Within and Without the Nation: Canadian History as Transnational History*. Toronto: University of Toronto Press, forthcoming.

Dueck, Arden M., Myron P. Loewen, Leslie L. Plett, and Eddy K. Plett. *Quellen Kolonie*. Torreon, Coahuila: Impresora Colorama, 1998.

Ens, Adolf. *Becoming a National Church: A History of the Conference of Mennonites in Canada*. Winnipeg: CMU Press, 2004.

– *Subjects or Citizens? The Mennonite Experience in Canada, 1970–1925*. Ottawa: University of Ottawa Press, 1994.

Ens, Adolf, Jacob E. Peters, and Otto Hamm. *Church, Family and Village: Essays on Mennonite Life on the West Reserve*. Winnipeg: Manitoba Mennonite Historical Society, 2001.

Epp, Frank H. *Mennonites in Canada, 1786–1920: The History of a Separate People*. Toronto: Macmillan, 1974.

– *Mennonites in Canada, 1920–1940: A People's Struggle for Survival*. Toronto: Macmillan, 1982.

Epp, Marlene. *Mennonite Women in Canada: A History*. Winnipeg: University of Manitoba Press, 2008.
– "Pioneers, Refugees, Exiles and Transnationalisms: Gendering Diaspora in an Ethno- Religious Context." *Journal of the Canadian Historical Association* 12, 1 (2001): 137–54. http://dx.doi.org/10.7202/031145ar.
Epp, Peter J. "Walking the Tightrope: Mennonite Entrepreneurs from Paraguay, Mexico and Belize in Manitoba." *Journal of Mennonite Studies* 22 (2004): 221–36.
Faist, Thomas. "Transnationalization in International Migration: Implications for the Study of Citizenship and Culture." *Ethnic and Racial Studies* 23, 2 (2000): 189–222. http://dx.doi.org/10.1080/014198700329024.
Fast, Kerry L. "Religion, Pain and the Body: Agency in the Life of an Old Colony Woman." *Journal of Mennonite Studies* 22 (2004): 103–40.
Fifer, J. "The Search for a Series of Small Successes: Frontiers of Settlement in Eastern Bolivia." *Journal of Latin American Studies* 14, 2 (1982): 407–32. http://dx.doi.org/10.1017/S0022216X00022471.
Flores, Gilberto. "A Third Way." *Mennonite Quarterly Review* 58 (1984): 399–409.
Flores, Ivonne. "Llegaron para quedarse: La colonizacion menonita en Chihuahua." *Cuadernos del norte* 11 (1990): 4–7.
Foner, Nancy. "Second Generation Transnationalism: Then and Now." In *The Changing Face of Home*, edited by Peggy Levitt and Mary C. Waters. New York: Russell Sage, 2002.
Fothergill, Robert A. *Private Chronicles: A Study of English Diaries*. London: Oxford University Press, 1974.
Foucault, Michel. *The Archaeology of Knowledge and the Discourse on Language*, translated by A.M. Sheridan Smith. New York: Pantheon, 1972.
Francis, E.K. "The Mennonite Commonwealth in Russia: A Sociological Interpretation." *Mennonite Quarterly Review* 25 (1951): 173–82.
– *In Search of Utopia: The Mennonites of Manitoba*. Altona, MB: D.W. Friesen and Sons, 1955.
Freund, Alexander, ed. *Beyond the Nation? Immigrants' Local Lives in Transnational Cultures*. Toronto: University of Toronto Press, 2012.
Friesen, Gerald A. *Citizens and Nation: An Essay on History, Communication, and Canada*. Toronto: University of Toronto Press, 2000.
Friesen, Gerald A., and Doug Owram, eds. *Thinkers and Dreamers: Historical Essays in Honour of Carl Berger*. Toronto: University of Toronto Press, 2009.
Friesen, John. *Field of Broken Dreams: Mennonite Settlement in Seminole, West Texas*. Winnipeg: Self-published, 1996.

Friesen, John J. *Building Communities: The Changing Face of Manitoba Mennonites*. Winnipeg: CMU Press, 2007.
– "Old Colony Theology, Ecclesiology and Experience of Church in Manitoba." *Journal of Mennonite Studies* 22 (2004): 131–44.
Friesen, Ralph. *Between Earth and Sky: Steinbach, the First 50 Years*. Steinbach, MB: Derksen Printers, 2009.
Friesen, Uwe. *Unter der Heizen Sonne des Suedens*. Loma Plata, Paraguay: Geschichtskomitee der Kolonie Menno, 2002.
Gabaccia, Dona R. "Is Everywhere Nowhere? Nomads, Nations and the Immigrant Paradigm of United States History." *Journal of American History* 86, 3 (1999): 1115–34. http://dx.doi.org/10.2307/2568608.
Gerber, David. "The Immigrant Letter Between Positivism and Populism: The Uses of Immigrant Personal Correspondence in 20th Century American Scholarship." *Journal of American Ethnic History* 16 (1997): 3–34.
Gerbrandt, Henry J. *Adventure in Faith: The Background in Europe and the Development in Canada of the Bergthaler Mennonite Church of Manitoba*. N.p.: Bergthaler Mennonite Church of Manitoba, 1970.
Glick Schiller, Nina, Linda Basch, and Cristina Szanton Blanc. "From Immigrant to Transmigrant: Theorizing Transnational Migration." *Anthropological Quarterly* 68, 1 (1995): 48–63. http://dx.doi.org/10.2307/3317464.
Good Gingrich, Luann, and Kerry Preibisch. "Migration as Preservation and Loss: The Paradox of Transnational Living for Low German Mennonite Women." *Journal of Ethnic and Migration Studies* 36, 9 (2010): 1499–1518. http://dx.doi.org/10.1080/1369183X.2010.494825.
Greer, Allan. "National, Transnational and Hypernational Historiographies: New France Meets Early American History." *Canadian Historical Review* 91, 4 (2010): 695–724. http://dx.doi.org/10.3138/chr.91.4.695.
Guenther, Alan M. "'Barred from Heaven and Cursed Forever': Old Colony Mennonites and the 1908 Commission of Inquiry regarding Public Education." *Preservings* 29 (2009): 4–13.
Guenther, Bruce L. "A Road Less Traveled: The Evangelical Path of the Kanadier Immigrants Who Returned to Canada." *Journal of Mennonite Studies* 22 (2004): 145–66.
Guenter, Jacob G., Leonard Doell, Dick Braun, Jacob L. Guenther, Henry A. Friesen, Jacob W. Loeppky, John P. Doell, Peter G. Giesbrecht, Anna Bueckert, and Anna Braun. *Hague-Osler Mennonite Reserve, 1895–1995I*. N.p.: Hague-Osler Reserve Book Committee, 1995.
Gutiérrez, González. "Fostering Identities: Mexico's Relations with Its Diaspora." *Journal of American History* 86, 2 (1999): 545–67. http://dx.doi.org/10.2307/2567045.

Hack, H. "Land Problems in the Paraguayan Chaco." *Boletin de Estudios Latinoamericanos y del Caribe* 34 (1983): 99–115.
Haniewicz, Joasia. *A Mennonite Story*. London: Self-published, 1991.
Harms, Jacob. *Das Hinterlassene Heft vom Verstorbenen Jacob Harms, 1914–1993*. Strassbourgo, Chihuahua: Strassbourg Platz, 2001.
Harms, Patricia. "'Gott es hiea uck': Gender and Identity in an Immigrant Family from Paraguay." *Journal of Mennonite Studies* 22 (2004): 39–58.
Harzig, Christine, and Dirk Hoerder with Donna Gabaccia. *What Is Migration History*. Malden, MA: Polity, 2009.
− "Transnationalism and the Age of Mass Migration, 1880s–1920." In *Transnational Identities and Practices in Canada*, edited by Vic Satzewich and Lloyd Wong. Vancouver: University of British Columbia Press, 2006.
Hedberg, Anna Sofia. *Outside the World: Cohesion and Deviation among Old Colony Mennonites in Bolivia*. Uppsala: ACTA Universitatis Upsaliensis, 2007.
Heppner, Jack. *Search for Renewal: The Story of the Rudnerweider / Evangelical Mennonite Mission Conference, 1937–1987*. Winnipeg: Evangelical Mennonite Mission Conference, 1987.
Higueros, Mario. "The Anabaptist Vision in the Church of Central America." *Mennonite Quarterly Review* 69 (1995): 389–404.
Hobsbawm, Eric. *The Age of Extremes: A History of the World, 1914–1991*. New York: Pantheon Books, 1994.
Hoerder, Dirk. "Historians and Their Data: The Complex Shift from Nation-State Approaches to the Study of People's Transcultural Lives." *Journal of American Ethnic History* 25 (2006): 85–96.
− "Transcultural States, Nations, and People." In *The Historical Practice of Diversity. Transcultural Interactions from the Early Modern Mediterranean to the Postcolonial World*, edited by Dirk Hoerder with Christiane Harzig and Adrian Schubert. New York: Berghahn Books, 2003.
Horst, Harder. *René D. The Stoessner Regime and Indigenous Resistance in Paraguay*. Gainsville, FL: University of Florida Press, 2007.
Horst, Isaac. *A Separate People: An Insider's View of Old Order Mennonite Customs and Traditions*. Kitchener, ON: Herald Press, 2000.
Hughes, Matthew. "Logistics and the Chaco War: Bolivia versus Paraguay, 1932–1935." *Journal of Military History* 69, 2 (2005): 411–37. http://dx.doi.org/10.1353/jmh.2005.0104.
Hurst, Charles E., and David L. McConnell. *An Amish Paradox: Diversity and Change in the World's Largest Amish Community*. Baltimore: Johns Hopkins University Press, 2010.
Iacovetta, Franca. *Gatekeepers: Reshaping Immigrant Lives in Cold War Canada*. Toronto: Between the Lines, 2006.

Iacovetta, Franca, with Paula Draper and Robert Ventresca, eds. *A Nation of Immigrants: Women, Workers and Communities in Canadian History, 1840s–1960s*. Toronto: University of Toronto Press, 1998.

Jackson, Michael. "Introduction." In *Politics of Storytelling: Violence, Transgression and Intersubjectivity*. Copenhagen: Museum Tusculanum, 2002.

Janzen, Abram G. *Aeltester Johan M. Loeppky, 1882–1950: Wie ich Ihm in Errinerung Habe*. Hague, SK: Self-published, 2003.

Janzen, Waldemar. "Geography of Faith." In *Still in the Image: Essays in Biblical Theology and Anthropology*. Winnipeg: Self-published, 1982.

Janzen, William. "Welcoming the Returning 'Kanadier' Mennonites from Mexico." *Journal of Mennonite Studies* 22 (2004): 11–24.

– *Build Up One Another: The Work of MCCO with the Mennonites from Mexico in Ontario, 1977–1997*. Kitchener, ON: Mennonite Central Committee Ontario, 1998.

– *Limits on Liberty: The Experience of Mennonite, Hutterite and Doukhobor Communities in Canada*. Toronto: University of Toronto Press, 1990.

– "Welcoming the Returning 'Kanadier' Mennonites from Mexico." *Journal of Mennonite Studies* 22 (2004): 11–24.

Juhnke, James C. *Vision, Doctrine, War: Mennonite Identity and Organization in America, 1890–1930*. Scottdale, PA: Herald Press, 1989.

Kampenhoefer, Walter. "The Volume and Composition of German American Return Migration." In *A Century of European Migrations, 1830–1930*, edited by Rudolph J. Vecoli and Suzanne Sinke. Urbana, Chicago: University of Illinois Press, 1991.

Kaplan, Caren. *Questions of Travel: Postmodern Discourses of Displacement*. Durham: Duke University Press, 1998.

Klassen, A.J., ed. *Alternative Service for Peace in Canada during World War II, 1941–1946*. Abbotsford: Mennonite Central Committee BC, 1998.

Klassen, Doreen Helen. "'I Wanted a Life of My Own': Creating Singlewoman Mennonite Identity in Mexico." *Journal of Mennonite Studies* 26 (2008): 49–68.

– *Singing Mennonite: Low German Songs among the Mennonites*. Winnipeg: University of Manitoba Press, 1989.

Klassen, Peter P. *The Mennonites in Paraguay*. Vol. I, *Kingdom of God and Kingdom of this World*, translated by Gunther H. Schmidt. Filadelfia, Paraguay: Self-published, 2004.

Koop, G.S. *Pioneer Jahre in British Honduras (Belize)*. Belize City: Self-published, n.d.

Kornelsen, Jacob U. *25 Jahre in Mexico: Beschreibung Von der Quellenkolonie, 1948–1973*. Cuauhtémoc, Mexico: Self-published, 1973.

Kraybill, Donald B. *The Riddle of Amish Culture*. Baltimore: Johns Hopkins University Press, 2001.

Kraybill, Donald B., and Carl F. Bowman. *On the Backroad to Heaven: Old Order Hutterites, Mennonites, Amish and Brethren*. Baltimore, MD: Johns Hopkins University Press, 2006. http://dx.doi.org/10.1525/nr.2006.9.4.122.

Kraybill, Donald B., Steven M. Nolt, and David L. Weaver-Zercher. *The Amish Way: Patient Faith in a Perilous World*. San Francisco: Josey Bass, 2010.

Kulig, Judith, and Barry L. Hall. "Health and Illness Beliefs among the Southern Alberta Kanadier Mennonite Immigrants." *Journal of Mennonite Studies* 22 (2004): 185–204.

Lehr, John C. *Community and Frontier: A Ukrainian Settlement in the Canadian Parkland*. Winnipeg: University of Manitoba Press, 2011.

Loewen, Jacob A. "A Mennonite Encounter with the 'Innermost' of the Lengua Indians." *Mennonite Quarterly Review* 39 (1965): 40–67.

Loewen, Royden. *Diaspora in the Countryside: Two Mennonite Communities and Mid-Twentieth Century Rural Disjuncture*. Toronto: University of Toronto Press and Urbana: University of Illinois Press, 2006.

– ed. *From the Inside Out: The Rural Worlds of Mennonite Diarists, 1863–1929*. Winnipeg: University of Manitoba Press, 1999.

– "Mennonite 'Repertoires of Contention': Church Life in Steinbach, Manitoba and Quellenkolonie, Chihuahua, 1945–1975." *Mennonite Quarterly Review* 72 (1998): 301–19.

– "To the Ends of the Earth: An Introduction to the Conservative Low German Mennonites in the Americas." *Mennonite Quarterly Review* 82 (2008): 427–48.

– "Trigo, mujeres, cosmovisiones: la historia social y los mennonitas en el oeste de Canada y de los Estados Unidos, 1850–1975," translated by Maria Bjerg. *Estudios Migratorios Latino Americanos (Buenos Aires, Argentina)* 31 (1996): 705–26.

Loewen, Royden, and Gerald Friesen. *Immigrants in Prairie Cities: Ethnic Diversity in 20th Century Canada*. Toronto: University of Toronto Press, 2009.

Loewen, Royden, and Steven M. Nolt. *Seeking Places of Peace: North America: A Global Mennonite History*. Intercourse, PA: Good Books, 2012.

Lowrey, Kathleen. "Ethics, Politics, and Host Space: A Comparative Case Study from the South American Chaco." *Comparative Studies in Society and History* 53, 4 (2011): 882–913. http://dx.doi.org/10.1017/S0010417511000442.

MacIntyre, Ben. *Forgotten Fatherland: The Search for Elisabeth Nietzsche*. New York: Farrar Straus Giroux, 1992.

MacMaster, Richard K. *Land, Piety Peoplehood: The Establishment of Mennonite Communities in America 1683–1790*. Scottdale, PA: Herald Press, 1985.

Marr, Lucille. *The Transforming Power of a Century: Mennonite Central Committee and its Evolution in Ontario*. Waterloo, ON: Pandora, 2003.

Marshall, T.H. *Class, Citizenship, and Social Development: Essays*. Garden City, NY: Doubleday, 1965.

Martens, Verna. *Beyond our Wildest Dream: Beginnings in Blue Creek*. N.p.: Jake Martens, 2007.

Mora, Frank O. "The Forgotten Relationship: United States-Paraguay Relations, 1937–89." *Journal of Contemporary History* 33 (1998): 451–73.

Morawska, Ewa. "'Diaspora' Diasporas' Representations of their Homelands: Exploring the Polymorphs." *Ethnic and Racial Studies* 34, 6 (2011): 1029–48. http://dx.doi.org/10.1080/01419870.2010.533783.

– "Return Migrations: Theoretical and Research Agenda." In *A Century of European Migrations, 1830–1930*, edited by Rudolph J. Vecoli and Suzanne Sinke. Urbana, Chicago: University of Illinois Press, 1991.

Myers, Thomas J., and Steven M. Nolt. *An Amish Patchwork: Indiana's Old Order in the Modern World*. Bloomington: University of Indiana Press, 2005.

Ngai, Mae M. *Impossible Subjects: Illegal Aliens and the Making of Modern America*. Princeton: Princeton University Press, 2004.

Niebuhr, Gundolf, Jakob Warkentin, and Hans Theodore Regier, eds. *Zur Geschichte der kanadischen Mennoniten in Paraguay*. Loma Plata, Paraguay: Jahrbuch fuer Geschichte und Kultur der Mennoniten in Paraguay, 2002.

Nisbet, Robert A. "Community as Typology – Toennies and Weber." In *The Sociological Tradition*. New York: Basic Books, 1966.

Nobbs-Thiessen, Ben. "Mennonites in Unexpected Places: Sociologist and Settlers in Latin America." *Journal of Mennonite Studies* 28 (2010): 203–24.

Osborne, Ken. "One Hundred Years of History Teaching in Manitoba Schools, Part I, 1897–1927." *Manitoba History* 36 (1998): 3–25.

Patel, Dhiru. "The Maple Neem Nexus: Transnational Links of South Asian Canadians." In *Transnational Identities and Practices in Canada*, edited by Vic Satzewich and Lloyd Wong. Vancouver: University of British Columbia Press, 2006.

Pauls, Karen. "Northfield Settlement, Nova Scotia: A New Direction for Immigrants from Belize." *Journal of Mennonite Studies* 22 (2004): 167–84.

Perry, Adele. "'Is Your Garden in England, Sir?': James Douglas's Archive and the Politics of Home." *History Workshop Journal* 70, 1 (2010): 67–85. http://dx.doi.org/10.1093/hwj/dbq024.

Peters, Jakob. "Mennonites in Mexico and Paraguay: A Comparative Analysis of the Colony Social System." *Journal of Mennonite Studies* 6 (1988): 198–214.

Plett, Delbert F., ed. *Old Colony Mennonites in Canada 1875 to 2000*. Steinbach, MB: Crossway Publications, 2001.

– *Saints and Sinners: The Kleine Gemeinde in Imperial Russia, 1812 to 1875*. Steinbach, MB: Crossway Publications, 1999.

Plett, Harvey. *Seeking to Be Faithful: The Story of the Evangelical Mennonite Conference*. Steinbach, MB: Evangelical Mennonite Conference, 1996.

Portelli, Alessandro. *The Death of Luigi Trastuli and Other Stories: Form and Meaning in Oral History*. Albano: SUNY, 1991.

Prieto Valladares, Jaime. *Mission and Migration: Global Mennonite History Series, Latin America*. Intercourse, PA: Good Books, 2010.

Quiring, David. "Intervention and Resistance: Two Mennonite Visions Conflict in Mexico." *Journal of Mennonite Studies* 22 (2004): 83–102.

– *The Mennonite Old Colony Vision: Under Siege in Mexico and the Canadian Connection*. Steinbach, MB: Crossway Publications, 2003.

Quiring, Walter. "The Canadian Mennonite Immigration into the Chaco, 1926–27." *Mennonite Quarterly Review* 8 (1934): 32–42.

– *Im Schweisse Deines Angesichts: Ein Mennonitisches Bilderbuch*. Steinbach, MB: Derksen Printers, 1953.

Rak, Julie. "Introduction, Widening the Field: Auto/biography Theory and Criticism in Canada." In *Auto/biography in Canada: Critical Directions*, edited by Julie Rak. Waterloo: Wilfrid Laurier University Press, 2005.

Ramirez, Bruno. *On the Move: French Canadian and Italian Migrants in the North Atlantic Economy 1860–1914*. Toronto: McClelland and Stewart, 1991.

Ramirez, Russo Manfredo. *El Chaco Paraguayo: Integración sociocultural de los Mennonitas a la sociedad nacional*. Asunción: Editorial El Foro, 1983.

Ratzlaff, Gerhard. *Entre dos fuegos: Los menonitas en el conflicto limitrofe entre Paraguay y Bolivia, 1932–1935*, Asunción: Self-published, 1993.

– *One Body, Many Parts: The Mennonite Churches in Paraguay*. Asunción: Evangelical Mennonite Association of Paraguay, 2001.

– *The Trans-Chaco Highway: How It Came to Be*, translated by Elizabeth Unruh Leite. Asunción: N.p., 2009.

Ratzlaff, Heinrich. *Äletester Martin C. Friesen: Ein Mann, den Gott brauchen konnte*. Loma Plata, Paraguay: Geschichtskomitee der Kolonie Menno, 2006.

– *Das Schulwesen der Kolonie Menno: Am Anfang der Siedlung bis zur Uebergabe der Vereinsschule an die Kolonie*. Loma Plata, Paraguay: Geschichtskomitee der Kolonie Menno, 2003.

Redekop, Calvin W. *The Old Colony Mennonites in Mexico: Dilemmas of Ethnic Minority Life*. Baltimore: Johns Hopkins University Press, 1969.

– "Religion and Society: A State within a Church." *Mennonite Quarterly Review* 47 (1973): 339–57.

Regehr, T. D. *Mennonites in Canada, 1939–1970: A People Transformed*. Toronto: University of Toronto Press, 1996.

– *Peace, Order and Good Government: Mennonites in Politics in Canada*. Winnipeg: CMBC Publications, 2000.

Reger, Adina, and Delbert Plett. *Diese Steine: Die Russlandmennoniten.* Steinbach, MB: Crossway, 2001.

Regier, Hans Theodore. "Die Altkolonier in Paraguay." *Jahrbuch fuer Geschichte und Kultur der Mennoniten in Paraguay* 1 (2000): 39–60.

Rempel, Gerhard, and Franz Rempel, eds. *75 Jahre Mennoniten in Mexiko.* Cuauhtémoc: Comite Pro Archivo Histórica y Museo Menonita,1998.

Reschly, Steven D. *The Amish on the Iowa Prairie, 1840–1910.* Baltimore: Johns Hopkins University Press, 2000.

Roessingh, Carel, and Tanja Plasil, eds. *Between Horse & Buggy and Four-Wheel Drive: Change and Diversity among Mennonite Settlements in Belize, Central America.* Amsterdam: VU University Press, 2009.

Sawatzky, Harry Leonard. *Mennonite Settlement in British Honduras.* Berkeley: University of California Press, 1969.

– *They Sought a Country: Mennonite Colonization in Mexico.* Berkeley: University of California Press, 1971.

Schartner, Sieghard, and Sylvia Bolivien. *Zufluschtsort der konservativen Mennoniten.* Santa Cruz, Bolivia: Self-published, 2009.

Schlabach, Theron F. *Peace, Faith, Nation: Mennonites and Amish in Nineteenth Century America.* Scottdale, PA: Herald Press, 1988.

Schmiedehaus, Walter. *Die Altkolonier-Mennoniten in Mexiko.* Winnipeg: CMBC Publications, 1982.

– *Ein feste Burg is unser Gott: der Wanderweg eines Christlichen Siedlervolkes.* Cuauhtémoc, Mexico: G.J. Rempel, 1948.

Schudson, Michael. *Discovering the News: A Social History of American Newspapers.* New York: Basic Books, 1978.

Shesko, Elizabeth. "Constructing Roads, Washing Feet, and Cutting Cane for the Patria: Building Bolivia with Military Labor, 1900–1975." *International Labor and Working Class History* 80, 1 (2011): 6–28. http://dx.doi.org/10.1017/S0147547911000056.

Smith, Mark M. "Old South Time in Comparative Perspective." *American Historical Review* 101, 5 (1996): 1432–69. http://dx.doi.org/10.2307/2170178.

Smith, Sidonie. *Subjectivity, Identity and the Body: Women's Autobiographical Practices in the Twentieth Century.* Bloomington: Indiana University Press, 1993.

Sneath, Robyn Dyck. "Imagining a Mennonite Community: The *Mennonitische Post* and a People of Diaspora." *Journal of Mennonite Studies* 22 (2004): 205–20.

Stoesz, Edgar. *Like a Mustard Seed: Mennonites in Paraguay.* Scottdale, PA: Herald Press, 2008.

Stoesz, Edgar, and Muriel T. Stackley. *Garden in the Wilderness: Mennonite Communities in the Paraguayan Chaco, 1927–1997*. Winnipeg: CMBC Publications, 1999.
Stolow, Jeremy. "Transnationalism and the New Religio-politics: Reflections on a Jewish Orthodox Case." *Theory, Culture & Society* 21, 2 (2004): 109–37. http://dx.doi.org/10.1177/0263276404042137.
Swyripa, Frances. *Storied Landscapes: Ethno-Religious Identity and the Canadian Prairies*. Winnipeg: University of Manitoba Press, 2010.
Takai, Yukari. *Gendered Passages: French-Canadian Migration to Lowell, Massachusetts, 1900–1920*. New York: Peter Lang, 2008.
Thiessen, Jack. *Mennonite Low German/Mennonitish-Plauttdeutsches Wörterbuch*. Madison: University of Wisconsin-Madison Max Kade Institute for German-American Studies, 2003.
Thiesen, John D. *Mennonite and Nazi? Attitudes Among Mennonite Colonists in Latin America, 1933–1945*. Kitchener, ON: Pandora Press, 1998.
Thompson, E.P. "Time, Work-Discipline and Industrial Capitalism." *Past & Present* 38, 1 (1967): 56–97. http://dx.doi.org/10.1093/past/38.1.56.
Tilly, Charles. "Contentious Repertoires in Great Britain, 1758–1834." *Social Science History* 17, 2 (1993): 253–80. http://dx.doi.org/10.2307/1171282.
Toews, Paul. *Mennonites in American Society, 1930–1970: Modernity and the Persistence of Religious Community*. Scottdale, PA: Herald Press, 1996.
Towell, Larry. *The Mennonites: A Biographical Sketch*. London: Phaidon Press, 2000.
Tsuda, Takeyuki. *Diasporic Homecomings: Ethnic Return Migration in Comparative Perspective*. Stanford: Stanford University Press, 2009.
Urry, James. *Mennonites, Politics and Peoplehood: Europe, Russia, Canada, 1525–1980*. Winnipeg: University of Manitoba Press, 2006.
– *None but Saints: The Transformation of Mennonite Life in Russia, 1789–1889*. Winnipeg: Hyperion, 1989.
Valverde, Mariana. *Law and Order: Images, Meanings, Myths*. New Brunswick, NJ: Rutgers, 2006.
Vertovec, Steven. *Transnationalism*. New York: Routledge, 2009.
Warkentin, Abe. *Dies und Das*. Steinbach: Verlag die Mennonitische Post, 1997.
– *Gäste und Fremdlinge: Hebräer 11:13; Strangers and Pilgrims: Hebrews 11:13*. Steinbach, MB: *Mennonitische Post*, 1987.
– *Reflections on Our Heritage: A History of Steinbach and Hanover from 1874*. Steinbach, MB: Derksen Printers, 1971.
Warkentin, J.W. "Carving a Home out of the Primeval Forest." *Mennonite Quarterly Review* 24 (1950): 142–8.

Weaver, John C. *The Great Land Rush and the Making of the Modern World: 1650–1900*. Montreal, Kingston: McGill-Queen's University Press, 2003.
Werner, Hans. *Living between Worlds: A History of Winkler*. Winkler, MB: Winkler Heritage Society, 2006.
Widdis, Randy W. *With Scarcely a Ripple. Anglo-Canadian Migration into the United States and Western Canada, 1880–1920*. Montreal, Kingston: McGill-Queen's University Press, 1998.
Will, Martina E. "The Mennonite Colonization of Chihuahua: Reflections of Competing Visions." *The Americas* 53, 3 (1997): 353–78. http://dx.doi.org/10.2307/1008029.
Wong, Lloyd L. "Transnationalism, Active Citizenship and Belonging in Canada." *International Journal (Toronto, Ont.)* 63 (2007/08): 83–94.
Yu, Henry. "Is Vancouver the Future or the Past? Asian Migrants and White Supremacy." *Pacific Historical Review* 75, 2 (2006): 307–12. http://dx.doi.org/10.1525/phr.2006.75.2.307.

Typescripts

Bjerg, Maria. "The Mennonites in the Agenda of the South American Social Sciences: A View from Argentina." Unpublished Literature Survey, ca. 2002, in possession of author.
Bushong, A.D. "Agricultural Settlement in British Honduras: A Geographical Interpretation." PhD dissertation, University of Florida, 1961.
Dueck, Alicia. "From Canada to Mexico and Back Again: The Transnational Lives of Willie and Elizabeth Dueck." Undergraduate research paper, University of Winnipeg, 2005.
Dyck, Andrea. "'And in Mexico We Found What We Had Lost in Canada': Mennonite Perceptions of Mexican Neighbours in *Die Steinbach Post*, 1922–1967." Master's thesis, University of Winnipeg, 2007.
Dyck, Isaak M. "Emigration from Canada to Mexico, Year 1922," translated by Robyn Dyck Sneath, 2005. Unpublished manuscript in possession of author.
Eicher, John. "'Wise as Serpents, Innocent as Doves': Mennonite Migrations, 1870–1943." Unpublished dissertation proposal, University of Iowa, 2012.
Eyford, Ryan. "An Experiment in Immigrant Colonization: Canada and the Icelandic Reserve, 1875–1897." PhD dissertation, University of Manitoba, 2011.
Fehr Kehler, Tina. "Mexican Mennonite Immigrant Women: Identity in Transition." Honours research paper, University of Winnipeg, 1999.
Friesen, Martin W. "Eine Neue Heimat in der Chaco Wildness," translated by Herman Rempel. Unpublished document in possession of author.

Hall, Catherine. Unpublished roundtable comments, at "Inside and Outside the Nation: Transnational Canadian History," Millennium Library, Winnipeg, 2009.

Hall, Jerry Alan. "Mennonite Agriculture in a Tropical Environment: An Analysis of the Development and Productivity of a Mid-Latitude Agricultural System in British Honduras." PhD dissertation, Clark University, 1970.

Hedges, Kelly. "'Plautdietsch' and 'Huuchdietsch' in Chihuahua: Language, Literacy and Identity among the Old Colony Mennonites in Northern Mexico." PhD dissertation, Yale University, 1996.

Kroeker, Peter J. "Lenguas and Mennonites: A Study of Cultural Change in the Paraguayan Chaco, 1928–1970." Master's thesis, Wichita State University, 1970.

Langemann, R. "The Development of a Model for the Life Cycle of a Closed Agricultural Colony: The Mennonite Colony of Spanish Lookout, British Honduras." Master's thesis, Simon Fraser University, 1971.

Lanning, James W. "The Old Colony Mennonites of Bolivia: A Case Study." Master's thesis, Texas A&M University, 1971.

Loeppky, Johan M. "A Travel Report to Mexico in the Year 1921," translated by Robyn Dyck Sneath. Unpublished manuscript in possession of author.

Palmer, Ronald. "Politics and Modernization: The Case of Santa Cruz, Bolivia." PhD dissertation, University of California, Los Angeles, ca. 1960.

Salomón Meraz, Liliana. *Historia de los Menonitas Radicados en Durango*. Durango: Programa de Apovo a Communicados Municipales y Communitarias, 2004.

Sawatzky, Roland. "The Control of Social Space in Mennonite Housebarns of Manitoba, 1874–1940." PhD dissertation, Simon Fraser University, 2004.

Thiessen, Lukas. "*Land*, and *Heimat*: The Concept of Home in the Letters of Low German-Speaking Mennonites from Bolivia in *Die Mennonitische Post*." Unpublished undergraduate essay, University of Winnipeg, 2009.

Van Dyck, Edward W. "Bluemenort: A Study of Persistence in a Sect." PhD dissertation, University of Alberta, 1972.

Warkentin, Karen. "'So ha' wie daut emma jedohne,' (that is how we have always done it): The Collective Memory and Cultural Identity of the Old Colony Mennonites in Bolivia." Master's thesis, University of Manitoba, 2010.

Wessel, Kelso Lee. "An Economic Assessment of Pioneer Settlement in the Bolivian Highlands." PhD dissertation, Cornell University, 1968.

Will, Martina. "The Old Colony Mennonite Colonization of Chihuahua and the Obregón Administration's Vision for the Nation." Master's thesis, University of California, San Diego, 1993.

Films

Klassen, Otto. *75th Anniversary Celebration of the Mennonites in Mexico, 1922–1997*, produced by Otto Klassen in collaboration with el Comité Pro Archivo Histórico y Museo Mennonita, 1977.
– *Old Colony Mennonites Emigrate from Canada to Mexico*. Winnipeg, Otto Klassen Productions, 1997.
Stellet Licht (*Luz Silencia*).
75 Jahre Kolonie Menno (in possession of author).

Correspondence

Luis Enrique Rivero Coimbra to Royden Loewen, 9 February 2010, translated by Gustavo Velasco.

Index

academics, 121–2, 130–50, 233
adaptation, 13, 51, 53, 54–5, 57, 61, 133–4, 168, 173, 204, 221
agriculture, 26, 30, 36, 38, 41–2, 49, 52, 59, 72, 113, 123–5, 130, 132–41, 146, 206. *See also* animals
Alberta. *See* Coaldale, Edmonton, La Crete, Peace River, Vauxhall
Altona, Manitoba, 22, 28, 33, 112, 114
Altona Echo, 97, 112–16, 153
Anderson, Benedict (historian), 176, 230
animals: cattle, 46, 50, 79, 113, 116, 156, 167, 211, 224, 229; chickens, 46, 77, 106, 167, 219; crocodiles, 61; dogs, 37, 46, 156, 263n14; horses, 32, 36, 40, 46, 50–1, 52, 79, 84, 108, 134, 142, 146, 156, 159, 166, 185, 210, 224; livestock, 156, 158, 167, 211; oxen, 36, 40, 50, 58, 62–3, 102–3, 105; tigers, 61, 116
Appadurai, Arjun (anthropologist), 154, 206
Argentina, 3, 5, 9, 15, 26–7, 40–1, 43, 111, 142, 175–6, 192, 199–200, 203–4, 230
Assman, Jan (historian), 154

Asunción, Paraguay, 34–5, 37, 40, 72, 101–3, 105, 112, 116–17, 180–1, 183, 229
Australia, 68, 88
Ayala, Eusebio (Paraguayan President), 35, 71
Aylmer, Ontario, 163, 165, 167, 171, 209

Banman, Anna and Heinrich (migrants), 155–8, 160–1, 166
Banman, H.H. (letter writer), 90
Banman, Johann and Katherina (letter writers), 181
Banman, John and Nettie (migrants), 157, 159, 162, 164, 172, 264n40, 26n50
Banman, "Frau" Klaas (letter writer), 185–6
Banman, Tina (child letter writer), 184
Barrientos Ortuño, René (Bolivian General), 141
Bartsch, Anna (pseudonym, migrant), 222–4
Bayly, C.A. (historian), 10
Belize (British Honduras), 3–5, 9, 12–13, 119–27, 130, 132–6, 149–50, 177–8, 190, 192, 228, 230

Belize Billboard, 122, 124–6
Belize Times, 122–3, 126
Bender, Harold S. (Mennonite scholar), 150
Bennett, R.B. (Canadian Prime Minister), 80, 85
Bentsen, Lloyd (Texan senator), 194
Bergen, A.A. (letter writer), 56
Bergen, Jacob (Minister), 103
Bergen, Margaretha (homemaker), 230, 232
Bergen, Mrs. Isaac F. (diarist), 102–6
Bergthal Colony, Paraguay, 116–17, 119, 138, 151, 177, 230, 253n1
Bergthaler Mennonite Church, Saskatchewan, 10, 24, 33, 37, 40, 71, 94, 102, 117, 253n2, 271–2
Blue Creek Colony, Belize, 119, 126, 132–4, 136
Boley, Oklahoma, 193–4
Bolivia, 4–5, 9, 12–13, 39, 74, 93, 119–22, 127–31, 136–50, 177–8, 192, 200–6, 225, 227–30
Borden, Robert L. (Canadian Prime Minister), 19
borders, 5, 7–8, 13, 32, 47–8, 64, 81, 84, 107, 125, 159–64, 171, 182, 186, 189, 193, 204, 232, 251n74, 252n93
Boschmann, Mrs. Peter (letter writer), 180
Bourdieu, Pierre (social scientist), 98
Brazil, 15, 24, 26–7, 43, 140
Breckenridge, Carol (anthropologist), 154
British Columbia, 100, 107, 120, 191, 228
Burns Lake, British Columbia, 100, 107–8.
Bushong, Allan D. (geographer), 130, 132–3

business, 11, 23, 25, 72, 79, 81–2, 85, 115, 147, 181, 190, 200, 214, 229, 251n74, 264n40; entrepreneurs, 91, 114, 135, 142, 198

Campeche, Mexico, 3, 5, 175, 183
California, 73, 115, 160, 192, 196
Canada, 79–85, 90–5, 120, 148–9, 232–3. *See also* migration
Cárdenas, Lázaro (Mexican President), 90–1
Carillon News, 97, 112, 113, 114, 115, 116, 153, 180
Carter, Jimmy (American President), 194
Casado, José (land owner), 34–7
Chihuahua (city), Mexico, 44, 53, 86, 88, 161, 183
Chihuahua (state), Mexico, 4, 37, 40, 46–7, 66, 68, 96, 113, 117, 119–20, 124, 126, 132–3, 139, 161, 171, 177, 186, 189, 193, 197–8, 208, 213, 228, 259n80, 264n40
childhood, 111, 154–7, 208–13, 228
children, 5, 14, 23, 28, 36, 57, 87–8, 90, 94, 143–4, 146, 148, 158, 161, 166, 168–9, 183–5, 188–9, 196, 205, 213–22, 226, 269n11
Chortitzer Mennonite Church, 10, 24, 33, 37–8, 40, 71, 94, 96, 117, 271
church. *See* Bergthaler Mennonite Church, Chortitzer Mennonite Church, Evangelical Mennonite Mission Church, Evangelical Mennonite Church, General Conference Mennonite Church, Kleine Gemeinde Mennonite Church, Mennonite Brethren

Church, Old Colony (Reinländer) Mennonite Church, Sommerfelder Mennonite Church
citizenship, 4–6, 8, 10–12, 27, 31, 49, 123, 130, 136, 160–1, 174, 177–9, 187–8, 190, 192–201, 203, 205–7, 209–10, 222, 224–5, 227, 230, 233, 252n93, 266n42, 269n11
class, 78, 135, 148, 157; middle-class, 13–14, 16, 20, 149, 207, 221, 231, 226; working class, 192, 218. *See also* poverty.
climate, 35, 48, 50–2, 56, 61, 66, 70, 77, 82, 94, 95, 115, 123, 181, 187, 203, 252n110
clothing, 3, 6, 20, 23, 80, 94, 101, 128, 143, 145, 169, 186, 189, 196, 212, 219, 221, 228, 231–2, 264n40
Coaldale, Alberta, 181
Cohen, Robin (social scientist), 68
Colonia Canadiense, 119, 128, 131, 136–8
Colorado, 192, 195
Curthoys, Ann (historian), 7

de Córdova, Roberto Lemaitre F. (official), 128–9
DeFehr, Cornelius (entrepreneur), 114
diaries, 12, 15–16, 21–39, 42–5, 97–106, 117
diaspora, 8, 10–13, 18, 41, 48, 55–6, 61, 64–5, 68–9, 95, 97–8, 154, 174, 177–8, 181–4, 187–8, 204, 205–7, 225, 227, 232, 233, 239n21, 272
Dick, Lyle, 41
Die Herald, 49
distance, 48, 56, 61, 64, 67, 83–4, 94, 140, 165, 218, 221, 230; space, 7–8, 11, 41, 48, 61, 96–7, 100–4, 117–18, 161, 206–8, 225, 233

Doerksen, Abraham (Ältester), 38, 170
Doerksen, Abram and Katherina (letter writers), 62
Doerksen, P.K. (letter writer), 49
Driedger, J.J. (letter writer), 200–1
Dueck, Peter R. (Ältester/diarist), 15, 21–4
Durango (city), Mexico, 31, 78
Durango (state), Mexico, 3, 32, 37, 40, 66, 68, 117, 197, 199, 264n40, 269n12
Durango Colony, Mexico, 3, 46, 85, 92–3, 107–8, 170, 176, 178, 183–4, 186, 213, 216, 264n12
Dyck, Anna (letter writer), 182
Dyck, Isaak F. (letter writer), 89–90
Dyck, Isaak M. (memoirist/Ältester), 14–15, 17–21, 23, 28, 109

East Reserve, Manitoba, 10, 21, 38, 47, 55, 58, 71
Edmonton, Alberta, 145
education, 5, 9–10, 20, 27–8, 33, 36, 39, 71, 91, 93–4, 109, 135, 138, 141, 144–5, 149, 194, 196, 231
El Diario, 127–8
Engen, Fred (land agent), 33–8, 57, 63, 72
Enns, William (reporter), 114
Ens, Gerhard (radio speaker), 191–2
environment, 10, 35, 41, 48, 62, 64, 68, 130, 133, 233, 236n7. *See also* climate.
Epp, Jake and Lydia (Member of Parliament), 199
Epp, Marlene (historian), 208
Esau, J.A. (letter writer), 75
Estenssoro, Victor Paz (Bolivian President), 127, 141

294   Index

evangelicalism, 34, 115, 145, 159, 168, 171–3, 177, 196–7, 205, 207, 221, 226, 231
Evangelical Mennonite Mission Church (EMMC), 3, 172–3, 263n33, 264n51
Evangelical Mennonite Church/ Conference (EMC), 173, 196, 217, 220, 223, 237n16, 264n51
excommunication, 23, 134, 148, 152, 159, 164, 168, 264n40; shunning, 148–9, 152

faith, 5–6, 17–19, 22, 28–9, 68, 80, 91–4, 97, 110, 112, 144–5, 147, 168, 171–3, 192, 196–7, 206, 225, 230
Falk, Aaron (return migrant), 114
Falk, Jacob W. (letter writer), 186
family. *See* gender, home, kinship, marriage
farming: crops, 51–2, 59, 62, 108, 115, 133, 142, 158, 183, 193, 203, 205, 208; dairy, 113, 139, 142, 176, 177, 229; poultry, 135, 177; tractors, 23, 46, 58, 115, 120, 134, 140, 143–4, 147, 158, 166, 228, 232, 260n81. *See also* agriculture, animals, business
Fast, Kerry L. (historian), 207
Fehr, Cornelius (pseudonym, Ältester), 229, 232
Fehr, J.J. (letter writer), 85
Fernheim Colony, Paraguay, 67, 70, 75, 138, 191
Foucault, Michael (philosopher), 121–2
Fretz, Winfield (Mennonite scholar), 150
Friesen, Abram D. (leader and diarist), 101–2
Friesen, Bernard (letter writer), 52

Friesen, Corny (migrant), 158, 161, 164, 166–7, 170–2, 263n14
Friesen, Franz and Margaretha (letter writers), 199
Friesen, Gerald (historian), 41
Friesen, Heinrich (letter writer), 54–5
Friesen, Isbrand (Ältester), 105
Friesen, Jacob N. (letter writer), 184
Friesen, Johan (Ältester, Old Colony), 19–21, 29
Friesen, John (Ältester, Sommerfelder), 170
Friesen, Katherina (letter writer), 60
Friesen, Martha (columnist), 116–17
Friesen, Martin W. (historian/ minister), 66, 115
Friesen, Peter (Minister), 20
Froese, Franz (letter writer), 63–4
Froese, Isaac and Lydia (entrepreneurs), 229, 232
Froese, Jacob J. (minister), 169
Funk, Franz (letter writer/farmer), 70–5

gender, 101, 150, 233; men, 11, 16, 20, 58, 78, 105, 123, 143, 183, 186, 216, 226; women, 8, 12, 75, 78, 100, 135, 143, 182, 184–6, 205, 207–26, 232, 268n6, 269n7
General Conference Mennonite Church, 10, 168
Giesbrecht, Peter (migrant), 156, 158, 162–3, 166–7, 171, 263n38, 264n41
Ginter, Johann P. (letter writer), 76, 79
globalization, 7–8, 11–13, 17, 120, 122, 126, 132, 137, 149, 206, 225, 227, 232
Goertzen, Abram (minister), 46, 50–1
Goertzen, Isaak (minister), 4, 227

Gondra Pereira, Manuel (Paraguayan President), 33, 35, 37, 39
Gretna, Manitoba, 43–4, 84, 155–6
Guenther, Eva (diarist), 100–1
Guenther, "Frau" (letter writer), 93–4

Hague, Saskatchewan, 9, 28, 82, 94, 155
Hall, Jerry A. (geographer), 130–1, 134–6, 257n33
Harder, Jakob D. (letter writer and memoirist), 76, 110
Harder, Johann (letter writer), 71, 74
Harder, Peter (Ältester), 170
Heide, Hein (farmer), 228, 232
Heide, Klaas and Katherina (letter writers), 108
Hiebert, G.G. (MCC leader), 73
Hiebert, I. and H. (letter writers), 54
Hiebert, Levi and Rosalie (teacher/homemaker), 229, 232
Hildebrandt, J. (letter writer), 85
Hoerder, Dirk (historian), 7, 84
Hofmeyr, Isabel (scholar), 7
home: heimat, 67, 69, 75–6, 79, 82, 95; homeland, 8, 11, 28, 41, 47–9, 60, 64, 66–9, 75, 84–5, 94–5, 109–10, 120, 128, 151–2, 159, 164, 174, 185–6, 201, 204, 206, 225, 233, 236n7; Vaterland, 67, 69, 76, 79, 95
horse and buggy (culture), 3, 119, 139, 177, 182, 183, 199, 200, 227, 228, 230, 260n81
hymns. *See* music

indigenous people, 37, 61–3, 73–4, 78, 106, 115, 125, 202, 247n82, 247n85, 271. *See also* race

industrialization, 10, 41, 98, 114, 173, 176, 217, 232
integration, 8–9, 13, 42, 54, 115, 122, 129, 136, 149, 154, 158, 173, 191, 195, 197, 226
Iowa, 192, 195–6
isolation, 3–4, 12, 38, 91, 119, 125, 128–9, 132–6, 142–3, 145–7, 183

Jackson, Michael (anthropologist), 206
Janzen, A.G. (letter writer), 179
Janzen, Waldemar (theologian), 41

Kanadier migrants, 151–3, 165, 173–4, 179, 195, 199
Kansas, 11, 21, 83–4, 102, 175, 192, 195–6, 206, 211, 225, 230
Kehler, Philip (letter writer/farmer), 70, 72–5
kinship, 41, 68, 76, 82, 84–5, 153, 172, 183, 207–9, 211, 213, 217, 222, 225–6, 231
Kitchener, Ontario, 171
Klassen, D. (letter writer), 107–8
Klassen, Doreen (anthropologist), 223
Klassen, Gerhard (Minister), 21
Klassen, Jakob T. (letter writer), 83–4
Klassen, Mrs. Derk (letter writer), 107, 109
Klassen, Susanna (letter writer), 183
Kleine Gemeinde Mennonite Church, 3, 4, 10, 15, 21–4, 32, 96, 99–100, 107, 117, 124, 134–5, 160, 190, 217, 220, 224, 254n3, 254n12, 257n11, 272
Klippenstein, David (minister), 181
Klippenstein, Johan G. (letter writer), 56–7

Klippenstein, Lisa (pseudonym, mother), 217, 220–2
Klippenstein, Martin (child), 228, 232
Knelsen, Gerhard (letter writer), 195
Knelsen, John (letter writer), 92–3
Krahn, Justina (pseudonym, mother), 217–20

La Crete, Alberta, 4, 107, 145, 230
La Honda Colony, Mexico, viii, 161, 162, 178, 203, 208, 210, 211, 229, 269n9
Lake, Marilyn (historian), 7
land. *See* environment, agriculture.
Lanning, James W. (anthropologist), 131, 139–44, 149
La Paz, Bolivia, 127–8, 140–1, 202
La Presencia, 127–8
Las Piedras Colony, Bolivia, 120, 137, 145
Las Virgénias Colony, Mexico, 178
Leamington, Ontario, viii, 3, 161, 167, 170–1, 221, 222, 264n50, 270n14
Lehr, John (geographer), 41
letters, 6, 12–13, 26, 42, 45–65, 67, 69–94, 97–8, 106–9, 116–17, 121, 152, 178–89, 195–6, 199–202, 204, 206, 255n12, 255n22
Loeppky, Cornelius (letter writer), 195
Loeppky, Johan M. (delegate/diarist), 15, 27–34, 113
Loewen, Abe (migrant), 158, 160, 162, 165, 167–8
Loewen, Cornie (radio host), 191
Loewen, Julius (Ältester), 30
Los Jagueyes Colony, Mexico, 4, 99, 113, 164, 177, 220, 228, 253n1, 254n3

Low German (Plaudietsch), 4, 6–7, 9, 13, 32, 38, 61, 64, 84, 100, 110, 131, 146, 152–4, 172, 175, 177–83, 187–92, 196, 198, 216, 219–20, 223, 231, 233, 272

Manitoba, Canada. *See* Altona, Steinbach, Winnipeg, Winkler.
Manitoba Colony, Mexico, 17, 46, 66, 88, 139, 176, 198, 230
marriage, 30, 53, 82, 100, 111, 146, 161, 164, 184–5, 191, 208–11, 218, 223, 226; elopement, 79
Martens, Elisabeth (child letter writer), 183
McRoberts, Samuel (financier), 25, 33–4, 37, 56, 63, 69
media, 7–8, 11–12, 116–18, 121–2, 128, 201, 233. *See also* diaries, letters, memoires, newspapers, radio, TV
Meighan, James (Belize politician), 125
memoirs, 6, 12, 14–17, 97–8, 104, 109–11, 117, 185, 255n36
memory, 16–17, 67, 154–7, 161, 174, 184, 207, 216–17, 233, 263n14; collective memory, 143, 154, 168, 173–4, 175, 233. *See also* oral history, nostalgia
Menem, Carlos (Argentine President), 203
Menno Colony, Paraguay, 37, 56, 63, 66–7, 70–4, 110–11, 114–15, 119, 138, 176, 199–200, 229, 246n45, 249n20, 266n41
Mennonite Brethren Church, 10, 115, 167, 237n16
Mennonite Central Committee (MCC), 71–3, 114–15, 131–2, 151,

153, 179–80, 188, 190, 192, 194, 228, 249n20, 258n63
Mennonitische Post, vii, 13, 175–91, 193–204
Mexico, 76–9, 86–8, 91–3, 197–9. *See also* migration
Mexico City, Mexico, 30, 37, 84–5, 88, 107, 140
migration: from Canada, 11–13, 14–39, 120, 130, 132, 138, 145–6, 154–7; from Mexico, 119, 123, 131–2, 139–40, 152–4, 157–74, 207–26; from Paraguay, 119, 138, 152; echo migration, 12, 233, migrant culture, 4–8, 97, 175–204; migration history (Canada), 10–11; return migration, 11–12, 52, 67–70, 85, 88–90, 95, 96–7, 120, 148–9, 153–74, 185, 233; to Argentina, 203; to Belize (British Honduras), 12, 119–27, 130, 132–6, 149–50; to Bolivia, 12, 119–22, 127–31, 136–50; to Canada, 15, 67–70, 76, 85, 88–95, 96–7, 149, 151–4, 157–74, 187–92, 207–26; to Mexico, 17–21, 27–33, 40, 42–54, 64–5, 76, 99, 113, 115, 117, 154–7; to Paraguay, 33–8, 40, 54–65, 96, 101–6, 110–17, 138; to United States, 93, 192–7
military: militarization, 10, 16, 27, 38, 86, 95, 149, 157, 188; military exemptions, 9, 14, 19, 20, 22, 25, 30–1, 35, 39, 87, 120, 125, 141, 200, 203; relations with military; 63, 74, 128–9, 147, 197
Miller, Orie O. (MCC leader), 102
modernity, 13, 16, 17, 19, 39, 97, 112, 120, 138, 140, 205; anti-modernity, 3, 8, 16, 96, 116, 120, 134,

Montreal, 102
Morawska, Ewa (sociologist/historian), 7, 67–8
music, 34, 74, 103–4, 145, 181, 191, 197, 231

nationalism, 5–6, 8–9, 13, 16–17, 20, 21, 38–9, 66–7, 69, 77–9, 95, 121, 122–3, 125–6, 136, 150, 179, 187, 188, 198, 204, 230, 231, 232, 249
nation-state, 5, 6, 13, 16, 39, 41, 42, 49, 65, 187, 197, 198, 199, 201, 204, 227, 236n7
Nebraska, 83, 192, 196
Neudorf, Rev. Jacob, 169, 172
Neudorf, Jacob (minister), 171
Neudorf, Johan (letter writer), 181
Neufeld, Gerhard D. (letter writer), 82
Neufeld, Maria (homemaker), 228, 232
newspapers, 6, 13, 41–2, 47–8, 64, 97–8, 112, 117, 122, 148, 153, 206, 231, 233, 254n7. See also *Altona Echo, Belize Billboard, Belize Times, Carillon News, Die Herald, El Diario, La Presencia, Mennonitische Post, Newsweek, Steinbach Post*
Newsweek, 193–4
New York City, United States, 25–6, 33–4, 37, 40, 104, 110, 113
Niverville, Manitoba, 48, 55, 99, 110
non-violence. *See* pacifism
nostalgia, 8, 66–9, 95, 126, 176, 186, 206, 225, 233
Nova Scotia, Canada, viii, 3, 4, 175, 190, 206, 227, 230

Obregón, Álvaro (Mexican President), 15, 30–3, 37, 39, 42, 86, 90, 198

Oklahoma, 175, 178
Old Colony (Reinländer) Mennonite Church, 3–4, 9, 14–15, 17–18, 20–1, 24, 27, 32–3, 40, 45–6, 91, 94, 119–20, 131, 139, 141, 143–9, 153, 159, 162, 164, 168–73, 182, 189, 191, 196–7, 200, 203, 206, 209, 216–20, 222, 226, 228–31, 243n61, 254n3, 254n12, 260n81, 262n3, 263n33, 264n40, 264n50
Ontario, 6, 11, 12, 135, 152–74, 184, 186, 188–9, 191, 193, 197, 205–26, 230. See also Aylmer, Leamington, Tillsonburg, Wheatley
Osler, Saskatchewan, 28–9, 113, 228
oral history, 13, 79, 153, 164, 173, 225–6, 255n22
Ordnung, 88, 98, 140, 272
Ottawa, 23, 25

pacifism, 6, 10, 13–14, 16, 20, 33, 38, 41, 74, 86–7, 128–9, 138, 187, 198–9, 231
Paraguay, 69–76, 199–200. See also migration
passports, 11, 85, 151–2, 160, 188, 197, 209–10, 232
Patel, Dhiru (scholar), 5, 235n7
Peace River, Alberta, 61, 89
Penner, Bernhard (letter writer), 80–1
Penner, D. (letter writer), 182–3
Penner, Heinrich C. (letter writer), 107–9
Penner, Maria (grandmother), viii, 3–4, 227
Peter, Jacob J. (diarist), 43–4
Peters, Anna and Cornelius (migrants), 155–7, 159, 163, 165–70
Peters, A.W. (letter writer), 83

Peters, Bernard F. (Ältester), 140
Peters, Johan (letter writer), 109
Peters, Wilhelm (letter writer), 108
People's United Party (PUP), 123, 125–6
Plett, Abram and Elisabeth (diarists), 99–100
poverty, 44, 70, 81, 89, 125, 129, 148, 152, 156–9, 169, 186, 195, 208, 218, 213, 217, 219, 225, 229
prayer, 25, 28, 33, 35, 38, 112, 144, 172, 196, 219–21
Price, George (Belizean Prime Minister), 123, 126
Privilegium, 9, 15, 33, 44, 141, 197, 198, 203, 272
Puerto Casado, Paraguay, 36–37, 40, 56–60, 63, 70, 72, 111, 184, 229

Quebec, 11, 24, 27, 93, 104
Quellenkolonie, Mexico. See Los Jagueyes Colony

race/racism, 10, 39, 49, 62, 65, 73, 78, 125, 143, 190, 199, 244n95. See also indigenous people
radio, 191, 201
Rak, Julie (scholar), 16
Redekop, Calvin (sociologist), 150
Redekop, John D. (letter writer), 107
Redekopp, David (letter writer), 52
Regina, Saskatchewan, 80
Reimer, Henry (Ältester), 170
religion. See evangelicalism, excommunication, faith, music, prayer, schism, sectarian, tradition
Rempel, Abram (letter writer), 46, 50
Rempel, David (diarist), 15, 24–8, 33–4, 43

Index   299

Rempel, Elisabeth (pseudonym, migrant), 208, 210–12
Rempel, Peter (entrepreneur, community leader), 198
reporters. *See* newspapers
Rio de Janeiro, Brazil, 26–7, 34, 102, 104
Riva Palacios Colony, Bolivia, 119, 137, 139–44, 147, 202, 228, 259n80
Rivero Coimbra, Luis Enrique (local historian), 127
Rodriguez, Abelardo L. (Mexican president), 80
Russländer migrants, 73, 152, 165, 168, 272

Salinas de Gortari, Carlos (Mexican President), 198
Santa Clara Colony, Mexico, 46, 66, 90, 139, 158
Santa Cruz, Bolivia, 119–20, 127–8, 131, 137–41, 143, 146–7, 177, 202, 228, 230
Santa Rita Colony, Bolivia, 119, 139, 202
Santa Rita Colony, Mexico, 46, 66, 259n80
Saskatchewan. *See* Hague, Osler, Saskatoon, Swift Current
Saskatoon, 58, 80, 123, 155
Sawatzky, Harry Leonard (geographer), 130–1, 133–4
Sawatsky, Ronald (oral historian), 153–4, 170, 173
Sawatsky, Susan (letter writer), 184–5
schism, 3, 10, 139
Schmidt, A.B. (writer), 85, 92–3

Schmiedehaus, Walter (German consul), 44–5, 91
Schulz, Peter (writer), 47–8, 50
Schudson, Robert (historian), 98
sectarian, 6, 9, 86, 98, 127, 138, 150
Seminole, Texas, 170, 192–7
separation: from family 38, 45, 55, 84, 103–4, 111, 152, 155, 177, 214; from outside world, 9, 17, 31, 41, 65, 67, 110, 132, 140, 149, 174, 187, 198–9, 201–3, 231
Shipyard Colony, Belize, 119, 132–4, 136
simplicity, 9–10, 13, 15, 21, 41, 111, 139–40, 171, 178, 231
Smith, Sidonie (theorist), 16
Sommerfeld Colony, Bolivia, 119, 139, 202
Sommerfeld Colony, Paraguay, 101, 103, 105, 151, 177, 253n1, 260n81
Sommerfelder Mennonite Church, 10, 15, 24, 33, 37–8, 40, 71, 94, 96, 102, 117, 119, 124, 139, 153, 162, 168, 171, 173, 257n11, 260n81, 262n3, 264n51, 272
South Africa, 68
South Dakota, 25, 84, 93
Spanish Lookout Colony, Belize, 3, 119, 125, 126, 130, 134, 135, 136, 257n33, 258n51
Steinbach, Manitoba, 21, 23, 55, 112, 114, 152, 200, 228
Steinbach Post, vii, 13, 42, 45–64, 67, 69–86, 94, 97, 101, 106–7, 116, 121, 152, 179, 180, 247n59, 248n4, 250n57, 251n91
Stolow, Jeremy (scholar), 5, 16, 236n7
Stroessner, Alfredo (Paraguayan President), 200

300   Index

suffering, 4, 17–18, 29, 91–3, 95, 112, 206, 213
Swift Current Colony, Bolivia, 119, 139, 202
Swift Current Colony, Mexico, 46, 66, 87, 259n80, 270n13
Swift Current, Saskatchewan, 7, 9, 28, 82, 92, 155, 230, 259n80
Swyripa, Frances (historian), 41

technology, 12, 17, 23, 32, 39, 98, 100, 117, 134, 138, 143, 145, 176, 232
Teichrob, Elisabeth (letter writer), 196
television (TV), 143, 189, 201, 213, 215, 219, 221, 229
Texas, 3, 83, 131, 139, 170, 175, 178, 182, 189, 192–7, 228
Thiessen, Aganetha (pseudonym, mother), 213–16
Thiessen, Helena (letter writer), 83
Thiessen, J.J. (MCC representative), 114
Thiessen, Johan A. (dairy farmer/diarist), 42–3, 98–9
Thiessen, Peter (letter writer), 107
Thompson, E.P. (historian), 98
Tillsonburg, Ontario, 164
Tilly, Charles (sociologist), 69
time, 8, 56, 70, 96–8, 100–9, 112, 117–18, 147, 154, 184–5, 206, 232–3, 254n4, 255n22
Toews, Bernard (diarist), 15, 33–8
Toews, Maria Wiebe (memoirist), 110–12
Toronto, 169, 173, 207, 210
Torrelio, Celso (Bolivian President), 201
tradition, 3, 6, 9, 41, 49, 55, 96–8, 100–1, 105–6, 113, 119–22, 134–5, 139, 143–50, 167–70, 178, 191, 196, 198–9, 205, 209, 212, 215, 222, 231–2, 236n7, 238n20
transnationalism, 4–5, 7–12, 17, 39, 40, 42, 45, 48, 64, 66, 84, 93, 97, 121–2, 129, 132, 137, 149, 156, 157, 174, 175–6, 180, 192, 202, 205–8, 213, 222, 224–6, 227, 230, 231–3, 238n19
transplantation, 42, 47–8, 55, 64, 66, 94, 98, 131, 134–6, 147, 165, 206, 226
transportation: Bennett Buggy, 85; boat, 35–6, 56, 72, 103–5, 140; bus, 82, 84, 89, 100–2; car, 23–4, 32, 43, 45–6, 49, 78, 82–4, 100, 133, 145–7, 151, 161–2, 168–9, 181, 214, 229, 264n40; cart, 40, 102–3, 105; horse-and-buggy, 134, 140, 159, 213, 229; plane, 101–2, 113, 140, 142, 175, 181, 199; streetcar, 25, 34; taxi, 84; train, 25, 32, 43–6, 55, 58, 72, 82, 84, 102–5, 165–6, 193, 208, 213, 229, 264n40
travelogue, 33, 44, 82–4, 97–8, 100–2, 117, 180–1, 254n12
Trudeau, Pierre Elliot (Canadian Prime Minister), 146
Tsuda, Takeyuki (anthropologist), 68

Unger, Cornelius (letter writer), 85
Unrau, P.A. (letter writer), 53
urbanization, 4, 10, 23, 26, 96, 100, 179, 217, 231–2

Vancouver, British Columbia, 100, 191
Van Dyck, Edward W. (anthropologist), 131, 145, 147–9
Vauxhall, Alberta, 190
Vertovec, Steven (anthropologist), 7, 11, 41, 168

village: imagined village, 4, 6, 8, 39, 42, 48, 64–5, 67, 84, 98, 106, 175–6, 179–80, 183–4, 188, 204–5, 224, 226–7, 230–3 ; village life; 4–6, 8, 40–1, 43, 47, 49–50, 57, 59, 63, 66, 72, 74, 87, 105–6, 108, 114, 120, 139, 144, 147–8, 159, 192, 197–8, 267n81
Voth, Heinrich and Maria (migrants), 155–6, 158, 171

Wall, Aron (migrant), 161–2, 171
Wall, David (letter writer), 107
Wall, Jakob (local historian), 3, 227
Wall, Johan (Minister), 26, 186
Warkentin, Abe (editor), 180
Watler, John A. (Belizean politician), 123
Weaver, John (historian), 41
Wessel, Kelso Lee (economist), 130–1, 137–9, 259n65
West Reserve, Manitoba, 9–10, 22, 38, 58, 71
Wheatley, Ontario, 182, 189
Wiebe, Jacob P.D. (letter writer), 186–7
Wiebe, Johan (Ältester), 19
Wiebe, Johan (letter writer), 57–8, 60–1
Wiebe, Julius (Ältester), 81
Wiebe, Nettie (pseudonym, migrant), 208–10
Wiebe, Peter (delegate), 124–5
Wiebe, Peter and Elisabeth (letter writers), 180
Wieler, D.D. (letter writer), 109
Wiens, Jacob (minister), 14–15
Will, Martina (historian), 39
Winkler, Manitoba, 28, 82, 152, 189, 191
Winland, Daphne (anthropologist), 176
Winnipeg, 4, 20, 22–3, 25, 29, 82, 103, 180, 229
Winnipeg General Strike, 80
Woelke, Helena (letter writer), 185
Wolf, Abram (letter writer), 77, 89
Wolf, Johann (letter writer), 88, 90

Zacharias, Aron (Ältester), 25
Zacharias, J.P. (reporter), 115
Zacharias, P.B. (letter writer), 51
Zuazo, Hernán Siles, (Bolivian President), 201